THE PRONUNCIATION

OF

10,000 PROPER NAMES

THE PRONUNCIATION

OF

10,000 PROPER NAMES

GIVING

FAMOUS GEOGRAPHICAL AND BIOGRAPHICAL
NAMES, NAMES OF BOOKS, WORKS OF ART,
CHARACTERS IN FICTION,
FOREIGN TITLES, ETC.

*NEW EDITION, WITH CORRECTIONS,
AND THE ADDITION OF IMPORTANT WORDS MAKING A
TOTAL OF 12,000 PROPER NAMES*

BY

MARY STUART MACKEY

AND

MARYETTE GOODWIN MACKEY, B.A.

NEW YORK
DODD, MEAD AND COMPANY
1922

Republished by Gale Research Company, Book Tower, Detroit, 1979

COPYRIGHT, 1922,
BY DODD, MEAD AND COMPANY, INC.

A Firenze Book

Library of Congress Cataloging in Publication Data

Mackey, Mary Stuart.
    The pronunciation of 10,000 proper names. . .

    Reprint of the ed. published by Dodd, Mead, New York.
    1. English language--Pronunciation. 2. Names--
Pronunciation. I. Mackey, Maryette Goodwin, joint
author. II. Title: The pronunciation of 10,000 proper
names. . .
PE1137.M5   1976   428'.1   70-167059
ISBN 0-8103-4137-9

PRINTED IN THE U. S. A.

To the Memory

OF

JOHN ROSEBERY MACKEY,

THIS LITTLE BOOK IS DEDICATED

PREFACE TO SECOND EDITION

THIS little book was first compiled in the hope of supplying some useful assistance to the reading public. The modest place which it has kept for more than twenty years seems to show that it has not been without its value.

It was not intended for scholars nor for linguists, who do not need it. It was planned to help the large number of readers who often wander far afield in the world of books, and who know but little of any language than their own. For them the signs and directions have been made as simple as possible, and it is hoped that they will be found clear.

The original edition contained considerably more than the 10,000 words claimed for it, and for this new edition about 1500 words have been added, and the whole work has been carefully revised. The new words are for the most part names of persons, places, characters in literature, etc., which have come into prominence since the publication of the first edition. It may safely be claimed that no other single work contains them all

THE AUTHORS

TABLE OF SIGNS, MARKS, AND ABBREVIATIONS

ā as in fāte, āte.
ă " făt, ăt.
ä " fäther, mämmä.
â " fâre, câre.
ȧ " sodȧ, ȧsk.
ē " mēte, wē.
ĕ " mĕt, bĕd.
ē̆ " hē̆r, fathē̆r.
ī " fīle, sīte.
ĭ " fĭll, sĭt.

ō as in nōte, ōpen.
ŏ " nŏt, bŏx.
ô " ôr, fôr.
ŏ̤ " whŏ̤lly.
ōō " fōōl, sōōth.
ŏŏ as in lŏŏk, bŏŏk.
ū " ūse, attenūated.
ŭ " ŭs, flŭsh.
ü " Fr. sur, Ger. über.

adj.	for	adjective.	Lat.	for	Latin.
Am.	"	American.	loc.	"	local.
Arab.	"	Arabic.	L.	"	Lake.
Bib.	"	Bible, Biblical.	mod.	"	modern.
Boh.	"	Bohemian.	n.	"	noun.
class.	"	classical.	Nor.	"	Norwegian.
D.	"	Dutch.	Pers.	"	Persian.
Dan.	"	Danish.	pop.	"	popularly.
Eng.	"	English, England.	Port.	"	Portuguese.
Fl.	"	Flemish.	R.	"	River.
Fr.	"	French.	Russ.	"	Russian.
Ger.	"	German.	Sc.	"	Scotch.
Gr.	"	Greek.	Shak.	"	Shakespeare.
Heb.	"	Hebrew.	Sp.	"	Spanish.
Hind.	"	Hindu.	Sw.	"	Swedish.
Hung.	"	Hungarian.	St.	"	Saint.
I.	"	Island.	Turk.	"	Turkish.
Ice.	"	Icelandic.			

SOUNDS AND MARKS USED IN GIVING PRONUNCIATION.

ch is pronounced as in **choose**.

ċh " " *Sc.* **loch,** *Ger.* **aċh.**

g is always hard in the pronunciation, as in **get.**

h " an aspirated sound.

᛫h is strongly aspirated, as in ᛫**hither,** ᛫**horrid.**

ng is pronounced as in **ring.**

ṅ " " " *Fr.* **boṅ-boṅ.**

oi " " " **oil.**

ow " " " **now.**

sh " " " **show.**

th " " " **thin.**

ṯh " " " **ṯhiṯher.**

y " " " a consonant, as in **you.**

zh " " " s in **treasure.**

- indicates a rapid pronunciation or running together of two syllables: as **Mercier, mârs-ē-ā′,** almost **mârs-yā.**

′ indicates the principal accent.

″ " " secondary, or weaker accent.

NOTES ON SOUNDS IN FOREIGN LANGUAGES:

In all cases foreign sounds should be learned from a native, if possible. In many cases they can be indicated only approximately by English sounds. Some have *no* equivalent in English.

French.

1. **e** and **eu** are both sounded peculiarly in French. They have been indicated in most cases by **ē** as in **hēr.** It should be remembered that this is *not the exact* sound.

xi

2. e at the end of a French word, and sometimes between two syllables, is pronounced very lightly. At the end of a word this has been indicated by the syllable **yu,** with the tie -. Example, **Allemagne, äl-män′-yŭ.** This slight sound is lost in rapid speech, but should be indicated, rather than pronounced, when the word is spoken deliberately.

3. u is pronounced like the German **ü.** These sounds are not heard in English, but are between **ū** in flūte, and **wee** in sweet. They are indicated by **ü.**

4. n in French has no equivalent in English. It is like a smothered **ng,** and is sometimes so indicated in dictionaries. But it is a worse fault to give it the full **ng** sound than to keep it a simple English **n.** It is indicated by **ṅ.**

5. r is rolled in the throat in a way difficult for an English-speaking person to acquire.

German.

1. ch is a strongly aspirated sound, and has no equivalent in English. If it is impossible to acquire this sound, it is perhaps best to use hard **c** or **k** instead. It is indicated by **ċh.** Ex. **Berchem, bĕr′-ċhĕm, — bĕr′-kĕm.**

2. g at the end of a word has nearly the same sound as **ch,** and has been indicated in the same way. In this case, however, one who cannot pronounce **ċh,** should use hard **g.** Ex. **Altenburg, äl′-tĕn-bo͞orċh, — äl′-tĕn-bo͞org.**

3. ö is different from any English sound, and resembles **eu** in French. It has been indicated by **ẽ** as in **hẽr,** but this is *not the exact* sound.

4. ü has no equivalent in English, but is like **u** in

French and in Dutch. It is a sound between ū in flute, and **wee** in sweet, and is indicated by **ü**.

Spanish.

1. Spanish vowels are all pronounced, though sometimes syllables are run together rapidly. Ex. **Caimanera, kä-ē-mä-nä-rä**. But the first two syllables are so rapidly spoken that they have the effect of **kī**, and the pronunciation is so given in some dictionaries. But here it has seemed best to keep the value of the vowels in most cases, according to Spanish rules. Sometimes this practice has appeared misleading; accordingly, **Aranjuez, ä-räng-chōō-ĕth′**, has been given **ä-räng-hwĕth′**, as less likely to be confusing.

2. **b** and **v** are often interchangeable, and have a sound between **b** and **v,** but as this is difficult for a foreigner, it has been given as a simple **b,** and may be pronounced **b** or **v** according to the letter employed in the Spanish word. It is **b** pronounced without closing the lips.

3. **d** is often softened or almost lost in Spanish, and in most dictionaries has been given as **ŧh.** But it has seemed better to indicate it here as a simple **d.**

4. **j** and **x** are interchangeable in Spanish, and have an aspirated sound much like the German **ch.** If this is not to be acquired, it is better to use an aspirated **·h** as in **·hither,** and the sound is indicated by both **ch** and **·h.**

5. **r** is rolled with the tip of the tongue.

Italian.

1. Double consonants in Italian are both pronounced, as the **d**'s in sand dune. Ex. **libretto, lē-brät′-tō.**

2. Before **t** the letter **n** is distinctly pronounced, the effect being of a pause between **n** and **t.**

10,000 PROPER NAMES

A

Aachen	ä′-chĕn.
Aar	är.
Aare	är′-ŭ.
Aaron	ăr′-ŭn, âr′-ŭn, ā′-rŭn.
Ab	äb.
Abaco	ä′-bä-kō.
Abaddon	ā-băd′-ŭn, ă-băd′-ŏn.
Abana	ăb′-à-nà.
Abassides, see Abbassides	ă-băs′-ĭdz, ăb′-à-sīdz.
Abate, see Abbate	ä-bä′-tĕ.
Abbas	äb′-bäs.
Abbassides, see Abassides	ă-băs′-ĭdz, ăb′-à-sīdz.
Abbate, see Abate	ä-bä′-tĕ.
Abbaye	ä-bā′.
Abbeokuta, see Abeokuta	ăb-ē″-ō-kōō′-tà.
Abbeville	ăb-vēl′.
Abbotsford	ăb′-ŏts-fŭrd.
Abdallah, see Abdullah	äbd-äl′-äh.
Abd-el-aziz, see Abdul-Aziz	äbd″-ĕl-ä-zēz′.
Abd-el-Kader, or Kadir	äbd-ĕl-kä′-dĕr.
Abd-el-Wahab	äbd″-ĕl-wä-häb′.
Abd-er-Rahman	äbd-ẹr-rä′-män.
Abdiel	ăb′-dĭ-ĕl.
Abdul-Aziz, see Abd-el-aziz	äbd″-ōōl-ä-zēz′.
Abdul-Kerim	äb-dōōl-kĕ-rēm′.
Abdullah, see Abdallah	äbd-ōōl′-ä.
Abdul-Medjid, or Mejid	äbd″-ōōl-mĕ-jēd′.

1

À Becket	à-bĕk'-ĕt.
Abednego	ă-bĕd'-nē-gō.
Abel	ā'-bel. *Nor.* ä'-bĕl.
Abelard. Fr. Abélard .	ăb'-ē-lärd. *Fr.* ä-bā-lär'.
Abelian	ā-bĕl'-ĭ-ăn.
	ăb-ĕn'-sĕ-rāj-ĕz.
Abencerrages	*Sp.* ä″-bĕn-thä-rä'-ċhĕs.
Abeokuta, see Abbeokuta	ăb-ē″-ō-kōō'-tà.
Abercrombie	ăb'-ēr-krŭm-bĭ.
Aberdeen	ăb-ēr-dēn'.
Abergavenny	ăb-ēr-gā'-nĭ, ăb″-ēr-gă-vĕn'ĭ.
Abernethy	ăb'-ēr-nĕth-ĭ, ăb'-ēr-nē-thĭ.
Abia, or Abiah	à-bī'-à.
Abiathar	à-bī'-à-thär.
Abib	ā'-bĭb.
Abiezar, or Abiezer . .	ā-bĭ-ē'-zēr.
Abigail	ăb'-ĭ-gāl.
Abihu	à-bī'-hū.
Abijah	à-bī'-jä.
Abila, see Abyla . . .	ăb'-ĭ-lä.
Abimelech	à-bĭm'-ĕ-lĕk.
Abo	ä'-bō. *Sw.* ô'-bō.
Abomey	ăb-ō'-mĭ, ä-bō-mä'.
Abonita	ä-bō-nē'-tä.
Abookeer, see Aboukir,	
Abukir	ä-bōō-kēr'.
Abou-ben-Adhem . . .	ä'-bōō-bĕn-ä'-dĕm.
Aboukir, see Abookeer,	
Abukir	ä-bōō-kēr'.
About, Edmond	ĕd-môṅd' ä-bōō'.
Abra	ăb'-rà.
Abrantès, (Duc) d' . .	dä-brän'-tĕz.
Abruzzi	ä-brŏŏtz'-sē.
Abruzzo	ä-brŏŏt'-sō.
Absalom	ăb'-sà-lŭm.
Abt	äpt.
Abu-Bekr	ä″-bōō-bĕk'-r.

Abukir, see Abookeer,
Aboukir . . . . . ä-boo-kēr'.
Abu-l-Hassan . . . . ä'-bool-häs'-än, häs-än'.
Abul-Kasim-Mansur . . ä'-bool-kä-sēm' (or
                        kä'-sēm) män-soor'.
Abydos . . . . . . ă-bī'-dŏs, ā-bī'dŏs.
Abyla, see Abila . . . ăb'-ĭ-lä.
Abyssinia . . . . . . ăb-ĭ-sĭn'-ĭ-à.
Académie Française, l' . lä-kă-dā-mē' frän-sĕz'.
Accademia delle Belle Arti äk-kä-dā'-mē-ä dĕl'-lĕ
                        bĕl'-lĕ är'-tē.
Academus . . . . . ăk-ā-dē'-mŭs.
Acadia . . . . à-kā'-dĭ-à.
Acadie . . . . ä-kä-dē'.
Acapulco . . . . . . ä-kä-pool'-kō.
Acbar, see Akbar . . . äk'-bēr. Hind. ŭk'-bĕr.
Accademia della Crusca . äk-kä-dā'-mē-à dĕl'-lä
                        kroos'-kä.
Acciajoli, or . . . . . ä-chä-yō'-lē.
Acciajuoli . . . . . . ä-chä-yoo-ō'-lē.
Accoramboni . . . . . äk-kō"-räm-bō'-nē.
Aceldama . . . . . . à-sĕl'dā-mà.
Acemetae, Acemeti, see
   Acoemitae . . . . . ă-sĕm'-ē-tē, ă-sĕm'-ē-tī.
Acemetic . . . . . . ăs-ē-mĕt'-ĭk.
Achaea, see Achaia . . ā-kē'-yà, ă-kē'-yà.
Achaean, see Achean . . ā-kē'-àn, ă-kē'-àn.
Achaia, see Achaea . . ā-kā'-yä, ă-kā'-yà.
Achaian, see Achean . . ā-kā'-yàn, ă-kā'-yàn.
Achan . . . . ā'-kăn.
Achates . . . . . . ă-kā'-tēz.
Achean, see Achaean . . ā-kē'-àn, ă-kē-àn.
Acheloös, or Achelous . ăk-ē-lō'-ŏs, ăk-ē-lō'-ŭs.
Acheron . . . . . . ăk'-ĕ-rŏn.
Achillean . . . . . . ăk-ĭl-ē'-àn.
Achilles . . . . . . ă-kĭl'-ēz.
Achitophel, see Ahithophel ā-kĭt'-ō-fĕl.

Achmet, see Ahmed . . ăċh'-mĕt.
Achray (Loch) . . . . ăk'-rā.
Acis . . . . ā'-sĭs.
Ackbar, see Akbar . . . äk'-bēr. *Hind.* ŭk'-bēr.
Acoemitae, see Acemetae ăs-ē-mī'-tē, *or* ă-sĕm'-ĭ-tē.
Adabazar . . . . . . ä-dä-bä-zär'.
Adelina . . . . . . ăd-ĕ-lī'-nà.
Adeline . . . . . . ăd'-ĕ-lĭn. *Fr.* ăd-lēn'.
Adis Abeba . . . . . ä'-dĭs ä-bä'-bä.
Adlai . . . . ăd'-lī.
Aegades (Is.) . . . . ē-gä'-dēz.
Aguada . . . . . . ä-gwād'-thà.
Aguilar . . . . . . ä-gē-lär'.
Aguinaldo . . . . . . ä-gē-näld'-thō.
Agulhas (Cape) . . . ä-gōōl'-yäs.
Acre . . . . ā'-kĕr, ä'-kĕr.
Acropolis . . . . . . ă-krŏp'-ō-lĭs.
Actaeon . . . . . . ăk-tē'-ŏn.
Actian . . . . ăk'-shĭ-àn.
Actium . . . . ăk'-shĭ-ŭm, ăk'-tĭ-ŭm.
Acuña . . . . ä-kōōn'-yà.
Adalbert . . . . . . ăd'-ăl-bērt.
Adam (Mme.) . . . . ä-däṅ'.
Adamawa . . . . . ä-dä-mô'-wä.
Adamic . . . . . . ă-dăm'-ĭk.
Adamowski . . . . . ä-dä-mŏf'-skĭ.
Adar . . . . ā'-där.
Ade (Geo.) . . . . . äd.
Adela . . . . ăd'-ē-là.
Adelaide . . . . . . ăd'-ĕ-lād.
Adélaïde (Princess) . . *Fr.* ä-dä-lä-ēd'.
Adelaïde (Beethoven) . . *Ger.* ä-dā-lä-ē'-dŭ.
Adelheid . . . . . . ä'-dĕl-hīt.
Adelphi, or Adelphoe . . ă-dĕl'-fī, ă-dĕl'-fē.
Aden . . . . ä'-dĕn, ā'-dĕn.
Adeona . . . . . . ăd-ē-ō'-nà.
Adige . . . . ăd'-ĭj-ē. *It.* ä'-dē-jĕ.

Adjanta, Adjunta, see
 Ajuntah . . . . . ă-jŭn'-tá.
Adjuntas . . . . . . äd-hōōn'-täs.
Adlai . . . . ăd'-lī, ăd'-lē-ī.
Adler . . . . äd'-lĕr.
Admetos, or Admetus . ăd-mē'-tŏs, ăd-mē'-tŭs.
Adonai . . . . ăd-ō-nā'-ī, ä-dō-nī'.
Adonais . . . . . . ăd-ō-nā'-ĭs.
Adonic . . . . à-dŏn'-ĭk.
Adonijah . . . . . . ăd-ō-nī'-jà.
Adoniram . . . . . . ăd-ō-nī'-răm.
Adonis . . . . ă-dō'-nĭs, ā-dō'-nĭs.
Adoni-zedec . . . . . à-dō'-nī-zē'-dĕk.
Adraste . . . . . . ä-dräst'.
Adrian . . . . ā'-drĭ-àn.
Adriana . . . . . . ā-drĭ-ā'-nà.
Adrianople . . . . . ā-drĭ-ăn-ō'pl.
Adriatic . . . . . . ā-drĭ-ăt'-ĭk, ăd-rĭ-ăt'-ĭk.
Adrienne Lecouvreur . . ä-drē-ĕn' lē-kōōv-rēr'.
Adullam . . . . . . à-dŭl'-àm.
Aeacides . . . . . . ē-ăs'-ĭ-dēz.
Aeacus . . . . ē'-à-kŭs.
Aegadian (Is.) . . . . ē-gā'-dĭ-àn.
Aegates . . . . . . ē-gā'-tēz.
Aegean, see Egean . . ē-jē'-àn.
Aegeria, see Egeria . . ē-jē'-rĭ-à.
Aegina, see Aigina . . . ē-jī'-nà.
Aeginetan . . . . . . ē-jĭ-nē'-tàn.
Aeginetic . . . . . . ē-jĭ-nêt'-ĭk.
Aegis . . . . ē'-jĭs.
Aeneas, see Eneas . . . ē-nē'às.
Aeneid . . . . ē-nē'-ĭd.
Aeolian, see Aiolian . . ē-ō'-lĭ-àn.
Aeolic, see Eolic . . . ē-ŏl'-ĭk.
Aeolis, see Eolis . . . ē'-ō-lĭs.
Aeolus . . . . ē'-ō-lŭs.
Aerschot . . . . . . är'-skŏt.

Aeschines	ĕs'-kĭ-nēz.
Aeschylean	ĕs-kĭ-lē'-ȧn.
Aeschylus	ĕs'-kĭ-lŭs.
Aesculapius, see Asklepios	ĕs-kū-lā'-pĭ-ŭs.
Aesir	ā'-sĕr, mod. ē'-sĕr. Ice. ī-sĕr.
Aesop, see Esop . . .	ē'-sŏp.
Aethelberht, see Ethelbert	ăth'-ĕl-bĕrht.
Aethelwulf, see Ethelwulf	ăth'-ĕl-wŏŏlf.
Aether	ē'-thĕr.
Aëtion	ā-ē'-shĭ-ŏn.
Aetna, see Etna . . .	ĕt'-nȧ.
Aetolian	ē-tō'-lĭ-ȧn.
Afer	ā'-fĕr.
Afghan	ăf'-găn.
Afghanistan	af-găn-ĭs-tän', af-gän-ĭs-tän'.
Afium-Kara-Hissar . .	ä-fē-ōōm'-kä-rä'-hĭs-sär'.
Africaine, L'	lăf-rē-kĕn'.
Africander, see Afrikander	ăf'-rĭ-kăn-dĕr.
Africanus	ăf-rĭ-kā'-nŭs.
Afridis	ä-frē'-dĭz.
Afrikander, see Africander	ăf'-rĭ-kăn-dĕr.
Agades, Agadez, see Agdas	ä'-gă-dĕz.
Agag	ā'-găg.
Agamemnon	ăg-ā-mĕm'-nŏn.
Agaña	ä-gän'-yä.
Agassiz	ăg'-ăs-sĭ, ăg'-ăs-ē. Fr.
	ä-gä-sē'.
Agdas, see Agades . . .	äg'-dȧs.
Agen	ä-zhŏṅ'.
Agenor	ă-jē'-nôr.
Agésilas	Fr. ä-zhä-sē-läs'.
Agesilaos, or	ă-jĕ-sĭ-lā'-ŏs.
Agesilaus	ă-jĕ-sĭ-lā'-ŭs.
Aghrim, see Aughrim . .	ôg'-rĭm.
Agincourt, see Azincourt .	ăj'-ĭn-kōrt. Fr.
	äzh-ăṅ-kōōr'.
Aglaia	ăg-lā'-yä.

Agnolo	än'-yō-lō.
Agnus Dei	ăg'-nŭs dē'-ī.
Agoncillo, Felipe . . .	fä-lē'-pä ä-gōn-thēl'-yō.
Agonistes	ăg-ŏn-ĭs'-tēz.
Agora	ăg'-ō-rȧ.
Agoult (Comtesse d') . .	dä-gōō'.
Agra	ä'-grȧ.
Agram	ä'-gräm.
Agricola	ă-grĭk'-ō-lä.
Agrigentum	ăg-rĭ-jĕn'-tŭm.
Agrippina	ăg-rĭ-pī'-nȧ.
Aguadilla	ä-gwä-dēl'-yä.
Aguado	ä-gwä'-dō.
Aguadores	ä-gwä-dō'-rās.
Aguas Buenas	ä'-gwäs bōō-ä'-näs.
Aguas Calientes . . .	ä'-gwäs kä-lē-ĕn'-tĕs.
Ahab	ā'-hăb.
Ahasuerus	ă-hăz-ū-ē'-rŭs.
Ahaz	ā'-hăz.
Ahimelech	ă-hĭm'-ĕ-lĕk.
Ahithophel, see Achitophel	ă-hĭth'-ō-fĕl, ā-hĭth'-ō-fĕl.
Ahmed, see Achmet . .	äh'-mĕd.
Ahmedabad	ä-mĕd-ä-bäd'.
Ahmednuggur	ä·mĕd-nŭg'-ēr.
Ahriman	ä'-rĭ-män.
Aï, see Ay	ä'-ē, ī. *Bib.* ā'-ī
Aibonito, see Aybonito .	ä-ē-bō-nē'-tō.
Aïda	ä-ē'-dä.
Aïdé	ä-ē-dä'.
Aidenn	ā'-dĕn.
Aidin	ī-dēn'.
Aigina, see Aegina . . .	ī'-gĭ-nä.
Aiglon, L'	lä-glôṅ'.
Aiguille du Midi . . .	ā gē'=yŭ dü mē dē'.
Aiguillon (Duc) d' . . .	dä-gē-yôn'
Aijalon, see Ajalon . .	ăj'-ȧ-lŏn.
Aintab	īn-täb'.

Aiolian, see Aeolian . . ā-ō′-lĭ-ȧn.
Aire . . . . âr.
Aisha . . . . ä′-ē-shä.
Aisne . . . . ĕn.
Aix . . . . island, ā. city, ĕks, ās.
Aix-la-Chapelle . . . . ĕks-lä-shä-pĕl′.
Aix-les-Bains . . . . ĕks-lā-băṅ′.
Ajaccio . . . . . . ä-yä′-chō.
Ajalon, see Aijalon . . ăj′-ȧ-lŏn.
Ajax . . . . ā′-jăks.
Ajmere, or Ajmir . . . äj-mēr′.
Ajuntah, see Adjanta . . ă-jŭn′-tȧ.
Akbar, or . . . . . .
Akber, see Ekber . . . äk′-bēr. _Hind._ ŭk′-bĕr.
Akiba (Rabbi) . . . . ä-kē′-bä.
Akimenko . . . . . ä-kē-mĕn′-kō.
Akra . . . . äk-rä′.
Aksakoff, or Aksakov . . äk-sä′-kŏf.
Akyab . . . . äk-yäb′.
Al Aaraaf, see Al Araf . äl-är′-äf.
Alabama . . . . . . ăl-ȧ-bä′-mȧ.
Alabamian . . . . . ăl-ȧ-bä′-mĭ-ȧn.
Alacoque . . . . . . ä-lä-kŏk′.
Aladdin, or Ala-ed-Din . ȧ-lăd′-ĭn, ä-lä′-ĕd-dēn′.
Alamanni, see Alemanni . ăl-ȧ măn′-ī.
Alamannic, see Alemannic ăl-ȧ-măn-ĭk.
Alameda . . . . . . ä lä-mā′-dä.
Alamo . . . . ä′-lä-mō.
Al Araf, see Al Aaraaf . äl är′-äf.
Alarcon y Mendoza . . ä-lär-kōn′ē mĕn-dō′-thä.
Alaric . . . . ăl′-ȧr-ĭk.
Alastor . . . . ă-lăs′-tôr.
Alba (Duke of), see Alva . ăl′-bȧ. _Sp._ äl′-bä.
Alba Longa . . . . . ăl′-bȧ lŏng′-gȧ.
Alban, St. . . . . . . ăl′-băn, ôl′ bȧn.
Albani (Mme.) . . . . äl-bä′-nē.
Albania . . . . . . äl-bā′-nĭ-ȧ.

Albano	äl-bä'-nō.
Albai, or Albay	äl-bä'=ē.
Alberic	ăl'-bĕr-ĭk.
Albert (of Belgium) . .	ăl-bâr'.
Albert, D'	däl-bâr'.
Albertinelli	äl-bâr-tē-näl'-lē.
Albertini	äl-bâr-tē'-nē.
Albert Nyanza	ăl'-bĕrt nyăn'-zȧ.
Albi, see Alby	äl-bē'.
Albigenses	ăl-bĭ-jĕn'-sēz.
Albion	ăl'-bĭ-ŏn.
Alboin	ăl'-boin.
Alboni (Mme.)	äl-bō'-nē.
Albrecht	äl'-brĕċht.
Albret, Jeanne d' . . .	zhän däl-brä'.
Albuera	äl-bōō-ä'-rä.
Albuquerque	ăl'-bū-kĕrk
	Sp. äl-bōō-kâr'-kä.
Alby, see Albi	äl-bē'.
Alcaeus	ăl-sē'-ŭs.
Alcalá de Henares . . .	äl-kä-lä' dä ä-nä'-räs.
Alcamenes	ăl-kăm'-ĕ-nēz.
Alcantara	äl-kän'-tä-rä.
Alcázar	äl-kä'-thär.
Alceste	ăl-sĕst'.
Alcibiades	ăl-sĭ-bī'-ȧ-dēz.
Alcinous	ăl-sĭn'-ō-ŭs.
Alcmaeon	ălk-mē'-ŏn.
Alcmaeonidae	ălk-mē-ŏn'-ĭ-dē.
Alcmene	ălk-mē'-nē.
Alcoran, see Alkoran . .	ăl'-kō-răn, ăl-kō-răn'.
Alcott, (Bronson) . . .	ôl'-kŭt.
Alcuin	ăl'-kwĭn.
Alcyone, see Halcyone .	ăl-sī'-ō-nē.
Aldebaran	äl-dĕb'-ȧ-rȧn, äl-dĕ-bä-rän'.
Alderney	ôl'-dĕr-nĭ.
Aldershot	ôl-dĕr-shŏt.

Aldine . . . . ăl'-dĭn, ôl'-dīn.
Aldobrandini . . . . . äl-dō-brän-dē'-nē.
Aldus Manutius . . . ăl'-dŭs mă-nū'-shĭ-ŭs.
Alecto . . . . ă-lĕk'-tō.
Aleksyeev, see Alexeieff . ä-lĕk-sā'-yĕf.
Alemanni, see Alamanni . ăl-ē-măn'-ī.
Alemannic, see Alamannic ăl-ē-măn'-ĭk.
Alembert, D' . . . . dä-lŏṅ-bâr'.
Alençon . . . . . . ä-lĕn'-sŭn. *Fr.* ä-lŏṅ-sôṅ'.
Alethea . . . . . . ăl-ē-thē'-à.
Aleutian . . . . . . ā-lū'-shĭ-ăn, ăl-ē-ū'-shĭ-ăn.
Aleuts . . . . ăl'-ē-ūts.
Alexeieff, see Aleksyeev . ä-lĕk-sā'-yĕf.
Alfadir . . . . äl-fà'-dĭr.
Alfieri, Vittorio . . . . vēt-tō'-rē-ō äl-fē-ā'-rē.
Alfio . . . . äl-fē'-ō.
Alfonso, see Alphonso . äl-fŏn'-sō, ăl-fŏn'zō. *Sp.*
äl-fōn'-sō.
Alford . . . . ôl'-fŭrd.
Alger . . . . ăl'-jĕr, ôl'-gĕr.
Algerian . . . . . . ăl-jē'-rĭ-àn.
Algerine . . . . . . ăl'-jĕ-rēn.
Algiers . . . . ăl-jērz'.
Algoa (Bay) . . . . . ăl-gō'-à.
Algonkin, or Algonquin . ăl-gŏn'-kĭn, ăl-gŏn'-kwĭn.
Alhambra . . . . . . ăl-hăm'-brà.
Ali Baba . . . . . . ä'-lē bä'-bä.
Alicante . . . . . . äl-ē-kän'-tä.
Alighieri . . . . . . ä-lē-gē-ā'-rē.
Aliwal . . . . äl-ē-wäl'.
Alkmaar . . . . . . älk-mär'.
Alkoran, see Alcoran . . ăl'-kō-ràn, ăl-kō-ràn'.
Allah . . . . ăl'-ä.
Allahabad . . . . . . äl-ä-hä-bäd'.
Alleghany, or Allegheny . ăl'-ē-gā-nĭ, ăl'-ē-gĕn-ĭ.
Allegri . . . . äl-lā'-grē.
Allemagne . . . . . ăl-măn'=yŭ.

Allenstein	äl'-ĕn-shtīn.
Alleyne	ăl'-ĕn.
Aller	äl'-ĕr.
Allobroges	ăl-ŏb'-rō-jēz.
Almacks	ôl'-măks.
Almagest	ăl'-má-jĕst.
Almahide	äl-mä-ēd'.
Almansa, see Almanza .	äl-män'-sä.
Al Mansour, Al Mansur .	äl män-sōōr'.
Almanza, see Almansa .	äl-män'-thä.
Alma-Tadema	äl'-mä tä'-dĕ-mä.
Almeida	äl-mä'-ē-dä.
Almeyda (Bay)	äl-mä'-dä.
Almirante Oquendo . .	äl-mē-rän'-tä ō-kĕn'-dō.
Almohades	ăl'-mō-hädz.
Almoravides	ăl-mō'-rá-vīdz.
Alnwick	ăn'-ĭk.
Aloiadae, or Aloidae . .	ă-lō-ī'-á-dē, ă-lō-ī'-dē
Aloysius	ăl-ō-ĭsh'-ĭ-ŭs.
Alpes-Maritimes . . .	älp-mär-ē-tēm'.
Alph	ălf.
Alpheius, or Alpheus . .	ăl-fī'-ŭs, ăl-fē'-ŭs.
Alphonse	ăl-fôns'.
Alphonso, see Alfonso .	ăl-fŏn'-sō, ăl-fŏn'-zō.
	Sp. äl-fōn'-sō.
Alpini	äl-pē'-nē.
Alpujarras, or Alpuxaras .	äl-pōō-chär'-räs.
Alsace-Lorraine	äl-zäs' lōr-rĕn'.
Al Sirat	äl sē-rät'.
Altai	äl-tī'.
Altaic	ăl-tä'-ĭk.
Alter Fritz	äl'-tĕr frĭts.
Althaea	ăl-thē'á.
Althing	äl'-tĭng.
Alton Locke	ôl'-tŭn lŏk.
Altstrelitz	ält-shträ'-lĭtz.
Alva, Duke of, see Alba .	ăl'-vá. Sp. äl'-bä.

Alvarado . . . . . . äl-bä-rä′-dō.
Alvares . . . . . . äl′-bä-rĕs.
Alvarez . . . . . . *Port.* äl′-vä-rĕz.
                    Sp. äl′-bä-rĕth.
Alvary . . . . äl-vä′-rĭ.
Alvinczy, or Alvinzi . . ôl′-vĭn-tsē.
Alwar, see Ulwar . . . äl′-wär.
Amadeo . . . . . . ä-mä-dā′-ō.
Amadeus . . . . . . ăm-à-dē′-ŭs.
Amadis of Gaul . . . . ăm′-à-dĭs ŭv gôl.
Amalfi . . . . ä-mäl′-fē.
Amalia, Anna . . . . än′-ä ä-mä′-lē=ä.
Aman-Jean . . . . . ä-män′-zhän′.
Amants Magnifiques, Les lä zä-män′ män-yē-fēk′.
Amaryllis . . . . . . ăm-à-rĭl′-ĭs.
Amasa . . . . ăm′-à-sà.
Amati . . . . ä-mä′-tē.
Amaury . . . . . . ă-mô′-rĭ. *Fr.* ä-mō-rē′.
Amazulu . . . . . . ä-mä-zoō′-loō.
Ambois . . . . . . än-bwä′.
Amboise . . . . . . än-bwäz′.
Ambrogio, San . . . sän äm-brō′-jŏ.
Ambrosius, (St.) . . . ăm-brō′-zhĭ-ŭs.
Ambur . . . . àm-boōr′.
Amenhotep . . . . . ä-mĕn-hō′-tĕp.
Amerigo Vespucci . . . ä-mĕr-ē′-gō vĕs-poō′-chē.
Amerongen . . . . . àm′-ĕr-ông-ĕn.
Amicis, De . . . . . dä ä-mē′-chēs.
Amiel . . . . ā′-mĭ-ĕl.
Amiel, Henri Frédéric . ŏn-rē′ frä-dä-rēk′ ă-mē-ĕl′.
Amiens . . . . . . ă-mē-än′.
Amistad . . . . . . *Sp.* ä-mēs-täd′.
Amlwch . . . . . . ăm′-loōk.
Amneris . . . . . . äm-nä′-rēs.
Amoor, see Amur . . . ä-moōr′.
Amor . . . . ā′-môr.
Amoret . . . . . . ăm′-ō-rĕt.

Amorites	ăm'-ō-rīts.
Amory (Blanche) . . .	ā'-mō-rĭ.
Amoskeag	ăm-ŏs-kĕg'.
Amoy	ä-moi'.
Ampère	äṅ-pâr'.
Amphictyonic	ăm-fĭk-tĭ-ŏn'-ĭk.
Amphictyony	ăm-fĭk'-tĭ-ŏn-ĭ.
Amphion	ăm-fī'-ŏn.
Amphipolis	ăm-fĭp'-ō-lĭs.
Amphitrite	ăm-fĭ-trī'-tē.
Amphitryon	ăm-fĭt'-rĭ-ŏn.
Amritsar, see Umritsir .	ȧm-rĭt'-sär.
Amundsen	ä'-mo͝ont-sĕn.
Amur, see Amoor . . .	ä-moōr'.
Amurath	ä-moō-rät'.
Amyot	ä-mē-ō'.
Anabasis	ȧ-năb'-ȧ-sĭs.
Anacreon, see Anakreon .	ă-năk'-rē-ŏn.
Anadyomene	ăn-ȧ-dĭ-ŏm'-ĕ-nē.
Anagni	än-än'-yē.
Anahuac	ä-nä'-wäk.
Anak	ā'-năk.
Anakim	ăn'-ă-kĭm.
Anakreon, see Anacreon .	ă-năk'-rē-ŏn.
Anam, see Annam . . .	ăn-ăm', än-äm'.
Ananias	ăn-ȧ-nī'-ȧs.
Añasco	än-yäs'-kō.
Anastasius	ăn-ăs-tā'-shĭ-ŭs.
Anathoth	ăn'-ȧ-thŏth.
Anatolian	ăn-ȧ-tō'-lĭ-ȧn.
Anaxagoras	ăn-ăks-ăg'-ō-rȧs.
Anaximander	ăn-ăks-ĭ-măn'-dĕr.
Anaximenes	ăn-ăks-ĭm'-ĕ-nēz.
Anchises	ăn-kī'-sēz.
Ancillon	äṅ-sē-yôṅ'.
Anckarström	äng'-kär-strĕm.
Ancona	än-kō'-nä.

Ancre (Marquis) d' . . däṅ'-kr.
Ancus Marcius . . . . ăng'-kŭs mär'-shĭ=ŭs.
Andalucia . . . . . . *Sp.* än-dä-lōō-thē'-ä
Andalusia . . . . . . ăn-dȧ-lū'-shĭ-ȧ,
   ăn-dȧ-lōō'-zĭ-ȧ.
Andaman . . . . . . ăn'-dȧ-mȧn.
Andelys, Les . . . . . lä zäṅ=dŭ-lē's
Andermatt . . . . . än'-dĕr-mät.
Andernach . . . . . än'-dĕr-näċh.
Andersen, Hans . . . häns än'-dĕr-sĕn.
Andes . . . . ăn'-dēz.
Andorra . . . . . . än-dŏr'-rä.
Andrássy . . . . . . ŏn'-drä-shē.
André . . . . än'-drā, ăn'-drĭ. *Fr.*
   äṅ-drā'.
Andrea del Sarto . . . än-drā'-ä dĕl sär'-tō.
Andrea Ferrara . . . . ăn'-drē-ȧ fĕr-rä'-rä.
Andrée . . . . . . äṅ'-drä.
Andreieff (-eyev) . . . ȧn-drā'-yĕf.
Androclus . . . . . . ăn'-drō-klŭs.
Andromache . . . . . ăn-drŏm'-ă-kē.
Andromaque . . . . . *Fr.* äṅ-drō-măk'.
Andromeda . . . . . ăn-drŏm'-ĕ-dȧ.
Andromède . . . . . äṅ-drō-mĕd'.
Andronicus . . . . . ăn-drō-nī'-kŭs.
   Shak. ăn-drŏn'-ĭ-кŭs.
Anelida . . . . . . ă-nĕl'-ĭ-dȧ.
Angara (R.) . . . . . än-gä-rä'.
Angelico, Fra . . . . frä än-jĕl'-ē-kō.
Angélique . . . . . . äṅ-zhä-lēk'.
Angelo . . . . ăn'-jĕ-lō. *It.* än'-jā-lō.
Angelus . . . . . . ăn'-jĕ-lŭs.
Angers . . . . ăn'-jērs. *Fr.* äṅ-zhä'.
Angevin, or Angevine . . ăn'-jē-vĭn, ăn'-jē-vīn.
Anghiari . . . . . . än-gē-ä'-rē.
Anglesea (-sey) . . . . ăng'-gl-sē.
Angra Pequeña . . . . äng'-grä pā-kän'-yȧ.

Annas . . . . ăn'-ȧs.
Annecy . . . . . . än-sē'.
Anse . . . . äṅs.
Antares . . . . . . ăn-tā'-rēz.
Antigone . . . . . . ăn-tĭg'-ō-nē.
Antigonus . . . . . . ăn-tĭg'-ō-nŭs.
Antigua . . . . . . än-tē'-gwä.
Antilles . . . . . . än-tĭl'-lēz. *Fr.* äṅ-tēl'.
Antilochus . . . . . ăn-tĭl'-ō-kŭs.
Anti-Macchiavel . . . ăn-tĭ-măk,-ĭ-ȧ-vĕl.
Antin (Duc) d' . . . . däṅ-tăṅ'.
Antinous . . . . . . ăn-tĭn'-ō-ŭs.
Antioch . . . . . . ăn'-tĭ-ŏk.
Antiochus . . . . . . ăn-tī'-ō-kŭs.
Antiope . . . . . . ăn-tī'-ō-pē.
Antipas, Herod . . . . hĕr'-ŏd ăn'-tĭ-păs.
Antipater . . . . . . ăn-tĭp'-ȧ-tĕr
Antiphanes . . . . . ăn-tĭf'-ă-nēz.
Antiphon . . . . . . ăn'-tĭ-fŏn.
Antipodes . . . . . . ăn-tĭp'-ō-dēz, ăn'-tĭ-pōds.
Antipolo . . . . . . än-tē-pō'-lō.
Antistates . . . . . . ăn-tĭs'-tă-tēz.
Antium . . . . . . ăn'-shĭ-ŭm.
Antivari . . . . . . än-tē'-vä-rē.
Antofagasta . . . . . än"-tō-fä-gäs'-tä.
Antoine de Bourbon . . äṅ-twăn' dĕ bōōr-bôṅ'.
Antokolsky . . . . . än-tō-kŏl'-skē.
Anton Ulrich . . . . . än'-tōn ōōl'-rĭch.
Antonelli Giaccomo (Cardinal) jä'-kō-mō än-tō-nĕl'-lē.
Antonello da Messina . än-tō-nĕl'-lō dämĕs-sē'-nä.
Antonina . . . . . . ăn-tō-nī-nä.
Antoninus Pius . . . . ăn-tō-nī'-nŭs pī'-ŭs.
Antonio . . . . . . än-tō'-nē-ō.
Antraigues, see Entraigues äṅ-trāg'.
Antwerp . . . . . . ănt'-wĕrp.
Anubis, see Anoobis . . ă-nū'-bĭs.
Anvers . . . . äṅ-vârs'.

Anzac	ăn'-zăk.
Aosta	ä-ŏs'-tä.
Apache, or	ä-pä'-chä.
Apaches	*pop.* ä-păch'-ēz.
Apari, or Aparri	ä-pär-rē'.
Apelles	ă-pĕl'-ēz.
Apemantus	ăp-ĕ-măn'-tŭs.
Apennines	ăp'-ĕ-nīnz.
Aphrodite	ăf-rō-dī'-tē.
Apia	ä'-pē-ä.
Apicius	ă-pĭsh'-ĭ=ŭs.
Apocalypse	à-pŏk'-à-lĭps.
Apocrypha	à-pŏk'-rĭ-fà.
Apollinare in Classe . .	ä-pōl-lē-nä'-rĕ ĭn kläs'-sĕ.
Apollino	ă-pŏl-lē'-nō.
Apollo Belvedere . . .	à-pŏl'-ō bĕl-vē-dēr'.
	It. ä-pōl'-lō bāl-vä-dä'-rĕ.
Apollo Chresterios . . .	à-pŏl'-ō krĕs-tē'-rĭ-ŏs.
Apollo Citharoedus . .	à-pŏl'-ō sĭth-à-rē'-dŭs.
Apollo Sauroktonos . .	à-pŏl'-ō sôr-ŏk'-tō-nŏs.
Apollodorus	à-pŏl''-ō-dō'-rŭs.
Apollonius	ăp-ŏl-ō'-nĭ-ŭs.
Apollyon	ă-pŏl'-yŏn, ā-pŏl'-ĭ-ŏn.
Apoxyomenos	ăp''-ŏks-ĭ-ŏm'-ĕ-nŏs.
Appalachian	ăp-à-lăch'-ĭ-ăn,
	ăp-ā-lā-chĭ-ăn.
Appii Forum	ăp'-ĭ-ī fō'-rŭm.
Appomattox	ăp-ō-măt'-ŏks.
Apponyi	ŏp'-pōn-yē.
Appuleius, see Apuleius .	ăp-ū-lē'-ŭs.
Apraxin	ä-präk'-sĭn.
Apries	ā'-prē-ēz.
Apuleius, see Appuleius .	ăp-ū-lē'-ŭs.
Apulia. It. Puglia . . .	à-pū'-lĭ-à.
Aquae Sextiae	ā'-kwē sĕk'-stĭ-ē.
Aquambo	ä-kwäm-bō'.
Aquapim	ä-kwä-pēm'.

Aquarius . . . . . . à-kwā'-rĭ-ŭs.
Aquednek, or . . . . ă-kwĕd'-nĕk.
Aquidneck . . . . . à-kwĭd'-nĕk.
Aquila . . . . ä'-kwē-lä.
Aquinas . . . . . . à-kwī'-nàs.
Aquitaine . . . . . ăk-wĭ-tān'. *Fr.* ä-kē-tän'.
Arab . . . . ăr'-àb.
Arabia Petraea . . . à-rā'-bĭ-ä pē-trē'-ä.
Arabic . . . . ăr'-à-bĭk.
Arabi Pasha . . . . . ä-rä'-bē păsh-ô', pà-shä',
　　　　　　　　　　or päsh'-à.
Araby . . . . ăr'-à-bĭ.
Ara Celi, or Coeli . . . ā'-rä sē'-lī.
Arachne . . . . . . à-răk'-nē.
Araf, Al, see Al Aaraaf . äl ä'-ràf.
Arafat . . . . ä-rä-fät'.
Arago . . . . är'-à-gō. *Fr.* ä-rä-gō'.
Aragon . . . . ăr'-à-gŏn. *Sp.* ä-rä-gōn'.
Araktcheyeff . . . . . ä-räk-chā'-yĕf.
Aral (Sea) . . . . . ăr'-àl.
Aram (Eugene) . . . . ā'-ràm.
Aramaic . . . . . . ăr-à-mā'-ĭk.
Aramis . . . . ä-rä-mēs'.
Aranjuez . . . . . . ä-räng-:'hwĕth'.
Arany János . . . . . ŏr-ŏn-yē' yä'-nōsh.
Arapaho, or Arapahoe . à-răp'-à-hō.
Arar . . . . ā'-rär.
Ararat . . . . ăr'-ă-răt.
Arayat . . . . ä-rä'=ē-ät.
Arbaces . . . . . . är'-bă-sēz, är-bā'-sēz.
Arbate . . . . är-bät'.
Arbela . . . . är-bē'-lä.
Arblay (Mme.) d' . . . där-blä'.
Arbois . . . . är-bwä'.
Arbuthnot . . . . . . är'-bŭth-nŏt. *Sc.*
　　　　　　　　　　är-bŭth'-nŏt.
Arcades . . . . . . är"-kà-dēz.

Arcady . . . . är'-kȧ-ŏĭ.
Arc de Triomphe de L'Étoile ärk dŭ trē-ôṅf' dŭ lä-twäl'.
Arc de Triomphe du Car- ärk dŭ trē-ôṅf' dü
  rousel . . . . . . kä-rōō-zĕl'.
Archangel . . . . . . ärk-ān'-jĕl.
Archangelsk . . . . . är-ćhäng'-gĕlsk.
Arcnelaus . . . . . . är-kē-lä'-ŭs.
Archias . . . . är'-kĭ-ȧs.
Archidamus . . . . . är-kĭ-dä'-mŭs.
Archilochus . . . . . är-kĭl'-ō-kŭs.
Archimage . . . . . är'-kĭ-mäj.
Archimago . . . . . . är-kĭ-mä'-gō.
Archimedean . . . . . är-kĭ-mē-dē'-ȧn.
Archimedes . . . . . är-kĭ-mē'-dēz.
Arcis-sur-Aube . . . . är-sē'-sür-ōb'.
Arcite . . . . är'-sīt.
Arco dei Leoni . . . . är'kō dä'-ē lä-ō'-nē.
Arco della Pace . . . . är'-kō dĕl'-lä pä'-chĕ.
Arcola, or Arcole . . . är'kō-lä, är'-kō-lĕ.
Arcot . . . . är-kŏt'.
Arcturus . . . . . . ärk-tū'-rŭs.
Arcueil . . . . är-kē'=yŭ.
Ardahan . . . . . . är-dä-hän'.
Ardennais . . . . . är-dĕn-nä'.
Ardennes . . . . . . är-dĕn'.
Arditi, Luigi . . . . . lōō-ē'-jē är-dē'-tē.
Ardres . . . . ärdr.
Ardrossan . . . . . . är-drŏs'-ȧn.
Arduin . . . . ärd'-wĭn.
Are, see Ari . . . . . ä'-rĕ.
Arecibo . . . . ä-rä-sē'-bō.
Arenas Gordas, Las . . läs ä-rä'-nȧs gōr'-dȧs.
Arensky . . . . . . ä-rĕn'-shkē.
Areopagite . . . . . ăr-ē-ŏp'-ȧ-jīt.
Areopagitica . . . . . ăr"-ē-ō-pă-jĭt'-ĭ-kä.
Areopagus . . . . . ā-rē-ŏp'-ă-gŭs.
Arequipa . . . . . . ä-rä-kē'-pȧ.

Ares	ā'rēz.
Arethusa	ăr-ē-thū'-sä.
Aretine	ăr'-ĕ-tĭn.
Aretino, Guido . . .	gwē'-dō ä-rä-tē'-nō.
Arezzo	ä-rĕt'-sō.
Argam, see Argaum . .	är-gäm'.
Argan	är-gäṅ'.
Argante (Spenser) . .	är-găn'tĕ.
Argante (Molière) . .	är-gäṅt'.
Argantes	är-gän'-tĕs.
Argaum, see Argam . .	är-gôm'.
Argenis	är'-jĕ-nĭs.
Argenson, d'	där-zhŏṅ-sôṅ'.
Argenteau	är-zhôṅ-tō'.
Argenteuil	är-zhŏṅ-tē'=yŭ.
Argentina	är-jĕn-tē'-nä. Sp.
	är-chĕn-tē'-nä.
Argentine	är'-jĕn-tīn, är'-jĕn-tēn.
Argives	är'-jīvz.
Argolis	är'-gō-lĭs.
Argonauts	är'-gō-nôtz.
Argonnes	är-gŏn'.
Argüelles	är-gwĕl'-yĕs.
Argyle, or Argyll . .	är-gīl'.
Ari, see Are	ä'-rē.
Ariadne	ăr-ĭ-ăd'-nē. ā-rĭ-ăd'-nē.
Arian	ā'-rĭ-ȧn.
Ariane	ä-rē-än'.
Arians	ā'-rĭ-ȧnz, ȧ'-rĭ-ȧnz.
Ariège	ä-rē-ĕzh'.
Ariel	ā'-rĭ-ĕl.
Aries	ā'-rĭ-ēz.
Ariete	ä-rē-ĕ'-tä.
Ariguanabo	ä-rē-gwä-nä'-bō.
Arimathaea, or Arimathea	ăr-ĭ-mä-thē'-ä.
Arion	ă-rī'-ŏn.
Ariosto	ăr-ĭ-ŏs'-tō. It. ä-rē-ŏs'-tō.

Arista (Gen.)	ä-rēs′-tä.
Aristagoras	ăr-ĭs-tăg′-ō-rås.
Aristarchus	ăr-ĭs-tär′-kŭs.
Ariste	ä-rēst′.
Aristeides, or Aristides .	ăr-ĭs-tī′-dēz.
Aristippus	ăr-ĭs-tĭp′-ŭs.
Aristobulus	ăr″-ĭs-tō-bū′-lŭs.
Aristodemus	ăr″-ĭs-tō-dē′-mŭs.
Aristogeiton, or Aristogiton	ăr″-ĭs-tō-jī′-tŏn.
Aristophanes	ăr-ĭs-tŏf′-å-nēz.
Aristotle	ăr′-ĭs-tŏtl.
Arius	ăr′-ĭ-ŭs, ā′-rĭ-ŭs.
Arjish	är-yĭsh′.
Arkansas	är′-kăn-sô, är-kăn′-zås.
Arles	ärlz. Fr. ärl.
Arlésienne, L'	lär-lä-zē=ĕn′.
Arline	är′-lēn.
Armada	är-mä′-dä.
Armado, Don	dŏn är-mä′-dō.
Armageddon	är-må-gĕd′-ŏn.
Armagh	är-mä′.
Armagnac	år-mån-yåk′.
Armande Béjart	är-mänd′ bā-zhär′.
Armentières	är-mŏṅ-tē=är′.
Armida	är-mē′-dä.
Armide et Renaud . . .	är-mēd′ ā rĕ-nō′.
Arminius	är-mĭn′-ĭ-ŭs.
Armorel of Lyonesse . .	är′-mō-rĕl ŭv lī′-ŏn-ĕs.
Armorica	är-mŏr′-ĭ-kä.
Armorican	är-mŏr′ĭ-kån.
Arnauld	är-nō′.
Arnaut	är′-nôt.
Arnim, Bettina von . .	bĕt-tē′-nä fŏn är′-nĭm.
Arno	är′-nō.
Arnolfo di Cambio . . .	är-nōl′-fō dē käm′-bē-ō.
Arnolfo di Lapo	är-nōl′-fō dē lä′-pō.
Arnolphe	är-nōlf′.

Arondight	ā'-rŏn-dīt.
Aroostook	ȧ-rōōs'-tŏŏk.
Arouet	ȧ-rōō-ā'.
Arpachshad, see Arphaxad	är-păk-shăd'.
Árpád	är'-päd.
Arphaxad, see Arpachshad	är-făk'-săd.
Arquà	är-kwä'
Arques	ärk.
Arras	är-räs'.
Arrhidaeus	ăr-ĭ-dē'-ŭs.
Arrivabene	är-rē-vä-bä'-nĕ.
Arroyo Molinos . . .	är-rō'yō mō-lē'nōs.
Arsaces	är'-să-sēz, är-sä'-sēz.
Arsacidae	är-săs'-ĭ-dē.
Arsames	är'-sä-mēz.
Arsenieff	är-sĕn'-yĕf.
Arsiero	är-sē-ā'-rō.
Arsinoë	är-sĭn'-ō-ē.
Ars Poetica	ärz pō-ĕt'-ĭ-kȧ.
Artachshast	är-tăk-shăst'.
Artagnan, D'	där-tän-yäṅ'.
Artamène	är-tä-mĕn'.
Artaphernes	är-tȧ-fēr'-nēz.
Artaxerxes	är-tăks-ērks'-ēz.
Artegal	är'-tē-gȧl.
Artemas	är'tē-mȧs.
Artemidorus	är-tē-mĭ-dō'-rŭs.
Artemis	är'-tē-mĭs.
Artemisia	är-tē-mĭsh'-ĭ=ä.
Artemisium	är-tē-mĭsh'-ĭ=ŭm.
Artevelde, Van	văn är'-tĕ-vĕl-dĕ.
Artiago	är-tē-ä'-gō.
Artichofsky	är-tē-shōv'-skē.
Artois	är-twä'.
Aruba	ä-rōō'-bä.
Arundel	ăr'ŭn-dĕl.
Aruwimi	är-ōō-wē'-mē.

Arviragus . . . . . . är-vĭr'-à-gŭs.
Aryan . . . . är'yàn, är'-ĭ=än.
Asaph . . . . ā'-sàf.
Asben . . . . äs-bĕn'.
Asboth . . . . ăs'-bŏth. *Hung.* ŏsh'-bōt.
Ascagne . . . . . . äs-kän'=yŭ.
Ascalon, see Askelon . . ăs'-kă-lŏn.
Ascanio . . . . . äs-kä'-nē=ō.
Aschaffenburg . . . . ä-shäf'-ĕn-bōōrċh.
Ascham . . . . . . ăs'-kăm.
Asdrubal, see Hasdrubal ăs'-drŭ-bàl.
Asenath . . . . . . ăs'ē-năth, ā-sē'-năth.
Aserraderos . . . . . ä-sâr-rä-dä'-rōs.
Asgard . . . . ăs'-gärd.
Ashango . . . . . . ä-shän'-gō.
Ashantee or Ashanti . . ä-shän'-tē, ă-shăn'-tē.
Ashby-de-la-Zouch . . ăsh'bĭ-dĕl-à-zōōch'.
Ashestiel . . . . . . ăsh'-ĕs-tēl.
Ashtaroth, Ashteroth . . ăsh'-tà-rŏth.
Ashtoreth, see Ashtaroth ăsh'tō-rĕth.
Asia . . . . ā'shĭ=ä, ā'-zhĭ=ä.
Asiago . . . . ä-sē-ä'-gō.
Asiatic . . . . ä-shĭ-ăt'-ĭk, ā-zhĭ-ăt'-ĭk.
Asisi, see Assisi . . . ä-zē'-zē.
Askabad . . . . . . äs-kä-bäd'.
Askelon, see Ascalon . . ăs'-kĕ-lŏn.
Askew (Anne) . . . . ăs'-kū.
Asklepios, see Aesculapius ăs-klē'pĭ-ŏs.
Asmodeus . . . . . ăs-mō-dē'-ŭs, ăs-mō'-dē-ŭs.
Asnières . . . . . . ä-nē=âr'.
Asola . . . . ä-zō'lä.
Asolando . . . . . . ăs-ō-lăn'-dō.
Asolo . . . . ä'-zō-lō.
Asolone . . . . . . ä-sō-lō'-nä.
Aspasia . . . . . . ăs-pä'-shĭ=à.
Aspromonte . . . . . äs-prō-mōn'-tĕ.
Asquith . . . . . . ăs'-kwĭth.

Assam	ăs-săm'.
Assaye, see Assye	äs-sī'.
Assen	äs'-ĕn.
Assini	äs-sē'-nē.
Assiniboia	ăs''-ĭn-ĭ-boi'-ä.
Assisi, see Asisi	ä-sē'-zē.
Assommoir, L'	lä-sŏm-wär'.
Assouan, Assuan, or Asswan	äs-swän'.
Assuay, see Azuay	äs-sōō-ī'.
Assye, see Assaye	äs-sī'.
Astarte	ăs-tär'tē.
Asterabad, see Astrabad	äs-tĕr-ä-bäd'.
Asti	äs'tē.
Astolat	ăs'-tō-lăt.
Astolfo, or Astolpho	ăs-tŏl'fō.
Astorga	äs-tōr'-gä.
Astrabad, see Asterabad	äs-trä-bäd'.
Astraea, or Astrea Redux	ăs-trē'ä rē'dŭks.
Astrakhan	äs-trä-ĉhän'.
Astrée	äs-trä'.
Astrolabe	ăs'-trō-läb.
Astrophel	ăs'-trō-fĕl.
Asturias	äs-tōō'-rē-äs.
Astyages	ăs-tī'á-jēz.
Astyanax	ăs-tī'-à-năks.
Asuncion	ä-sōōn-thē-ōn'.
Asurbanipal	ä-sōōr-bä'-nĭ-päl.
Atacama	ä-tä-kä'-mä.
Atahualpa	ä-tä-wäl'pä.
Atak, see Attock	ăt-ăk'.
Atala	ä-tä-lä'.
Atalanta in Calydon	ăt-à-lăn'-tä ĭn kăl'-ĭ-dŏn.
Ataliba	ăt-ă-lē'-bä.
Atalide	ăt-ä-lēd'.
Atbara	ät-bä'-rä.
Ate	ā'-tē.
Aterno	ä-tĕr'-nō.

Athalaric, see Athalric	ăth-ăl'-à-rĭk.
Athaliah	ăth-à-lī'-ä.
Athalie	ä-tä-lē'.
Athalric, see Athalaric	ăth-ăl'-rĭk.
Athanasian	ăth-à-nā'-zhĭ-zàn.
Athanasius	ăth-à-nā'-shĭ=ŭs.
Atharvaveda	ăt-här-vä-vā'-dä.
Athena	ă-thē'-nä.
Athenaeum, see Atheneum	ăth-ĕ-nē'-ŭm.
Athene	ă-thē'-nē.
Athene Parthenos . . .	ă-thē'-nē pär'-thĕ-nŏs.
Athene Polias	ă-thē'-nē pŏl'-ĭ-ăs.
Atheneum, see Athenaeum	ăth-ĕ-nē'-ŭm.
Athol	ăth'-ŏl.
Athos (Mt.)	ăth'ŏs.
Athos (Dumas)	ä-tōs'.
Atlantean	ăt-lăn-tē'-àn.
Atlantides	ăt-lăn'-tĭ-dēz.
Atreus	ā'-trūs, ā'-trē-ŭs.
Atri	ä'-trē.
Atria	ä'-trē-ä.
Atridae	ă-trī'dē.
Atropos	ăt'-rō-pŏs.
Attalia	ăt-à-lī'-ä.
Attalus	ăt'-à-lŭs.
Attar	ăt-tär'.
Atticus	ăt'-ĭ-kŭs.
Attila	ăt'-ĭ-lä.
Attis, see Atys . . .	ăt'-ĭs.
Attock, see Atak . . .	ăt-tŏk'.
Atys, see Attis . . .	ăt'-ĭs.
Aubanel	ō-bä-nĕl'.
Aubé, Jean Paul . . .	zhŏn pōl ō-bā'.
Auber (D. F. E.) . . .	ō-bâr'.
Auberge Rouge	ō-bârzh' rōōzh'.
Aubert	ō-bâr'.
Aubigné, D'	dō-bēn-yä'.

Aubusson . . . . . . ō-büs-ôṅ'.
Aucassin et Nicolette . . ō-kă-săṅ'nā nē-kō-lĕt'.
Auch . . . . ōsh.
Aude . . . . ōd.
Audefroy le Bastard . . ōd-frwä' lĕ bås-tär'.
Audenarde, see Oudenarde ōd-närd'.
Audh, see Oudh, Oude . owd.
Audouin . . . . . . ō-dōō-ăṅ'.
Audran . . . . . . ō-dräṅ'.
Audrey . . . . . . ôd'-rĭ.
Aue, Hartmann von . . härt'män fŏn ow'-ŭ.
Audubon . . . . . . ô'-dū-bŏn.
Auerbach . . . . . . ow'-ĕr-bäċh.
Auersperg . . . . . ow'-ĕrs-pĕrċh.
Auerstädt or Auerstedt . ow'ĕr-stĕt.
Auf der Höhe . . . . owf dĕr hē'-yŭ.
Augarten . . . . . . ow'-gär-tĕn.
Augean . . . . . . ô-jē'-ȧn.
Augeas . . . . . . ô'-jē-ăs, ô-jē'-ăs.
Auger . . . . Fr. ō-zhä'.
Augereau . . . . . . ōzh-rō'.
Aughrim, see Aghrim . . ôg'-rĭm.
Augier, Émile . . . . ā-mēl' ō-zhē=ā'.
Augsburg . . . . . . ôgz'-bērg. Ger.
    owgs'-bōōrċh.
Augusta Victoria . . . ô-gŭs'tä vĭk-tō'-rĭ-à.
    Ger. ow-gōōs'-tä,
    fēk-tō'-rē-ä.
Augustenburg . . . . ow-gōōs'tĕn-bōōrċh.
Augustine . . . . . . ô-gŭs'-tĭn, ô'-gŭs-tĭn.
Augusti y Davila . . . ä=ōō-gōōs'-tē ē dä'-bē-lä.
Augustovo . . . . . ow-gōōs-tō'-vō.
Augustulus . . . . . ô-gŭst'-yū-lŭs.
August Wilhelm . . . Ger. ow'-gōōst vĭl'-hĕlm.
Aulis . . . . ô'-lĭs.
Aulnoy, or Aunoy . . . ō-nwä'.
Aumale, Duc d' . . . . dük dō-măl'.

Aurangabad, see Aurengabad	ow-rŭng-gȧ-bäd'.
Aurelle de Paladines	ō-rĕl'dŭ pä-lä-dēn'.
Aurengabad, or Aurungabad	ow-rŭng-gȧ-bäd'.
Aureng-zebe, or Aurung-zeb	ô'-rŭng-zĕb'.
Aurigny	ō-rēn-yē'.
Aus der Ohe	ows dĕr-ō'-ŭ.
Aussa	ow'-sä.
Austerlitz	ows'-tĕr-lĭts.
Austrasia	ôs-trä'-shĭ=ȧ, ôs-trä'-zhĭ=ȧ
Austria-Hungary	ôs'-trĭ-ä-hŭng'-gä-rĭ.
Auteuil	ō-tē'=yŭ.
Autolycus	ô-tŏl'-ĭ-kŭs.
Automedon	ô-tŏm'-ĕ-dŏn.
Autriche	ō-trēsh'.
Auvergnat	ō-vȃrn-yä'.
Auvergne	ō-vȃrn'=yŭ.
Aux Cayes, see Cayes	ō kä.
Auxerre	ōks-ȃr'.
Auxerrois	ōks-ȃr-wä'.
Avalon or Avallon	ăv'-ă-lŏn.
Avalos, D'	dä-vä'-lŏs.
Avare, L'	lă-vȧr'.
Ave Maria	ä'-vē mȧ-rī'-ȧ. *It.* ä'-vä mä-rē'-ä.
Avenel	äv'-nĕl.
Aventine	ăv'-ĕn-tĭn.
Avenue de l'Opéra	ăv-nü' dŭ lō-pä-rä'.
Ave Roma Immortalis	ä'-vē rō'-mȧ ĭm-ôr-tä'-lĭs.
Averrhoës or Averroës	ă-vĕr'-ō-ĕz.
Avesnes	ä-vän'.
Avicenna	ăv-ĭ-sĕn'-ä.
Avignon	ä-vēn-yôṅ'.
Avila	ä'-vē-lä.
Avilion, see Avalon	ă-vĭl'yŏn.
Aviz	*Port.* ä-vēz'; *Sp.* ä'-vĭth.
Avlona	äv-lō'-nä.

Avogadro	ä-vō-gä′-drō.
Avon	ā′-vŏn, *local Am.* ăv′-ŏn.
Avre	ävr.
Ayala, Pero López	pä′-rō lō′-pĕth ä-yä′-lä.
Axayacatl, or	ă-tchä-yä-kä′-tl.
Axayacatzlin	ä-tchä-yä-kătz-lēn′.
Axim	äks′-ĭm, ä-shēng′.
Axminster	ăks′-mĭn-stēr.
Ay, see Aï	ä′=ē.
Ayacucho	ä=ē-ä-kōō′-chō.
Ayala	ä-yä′-lä.
Aybonito, see Aibonito	ä=ē-bō-nē′-tō.
Ayesha	ä-yĕ′-shä.
Aymon	ā′-mōn.
Ayoub Khan, see Ayub Khan	ä-yōōb′ khän.
Ayr	âr.
Ayscue	ās′-kū.
Aytoun	ā′-tōōn.
Ayub Khan, see Ayoub Khan	ä-yōōb′ khän.
Azarael, or Azareel	ăz′-á-rā-ĕl, äz′-á-rĕ-ĕl.
Azarias	ăz-á-rī′-ás.
Azazel	ă-zä′-zĕl.
Azaziel	ă-zā′-zĭ-ĕl.
Azeglio, D′	däd-zāl′-yō.
Azerbaijan	äz-ĕr-bī-jän′.
Azimgarh	ă-zĭm-gŭr′.
Azincourt, see Agincourt	ăz′-ĭn-kōrt. *Fr.* äzh-ăṅ-kōōr′.
Azof, or Azoff, see Azov	ä′-zŏf.
Azor	*Sp.* ä-thōr′.
Azores	ă-zōrz′.
Azorin	ä-sō-rēn′.
Azov, see Azof	ä′-zŏf.
Azrael, or Azrail	ăz′-rā-ĕl, äz′-rā-ĭl.
Aztecas	ăz′-tĕk-áz.
Azuay, see Assuay	ä-thōō-ī′.
Azucena	äd-zōō-chä′-nä.

B

Baal	bā'-ȧl.
Baalbac, or Baalbak . .	bäl'-bắk, bäl-bắk'.
Baalbec, or Baalbek . .	bäl'-bĕk, bäl-bĕk'.
Baalim	bā'-ȧ-lĭm.
Bab	bäb.
Baba, Ali	ä'-lē bä'-bä.
Bab-el-Mandeb	bäb-ĕl-män'-dĕb.
Baber, see Babur . . .	bä'-bēr.
Babieca, see Bavieca . .	bä-bē=ā'-kä.
Babington	bắb'-ĭng-tŏn.
Babist	bäb'-ĭst.
Babur, see Baber . . .	bä'-bēr.
Babúyan (Is.)	bä-bōō'-yän.
Babylonic	bắb-ĭ-lŏn'-ĭk.
Bacchae	bắk'-ē.
Bacchante	bắk-kắn'-tē.
Bacchus	bắk'-ŭs.
Bacchylides	bắ-kĭl'-ĭ-dēz.
Bacciochi	bä-chŏk'-kē.
Baccio della Porta . . .	bä'-chō dĕl'-lä pōr'-tä.
Bach, J. S.	bäċh.
Bache	bāch.
Backergunge, see Baker- ganj	bäk-ĕr-gŭnj.
Backhuysen	bäk'-hoi-zĕn.
Bacolod	bä-kō-lōd'.
Bacolor	bä-kō-lōr'.
Bacoor, see Bakoor . .	bắ-kōōr'.
Bacsânyi	bä'-chän-yē.
Bactriana	bắk-trĭ-ā'-nä.
Badagry	bä-dä-grē'.
Badajos, or Badajoz . .	bäd-ä-hōs'. Sp. bä-dä-hōth.
Badebec	bäd-bĕk'.
Baden	bä'-dĕn.

Baden-Powell . . .	bā-dĕn-powl'.
Badinguet-Radot . . .	bä-dăṅ-gä' rä-dō'.
Badon (Mt.)	bā'-dŏn.
Badoura	bă-dōō'-rä.
Baedeker	bā'-dĕk-ēr. *Ger.* bâ'-dĕk-ĕr.
Baena	*Sp.* bä-ā'-nä; *Port.*
	bä-yā'-nä.
Baer, Von	fōn bâr.
Baez	bä'-āth.
Bafing, Ba-Fing	bä-fēng'.
Bagalor	bä-gä-lōr'.
Bagamoyo	bä-gä-mō'-yō.
Bagdad or Baghdad . .	bäg-däd', *commonly*
	băg'-dăd.
Bagehot	băj'-ŏt.
Baghdad or Bagdad . .	bäg-däd'₂ *commonly*
	băg'-dăd.
Bagheria	bä-gä-rē'-ä.
Baguio	bä'-gē-ō.
Bagnacavallo . . .	bän''-yä-kä-väl'-lō.
Bagni di Lucca	bän'-yē dē lōōk'-kä.
Bagration	bä-grä-tsē-ōn', bȧ-grä'-shŭn.
Bahamas	bā-hä'-mȧz.
Bahar, see Behar, Bihar .	bă-här'.
Bahari	bä-hä-rē'.
Bahawalput	bä-hä-wäl-pōōr'.
Bahia	bä=ē'-ä.
Bahia Honda . . .	bä=ē'-ä ōn'-dä.
Baiae	bā'-yē.
Baikal	bī'-käl, bī-käl'.
Bailleul	bä=ē-yēl'.
Baillie	bā'-lē.
Baillot	bä=ē-yō'.
Bailly	bā'-lē. *Fr.* bä-yē'.
Baiquiri	bä=ē-kē'-rē.
Bairam, see Beiram . .	bī-räm'.
Baireuth, see Bayreuth .	bī'rūth. *Ger.* bī-roit'.

Bairut, see Beirut, or Bey-
rout . . . . bā-rōōt'.
Baja . . . . bä'-yä.
Bajazet, see Bayazid . . băj'-ā-zĕt, băj-ā-zĕt'.
Bajza . . . . bŏy'-zä.
Bakerganj, see Backergunge bäk'-ēr-gȧnj.
Bakhuyzen . . . . . bäk'-hoi-zĕn.
Bakoor, or Bakor, see Bacoor bă-kōōr'.
Baku . . . . bä-kōō'.
Balaam . . . . . . bā'-lăm.
Balábac . . . . . . bä-lä'-bäk.
Balaclava, or Balaklava . bä-lä-klä'-vä.
Balafré, Le . . . . . lŭ bä-lä-frä'.
Balaguer . . . . . . bä-lä-gâr'.
Balakireff . . . . . . bä-lä-kēr'-ĕf.
Balaklava, or Balaclava . bä-lä-klä'-vä.
Balasore, Balasur . . . băl-ȧ-sōōr'.
Balaustion . . . . . bă-lôs'-chŏn.
Balbek, see Baalbec . . bäl'-bĕk, bäl-bĕk'.
Balbo . . . . bäl'-bō.
Balboa, De . . . . . dä bäl-bō'-ä.
Balchen (Admiral) . . . bôl'-chĕn.
Baldassare . . . . . bäl-däs-sä'-rä.
Balder, Baldur . . . . bôl'-dēr.
Bâle, see Basle . . . . bäl.
Baleares . . . . . . bā-lē-ä'-rēz.
Balearic . . . . . . băl-ē-ăr'-ĭk.
Baléchou . . . . . . bä-lä-shōō'.
Baler . . . . bä-lâr'.
Balestier . . . . . . băl-ĕs-tēr'.
Balfe . . . . bălf.
Balfour . . . . . . băl'-fōōr, băl'-fēr.
Balimghem . . . . . bä-lăṅ-găṅ'.
Balin and Balan . . . bā'-lĭn, ănd bā'-lăn.
Baliol, see Balliol . . . bā'-lĭ-ŏl. *Fr.* bäl-yōl'.
Baliuag . . . . . . bäl-ē'-wäg.
Balize . . . . bä-lēz'.

Balkan	bôl'-kăn, bäl-kän'.
Ballarat	băl-à-răt'.
Ballari	bäl-lä'-rē.
Ballesteros	bäl-yĕs-tä'-rōs.
Balliol, see Baliol . . .	bä'-lĭ-ŏl. *Fr.* bäl-yōl'.
Balliol (College) . . .	bāl'-yĕl.
Ballo in Maschera . . .	bäl'-lō ēn mäs'-kä-rä.
Balmaceda	bäl-mä-thä'-dä.
Balmoral	băl-mŏr'-ăl, băl-mō'-răl.
Balmung	bäl'-mo͞ong.
Balsamo	băl-sä'-mō. *Fr.* bäl-sä-mō'.
Balthasar, or Balthazar .	băl-thä'-zär, bäl'-tä-zär.
Baluchistan, see Beluchistan, or Beloochistan .	băl-o͞o-chĭs-tän'.
Balwhidder	băl-whĭt͡h'-ēr.
Balzac	băl-zăk', *commonly* băl'zăk.
Bamberg	bäm'-bĕrċh.
Banana	bä-nä'-nä.
Banaras, see Benares . .	bă-nä'-räs.
Banat	bä'-nät.
Bancroft	băn'-krŏft.
Banér, see Banner . . .	bä-nâr'.
Bangkok	băng-kŏk'.
Bangor (Me.)	băn'-gŏr.
Bangor (Wales)	băng'-gēr.
Bangweolo	băng-wē-ō'-lō.
Banner, see Banér . . .	bä-nâr'.
Banquo	băn'-kwō, băng'-kwō.
Bantam	bän-täm'.
Bantu	băn'-to͞o.
Banville (Théodore de) .	bäṅ-vēl'.
Banyoro	bä-nyō'-rō.
Bapaume	bă-pōm'.
Bara Banki	bä'-rä băn'-kē.
Barabas, or Barabbas . .	bä-răb'-às.
Barabra, see Berabra . .	bä-rä'-brä.
Baracoa	bä-rä-kō'-ä.

Baraguay d'Hilliers . . bä-rä-gā′ dē-yā′.
Barataria . . . . . . băr-à-tā′-rĭ-ä. *Sp.*
  bä-rä-tä-rē′-ä.
Barbadoes, or Barbados . bär-bā′-dōz.
Barbarelli . . . . . . bär-bä-rĕl′-lē.
Barbarossa . . . . . bär-bà-rŏs′-ä.
Barbaroux . . . . . bär-bä-rōō′.
Barbary . . . . . . bär′-bà-rĭ.
Barbauld . . . . . . bär′-bôld. *Fr.* bär-bō′.
Barbazon, see Barbison . bär-bä-zôn′.
Barberini . . . . . . bär-bā-rē′-nē.
Barbey d'Aurevilly . . . bär-bā′ dō=rĕ-vē-yē′.
Barbier de Séville, Le . lŭ bär-bē=ā′ dŭ sā-vēl′.
Barbiere de Seviglia, Il . ēl bär-bē-ä′-rĕ dä sä-vēl′-yä.
Barbison, see Barbazon . bär-bē-zôn′.
Barbusse, Henri . . . ôn-rē′ bär-büs′.
Barcellona . . . . . bär-chĕl-lō′-nä.
Barcelona . . . . . . bär-sĕ-lō′-nä. *Sp.*
  bär-thä-lō′-nä.
Barclay de Tolly . . . bär-klā′ dŭ tō-lē′.
Bardera . . . . . . bär-dä′-rä.
Bardi, Bardo de' . . . bär′-dō dä bär′-dē.
Bardolph . . . . . . bär′-dŏlf.
Bardwan, see Burdwan . bàrd-wän′.
Bareja . . . . bä-rā′-ċhä.
Barère de Vieuzac . . . bä-râr′ dŭ vē=ē-zä′.
Baretti . . . . bä-rät′-tē.
Barfleur . . . . . . bär-flēr′.
Bargello . . . . . . bär-jĕl′-lō.
Bargiel . . . . bär′-gēl.
Bariatinski . . . . . bär-yä-tēn′-skē.
Baring . . . . bā′-rĭng, bâr′-ĭng.
Baring-Gould . . . . bâr′-ĭng-gōōld′.
Barlaymont . . . . . bär-lä-môn′.
Bar-le-Duc . . . . . bär-lē-dük′.
Barmecides . . . . . bär′-mē-sīdz.
Barnabas . . . . . . bär′-nà-bàs.

Barnato	bär-nä′-tō.
Barnay	Ger. bär′-nī.
Barnett	bär′-nĕt.
Barneveld	bär′-nĕ-vĕlt.
Baroccio, see Barozzio	bä-rŏch′-ō.
Baroda	bä-rō′-dä.
Baroja	bä-rō′-chȧ.
Baron	Fr. bä-rôṅ′. Ger. bä-rōn′.
Baronin	bä-rō′-nēn.
Baronne	bä-rŏn′.
Baroque	bä-rŏk′.
Barotse Land	bȧ-rŏt′-sĕ-lȧnd.
Barozzi	bä-rŏt′-sē.
Barozzio, see Baroccio	bä-rŏt′-sē-ō.
Barrackpur	bär-äk-pōōr′.
Barradas	bär-rä′-däs.
Barragan	bär-rä-gän′.
Barranquilla	bär-rän-kēl′-yä.
Barranquitas	bär-rän-kē′-täs.
Barras	bä-räs′. Fr. bä-rä′.
Barré	bä-rä′.
Barrès, Maurice	mō-rēs′ bär-rĕz′.
Barrie	bắr′-ĭ.
Barrili	bär-rē′-lē.
Barrot	bä-rō′.
Barrundia	bä-rōōn′-dē-ä.
Barry, Mme. du	mä-dăm′ dü bär-rē′.
Bar-sur-Aube	bär-sür-ōb′.
Bartas	bär-tä′.
Barth	bärt.
Barthélemy-Saint-Hilaire	bär-tāl-mē′-săṅ-tē-lâr′.
Bartholdi	bär-tōl-dē′.
Bartholo	bär-tō-lō′.
Bartholomé	bär-tō-lō-mä′.
Bartimeus	bär-tĭm-ē′-ŭs.
Bartol	bär-tŏl′.
Bartoli	bär′-tō-lē.

Bartolommeo . . . . . bär-tō-lŏm-mä'-ō.
Bartolozzi . . . . . . bär-tō-lōt'-sē.
Baruch . . . . bā'-rŭk.
Bärwalde . . . . . . bâr'-väl-dŭ.
Barye . . . . bä-rē'.
Barzillai . . . . . . bär-zĭl'-ä-ī, bär'-zĭl-ä.
Baseelan, see Basilan . bä-sē'-län.
Basel . . . . bä'-zĕl.
Bashan . . . . . bā'-shȧn.
Bashee, or Bashi (I.) . . bä-shē'.
Bashi-Bazouk . . . . bȧsh'-ĭ-bȧ-zōōk'.
Bashkirtseff, Marie . . mȧ-rē' bäsh-kērt'-sĕf.
Basil . . . . . . bā-'zĭl, bȧz'-ĭl.
Basilan, see Baseelan . bä-sē'-län.
Basilicon Doron . . . bȧ-sĭl'-ĭ-kŏn dō'-rŏn.
Baskunchak . . . . . bäs-kōōn-chäk'.
Basque . . . . . . bȧsk.
Basra, see Bussora . . bäs'-rä.
Bassanio . . . . . bä-sä'-nĭ-ō.
Bassano (Duke of) . . bäs-sä'-nō.
Basses-Alpes . . . . bäs-zälp'.
Basses-Pyrénées . . . bäs-pē-rä-nä'.
Basse-Terre . . . . . bäs-târ'.
Bassi . . . . bäs'-sē.
Bassompierre . . . . bä-sôṅ-pē=âr'.
Bastian . . . . . . bäs'-tē=än.
Bastiat . . . . . . bäs-tē=ä'.
Bastien-Lepage . . . . bäs-tē=ĕṅ' lē-pȧzh'.
Bastile, or Bastille . . . bȧs'-tēl. *Fr.* bäs-tē'=yŭ.
Basundi . . . . . . bä-sōōn'-dē.
Basutoland . . . . . bä-sōō'-tō-lȧnd.
Bataan . . . . bä-tä-än'.
Batabano . . . . . bä-tä-bä'-nō.
Batalha . . . . . bä-täl'-yä.
Batan (I.) . . . . . . bä-tän'.
Batanes . . . . . . bä-tä'-nĕs.
Batangas . . . . . . bä-tän'-gäs.

Batavia . . . . . . bȧ-tā'-vĭ-ȧ. *Jav.* bä-tä'-vĭ-ȧ.
Báthori, see Batory . . bä'-tō-rē.
Bathsheba . . . . . băth-shē'-bä, băth'-shĕ-bȧ.
Batignolles . . . . . bȧ-tēn-yŏl'.
Baton Rouge . . . . . băt'-ŭn rōozh. *Fr.* bä-tôṅ' rōozh.
Batory, see Báthori . . bä'-tō-rē.
Battenberg . . . . . băt'-tĕn-bĕrg. *Ger.* bät'-tĕn-bĕrċh.
Battersea . . . . . . băt'-ēr-sē.
Batthyányi . . . . . 'bŏt'-yän-yē.
Batum, or Batoum . . . bä-tōom'.
Baucis . . . . bô'-sĭs.
Baudelaire . . . . . bōd-lâr'.
Baudissin . . . . . . bow'-dĭs-sēn.
Baudricourt . . . . . bō-drē-kōor'.
Baudry . . . . . . bō-drē'.
Bautista . . . . . . bä=ōo-tēs'-tä.
Bautzen . . . . . . bowt'-sĕn.
Bavieca, see Babieca . . bä-bē=ä'-kä.
Bayambang . . . . . bī-äm-bäng'.
Bayamo . . . . . . bä-yä'-mō.
Bayamon . . . . . . bä-yä-mōn'.
Bayard (Chevalier) . . . bä'-ärd. *Fr.* bä-yär'.
Bayard (James A.) . . . bī'-ärd.
Bayazid, see Bajazet . . bä-yä-zēd'.
Bayeux . . . . . . bä-yẽ'.
Bayle . . . . bāl.
Bayombong . . . . . bä=ĕŏm-bōng'.
Bayonne . . . . . . bā-yŏn', bī'-yŭn. *Fr.* bä-yŏn'.
Bayreuth, see Baireuth . bī'-rŭth. *Ger.* bī-roit'.
Baza . . . . bä'-thä.
Bazaine . . . . . . bȧ-zĕn'.
Bazalgette, Léon . . . lä-ōṅ' bȧ-zȧl-zhĕt'.
Bazan, Don Cesar de . . dôṅ sä-zär' dŭ bä-zäṅ'.
Bazán, Emilia . . . . ā-mēl'-ē-ä bä-thän'.

Bazarof	bä-zär'-ŏf.
Bazin	bă-zăṅ'.
Beaconsfield	bē'-kŏnz-fēld, bĕk'-ŏnz-fēld,
Béarn	bā-är'.
Béarnais, Le	lē bā-är-nā'.
Beata Beatrix . . .	bē-ā'-tä bē'-ä-trĭks.
Beaton	bē'-tŏn. *Sc.* bā'-tŏn.
Beatrice	bē'-à-trĭs. *Fr.* bā-ä-trēs'.
	It. bā-ä-trē'-chĕ.
Beatrice Cenci	bā-ä-trē'-chĕ chĕn'-chē.
Beatrice Portinari . . .	bā-ä-trē'-chĕ pōr-tē-nä'-rē.
Beatrix	bē'-à-trĭks.
Béatrix	bē'-à-trĭks. *Fr.* bā-ä-trēks'.
Beattie	bē'-tĭ. *Sc.* bā'-tĭ.
Beau Brummel	bō brŭm'-ĕl.
Beaucaire	bō-kâr'.
Beauchamp (Alphonse de)	*Fr.* bō-shäṅ'.
Beauchamp (Philip) . .	*Eng.* bē'-chăm.
Beauclerc, or Beauclerk .	bō-klärk', bō'-klärk.
Beaufort	*Eng.* bō'-fŭrt. *Fr.* bō-fōr'.
Beaufort-en-Vallée . .	bō-fōr'-tôṅ-väl-lā'.
Beaufort (Sir Francis) .	bŭ'-fŭrt.
Beaugency	bō-zhŏṅ-sē'.
Beauharnais, Eugène de .	ē-zhĕn' dŭ bō-är-nā'.
Beauharnais, Joséphine de	zhō-zā-fēn' dŭ bō-är-nā'.
Beauharnais, Hortense de	ōr-tŏṅs' dŭ bō-är-nā'.
Beaujeu, Anne de . . .	ăn dē bō-zhē'.
Beaulieu	bō-lē=ē'.
Beaumanoir	bō-mä-nwär'.
Beaumarchais	bō-mär-shā'.
Beaumont	*Eng.* bō'-mŏnt, *or*
	bū'-mŏnt. *Fr.* bō-môṅ'.
Beaumont-sur-Oise . .	bō-môṅ'-sür-wäz'.
Beaune	bōn.
Beaune-la-Rolande . .	bōn-lä-rō-läṅd'.
Beauregard	bō'-rĕ-gärd. *Fr.* bō=rĕ-gär'.
Beaurepaire	bō=rē-pâr'.

Beauvais	bō-vā'.
Beaux	bō.
Bebel	bā'-bĕl.
Beccafumi	bĕk-kä-fōō'-mē.
Beccari	bĕk'-kä-rē.
Beccaria	bĕk-kä-rē'-ä.
Becher	bĕċh'-ĕr.
Bechuanaland	bĕt-chōō-ä'-nä-lănd.
Bechuanas	bĕt-chōō-ä'-näs.
Becket (Thomas) à	à bĕk'-ĕt.
Bécquer	bā'-kĕr.
Becquerel	bĕk-rĕl'.
Bedaween, see Bedouin	bĕd'-à-wēn.
Bede	bēd.
Bedel (Timothy)	bē'-dĕl.
Bedivere	bĕd'-ĭ-vēr.
Bedouin, see Bedaween	bĕd'-ōō-ĭn.
Bedreddin Hassan	bĕd-rĕd-dēn' häs'-sän.
Beelzebub, see Belzebub	bē-ĕl'-zē-bŭb.
Beerbohm	bēr'-bōm.
Beersheba	bē-ēr-shē'-bà, bē-ēr'-shĕ-bà.
Beethoven, Van	fän bā'-tō-vĕn.
Befana	bā-fä'-nä.
Béguinage	bā-gē-näzh'.
Beguins, or Béguines	bĕg'-ĭnz or bā'gĭnz.
Behaim	bā'-hīm.
Behar, see Bahar, Bihar	bĕ-här'.
Behechio	bā-ā'-chē=ō, bā-ĕ-chē'-ō.
Behn (Mrs. Aphra)	bān.
Behring, see Bering	bē'-rĭng. Dan. bā'-rĭng.
Beira	bā'-rä.
Beiram, see Bairam	bī-räm'.
Beirut, see Bairut and Bey-rout	bā-rōōt'.
Béjart, Armande	är-mäṅd' bā-zhär'.
Bejol	bā-ċhōl'.
Bejucal	bā-ċhōō-käl'.

Belarius . . . . . . bĕ-lā'-rĭ-ŭs.
Belaspoor, see Bilaspoor . bē-läs-poōr'.
Belchite . . . . . . bĕl-chē'-tā.
Beleek . . . . bĕl-ēk'.
Belfagor, see Belphegor . bĕl'-fȧ-gôr.
Belfast (Ireland). . . . bĕl-fäst', bĕl-fȧst'.
Belfast (Maine) . . . . bĕl'-fȧst, bĕl-fȧst'.
Belfort . . . . Fr. bĕl-fōr'.
Belgian . . . . . . bĕl'-jĭ-ȧn.
Belgiojoso . . . . . bĕl-jō-yō'-zō.
Belgique . . . . . . bĕl-zhēk'.
Belgium . . . . . . bĕl'-jŭm.
Belgrad . . . . . . bĕl-gräd'.
Belgrade . . . . . . bĕl-grād'.
Belial . . . . bē'-lĭ=ăl.
Belianis (of Greece) . . bā-lē-ä'-nēs.
Belisario . . . . . . bā-lē-zä'-rē-ō.
Belisarius . . . . . . bĕl-ĭ-sā'-rĭ-ŭs.
Bélise . . . . bā-lēz'.
Beliza . . . . bĕ-lē'-zä.
Bellagio . . . . . . bĕl-lä'-jō.
Bellario . . . . . . bĕl-lä'-rĭ-ō.
Bellarmine . . . . . bĕl-lär-mēn'.
Bellatrix . . . . . . bĕl'-ȧ-trĭks, bĕl-lā'-trĭks.
Bellay . . . . bĕ-lā'.
Belle Alliance, La . . . lä bĕl äl-lē-äṅs'.
Belleau . . . . . . bĕl-lō'.
Belle Île, or Belle Isle-en-
Mer . . . . bĕl ēl' ôṅ mâr'.
Belle-Isle (Newfoundland) bĕl-īl'.
Belle Jardinière, La . . lä bĕl zhär-dēn-ē=âr'.
Belle Laitière, La . . . lä bĕl lâ-tē=âr'.
Bellerophon . . . . . bĕ-lĕr'-ō-fŏn.
Belliard . . . . . . bĕl-yär'.
Bellingham . . . . . bĕl-ĭng-ȧm.
Bellini . . . . bĕl-lē'-nē.
Bello, Andres . . . . bĕl'-yō. Sp.än-drĕs'bäl'-yō.

Belloc, Hilaire	ē-lâr′ bĕl-ŏk′.
Bellona	bĕl-ō′-nȧ.
Beloeil	bĕl-ē′=yŭ.
Belon	bĕ-lôṅ′, blôṅ.
Beloochistan, see Beluchis-	
tan, Baluchistan . . .	bĕl-ōō-chĭs-tän′.
Belphegor, see Belfagor .	bĕl′-fĕ-gôr.
Belphoebe	bĕl-fē′-bē.
Belshazzar	bĕl-shăz′-är.
Beluchistan, see Baluchis-	
tan, Beloochistan . .	bĕl-ōō-chĭs-tän′.
Belvedere	bĕl-vĕ-dēr′. *It.*
	bāl-vā-dā′-rĕ.
Belvoir	*Eng.* bē′-vēr.
Belzebub, see Beelzebub .	bĕl′-zē-bŭb.
Belzoni	bĕl-tsō′-nē.
Bemba (L.)	bĕm′-bä.
Bembesi	bĕm-bā′-zē.
Benaiah	bĕ-nā′-yä.
Benalcazar, see Velalcazar	bā-näl-kä′-thär.
Benares, see Banaras . .	bĕ-nä′-rĕz.
Benbow (Admiral) . . .	bĕn′-bō.
Bendavid	bĕn-dä′-fĭd.
Bender-Abbas, or . . .	bĕn′-dĕr-äb′-bäs.
Bender Abbasi . . .	bĕn′-dĕr-äb-bä-sē′.
Benedetto da Majano . .	bā-nā-dāt′-tō dä mä-yä′-nŏ.
Benedicite	bĕn-ĕ-dĭs′-ĭ-tē.
Beneke	bĕ′-nĕ-kŭ.
Benevento	bĕn-ĕ-vĕn′-tō. *It.*
	bā-nā-vän′-tō.
Bengal	bĕn-gôl.
Bengali	bĕn-gô-lē′.
Benguela	bĕng-gā′-lä.
Ben-hadad	bĕn-hā′-dăd.
Benicia	bē-nĭsh′-ĭ-ȧ.
Beni-Mansur	bā-nē-män-sōōr′.
Benin	bĕ-nēn′.

Ben Ledi	bĕn lĕd'-ĭ.
Ben Nevis	bĕn nĕv'-ĭs.
Bennigsen	bĕn'-nĭg-sĕn.
Benoît	bĕ-nwä'.
Ben-oni	bĕn-ō'-nĭ.
Bentham	bĕn'-thȧm, bĕn'-tȧm.
Bentinck	bĕn'-tĭngk.
Bentivoglio	bĕn-tē-vōl'-yō.
Bentzon, Théodore . .	tä-ō-dōr' bôṅt-zôṅ'.
Benue, see Binue . . .	bĕn-wē'.
Benvenuto Cellini . . .	bän-vä-nōō'-tō chĕl-lē'-nē.
Ben Vorlich	bĕn vôr'-lĭċh.
Beowulf	bā'-ō-wŏŏlf, bē'-ō-wŏŏlf.
Berabra, see Barabra . .	bĕ-rä'-brä.
Béranger, de	dŭ bā-räṅ-zhä'.
Berar	bā-rär'.
Berat	bā-rät'.
Berber	bēr'-bēr.
Berbera	bēr-bä'-rä.
Berceo, Gonzalo de . .	gŏn-thä'-lō dä bâr-thä'-ō.
Berchem, see Berghem .	bĕrċh'-hĕm.
Berea	bĕ-rē'-ȧ.
Berengaria	bĕr-ĕn-gâr'-ĭ-ȧ,
	bā-rĕn-gä'-rē-ä.
Berengarius	bĕr-ĕn-gâr'-ĭ-ŭs.
Bérenger	bā-rŏṅ-zhä'.
Berenice	bĕr-ĕ-nī'-sē.
Bérénice	bā-rä-nēs'.
Beresford	bĕr'-ĕs-fŭrd.
Beresina, or Berezina . .	bĕr-ĕ-zē'-nä.
Bergami, Bartolomeo . .	bär"-tō-lō-mä'-ō bâr'-gä-mē.
Bergamo	bâr'-gä-mō.
Bergen-op-Zoom . . .	bĕr'-ċhĕn-ŏp-zōm'.
Bergerac, Cyrano de . .	sĭr-ä-nō' dŭ bĕrzh-răk'.
Berghem, see Berchem .	bĕrċh'-hĕm.
Bergsö	bĕrg'-sē.
Bergson, Henri	ôṅ-rē' bârg-sôṅ'.

Berhampur	bẽr'-àm-pōōr.
Bering, see Behring . .	bā'-rĭng, *or* bē'-rĭng. *Dan.* bā'-rĭng.
Bériot	bā-rē-ō'.
Berkeley	bẽrk'-lĭ, bärk'-lĭ.
Berlichingen, Götz von	gẽts fŏn bĕr'-lĭċh-ĭng-ĕn.
Berlin	bẽr-lĭn'. *Ger.* bĕr-lēn'.
Berliner Tageblatt . . .	bâr-lē'-nĕr tä'-gä-blät.
Berlioz	bĕr-lē-yŏz'.
Bermoothes	bẽr-mōō'-t͡hĕs.
Bermudas	bẽr-mū'-dàz.
Bern, see Berne . . .	bẽrn. *Ger.* bĕrn.
Bernadotte	bẽr'-nà-dŏt. *Fr.* bĕr-nä-dŏt'.
Bernard	bẽr'närd, bēr-närd'. *Fr.* bâr-när'.
Bernardin de St. Pierre .	bĕr-när-dăṅ' dŭ săṅ pē=âr'.
Bernardine	bẽr'-när-dĭn.
Bernardo del Carpio . .	bĕr-när'-dō dĕl kär'-pē=ō.
Berne, see Bern . . .	bẽrn. *Fr.* bĕrn.
Bernese	bẽr-nēs', bēr-nēz'.
Bernhardi	bârn-här'-dē.
Bernhardt, Sarah . . .	sā'-rä bẽrn'-härt. *Fr.* sä-rä' bâr-när'.
Bernice	bẽr-nĭ'-sē.
Bernini	bĕr-nē'-nē.
Bernoulli, or Bernouilli .	bĕr-nōō'-yē.
Bernson, Bernhardt . .	bârn'-härt bârn'-sŏn.
Bernstorff	bârns'-tôrf.
Berri, or Berry	bĕr'-ĭ. *Fr.* bĕr-rē'.
Berruguete	bĕr-ōō-gā'-tĕ.
Bertha	*Ger.* bâr'-tä.
Berthelot	bĕr=tĕ-lō'.
Berthier	bĕr-tē=ā'.
Berthollet	bĕr-tō-lä'.
Bertin	bĕr-tăṅ'.
Bertrand	bĕr-träṅ'.
Bertuccio	bâr-tōōch'-ō.

Berwick	bĕr′-ĭk.
Berzelius	bēr-zē′-lĭ-ŭs. *Sw.*
	bĕr-zĭl′-ĭ-ŏŏs.
Besançon	bĕ-zän-sôṅ′.
Besant (Walter) . . .	bĕs′-ȧnt.
Besant (Annie)	bĕz′-ȧnt.
Besnard	bĕs-när′.
Bessaraba	bĕs-ä′-rä-bä.
Bessarabia	bĕs-ȧ-rä′-bĭ-ȧ.
Bessières	bĕs-ē=âr′.
Betelgeux, or	bĕt-ĕl-gē′.
Betelgeuze	bĕt-ĕl-gēz′.
Betelguese	bĕt-ĕl-gēz′, bĕt′-ĕl-gēz,
	or -gēs.
Bethabara	bĕth-ăb′-ȧ-rȧ.
Bethesda	bĕ-thĕz′-dȧ, bĕ-thĕs′-dȧ.
Bethincourt	bĕ-tăṅ-kŏŏr′.
Bethlehem	bĕth′-lē-ĕm, bĕth′-lē-hĕm.
Bethmann-Hollweg . .	bät′-män hŏl′-väċh.
Bethpeor	bĕth-pē′-ôr.
Bethphage	bĕth′-fä-jē, bēth′-fäj.
Bethsaida	bĕth-sä′-ĭ-dȧ, bĕth-sä′-dȧ.
Bethuel	bē-thū′-ĕl.
Bethune	bĕ-thūn′.
Béthune	bä-tün′.
Bettina von Arnim . . .	bĕt-tē′-nä fŏn är′-nĭm.
Bettws-y-Coed	bĕt″-üs-ē-kō′-ĕd.
Beulah	bū′-lä, bē-ū′-lä.
Beust, von	fŏn boist.
Bevis	bē′-vĭs.
Bewick	bū′-ĭk.
Bey	bä.
Beyle	bäl.
Beyle, Henri	ôṅ-rē′ bĕl.
Beyme, von	fŏn bī′-mŭ.
Beyrout, see Bairut, Beirut	bä′-rŏŏt. *Turk.* bī′-rŏŏt.
Beza	bē′-zȧ.

Bezaleel	bĕ-zăl'-ē-ĕl.
Bèze, or Besze	bĕz.
Béziers	bā-zē=ā'.
Bhagalpur, see Boglipoor .	bhä-gäl-po͞or', bôg-ŭl-po͞or'.
Bhagavadgita	bhă"-gă-văd-gē'-tä.
Bhagavatapurana . . .	bhä"-gȧ-vă-tȧ-poͦo-rä'-nä.
Bhartpur, see Bhurtpore .	bhŭrt-po͞or'.
Bhawalpur	bhä'-wäl-poͦor.
Bheel, or Bhil	bēl.
Bhopal	bhō-pôl'.
Bhurtpore, see Bhartpur .	bhērt-pōr'.
Biafra	bē-ä'-frä.
Biagrassa	bē-ä-gräs'-sä.
Bianca Capello	bē-än'-kä kä-pāl'-lō.
Bianchi	bē-än'-kē.
Biarritz	bē-är-rēts'.
Bias	bī'-ȧs.
Bibbiena	bēb-bē-ā'-nä.
Biblical	bĭb'-lĭ-kl.
Bibliothèque Nationale .	bēb-lē-ō-tĕk' năs-ĭ=ō-năl'.
Bicester	bĭs'-tēr.
Bichat	bē-shä'.
Bicor	bē-kŏr'.
Bidassoa	bē-däs-sō'-ä.
Biddeford (Me.) . . .	bĭd'-ĕ-fōrd.
Bideford (Eng.)	bĭd'-ĕ-fŭrd.
Biela	bē'-lä.
Bierstadt	bēr'-stät.
Bigelow	bĭg'-lō.
Bigod	bĭg'-ŏd.
Bihac	bē'-häċh.
Bihar, see Bahar, Behar .	bĭ-här'.
Bilaspoor, see Belaspoor .	bē-läs-poͦor'.
Billardière	bē-yär-dē=âr'.
Billot (Gen.)	bē-yō'.
Bimani, or	bē-mä-nē'.
Bimini	bē-mē-nē'.

Bingen	bǐng'-ĕn.
Biondi	bē-ōn'-dē.
Binondo	bē-nŏn'-dō.
Binue, see Benue . . .	bǐn'-wē.
Biot	bē-ō'.
Birejik	bēr-ĕ-jǐk'.
Birmingham	bēr'-mǐng-àm.
Birnam	bēr'-nàm.
Biron	bǐr'-ŏn. *Fr.* bē-rôṅ'.
Bisayas	bē-sä'-yäs.
Bismarck, or Bismarck-	
Schönhausen	bǐz'-märk shĕn'-how-zĕn.
Bithynia	bǐ-thǐn'-ǐ=à.
Bitolj	bē-tŏl'=yǔ.
Biton	bī'-tŏn.
Bivar, Rodrigo de . . .	rōd-rē'-gō dä bē-bär'.
Bizet	bē-zā'.
Björnson, Björnstjerne .	be=ẽrn'-shâr-nǔ bē-ẽrn'-sŏn.
Blackstone	blăk'-stǔn.
Blaise	blĕz.
Blanc	bläṅ.
Blanchard	bläṅ-shär'.
Blanche	blănch. *Fr.* bläṅsh.
Blanco	blän'-kō.
Blandamour	blän'-dä-mōōr.
Blanqui	bläṅ-kē'.
Blasius	blä'-zǐ-ǔs.
Blavatsky	blä-vät'-skǐ.
Blaze de Bury	blăz dǔ bü-rē'.
Bléneau	blä-nō'.
Blenheim, see Blindheim	blĕn'-ǐm.
Blida, Blidah	blē'-dä.
Blifil	blī'-fǐl.
Blind	*Ger.* blǐnt.
Blindheim, see Blenheim	*Ger.* blǐnt'-hǐm.
Bloemaert	blōō'-märt.
Bloemen	blōō'-mĕn.

Bloemfontein	blo̅o̅m'-fŏn-tīn.
Blois	blwä.
Bloomfield-Zeisler . . .	blo̅o̅m'-fēld-tsīs'-lĕr.
Blouet	blo̅o̅-ā'.
Blowitz	blō'-vĭts.
Blücher	blo̅o̅'-kĕr. *Ger.* blü'-ċhĕr.
Blum	blo̅o̅m.
Blumenbach	blo̅o̅'-mĕn-bäċh.
Blumenthal	blo̅o̅'-mĕn-täl.
Blythe	*Eng.* blī.
B'nai B'rith	b'-nā brĭth.
Boabdelin	bō-äb'-dĕ-lĭn.
Boabdil	bō-äb-dēl'.
Boadicea	bō-à-dĭ-sē'-à.
Boanerges	bō-à-nēr'-jēz.
Boas	bō'-äs.
Boaz	bō'-ăz.
Bobadil	bŏb'-à-dĭl.
Bobadilla	bō-bä-dēl'-yä.
Boboli	bō'-bō-lē.
Boca Chica	bō'-kà chē'-kà.
Boca del Drago . . .	bō'-kä dĕl drä'-gō.
Boca del Sierpe	bō'-kä dĕl sē-ĕr'-pä.
Boccaccio	bŏk-käċh'-ō.
Boccardo	bŏk-kär'-dō.
Boccherini	bŏk-kä-rē'-nē.
Boche	bŏsh
Böckh	bēk.
Böcking	bēk'-ĭng.
Böcklin	bēk'-lēn.
Bode	bō'-dŭ.
Bodin	bō-dăṅ'.
Bodleian	bŏd-lē'-àn, bōd'-lē-àn.
Boece	bō-ēs', bois.
Boehm	bēm.
Boellmann	bēl'-män.
Boeotia	bē-ō'-shà.

Boeotian . . . . . bē-ō'-shȧn.
Boer . . . . . . bōōr.
Boerhaave . . . . bōr'-häv. *D.* bōōr'-hä-vĕ.
Boethius . . . . . bō-ē'-thǐ-ŭs.
Bogdanovitch . . . bŏg-dä-nō'-vǐch.
Boglipoor, see Bhagalpur . bôg-lǐ-pōōr'.
Bogotá . . . . . . bō-gō-tä'.
Bogra . . . . . . bŏg-rä'.
Bohemond, Bohemund . bō'-hē-mŭnd.
Bohio . . . . . . bō-yō'.
Böhme . . . . . . bē'-mŭ.
Bohol, see Sp. Bojol . . bō-hŏl'.
Bohun . . . . . . bō'-ŭn.
Boiardo, Bojardo . . . bō-yär'-dō.
Boiëldieu . . . . . bwä=ĕl-dē=ŭ'.
Boii . . . . bō'-ǐ-ī.
Boileau-Despréaux . . bwä-lō'-dä-prä-ō'.
Bois de Boulogne . . . bwä dŭ bōō-lōn'=yŭ.
Boisdeffre . . . . bwä-dĕfr'.
Bois de Vincennes . . . bwä dŭ väṅ-sĕn'.
Boise (Montana) . . . boi'-zĕ.
Bois Guilbert . . . bwä gēl-bâr'.
Boisrobert . . . . . bwä-rō-bâr'.
Boito . . . . . . bō-ē'-tō.
Bojador (Cape) . . . . bŏj-à-dōr'.
Bojer . . . . . . bô'-yĕr.
Bojol, see Bohol . . . bō-hŏl'.
Bokhara, see Bukhara, Bu-
 charia . . . . . . bōk-hä'-rä, bō-ċhä'-rä.
Boldini . . . . . . bōl-dē'-nē.
Boleyn, or Bellen . . . bōŏl'-ĕn.
Bolingbroke . . . . bŏl'-ǐng-brŏŏk.
Bolívar . . . . . . *Sp.* bō-lē'-vär.
Bologna . . . . . bō-lōn'-yä.
Bolognese . . . . bō-lōn-yēs', bō-lōn-yēz'.
Bolsena . . . . . bŏl-sä'-nä.
Bolshevik . . . . . bŏl'-shĕ-vēk.

Bolsheviki	bŏl'-shĕ-vē-kē.
Bolshevist	bŏl'-shĕ-vĭst.
Bolshevism	bŏl'-shĕ-vĭzm.
Bolsover (Castle) . . .	bŏl'-sō-vẽr, bow'-zẽr.
Bombastes Fùrioso . .	bŏm-băs'-tēz fū-rĭ-ō'-sō.
Bom Jesus	Port. bŏṅ zhā'-zŏŏsh.
Bonaca, or Bonacca . .	bŏn-ăk'-kä.
Bonacieux	bō-nä-sē=ẽ'.
Bonalde, Pérez	pā'-rĕs bō-näl'-dä.
Bonaparte, see Buonaparte	bō'-nȧ-pärt. It.
	bō-nä-pär'-tĕ.
Bonapartist	bō'-nȧ-pärt"-ĭst.
Bonaventura	bō"-nä-vän-tōō'-rä.
Bonci	bōn'-chē.
Bonheur	bŏn-ẽr'.
Bonhomme Richard . .	bŏn-ŏm' rē-shär'.
Boniface	bŏn'-ĭ-fās.
Bonifacio	bō-nē-fä'-chō.
Bonn	bŏn. Ger. bŏn.
Bonnat	bŏn-nä'.
Bonnivard	bŏ-nē-vär'.
Bonnivet	bŏ-nē-vä'.
Bononcini, see Buononcini	bōn-ōn-chē'-nē.
Bonpland	bôṅ-pläṅ'.
Bon Silène	bôṅ sē-lĕn'.
Bontemps	bôṅ-tôṅ'.
Bony	Fr. bō-nē'.
Boomplaats	bōm'-pläts.
Boötes	bō-ō'-tēz.
Booth	bōōth.
Borachio	bō-rä'-chē=ō, bō-rä'-chō.
Bordeaux	bōr-dō'.
Bordereau (The) . . .	bōr=dĕ-rō'.
Bordone	bōr-dō'-nĕ.
Boreas	bō'-rē-ȧs.
Borghese	bōr-gā'-zĕ.

Borgia	bōr′-jä.
Borgo	bōr′-gō.
Borneo	bôr′-nē-ō.
Borodin	bō-rō-dēn′.
Borodino	bōr-ō-dē′-nō.
Borrioboola-gha	bŏr″-ĭ-ō-bōō′-lä-gä′.
Borromean (Is.)	bŏr-ō-mē′-àn.
Borromée	bŏr-rō-mä′.
Borromeo	bŏr-rō-mä′-ō.
Borromini	bŏr-rō-mē′-nē.
Bosanquet	bō′-zăn-kĕt.
Bosboom	bŏs′-bōm.
Boscawen (Admiral)	bŏs′-kȧ-wĕn.
Boscobel	bŏs′-kō-bĕl.
Boshof	bŏs′-hŏf.
Bosna-Serai	bŏs″-nä-sĕ-rī′.
Bosnia	bŏz′-nĭ-ä.
Bosphorus, or	bŏs′-fō-rŭs.
Bosporus	bŏs′-pō-rŭs.
Bossuet	bŏ-sü=ä′.
Boston	bŏs′-tŭn, bôs′-tŭn.
Boswell	bŏz′-wĕl.
Botetourt	bŏt′-ĕ-tōōrt.
Botha (Gen.)	bō′-tă.
Bothwell	bŏth′-wĕl, bŏth′-wĕl.
Botolph (St.)	bō-tŏlf′, bō′-tŏlf.
Botticelli	bŏt-tē-chĕl′-lē,
	bŏt-tē-shĕl′-lē
Boturini Benaduci	bō-tōō-rē′-nē bä-nä-dōō′-chē.
Botzaris, see Bozzaris	bŏt′-sä-rēs, pop. bŏ-zăr′-ĭs.
Botzen, Bozen	bŏts′-ĕn.
Boucher de Perthes	bōō-shä′ dŭ pârt′.
Boucicault	bōō′-sē-kō.
Boudinot	bōō′-dĭ-nŏt.
Boufflers	bōō-flâr′.
Bougainville	bōō-găṅ-vēl′.
Bouguereau	bōōg-rō′, bōō-gĕr=ō′

Bouillé	bōō-yā′.
Bouillon	bōō-yôṅ′, bōōl-yôṅ′.
Boulainvilliers . . .	bōō-lăṅ-vē-yā′.
Boulak, see Bulak . . .	bōō-läk′.
Boulanger	bōō-läṅ-zhā′.
Boulevard des Italiens	bōōl-vär′ dä zē-täl-ē=ěṅ′.
Boulogne, or	bōō-lōn′. *Fr.* bōō-lōn′=yŭ.
Boulogne-sur-Mer . . .	bōō-lōn′-sür-mâr′.
Bourbon	bōōr′-bŭn. *Fr.* bōōr-bôṅ′.
Bourbon (Kentucky) . .	*pop.* bēr′-bŭn.
Bourbon l'Archambault .	bōōr-bôṅ′ lär-shäm-bō′.
Bourdaloue	bōōr-dä-lōō′.
Bourdon	bōōr-dôṅ′.
Bourgeois (Sir Francis) .	bŭr-jois′.
Bourgeois (François) . .	bōōr-zhwä′.
Bourgeois Gentilhomme, Le	lē bōōr-zhwä′ zhôṅ-tēl-ŏm′.
Bourges	bōōrzh.
Bourget, Paul	pōl bōōr-zhā′.
Bourgogne	bōōr-gōn′=yŭ.
Bourrienne, de	dŭ bōō-rē-ěn′.
Bourse, La	lä bōōrs.
Boutet de Monvel . . .	bōō-tā′ dŭ môṅ-věl′.
Bouvier	bōō-vēr′. *Fr.* bōō-vē=ā′.
Bouvines, see Bovines .	bōō-vēn′.
Bovary, Madame . . .	mä-dăm′ bō-vä-rē′.
Bovines, see Bouvines .	bō-vēn′.
Bowditch	bow′-dǐch.
Bowdoin	bō′-dn.
Bowring	bow′-rǐng.
Boyacá	bō-yä-kä′.
Boyesen	boi′-ě-sěn.
Boylesve, René	rē-nā′ bwä-läv′.
Boz	bŏz.
Bozzaris, see Botzaris .	bōt′-sä-rēs, *pop.* bŏ-zăr′-ĭs.
Brabançonne, La . . .	lä brä-bäṅ-sŏn′.
Brabant	brä-bănt′, brä′-bȧnt. *Fr.* brä-bäṅ′.

Brabant (Gen.)	brä′-bănt.
Brabantio	bră-băn′-shĭ=ō.
Bracciano	bräch-ä′-nō.
Bradlaugh	brăd′-lô.
Braccio da Montone . .	bräch′-ō dä mŏn-tō′-ně.
Bradwardine	brăd′-wär-dĭn.
Bragança	brä-gän′-sä.
Braganza	brä-gän′-zä.
Bragelonne	brăzh=ĕ-lŏn′.
Braham	brā′-ȧm.
Brahe, Tycho	tī′-kō brā or brä. *Dan.* brä′-ĕ.
Brahma	brä′-mä.
Brahman	brä′-mȧn.
Brahmaputra	brä-mȧ-pōō′-trȧ.
Brahmasamaj, see Brahmosomaj	brä″-mä-sä-mäj′.
Brahmin	brä′-mĭn.
Brahminism	brä′-mĭn-ĭzm.
Brahmosomaj, see Brahmasamaj	brä″-mō-sō-mäj′.
Brahms	brämz.
Braila	brȧ-ē′-lȧ.
Bramante	brä-män′-tä.
Brandegee	brăn′-dĕ-gē.
Brandeis	brăn′-dīs.
Brandenburg	brän′-dĕn-bōōrch.
Brandes, Georg	yä-ôrch′ brän′-dĕs.
Branicki	brän=yĭt′-skē.
Brantôme	brän-tōm′.
Brasenose (Coll.) . . .	brāz′-nōz.
Brassington	brȧs′-n.
Brauwer, see Brouwer .	brow′-ẽr.
Bravo	brä′-vō.
Brazil. Sp. Brasil . . .	bră-zĭl′. *Port.* brä-zēl′.
Brazos	brä′-zōs.
Brazza	brät′-sä.

Breadalbane	brĕd-ôl'-bān.
Brébeuf	brä-bĕf'.
Breda	D. brā-dä'.
Brederode	brā'-dä-rō″-dĕ.
Bregenz	brä-gĕnts'.
Breisgau	brīs'-gow.
Breitenfeld	brī'-tĕn-fĕlt.
Breitmann, Hans . .	hänts brīt'-män.
Brema, Marie	mä-rē' brā'-mä.
Bremen	brĕm'-ĕn. Ger. brā'-mĕn.
Bremer (Frederika) . .	brām'-ēr. Sw. brĭm'-ēr.
Bremerhafen, or . . .	brā'-mēr-hä″-fĕn.
Bremerhaven	brĕm'-ēr-hā″-vĕn.
Brentano	brĕn-tä'-nō.
Brera	brā'-rä.
Brescia	brĕ'-shä.
Breshkovskaya (-ia) . .	brĕsh-kŏf'-skä-yä.
Breslau	brĕs'-low, brĕs'-lō.
Brest	brĕst
Brest-Litovsk	brĕst-lē-tofsk'.
Bretagne	brĕ-tän'=yŭ.
Breteuil	brē-tē'=yŭ.
Bretigny	brĕ-tēn-yē'.
Breton (Cape)	brĭt'ŭn, brĕt'-ŭn.
Breton, Jules	zhül brĕ-tôṅ'.
Breughel	brē'-ċhĕl.
Brian Borohma, Boroihme,	
or Boru	brī'-àn bŏ-rō'-mä, bŏ-rōō'.
Briance	brē-än'-chĕ.
Briançon	brē-äṅ-sôṅ'.
Briand	brē-äṅ'.
Brian de Bois Guilbert .	brē-äṅ' dĕ bwä gēl-bâr'.
Briareus	brī-ā'-rē-ŭs, brī'-ā-rūs.
Bridlington	bĕr'-lĭng-tŭn.
Brie	brē.
Briel	brēl.
Brieux, Édouard . . .	ā-dōō-är' brē-ē'.

Brighthelmstone, Brighton brī'-tŭn.
Brignoli . . . . . . brēn-yō'-lē.
Brihuega . . . . . brē-wā'-gä.
Bril . . . . brēl.
Brilessus . . . . . brĭ-lĕs'-ŭs.
Brillant . . . . . brē-yäṅ'.
Brillat-Savarin . . . brē-yä' sä-vä-räṅ'.
Brindisi . . . . . . brēn'-dē-zē.
Brinvilliers . . . . . brăṅ-vēl-yä'.
Briseis . . . . brī-sē'-ĭs.
Brissot de Warville . . brē-sō' dŭ vär-vēl'.
Britannia . . . . . . brĭ-tăn'-ĭ-à.
Britomart, or Britomartis . brĭt'-ō-märt, brĭt-ō-mär'-tĭs.
Brobdingnag . . . . . brŏb'-dĭng-năg. [-nä'-jĭ-ăn.
Brobdingnagian . . . . brŏb-dĭng-năg'-ĭ-ăn,
Brody . . . . brō-dē'.
Broek . . . . bro͞ok.
Broglie, de . . . . . dŭ brōg-lē   Fr. dŭ brôg-lē'.
Broke (Sir Philip) . . . bro͝ok.
Bromley . . . . . . brŭm'-lĭ.
Brontë . . . . brŏn'tē, brŏn'-tĕ.
Brough . . . . . . brŭf.
Brougham . . . . . bro͞o'-àm, bro͞om, brō'-àm.
                     Sc. bro͞oċh'-àm.
Broughton (Hugh & Thos.) brô'-tŭn.
Broughton (Rhoda) . . brow'-tŭn.
Brougniart . . . . . bro͞on-ē=är'.
Brouwer, see Brauwer . brow'-ẽr.
Brown-Séquard . . . . brown-sä-kär'.
Bruch . . . . bro͝oċh.
Brueys . . . . brü-ā'.
Bruges . . . . bro͞o'-jĕz.   Fr. brüzh.
Brugsch Bey . . . . . bro͞oksh, or bro͞osh bā.
Brühl . . . . brül.
Bruis, see Bruys . . . brü-ē'.
Brumaire . . . . . . brü-mâr'.
Brummell . . . . . . brŭm'-ĕl.

Brunehaut	brün-ŭ=ō'.
Brunehild	broō'-nŭ-hĭlt.
Brunehilde, see Brunhild	broō''-nŭ-hĭl'-dŭ.
Brunelleschi	broō''-nĕl-lĕs'-kē.
Brunetière	brün-tē=âr'.
Brunetto Latini	broō-nāt'-tō lä-tē'-nē.
Brunhild, see Brunehild .	broōn'-hĭlt.
Brunhilde	broōn-hĭl'-dŭ.
Brünig	brü'-nĭċh.
Brunn	brün.
Bruno	broō'-nō.
Brunswick-Wolfenbüttel .	brŭnz'-wĭk-vŏl'-fĕn-büt''-tĕl.
Brussiloff (-ov)	broō-sē'-lŏf.
Brut	broōt.
Bruxelles	brüs-sĕl', brüks-ĕl'.
Bruycker, Jules de . .	zhül dĕ broi'-kĕr.
Bruys, see Bruis . . .	brü-ē'.
Brydges	brĭj'-ĕz.
Bryn Mawr (Pa.) . . .	pop. brĭn mär'.
Bryn Mawr (Wales) . .	brŭn-mowr'.
Buccleugh	bŭ-klū'.
Bucentaur	bū-sĕn'-tôr.
Bucephalus	bū-sĕf'-à-lŭs.
Bucer, see Butzer . . .	bū'-sĕr.
Buch, von	fŏn boōċh.
Buchanan	bŭk-ăn'-ăn, bū-kăn'-ăn.
Bucharest, see Bukharest	boō-kà-rĕst', bū-kà-rĕst'.
Bucharia, see Bokhara .	bū-kä'-rĭ-à.
Büchner	büċh'-nĕr.
Buckingham	bŭk'-ĭng-àm.
Bucolics	bū-kŏl'-ĭks.
Buczacz	boōch'-äch.
Buda Pesth	bū'-dà-pĕst. *Hung.*
	boō'-dä-pĕsht.
Budaun	boō-dä-oōn'.
Buddha	boŏd'-à, boō'-dä, bŭd'-à.
Buddhist	boŏd'-ĭst, boōd'-ĭst, bŭd'-ĭst.

Buddism . . . . . . boŏd'-ĭzm, boōd'-ĭzm,
                    bŭd'-ĭzm.
Budweis . . . . . . boŏd'-vīs.
Buena Vista . . . . . bū'-nȧ vĭs'-tȧ. *Sp.*
                    bwā'-nä vĭs'-tä.
Buen Ayre . . . . . bwān ī'-rā.
Buencamino . . . . . bwān-kä-mē'-nō.
Buenos Aires . . . . bō'-nŭs ā'-rĭz. *Sp.*
                    bwā'-nōs ī'-rĕs.
Buffon . . . . bŭf'-ŭn. *Fr.* büf-ôṅ'.
Bugeaud de la Piconnerie bü-zhō' dŭ lä pē-kŏn=ē-rē'.
Bug Jargal . . . . . büg zhär-gäl'.
Buitenzorg . . . . . boi'-tĕn-zôrk.
Bukhara, see Bokhara, Bu-
  charia . . . . . . boō-ċhä'-rä.
Bukharest, see Bucharest boō-kä-rĕst', bū-kä-rĕst'.
Bukowina . . . . . . boō-kō-vē'-nä.
Bulacan . . . . . . boō-lä-kän'.
Bulak, see Boulak . . . boō-läk'.
Bulawayo, see Buluwayo . boō-lä-wä'-yō.
Bulgaria . . . . . . boŏl-gā'rĭ-ȧ.
Bullen, see Boleyn . . . boŏl'-ĕn.
Buller (Gen.) . . . . boŏl'-ĕr.   [bü'-lŏv.
Bülow, Hans von . . . hänts fŏn bü'-lō. *Ger.*
Bultfontein . . . . . bŭlt'-fŏn-tīn.
Buluwayo, see Bulawayo . boō-loō-wä'-yō.
Bundelcund, Bundelkhand bŭn-dĕl-kŭnd',
                    bŭn-dĕl-känd'.
Bundesrath . . . . . boŏn'-dĕs-rät.
Bunsen . . . . . . bŭn'-sĕn. *Ger.* boŏn'-zĕn.
Bunwool . . . . . . bŭn'-woŏl.
Buola . . . . boō-ō'-lä.
Buonaparte, see Bonaparte boō=ōn-ä-pär'-tĕ.
Buonarroti . . . . . boō=ōn-är-rō'-tē.
Buononcini, see Bononcini boō=ōn-ōn-chē'-nē.
Buonsignori . . . . . boō=ōn-sēn-yō'-rē.
Burano . . . . . . boō-rä'-nō.

Burbon	bêr′-bun.
Burdett-Coutts	bêr-dĕt′-kōōts′.
Burdwan, see Bardwan	bŭrd-wän′.
Burgdorf	bōōrg′-dôrf.
Bürger	bürg′-ĕr.
Burgh, Hubert de	hū′-bêrt dĕ bêrg or bōōrg.
Burghley, see Burleigh	bŭr′-lĭ.
Burgkmair	bōōrk′-mīr.
Burgos	bōōr′-gōs.
Burgundy	bŭr′-gŭn-dĭ.
Burleigh, see Burghley	bŭr′-lĭ.
Burleson	bêr′-lĕ-sŭn.
Burrhus, or Burrus	bŭr′-ŭs.
Burschenschaft	bōōr′-shĕn-shäft.
Bury, Blaze de	blăz dŭ bü-rē′.
Busento	bōō-sĕn′-tō.
Bushiri bin Salim	bōō-shē′-rē bĭn sä-lēm′.
Busiris	bū-sī′-rĭs.
Bussorah, see Basra	bŭs′-sō-rä.
Busuanga	bōō-swäng′-gȧ.
Bussy-Rabutin	büs-ē′-rä-bü-tăṅ′.
Bustamante	bōōs-tä-män′-tĕ.
Bustee	bŭs′-tē.
Butauan	bōō-tä=ōō-än′.
Buteshire	būt′-shĭr.
Butte	būt.
Buttes de Chaumont	büt dĕ shō-môṅ′.
Buturlin	bōō-tōōr-lēn′.
Butzer, see Bucer	bōōt′-zĕr.
Buxhöwden	bōōks-hĕv′-dĕn.
Byblis	bĭb′-lĭs.
Byelostok	b-yĕ-lŏs-tŏk′.
Bysshe	bĭsh.
Byzantian	bī-zăn′-shĭ-ȧn.
Byzantine	bĭ-zăn′-tĭn, bĭz′-ȧn-tĭn, bī-zăn′-tĭn.
Byzantium	bĭ-zăn′-shĭ-ŭm.

C

Caaba, see Kaaba . . .	kä'-bȧ, kā'-ȧ-bȧ.
Cabal	kǎ-bǎl'.
Cabala, see Kabbala . .	kǎb'-ȧ-lä.
Caballero, Fernan . . .	fâr-nän' kä-bäl-yā'-rō.
Caballos	kä-bäl'-yōs.
Cabanagem	kä-bä-nä'-zhām.
Cabañas	kä-bän'-yäs.
Cabanel	kä-bä-nĕl'.
Cabanilla	kä-bä-nēl'-yä.
Cabanis	kä-bä-nēs'.
Cabanos	kä-bä'-nŏs.
Cabatuan	kä-bä-tōō-än'.
Cabazera	kä-bä-thā'-rä.
Cabeça de Vaca, see Cabeza	kä-bā'-thä dā bä'-kä.
Cabell	kǎ'-bĕl.
Cabet	kä-bā'.
Cabeza de Vaca, see Cabeça	kä-bā'-thä dā bä'-kä.
Cabezas	kä-bā'-thäs.
Cabiao	kä-bē-ä'=ō.
Cabiria	kȧ-bē'-rĭ-ȧ.
Cabo Rojo	kä'-bō rō'ċhō.
Cabot	kǎb'-ŏt.
Cabral	kä-bräl'.
Cabrera	kä-brä'-rä.
Cabul, see Kabul . . .	kä-bōōl'.
Cacama	kä'-kä-mä.
Cáceres	kä'-thä-rĕs.
Cadena	kä-dä'-nä.
Cadenus	kǎ-dē'-nŭs.
Caderousse	käd-rōōs'.
Cadillac	kǎd'-ĭl-ǎk. *Fr.* kǎ-dē-yǎk'.
Cadiz	kā'-dĭz. *Sp.* kä'-dēth.
Cadmean	kǎd-mē'-ȧn.
Cadorna	kä-dōr'-nä.
Ca' d'Oro	kä dō'-rō.

Cadoudal	kă-dōō-däl'.
Cadwalader	kăd-wäl'-à-dēr.
Caedmon	kăd'-mŏn, kĕd'-mŏn.
Caelian	sē'-lĭ-àn.
Caen	kän.
Caerleon	kär-lē'-ŏn.
Caernarvon, see Carnarvon	kär-när'-vŏn.
Caesalpinus	sĕs-ăl-pī'-nŭs.
Caesarea	sĕs-ā-rē'-à, sĕz-à-rē'-ä.
Caesarian, see Cesarian .	sē-zā'-rĭ-ăn.
Caesarion	sē-zā'-rĭ-ŏn.
Caffarelli	käf-fä-rĕl'-lē.
Caffre, see Kaffir . . .	kăf'-ēr.
Cagayan	kä-gä-yän'.
Cagliari	käl-yä'-rē.
Cagliostro	käl-yōs'-trō. *Fr.* kä-yō-trō'.
Cagnes	kän'=yŭ.
Caguas	kä'-gwäs.
Cahors	kä-ōr'.
Cahuenga	kä-wĕng'-gà.
Caiaphas	kā-yà-fàs, kī'-à-fàs.
Caibarien	kä=ē-bä'rē=ĕn.
Caicos, see Caycos . .	kī'-kōs. *Sp.* kä'=ē-kōs.
Caillou, Le	lē kä=ē-yōō'.
Caillebotte	kä=ē-yē-bŏt'.
Caimanera	kä=ē-mä-nā'-rä.
Caimanes	kä=ē-mä'-nĕs.
Ca ira	sä ē-rä'.
Cairo (Egypt)	kī'-rō.
Cairo (U. S.)	kā'-rō.
Caius Cestius	kā'-yūs sĕst'-ĭ=ŭs.
Caius (College)	kēz, kēs.
Cajetan, or	kăj'-ĕ-tăn.
Cajetano, or	*It.* kä-yä-tä'-nō.
Cajetanus	kăj-ĕ-tā'-nŭs.
Cajigal	kä-ćhē-gäl'.
Calabar	kăl-à-bär', kä-lä-bär'.

Calabria	kă-lā′-brĭ-à.
Calais	kăl′-ĭs. *Fr.* kä-lā′.
Calajan	kä-lä- hän′.
Calame	kä-läm′.
Calamianes	kä″-lä-mē-ä′-nĕs.
Calaveras	kăl-à-vā′-ràs, kà-lä-vā′-räs.
Calayan	kä-lä-yän′.
Calchas	kăl′-kàs.
Calderari	käl-dā-rä′-rē.
Calderon	kăl′-dĕr-ŏn. *Sp.*
	käl-dā-rōn′.
Calderon de la Barca . .	kăl′-dĕr-ŏn dŭ lä bär′-kà.
	Sp. käl-dā-rōn′ dā lä
	bär′-kä.
Caldiero	käl-dē-ä′-rō.
Calgary	kăl′-găr-ĭ.
Caliban	kăl′-ĭ-băn.
Calif, see Caliph, Khalif .	kā′-lĭf.
Caligula	kă-lĭg′-ū-là.
Caliph, see Calif, Khalif .	kā′-lĭf.
Callao	käl-lä′-ō, käl-yä′-ō, *pop.*
	kăl-lä-o′.
Calle Obispo	käl′-yĕ ō-bēs′-pō.
Callias	kăl′-ĭ-ăs.
Callicrates	kăl-lĭk′-rà-tēz.
Callimachus	kăl-lĭm′-à-kŭs.
Calliope	kăl-lī′-ō-pē.
Callirrhoë	kăl-lĭr′-ō-ē.
Callisthenes	kăl-lĭs′-thĕ-nēz.
Callisto	kăl-lĭs′-tō.
Callistratus	kăl-lĭs′-trà-tŭs.
Callot	kä-lō′.
Calmar, see Kalmar . .	käl′-mär.
Calne	kôn.
Calpurnia	kăl-pẽr′-nĭ-à.
Caltagirone	käl-tä-jē-rō′-nä.
Caltanissetta	käl″-tä-nē-sät′-tä.

Calumet	kăl'-ū-mĕt.
Calvados	käl-vä-dōs'.
Calvart, Calvaert . . .	käl'-värt. *Fr.* käl-vär'.
Calvé	käl-vä'.
Calvo, Baldassare . . .	bäl-dä-sä'-rĕ käl'-vō.
Calydon	kăl'-ĭ-dŏn.
Calypso	kă-lĭp'-sō.
Camacho	kä-mä'-chō.
Camaguey	kä-mä-gä'=ē.
Camanche, see Comanche	kă-măn'-chē.
Cámara (Admiral) . . .	kä'-mä-rä.
Camaralzaman	kăm-à-răl'-zà-măn.
Cambacerès	käṅ-bä-sä-rĕs'.
Cambay	kăm-bā'.
Cambert	käṅ-bâr'.
Cambon, Jules	zhül käṅ-bôṅ'.
Cambrai (-bray) . . .	kăm-brä. *Fr.* käṅ-brâ'.
Cambria	kăm'-brĭ-ä.
Cambronne	käṅ-brōn'.
Cambuscan	kăm-bŭs-kăn',
	kăm-bŭs'-kàn.
Cambyses	kăm-bī'-sēz.
Camelot	kăm'-ĕ-lŏt.
Camerarius	kä-mä-rä'-rē-ōōs.
Cameroon, see Kamerun .	kăm-ēr-ōōn', kä-mĕ-rōōn'.
Camille	kä-mēl'.
Camillo	*It.* kă-mĭl'-lō. *Sp.*
	kä-mĭl-yo.
Caminha	kä-mēn'-yä.
Camino Real	kä-mē'-nō rä-äl'.
Camisards	kăm'-ĭ-zärdz.
Camoens, or	kăm'-ō-ĕns.
Camões	*Port.* kä-môṅ'-ēsh.
Camorra	kä-mōr'-rä.
Campagna di Roma . .	käm-pän'-yä dē rō'-mä.
Campan	käṅ-päṅ'.
Campanini	käm-pä-nē'-nē.

Campaspe	kăm-păs'-pē.
Campbell	kăm'-bĕl. *Sc.* kăm'-ĕl.
Campeador, El	āl käm″-pā-ä-dōr'.
Campeachy, or Campeche	kăm-pē'-chĭ, käm-pā'-chā.
Campeggio	käm-pĕj'-ō.
Camperdown	kăm-pēr-down'.
Campo Formido . . .	käm'pō fōr-mē'-dō.
Campo Formio	käm'-pō fōr'-mē-ō.
Campo Santo	käm'-pō sän'-tō.
Campos, Martínez . . .	mär-tē'-nĕth käm'-pōs.
Campus Martius . . .	kăm'-pŭs mär'-shĭ-ŭs.
Camtoos	käm-tōs', käm-tōōs'.
Canaan	kā'-nȧn, kā'-nä-ăn.
Canale, or Canaletto . .	kä-nä'-lĕ, kä-nä-lät'-tō.
Canalizo	kä-nä-lē'-thō.
Canaris, see Kanaris . .	kä-nä'-rĭs.
Cancao, see Kang-Kao .	kän-kow'.
Cancelleria	kän″-chĕl-lä-rē'-ä.
Candace	kăn'-dȧ-sē.
Candahar, see Kandahar .	kän-dä-här', kăn-dȧ-här'.
or Candehar . . .	kän-dĕ-här', kăn-dĕ-här'.
Candeish, see Khandesh .	khän-dāsh'.
Candide, ou l'Optimisme .	käṅ-dēd' ōō lŏp-tē-mēs'=mŭ.
Candolle	käṅ-dŏl'.
Canea, see Khania . .	kă-nē'-ä.
Caney, El	āl kä'-nä.
Can Grande	kän grän'-dä.
Canisius	kä-nē'-sē=ŭs.
Cannæ	kăn'-ē.
Cannes	kän.
Canon, Hans	hänts kä'-nōn.
Canopus	kä-nō'-pŭs.
Canossa	kä-nŏs'-sä.
Canova	kä-nō'-vä.
Cánovas del Castillo . .	kä'-nō-väs dāl käs-tēl'-yō.
Canrobert	käṅ-rō-bâr'.
Cantabrian (Mts.) . . .	kăn-tä'-brĭ-ȧn.

Cantacuzene	kăn″-tȧ-kū-zēn′. *Gr.*
	kän-tä-kōō′-zĕ-nĕ.
Cantacuzenus	kăn″-tȧ-kū-zē′-nŭs.
Cantal	käṅ-täl′.
Canto	kän′-tō.
Canton (China) . . .	kăn-tŏn′.
Canton (Ohio) . . .	kăn′-tŭn.
Cantú, Cesare . . .	chā′-zä-rĕ kän-tōō′.
Canuck, see Kanuck . .	kă-nŭk′.
Canute, see Cnut . . .	kȧ-nūt′.
Capaneus	kȧ-pā′-nūs.
Cape Breton	brĭt′-ŏn, brĕt′-ŏn.
Capel	kăp′-ĕl.
Capella	kă-pĕl′-lȧ.
Capelle, von	fŏn kä-pĕl′-ȧ.
Capello	kä-päl′-lō.
Capernaum	kă-pêr′-nā-ŭm.
Capet	kăp′-ä, *or* kā′-pĕt. *Fr.*
	kä-pä′.
Capetian	kȧ-pē′-shȧn.
Cape Verd, or Verde . .	kāp vêrd.
Cap Haitien	kăp ä=ē-sē-ĕṅ′.
Capistrano	kä-pĭ-strä′-nō.
Capitoline	kăp′-ĭ-tō-līn′.
Capitolinus	kăp-ĭ-tō-lī′-nŭs.
Capiz	kä-pēth′.
Capo d'Istria, or . . .	kä′-pō dēs′-trē-ä.
Capodistrias	kä-pō-dēs′-trē-ȧs.
Caponsacchi	kä-pōn-säk′-kē.
Caporetto	kä-pō-rät′-tō.
Cappadocia	kăp-ȧ-dō′-shĭ=ȧ.
Cappello, see Capello . .	kä-päl′-lō.
Capreae	kā′-prē-ē.
Caprera	kä-prä′-rä.
Capri	kä′-prē.
Capricornus	kăp-rĭ-kôr′-nŭs.
Caprivi, von	fŏn kä-prē′-vē.

Capua . . . . kăp'-ū-ȧ. *It.* kä'-pōō-ä.
Capuchins . . . . . kăp'-ū-chĭnz.
Capucines . . . . . kȧ-pü-sēn'.
Capulet . . . . . . kăp'-ū-lĕt.
Capus, Alfred . . . . ăl-frĕd' kȧ-pü'.
Carabagh, see Kara-Bagh,
  or Karabagh . . . . kä-rä-bäg'.
Caracalla . . . . . . kăr-ȧ-kăl'-ȧ.
Caracallus . . . . . kăr-ȧ-kăl'-ŭs.
Caracas . . . . . . kä-rä'-käs.
Caractacus . . . . . kăr-ăk'-tȧ-kŭs.
Cara-Mustafa, see Kara
  Mustapha . . . . . kä'-rä *or* kä-rä' mŏōs'-tä-fä.
Caravaca . . . . . . kä-rä-vä'-kä.
Caravaggio . . . . . kä-rä-väd'-jō.
Carbonari . . . . . . kär-bō-nä'-rē.
Carcassonne . . . . . kär-käs-sŏn'.
Cárdenas . . . . . . kär'-dä-näs.
Cardonnel . . . . . kär-dŏn'-ĕl.
Carducci . . . . . . kär-dōōch'-ē.
Carême . . . . . . kă-rĕm'.
Carib . . . . kăr'-ĭb.
Caribbean . . . . . kăr-ĭ-bē'-ȧn.
Caribbees . . . . . . kăr'-ĭ-bēz.
Carignan . . . . . . kä-rēn-yäṅ'.
Carisbrooke . . . . . kăr'-ĭs-brŏōk.
Carlén (Madame) . . . kär-län'.
Carlier, Don Diego . . dōn dē-ä'-gō kär-lē=âr'.
Carlisle . . . . . . kär-līl'.
Carlovingian, see Karlovin-
  gian . . . . kär-lō-vĭn'-jĭ-ȧn.
Carlowitz, see Karlowitz . kär'-lō-vĭts.
Carlsbad, see Karlsbad . kärlz'-bät.
Carlsruhe, see Karlsruhe kärlz'-rōō-ŭ.
Carlyle . . . . kär-līl'.
Carmagnole, La . . . . lä kär-män-yŏl'.
Carnarvon, see Caernarvon kär-när'-vŏn.

Carnaval de Venise . . kär-nä-väl' dŭ vĕ-nēz'.
Carnegie . . . . . . kär'-nĕ-gĭ, kär-nä'-gĭ,
kär-nĕg'-ē.
Carniola . . . . . . kär-nĭ-ō'-lä.
Carnot, Sadi- . . . sä-dē'-kär-nō'.
Carolina . . . . . . kăr-ō-lī'-nȧ.
Carolinian . . . . . kăr-ō-lĭn'-ĭ-ȧn.
Carolus Duran . . . kăr-ō-lüs' dü-räṅ'.
Carpaccio . . . . . kär-päch'-ō
Carpeaux . . . . . . kär-pō'.
Carpio, Bernardo del . . bĕr-när'dō dĕl kär'-pē=ō.
Carracci, Agostino . . . ä-gōs-tē'-nō kär-räch'-ē.
Carracci, Annibale . . . än-nē-bä'-lĕ kär-räch'-ē.
Carranza . . . . . . kär-rän'-sä.
Carrara . . . . . . kär-rä'-rä.
Carreño, Teresa . . . tä-rä'-sȧ kär-rĕn'-yō.
Carrière . . . . . . kăr-rē=âr'.
Carriès, Jean . . . . zhäṅ kăr-rē=ĕs'.
Carrousel . . . . . . kär-ōō-zĕl'.
Cartagena, see Carthagena kär-tȧ-jē'-nȧ. Sp.
kär-tä-ċhä'-nä.
Cartesian . . . . . . kär-tē'-zhĭ=ȧn.
Carthagena, see Cartagena kär-thȧ-jē'-nȧ. Sp.
kär-tä-ċhä'-nä.
Carthaginian . . . . . kär-thȧ-jĭn'-ĭ-ȧn.
Carthusian . . . . kär-thū'-zhĭ=ȧn.
Cartier, Jacques . . . zhäk kär-tē=ä'.
Caruso . . . . kä-rōō'-sō.
Caryatides . . . . . kă-rĭ-ăt'-ĭ-dēz.
Casabianca . . . . . kä"-zä-bē=än'-kä.
Casa Braccio . . . . . kä'-zä bräch'-ō.
Casa d'Oro . . . . . kä'-zä dō'-rō.
Casa Guidi . . . . . kä'-zä gwē'-dē.
Casas, Las . . . . . läs kä'-säs.
Casaubon . . . . . . kă-sô'-bŏn. Fr. kä-zō-bôṅ'.
Cascine . . . . . . kä-shē'-nä.
Caserta . . . . . . kä-zâr'-tä.

Cases, Las . . . . . läs käz.
Cashmere, see Kashmere,
  Kashmir . . . . . kăsh-mēr'.
Casiguran (Bay) . . . kä"-sē-gōō-rän'.
Casimir . . . . . . kăs'-ĭ-mēr.
Casimir-Périer . . . . kăz-ē-mēr' pā-rē=ā'.
Cassagnac, Granier de . grä-nē=ā' dŭ kăs-sän-yäk'.
Cassibelaunus, see Cassi-
  vellaunus . . . . . kăs"-ĭ-bĕ-lô'-nŭs.
Cassiepeia . . . . . kăs"-ĭ-ĕ-pē'-yȧ.
Cassio . . . . kăsh'-ō.
Cassiopeia . . . . . kăs-ĭ-ō-pē'-yȧ.
Cassius . . . . . . kăsh'-ŭs.
Cassivellaunus, see Cassi-
  belaunus . . . . . kăs"-ĭ-vĕ-lô'-nŭs.
Castagno . . . . . . käs-tän'-yō.
Castaigne . . . . . . käs-tän'.
Castaños . . . . . . käs-tän'-yōs.
Castelar . . . . . . käs-tä-lär'.
Castelfranco . . . . . käs-tĕl-frän'-kō.
Castellamare . . . käs'-tĕl-lä-mä'-rä.
Castellane, de . . . . dē kăs-tĕl-ăn'.
Castellon . . . . . . käs-tĕl-yōn'.
Castelnau . . . . . . käs-tĕl-nō'.
Castelnaudary . . . . käs-tĕl"-nō-dä-rē'.
Castiglione . . . . . käs-tēl-yō'-nĕ.
Castilla, Sp. for Castile . käs-tēl'-yä.
Castillejo . . . . . . käs-tēl-yä'-ċhō.
Castillo . . . . . . käs-tēl'-yō.
Castlereagh . . . . . kăs'-ĕl-rä.
Castro del Rio . . . . käs'-trō dĕl-rē'-ō.
Catanduanes . . . . . kä"-tän-dōō-ä'-nĕs.
Catania . . . . . . kä-tä'-nē-ä.
Catarina Cornaro . . . kä-tä-rē'-nä kōr-nä'-rō.
Catawba . . . . . . kȧ-tô'-bȧ.
Cateau Cambrésis . . . kă-tō' kän-brä-zē'.
Cathay . . . . kă-thä'.

Catiline	kăt'-ĭ-lĭn.
Cattack, see Cuttack, Katak	kŭt-tăk', kŭt-täk'.
Cattaro	kät-tä'-rō.
Cattegat, see Kattegat	kăt'-ĕ-găt.
Caucasians	kô-kā'-shȧnz, kô-kăsh'-ȧnz.
Caucasus (Mts.) . . .	kô'-kȧ-sŭs.
Cauldon	kôl'-dŭn.
Caulincourt, de	dŭ kō-lăṅ-kōōr'.
Cauterets	kōt-rā'.
Cauto (River)	kä'=ōō-tō.
Cavaignac	kä-vän-yăk'.
Cavalcanti, Guido . . .	gwē'-dō kä-väl-kän'-tē.
Cavalieri, Lina	lē'-nä kä-vä-lē-ä'-rē
Cavalleria Rusticana . .	kä″-väl-lä-rē'-ä rŏŏs-tē-kä'-nä.
Cavan	kăv'-ȧn.
Cavaradossi	kä″-vä-rä-dōs'-sē.
Cavell	kȧ-vĕl'.
Cavendish	kăv'-ĕn-dĭsh, kăn'-dĭsh.
Cavey	kä-bā'=ē.
Caviedes	kä-bē=ĕd'-äs.
Cavité	kä-bē-tä'.
Cavour	kä-vōōr'.
Cawein (Madison) . . .	kā-wīn'.
Cawnpore, or Cawnpur	kôn-pōr', kôn-pōōr'.
Cay	kä'=ē.
Caycos, see Caicos . .	kī'-kōs. Sp. kä'=ē-kōs.
Cayenne	kā-yĕn', kī-ĕn'.
Cayes, see Aux Cayes .	ō kä.
Cayister	kā-ĭs'-tẽr.
Caylus	kā-lüs'.
Caymans	kī'mȧnz. Sp. kä=ē-mänz'.
Cayo Cocas	kī'-ō kō'-käs.
Cayor, see Kayor . . .	kī-ōr', or kī-ôr'.
Cay Smith	kī smĭth.
Cayster	kā-ĭs'-tẽr.
Cazembe	kä-zĕm'-bĕ.

Cazin	kä-zăṅ'.
Ceadda, see Chad . . .	kĕ=äd'-dä.
Cean-Bermudez . . .	thā-än' bĕr-mōō'-thĕth.
Ceará	sē-ä-rä'.
Ceballos	thā-bäl'-yōs.
Cebú, see Zebú	sĕ-bōō'. *Sp.* thā-bōō .
Cecil	sĕs'-ĭl, sĭs'-ĭl.
Cécile	*Fr.* sä-sēl'.
Cecilia	sē-sĭl'-ĭ-ȧ. *It.* chā-chēl'-yä.
Cecily	sĕs'-ĭ-lĭ.
Cecrops, see Kekrops . .	sē'-krŏps.
Ced (St.), or	kĕd.
Cedda	kĕd'-dȧ.
Cedric of Rotherwood .	kĕd'-rĭk, sĕd'-rĭk ŭv
	rŏth'-ēr-wŏŏd.
Cedron, see Kedron, Kidron	sē'-drŏn.
Cefalú	chā-fä-lōō'.
Celadon	sĕl'-ȧ-dŏn.
Celebes (Is.)	sĕl'-ĕ-bĕs, *or* sĕl'-ĕ-bēz.
Celia	sē'-lĭ-ä.
Célimène	sä-lē-mĕn'.
Cellini, Benvenuto . . .	bān-vā-nŏŏ'-tō chĕl-lē'-nē.
Celsius	sĕl'-sĭ-ŭs, sĕl'-shĭ=ŭs
Celts, see Kelts	sĕlts, kĕlts.
Cenci	chĕn'-chē.
Cendrillon	sôṅdrē-yŏṅ'.
Cenis, Mont	môṅ sĕ=nē'.
Cephalonia	sĕf-ȧ-lō'-nĭ-ȧ.
Cephas	sē'-fȧs.
Cephisodotus . . .	sĕf-ĭ-sŏd'-ō-tŭs.
Cerberian	sēr-bē'-rē-ȧn.
Cerberus	sēr'-bĕ-rŭs, sēr'-bē-rŭs.
Cerdic	kēr'-dĭk.
Ceres	sē'-rēz.
Ceri, di	dē chā'-rē.
Cernawoda (-voda) . .	chĕr'-nä-vō-dä.
Cerquozzi	chär-kwŏt'-zē.

Cerro (The) . . . . . thĕr'-rō.
Cerro Gordo . . . . . sĕr'-rō gôr'-dō. *Sp.*
     thĕr'-rō gōr'-dō.
Certosa, La . . . . . lä chĕr-tō'-zä.
Cervantes Saavedra . . sēr-văn'-tēz, sä-ä-vä'-drä.
     Sp. thâr-bän'-tĕs
     sä-ä-bā'-drä.
Cervera . . . . . . thâr-bā'-rä.
César Birotteau . . . sā-zär' bē-rŏt-tō'.
Cesare . . . . . . chā'-zä-rĕ.
Cesari . . . . chā'-zä-rē.
Cesarian, see Caesarian . sē-zā'-rĭ-án.
Cesario . . . . . sĕ-zä'-rĭ-ō.
Cesnola . . . . . chĕs-nō'-lä.
Céspedes, de . . . . dā thĕs'-pä-dĕs.
Cetewayo, see Cettiwayo,
  Ketshwayo . . . . sĕt ĭ wä'-yō.
Cetigne, or Cettinje, or tsĕt-tĭn'-yĕ, *or* chĕ-tēn'-yā.
Cettigno . . . . . . *It.* chĕt-tēn'-yō.
Cettiwayo, see Cetewayo,
  Ketshwayo . . . . sĕt-ĭ-wä'-yō.
Ceuta . . . . sū'-tä. *Sp.* thā'=ōō-tä.
Cévennes . . . . . . sā-vĕn'.
Ceylon . . . . . . sē-lŏn', sĕ-lŏn'.
Cézanne . . . . . . sā-zăn'.
Chabaud . . . . . . shă-bō'.
Chabert, Le Colonel . . lĕ kō-lō-nĕl' shä-bâr'.
Chablis . . . . . shä-blē'.
Chabot . . . . shä-bō'.
Chachapoyas . . . . . chä-chä-pō'-yäs.
Chacon y Castellon . . chä-kōn' ē käs-tāl-yōn'.
Chad (Lake), see Tchad,
  Tsad, Tschad . . . . chäd.
Chad (St.), see Ceadde . chăd.
Chaeronea, or . . . . kĕr-ō-nē'-á.
Chaeroneia . . . . . kĕr-ō-nē'-yá.
Chagres . . . . . . chä'-grĕs.

Chaillé-Long . . . . . shä̤-yā′-lôǹ′.
Chaillu, du . . . . . dü shä-yü′.
Chalcis . . . . . . kăl′-sĭs.
Chaldea . . . . . . kăl-dē′-a̤.
Chaldean . . . . . kăl-dē′-an.
Chaldee . . . . . . kăl′-dē.
Chalgrin . . . . . . shäl-grăǹ′.
Challemel-Lacour . . . shăl-mĕl′-lä-kōōr′.
Chalmers . . . . . . chăl′-mērz, chä′-mērz.
            Sc. chô′-mērz.
Châlons . . . . . . shä-loǹ′.
Cham . . . . . . kăm.
Chamba . . . . . . chăm′-ba̤.
Chambertin . . . . . shäǹ-bĕr-tăǹ′.
Chambéry . . . . . shäǹ-bā-rē′.
Chambezi . . . . . . chăm-bē′-zĭ.
Chambord . . . . . shäǹ-bōr′.
Chaminade . . . . shă-mē-năd′.
Chamisso . . . . . shä-mēs′-ş̌ō.
Chamonix, or . . . . shä-mō-nē′.
Chamouni, or Chamouny . shä-mōō-nē′.
Champagne . . . . . shăm-pān′. Fr.
            shäǹ-pän′=yŭ.
Champaigne, de . . . dŭ shäǹ-pān′=yŭ.
Champaran, see Chumparun chŭm-pä-rŭn′.
Champ-de-Mars . . . shäǹ-dŭ-märs′.
Champfleury . . . . . shäǹ-flĕ-rē′.
Champigny . . . . . shäǹ-pēn-yē′.
Champlain . . . . . shăm-plān′. Fr. shäǹ-plăǹ′.
Champollion . . . . . shăm-pōl′-ĭ-ŏn. Fr.
            shäǹ-pŏl-yôǹ′.
Champs-Élysées . . . shäǹ-zä-lē-zā′.
Chanda . . . . . . chän′-dä.
Chang Chau . . . . . chäng′-chow′.
Changsha . . . . . . chäng′-shä′.
Chanoine . . . . . shä-nwăn′.
Chanson de Geste . . . shäǹ-sôǹ′ dŭ zhĕst′.

Chanson de Roland . .	shän-sôn' dŭ rō-län'.
Chanson de Roncevaux .	shän-sôn' dŭ rôns-vō'.
Chantecler	shän=tē-klĕr'.
Chantilly	shän-tē-yē'.
Chapdelaine	shäp=dĕ-lĕn'.
Chapelain	shăp-län'.
Chapu	chä-pōō', shä-pōō'.
Chapultepec	chä-pōōl"-tĕ-pĕk'.
Chardin	shär-dän'.
Chardonne, Jacques . .	zhăk shär-dŏn'.
Charente	shä-rŏnt'.
Chargé d'Affaires . . .	chär-zhä' dăf-fâr'.
Charlemagne	shär'-lĕ-mān. Fr.
	shärl-män'=yŭ.
Charleroi	shär=lĕ-rwä'.
Charleville	shärl-vēl'.
Charlevoix	shär=lĕ-vwä'.
Charmian	kär'-mĭ-ȧn.
Charon	kā'-rŏn.
Charpentier	shär-pôn-tē=ä'.
Chartier, Alain	ä-län' shär-tē=ä'.
Chartism	chär'-tĭzm.
Chartres	shärtr.
Chartreuse	shär-trēz'.
Charybdis	kā-rĭb'-dĭs.
Chasles	shäl.
Chasseloup-Laubat . .	shäs-lōō'-lō-bä'.
Chassepot	shäs-pō'.
Chastelard, de	dŭ shät-lär'.
Chasteler, du	dü shät-lä'.
Châtaignerie, La . . .	lä shä-tān=yŭ-rē'.
Chateaubriand	shä-tō-brē-än'.
Château d'If	shä-tō' dēf'.
Château Lafitte	shä-tō'lä-fēt'.
Château Margaux . . .	shä-tō' mär-gō'.
Châteauroux	shä-tō-rōō'.
Château-Thierry . . .	shä-tō'-tē=âr-rē'.

Châtelet . . . . . . shät-lā′.
Chatham . . . . . ′ . . chăt′-ảm.
Châtillon . . . . . . shä-tē-yôṅ′.
Châtillon-sur-Seine . . shä-tē-yôṅ′-sür-sĕn′.
Chatrian . . . . . . shä-trē-äṅ′.
Chaucer . . . . . . chô′-sẽr.
Chaulnes . . . . . . shōn.
Chaumont . . . . shō-mŏṅ′.
Chautauqua . . . . shô-tô′-kwả.
Chauvinism . . . . . shō′-vĭn-ĭzm.
Chavannes, Puvis de . . pü-vēs′ dŭ shä-vän′.
Chedorlaomer . . . . kē″-dôr-lä-ō′-mẽr,
                      lä′-ō-mẽr.
Che-kiang . . . . . chē-kyäng′.
Chemin des Dames . . shē-măṅ′ dā dăm′.
Chenab, Chenaub,   see
  Chinab . . . . . . chē-nôb′.
Chénier . . . . . . shä-nē=ā′.
Cheops . . . . . . kē′-ŏps.
Chephren . . . . . . kĕf′-rĕn.
Cher . . . . shâr.
Cherbourg . . . . shẽr′-bẽrg. Fr. shâr-bōōr′.
Cherbuliez . . . . . shâr-bü-lē=ā′.
Cherniavsky . . . . . tschĕr-nĭ-äf′-skĭ.
Chersonesus . . . . . kẽr-sō-nē′-sŭs.
Chertsey . . . . . . chĕs′-sĭ, chĕrt′-sĭ.
Cherubini . . . . . . kā-rōō-bē′-nē.
Chevalier . . . . . . shĕ-vä-lē=ā′.
Chevalier de Maison-Rouge shĕ-vä-lē=ā′ dŭ mā-zôṅ′-
                      rōōzh.
Chevalier de Saint George shĕ-vä-lē=ā′ dŭ săṅ zhŏrzh′.
Chevalier d'Harmental . shĕ-vä-lē=ā′ där-mŏṅ-täl′.
Chevillard . . . . . shĕ-vē-yär′.
Cheviot . . . . . . chĕv′-ĭ-ŭt, chĭv′-ĭ-ŭt.
Chevreuse . . . . . shĕv-rēz′.
Chevy Chase . . . . chĕv′-ĭ-chās.
Cheyenne . . . . . . shī-ĕn′.

Cheyne	chān, chīn.
Chhatisgarh	chŭt-tēs-gär'.
Chiaja, La	lä kē-ä'-yä.
Chianti	kē-än'-tē.
Chicago	shĭ-kô'-gō.
Chichester	chĭ'-chĕs-tēr.
Chicot	shē-kō'.
Chienne	shē-ĕn'.
Chieveley	chĭv'-lĭ'.
Chih-li, see Chi-li . . .	chē'-lē'.
Chihuahua	chē-wä-wä.
Chi-li, see Chih-li . . .	chē'-lē'.
Chile or Chili	chĭl'-ĕ, chĭl'-ĭ. *Sp.* chē'-lĭ.
Chilkat	chĭl'-kăt.
Chillon	shĭl'-ŏn. *Fr.* shē-yôṅ'.
Chilpéric	chĭl'-pĕ-rĭk. *Fr.* shēl-pä-rēk'.
Chimæra	kī-mē'-rä.
Chimay	shē-mä'.
Chimborazo	chĭm-bō-rä'-sō.
Chinab, see Chenab . .	chē-nôb'.
Chinese	chī-nēz', chī-nēs'.
Chingachgook	chĭn-gäk'-gō̄k.
Chingleput	chĭng-glĕ-pŭt'.
Chin-kiang	chĭn-kē-äng'.
Chinon	shē-nôṅ'.
Chinook	chĭ-nō̄k'.
Chioggia, see Chiozza .	kē-ŏd'-jä.
Chios, see Scio	kī'-ŏs.
Chiozza, see Chioggia .	kē-ŏt'-sä.
Chippewa, or	chĭp'-pē-wä, chĭp'-pē-wä.
Chippeway	chĭp'-ĕ-wä.
Chiron	kī'-rŏn.
Chisholm	chĭzm.
Chisleu	kĭs'-lū.
Chiswick	chĭz'-ĭk.
Chita	ċhē'-tä.

Chitral . . . . chĭt-räl', *or* chī'-tràl.
Chittagong . . . . . chĭt-tȧ-gŏng'.
Chittim, see Kittim . . kĭt'-ĭm.
Chivery . . . . . . chĭv'-ĕ-rĭ.
Chloe . . . . klō'-ē, *or* klō'-ĭ.
Chlom . . . . ċhŏlm.
Chlopicki . . . . . . ċhlō-pĭt'-skē.
Chlotar, see Clotaire . . ċhlō'-tär.
Chmielnicki . . . . . ċhmē=ĕl-nĭt'-skē.
Chocano, Santos . . . sän'-tōs chō-kä'-nō.
Cho-Cho-San, (see Cio-Cio) chō-chō-sän.
Choiseul . . . , . . shwä-zēl'.
Choiseul-Praslin . . . shwä-zēl'-prä-lăṅ'.
Choisy . . . . shwä-zē'.
Cholmondeley . . . . chŭm'-lĭ.
Chopin . . . . shō-păṅ'.
Chorazin . . . . . . kō-rā'-zĭn.
Chosroes . . . . . . kŏs'-rō-ēz, kŏs'-rō-ĕz.
Chota, see Chutia . . . chō'-tä.
Chouans . . . . . . shoō'-ȧnz. *Fr.* shoō-äṅ'.
Chrestien, or Chrétien de
Troyes . . . . . . krä-tē-ĕṅ' dŭ trwä'.
Chriemhild, see Kriemhild krēm'-hĭlt.
Christe eleïson . . . . krĭs'-tē ĕ-lā'-ĭ-sŏn.
Christian . . . . . . krĭst'-yăn, *or* krĭst'-ĭ=ȧn.
Christianity . . . . . krĭst-yăn'-ĭ-tĭ,
                    krĭst-ē=ăn'-ĭ-tĭ.
Christus . . . . . . krĭs'-tŭs.
Chronos . . . . . . krō'-nŏs.
Chryseis . . . . . . krī'-sē-ĭs.
Chrysostom . . . . . krĭs'-ŏs-tŏm, krĭs-ŏs'-tŏm.
Chumie . . . . . . choō'-mē.
Chumparun, see Champaran chŭm-pȧ-rŭn'.
Chur, see Coire . . . . koōr.
Churubusco . . . . . choō-roō-boōs'-kō.
Chusan . . . . . . choō-sän'.
Chutia, see Chota . . . choō'-tē-ä.

Cialdini	chäl-dē'-nē.
Cibo (Cardinal) . . .	thē'-bō.
Cibola, see Sibola . . .	sē'-bō-lä.
Cibrario	chē-brä'-rē-ō.
Cicero	sĭs'-ĕ-rō.
Cid, El	ĕl sĭd. *Sp.* äl thĭd.
Cid, Le	*Fr.* lē sēd.
Cienfuegos	thē-än"-fōō=ā'-gōs.
Ciergnon	sē-ârn-yôn'.
Cifuentas	thē-fōō=ĕn'-täs.
Cimabue	chē-mä-bōō'-ä.
Cima da Conegliano . .	chē'-mä dä kō-näl-yä'-nō.
Cimarosa	chē-mä-rō'-zä.
Cimmeria	sĭ-mē'-rĭ-å.
Commerian	sĭm-mē'-rĭ-ån.
Cimon	sī'-mŏn.
Cincinnati	sĭn-sĭn-nä'-tĭ.
Cincinnatus	sĭn-sĭn-nā'-tŭs.
Cingalon	thēn-gä-lōn'.
Cinq-Mars	săṅ-mär'.
Cinque Ports	sĭngk pōrts.
Cintra	sēn'-trä.
Cio-Cio-San, (see Cho-Cho)	chō-chō-sän.
Cipango	sĭ-păng'-gō.
Cipriani	chē-prē-ä'-nē.
Circaean, see Circean . .	sẽr-sē'-ån.
Circe	sẽr'-sē.
Circean, see Circaean . .	sẽr-sē'-ån.
Cisleithania	sĭs-lī-thä'-nĭ-å, sĭs-lī-tä'-nĭ-ä.
Cisneros	thēs-nä'-rŏs.
Cispadane	sĭs-pä'-dän.
Cissey	sē-sā'.
Città della Pieve . . .	chēt-tä' dĕl'-lä pē=ā'-vĕ.
Ciudad Bolívar	sē-ōō-däd' bō-lē'-vär.
Ciudad de Cadiz . . .	thē=ōō-däd' dä kä'-dĭth.
Ciudad Real	thē=ōō-däd' rä-äl'.
Ciudad Rodrigo	thē=ōō-däd' rōd-rē'-gō.

Cività Vecchia, Civitavecchia   chē-vē-tä' věk'-kē-ä.

Claes . . . . . .   kläz.
Clairault, or Clairaut . .   klä-rō'.
Clairvaux . . . . .   klâr-vō'.
Claretie . . . . .   klăr-tē'.
Claude, Georges . . .   zhōrzh klōd.
Claudel, Paul . . . .   pōl klō-děl'.
Claude Lorraine . . .   klōd lō-rěn'.
Claverhouse . . . .   klăv'-ēr-ŭs.
Cléante . . . . . .   klä-äṅt'.
Cleishbotham . . . .   klēsh'-bŏth-àm.
Cleisthenes, see Clisthenes   klīs'-thě-nēz.
Clélie . . . . . .   klä-lē'.
Clémenceau . . . .   klä-mŏṅ-sō'.
Clément . . . . .   klä-môṅ'.
Clemente, San . . .   sän klä-měn'-tě.
Clementi . . . . .   klä-měn'-tē.
Clementine . . . .   klěm'-ěn-tĭn, klěm'-ěn-tēn,
     or klěm-ěn-tēn'.
Cleobis . . . . . .   klē'-ō-bĭs.
Cleopas . . . . . .   klē'-ō-păs.
Cleopatra . . . . .   klē-ō-pā'-trà.
Cléopâtre . . . . .   klä-ō-pătr'.
Cleves, or . . . . .   klēvz.
Clèves . . . . . .   Fr. klâv.
Clio . . . .   klī'-ō.
Clisthenes, see Cleisthenes   klĭs'-thě-nēz.
Clitandre . . . . .   klē-täṅdr'.
Clive . . . . . .   klīv.
Cloaca Maxima . . .   klō-ā'-kà măk'-sĭ-mà.
Cloisonné . . . . .   klwä-zŏn-nā'.
Clonmel . . . . .   klŏn-měl'.
Clos Vougeot . . .   klō vōō-zhō'.
Clotaire, see Chlotar . .   klō-târ'.
Clouet . . . . . .   klōō-ā'.
Clough . . . . . .   klŭf.
Cluseret (Gen.) . . .   klü=zē-rä'.

Clusium . . . . . . klū'-sǐ-ŭm, klū'-shǐ-ŭm.
Cnidian . . . . . . nǐd'-ǐ-àn.
Cnidus . . . . nī'-dŭs.
Cnut, see Canute . . . knōōt.
Coachella . . . . . . kō-à-chĕl'-à.
Coahuila . . . . . . kō-à-wē'-là.
Coamo . . . . kō-ä'-mō.
Coanza, see Kuanza, Quanza kō-än'-zä.
Cobi, see Gobi . . . . kō'-bē.
Coblenz, or Coblentz . . kō'-blĕnts.
Cobre, El . . . . . . ĕl kō'-brä.
Cochin China . . . . kō'-chǐn chī'-nà.
Cockagne, or Cockaigne . kŏk-än'.
Cockburn . . . . . . kō'-bŭrn.
Cocles . . . . kō'-klēz.
Cocytus . . . . kō-sī'-tŭs.
Codrus . . . . kō'-drŭs.
Cœlebs . . . . sē'-lĕbz.
Coelho, or Coello . . . kō-ĕl'-yō.
Coelian Hill . . . . . sē'-lǐ-àn.
Coeur d'Alène . . . . kĕr dă-lĕn'.
Coeur de Lion . . . . kĕr dŭ lī'-ŏn. *Fr.* kĕr dŭ
lē-ôn'.
Cognac . . . . kōn-yäk'.
Cohoes . . . . kō-hōz'.
Coimbatore, see Koimbatur kō-ĭm''-bà-tōr'.
Coire, see Chur . . . . kwär.
Coke . . . . kōk, *originally* kŏŏk.
Colapur, see Kolhapur . kō-lä-pōōr'.
Colbert . . . . *Fr.* kōl-bâr'.
Colenso . . . . kō-lĕn'-sō.
Coleone, see Colleoni . . kō-lä-ō'-nä.
Colesberg . . . . . . kōlz'-bĕrg.
Colet . . . . kŏl'-ĕt.
Coligni, or Coligny . . . kō-lēn'-yē. *Fr.* kō-lēn-yē'.
Colin Clout . . . . . kŏl'-ĭn klowt.
Coliseum, see Colosseum . kŏl-ĭ-sē'-ŭm.

Colleoni, see Coleone . . kōl-lā-ō'-nē.
Colletta . . . . . . kŏl-lĕt'-tä.
Colmar, see Kolmar . . kōl-mär'.
Cologne . . . . . kä-lōn'. *Fr.* kō-lōn'=yŭ.
Colon . . . . . . kŏ-lŏn'. *Sp.* kō-lōn'.
Colon Cristóbal . . . . krēs-tō'-bäl kō-lōn'.
Colonel Chabert . . . kō-lō-nĕl' shä-bâr'.
Colonna . . . . . . kō-lŏn'-nä.
Coloocan . . . . . kŏl-ō'-kăn.
Colorado . . . . . . kŏl-ō-rä'-dō.
Colosse . . . . kō-lŏs-sē.
Colosseum, see Coliseum kŏl-ō-sē'-ŭm.
Colquhoun . . . . . kŏ-hōōn'.
Comacchio . . . . . kō-mäk'-kē=ō.
Comanche, see Camanche kō-măn'-chē.
Combe . . . . . . kōm, kōōm.
Comédie Française . . . kō-mā-dē' fräṅ-sĕz'.
Comédie Humaine . . . kō-mā-dē' ü-mĕn'.
Comeiro . . . . . . kō-mā'=ē-rō.
Comines, or Commines . kŏ-mēn'.
Commodus . . . . . kŏm'-mō-dŭs.
Commune . . . . . . kŏm'-yūn. *Fr.* kŏm-ün'.
Comneni . . . . . . kŏm-nē'-nī.
Comnenus . . . . . kŏm-nē'-nŭs.
Comorin . . . . . . kŏm'-ō-rĭn.
Compagnie G é n é r a l— kôṅ-pän-yē' zhā-nā-răl'
 Transatlantique . . . träṅz-ät-läṅ-tēk'.
Compiègne. . . . . . kôṅ-pē-ān'=yŭ.
Comte . . . . kôṅt.
Comtesse de Rudolstadt . kôṅ-tĕs' dŭ rü-dŏl-stät'.
Comtist . . . . . . kŏm'-tĭst. *Fr.* kôṅ-tēst'.
Comus . . . . kō'-mŭs.
Concas . . . . kōng'-käs.
Concepcion . . . . . kŏn-sĕp'-shŏn. *Sp.* kōn-
 thāp''-thē-ōn'.
Conchita . . . . . . kōn-chē'-tȧ.
Conciergerie . . . . . kōn-sē=ĕr-zhē-rē'.

Concini . . . . . . *It.* kōn-chē'-nē. *Fr.*
    kŏn-sē-nē'.
Concone . . . . . . kōn-kō'-nä.
Concordat . . . . . kŏn-kôr'-dăt. *Fr.*
    kŏṅ-kōr-dä'.
Condé . . . . kôṅ-dä'.
Condé-sur-Noireau . . kôṅ-dä'-sür-nwä-rō'.
Condillac . . . . . . kôṅ-dē-yäk'.
Condorcet, de . . . . du kôṅ-dōr-sä.
Conegliano, Cima da . . chē'-mä dä kō-nāl-yä'-no.
Confessio Amantis . . . kŏn'-fĕsh'-ō ä-mǎn'-tĭs.
Conflans . . . . . . kôn-fläṅ'.
Congreve . . . . . . kŏng'-grev.
Coniston . . . . . . kŏn'-ĭs-tŭn.
Connaught . . . . . kŏn'-nôt.
Conradin . . . . . . kōn'-rä-dēn.
Consalvi . . . . . . kōn-säl'-vē.
Constable . . . . . . kŭn'-stà-bl.
Constant de Rebecque . kôṅ-stäṅ' dŭ rē-bĕk'.
Constantine (Emperor) . kŏn'-stàn-tīn.
Constantine (Algeria) . . kôn-stäṅ-tēn'.
Constanza . . . . . . kŏn-stän'-zä.
Consuelo . . . . . . kŏn-sōō-ä'-lo. *Fr.*
    kŏṅ-sü=ä-lō'.
Conte . . . . kōn-tä.
Contel . . . . kŏn-tĕl'.
Contes d'Hoffmann . . kōnt dŏf-mäṇ'.
Contessa . . . . . . kōn-tĕs'-sä.
Conti . . . . kônt-tē'.
Contreras . . . . . . kōn-trä'-räs.
Conybeare . . . . . . kŭn'-i-bĕr.
Coomassie, see Kumassi . kōō-mäs'-sē.
Coombe . . . . . . kōōm.
Copenhagen . . . . . kō-pĕn-hä'-gĕn. *Dan.*
    kō-pĕn-hä'-gĕn
Copernicus . . . . . kō-pēr-'nĭ-kŭs.
Cophetua . . . . . . kō-fĕt'-ū-à.

Coppée François	frän-swä′ kŏp-pä′.
Coquelin	kōk-lăṅ′.
Corcyra	kôr-sī′-rȧ.
Corday d'Armans . . .	kôr-dā där-mäṅ′.
Cordeliers	kōr-dĕ-lē=ā′.
Cordilleras	kôr-dĭl′-ēr-ȧz. *Sp.*
	kōr-dĕl-yā′-räs.
Córdoba, or Cordova . .	kôr′-dō-vä. *Sp.*kōr′-dō-bä.
Cordovan	kôr′-do-vȧn.
Corea, see Korea . . .	kō-rē′-ȧ.
Corean, see Korean . .	kō-rē′-ȧn.
Corfu	kōr-fōō′, kŏr-fŭ′.
Cori	kō′-rē
Coriolanus	kō″-rĭ-ō-lä′-nŭs.
Corioli	kō-rī′-ō-lē.
Corleone	kōr-lä-ō′-nä.
Cornaro	kōr-nä′-rō.
Corneille	kŏr-nāl. *Fr.* kōr-nā′=yŭ.
Cornelis	kŏr-nä′-lĭs.
Cornice, or	*It.* kōr′-nē-chä.
Corniche	*Fr.* kôr-nēsh′.
Corona Borealis . . .	kō-rō′-nä bō-rē-ä′-lĭs.
Corozal	kō-rō-säl′.
Corot	kō-rō′.
Correa	kōr-rä′-ä.
Correggio	kŏr-rĕd′-jō.
Corregidor	kŏr″-rä¢h-ē-dōr′
Corrèze	kŏr-râz′.
Corrientes	kŏr-rē-ĕn′-tĕs.
Cortes (The)	kŏr′-tĕs.
Cortés (Fernando) or . .	kŏr täs′.
Cortez	kŏr′-tĕz.
Coruña, La	lä kō-rōōn′-yä.
Corunna	kō-rŭn′-ȧ.
Corvisart-Desmarets . .	kōr-vē-zär′ dä-mä-rä′.
Corydon	kŏr′-i-dŏn
Cosette	kō-zet′.

Cosimo	kō'-zē-mō.
Cosmati	kōs-mä'-tē.
Cosmo de Medici . . .	kōs'-mō dä mä'-dē-chē.
Cossack	kŏs'-ăk, kŏz-ăk'.
Costa Rica	kŏs'-tä rē'-kä. *Sp.*
	kōs'-tä.
Costis	kŏs'-tĭs.
Côte d'Azur	kŏt dă-zür'.
Côte d'Or	kŏt'- dōr'.
Cotes du Nord . . .	kŏt'-dü-nōr'.
Cottin	kōt-tăn'.
Coucy	kōō-sē'.
Coulanges	kōō-länzh'.
Coulommiers	kōō-lŏm-ē=ā'.
Couperin	kōō-pē-răn'.
Couperus	kōō-pâr'-ōōs.
Courbet	kōōr-bā'.
Courcelles	kōōr-sĕl'.
Courcy	kōōr-sē'.
Courland	kōōr'-lănd.
Courtenay	kĕrt'-nā, kŏŏrt'-nā.
Courtois	kōōr-twä'.
Courtrai, or Courtray . .	kōōr-trä'.
Cousin, Victor	vēk-tōr' kōō-zăn'
Cousin Pons	kōō-zăn' pôn.
Cousine Bette	kōō-zēn' bĕt.
Coutances	kōō-täns'.
Coutras	kōō-trä'.
Couture	kōō-tür'.
Covent (Garden) . . .	kŭv'-ĕnt.
Coventry	kŭv'-ĕn-trĭ.
Correa	kŏr-rā'-ä.
Correggio . . ˙ . . .	kŏr-rĕd'-jō.
Corregidor	kŏr"-rāċh-ē-dōr'.
Corrèze	kŏr-rĕz'.
Coxsackie	kŏŏk-sô'-kĭ.
Coysevox	kwäz-vŏks'.

Craigenputtoch, or . . . . _Sc._ krā-gĕn-pŭt'-ŏċh.
Craigenputtock . . . . krā-gĕn-pŭt'-ŏk.
Cramer . . . . _Ger._ krä'-mĕr.
Cranach (Lucas), see Kranach krăn'-ȧk, krä'-näċh.
Craonne . . . . . . krä-ŏn'.
Crapaud . . . . . . kră-pō'.
Cratylus . . . . . . krăt'-ĭ-lŭs.
Crébillon . . . . . . krā-bē-yôn'.
Créçy, see Cressy . . . krĕs'-ĭ. _Fr._ krā-sē'.
Credi . . . . krā'-dē.
Crédit Lyonnais . . . krā-dē' lē-ŏn-ĕ'.
Crédit Mobilier . . . . krĕd'-ĭt mō-bē'-lĕ-ēr. _Fr._
  krā-dē' mō-bē-lē=ā'.
Crémieux . . . . . . krā-mē-ē'.
Cremona . . . . . . krē-mō'-nä. _It._ krā-mō'-nä.
Crespy, or Crêpy-en-
  Laonnais . . . . . krā-pē' ôn lä=ō-nä'.
Cressida . . . . . . krĕs'-ĭ-dȧ.
Cressy, see Créçy . . . krĕs'-ĭ.
Creusa . . . . krē-ū'-sȧ.
Creuse . . . . krĕz.
Creusot, or Creuzot . . krē-zō'.
Crèvecœur . . . . . krāv-kēr'.
Crichton . . . . . . krī'tŏn.
Crillon . . . . krē-yôn'.
Crimea . . . . krĭ-mē'-ȧ, krī-mē'-ȧ.
Crispi . . . . krĭs'-pē.
Cristóbal Colón . . . . krēs-tō'-bäl kō-lōn'.
Cristofori . . . . . . krĭs-tō-fō'-rē.
Critias . . . . krĭsh'-ĭ-ȧs.
Crito . . . . krī'-tō.
Crivelli . . . . krē-vel'-lē.
Crna Gora, see Czernagora chĕr'-nä gō'-rä.
Croat . . . . krō'-ăt.
Croatia . . . . . . krō-ā'-shē=ȧ.
Cromwell . . . . . . krŏm'-wĕl, krŭm'-wĕl.
  pop. krŭm'-l.

Cronaca	krōn'-ä-kä.
Cronjé	krŏn'-yĕ.
Cronstadt, see Kronstadt .	krŏn'-stăt. *Ger.* krōn'-stät.
Cronus, or Cronos, see	
Kronos	krō'-nŭs.
Cruz	krōōth.
Ctesias	tē'-shĭ=às.
Cuba	kū'-bä. *Sp.* kōō'-bä.
Cuchulain, (or -lin, etc.) .	kōō-'hōō'-lĕn.
Cuddalore	kŭd-dȧ-lōr'.
Cuddapah, see Kadapa .	kŭd'-dȧ-pä.
Cuenca	kōō=ĕn'-kä.
Cuernavaca	kwĕr-nä-vä'-kä.
Cui, César	tsä'-zär kwē.
Culebra	kōō-lä'-brȧ.
Culiacan	kōō-lē-ä-kän'.
Culion	kōō-lē-ōn'.
Culloden	kŭl-lō'-dĕn.
Culmbach, see Kulmbach	kŏŏlm'-bäċh.
Cumae	kū'-mē.
Cumaean	kū-mē'-ȧn.
Cumières	kü-mē=âr'.
Cunctator	kŏŏngk-tä'-tôr.
Cuneo	kōō-nä'-ō.
Cupey	kōō-pä'=ē.
Curaçao, or Curazao, or .	kōō-rä-sä'-ō, kū'-rȧ-sō,
Curaçoa	kū'-rȧ-sō"-a, kōō-rä-sō'-ä,
	kōō-rä-sō'.
Curico	kōō-rē-kō'.
Curie	kü-rē'.
Curtius	*Ger.* kōōr'-tsē-ŏŏs. *Lat.*
	kĕr'-shĭ-ŭs.
Curzon	kĕr'-zŭn.
Cush	kŭsh.
Custine	küs-tēn'.
Custoza, or	kŏŏs-tōd'-sä.
Custozza	kŏŏs-tōt'-zä.

Cüstrin, see Küstrin . . küs-trēn'.
Cuttack, see Cattack, Kutak kŭt-tăk', kŭ-täk'.
Cuvier . . . . kü-vē=ā'.
Cuxhaven . . . . . kŭks-hā'-věn. Ger.
           kōōks'-hä-fěn.
Cuyo . . . . kōō'-yō.
Cuyos . . . . kōō'-yōs.
Cuyp, see Kuyp . . . koip.
Cuzco . . . . kōōz'-kō.
Cwm . . . . kōōm.
Cyaxares . . . . . . sī-ăx'-ā-rēz.
Cybele . . . . sĭb-ē'-lē, sĭb'-ĕ-lē.
Cyclades . . . . . . sĭk'-lā-dēz.
Cyclop . . . . sī'-klŏp.
Cyclopean . . . . . sī-klō-pē'-àn.
Cymbeline . . . . . sĭm'-bĕ-lĭn, or sĭm'-bĕ-līn.
Cymry, see Kymry . . kĭm'-rĭ.
Cynewulf . . . . . . kĭn'-ĕ-wōŏlf.
Cyprian . . . . . . sĭp'-rĭ-àn.
Cyrano de Bergerac . . sĭr-ä-nō' dŭ bâr=zhĕ-räk'.
Cyrene . . . . sī-rē'-nē.
Cyrenian . . . . . . sī-rēn'-ĭ-àn.
Cyril . . . . sĭr'-ĭl.
Cythera . . . . . . sī-thē'-rȧ.
Cytherean . . . . . sĭth-ēr-ē'-àn.
Cyzicus . . . . . . sĭz'-ĭ-kŭs.
Czajkowski, Czaykowski . chī-kŏv'-skē.
Czar . . . . zär, tsär.
Czardas . . . . . . chär'-däsh.
Czarevitch, see Tsarovitch zär'-ĕ-vĭch, tsär'-ĕ-vĭch.
Czarevna, see Tsarevna . zär-ĕv'-nä, tsär-ĕv'-nä.
Czarina, see Tsarina . . zär-ē'-nä, tsär-ē'-nä.
Czaritza . . . . . . zär-ĭt'-zä, tsär-ĭt'-zä.
Czarniecki . . . . . chärn-yĕt'-skē.
Czarowitch . . . . . zär'-ō-vĭch, tsär'-ō-vĭch.
Czarowitz, see Tsarowitz . zär'-ō-vĭtż, tsär'-ō-vĭtz.
Czartoryski . . . . . chär-tō-rĭ'-skē.

Czaykowski, Czajkowski . chī-kŏv′-skē.
Czecho-Slovak . . . . chĕk′-ō slō′-văk.
Czechs, see Tsech . . . chĕċhs, chĕks.
Czermak . . . . . . chĕr-mäk′.
Czernagora, or Crna Gora chĕr″-nä-gō′-rä.
Czernin . . . . . . tchĕr-nēn′.
Czernowitz . . . . . chĕr′-nō-vĭts.
Czerny . . . . chĕr′-nē.
Czibulka . . . . . . chē-bōōl′-kä.

D

Dablon . . . . . . dä-blôṅ′.
Dacca, see Dhaka . . . dăk′-ȧ.
Dacia . . . . dā′-shĭ=ä.
Daedalian . . . . . dē-dā′-lĭ-ȧn.
Daedalus . . . . . . dē′-dȧ-lŭs, dĕd′-ȧ-lŭs.
Daeye, Hippolyte . . . ēp-ō-lēt′ dä′=yŭ.
Daghestan . . . . . dä-gĕs-tän′.
Dagnan-Bouveret . . . dän-yäṅ′-bōōv-rä′.
Dagobert . . . . . . dăg′-ō-bĕrt. Fr. dä-gō-bâr′.
Dagon . . . . dā′-gŏn.
Dagonet, or Daguenet . dăg′-ō-nĕt, or dăg′-ĕ-nĕt.
Daguerre . . . . . . dä-gâr′.
Dagupan or Dagúpan . . dä-gōō-pän′, dä-gōō′-pän.
Dahlgren . . . . . . dăl′-grĕn. Sw. däl′-grĕn.
Dahn . . . . dän.
Dahomey . . . . . . dä-hō′-mĭ, dä-hō′-mä.
Dail Eareann . . . . dīl ē′-rän.
Daimio . . . . . . dī′-mē=ō.
Daiquiri . . . . . . dä=ē-kē′-rē.
D'Albert . . . . . . däl-bâr′.
D'Alembert . . . . . dä-lôṅ-bâr′.
Dalgetty . . . . . . dăl′-gĕt-ĭ.
Dalgleish . . . . . . dăl-glēsh′.
Dalhousie . . . . . . dăl-hōō′-zĭ, dăl-how′-zĭ.
Dalida . . . . dăl′-ĭ-dȧ.

Dalin . . . . dä'-lǐn.
Dalkeith . . . . . . dăl-kēth'.
Dalles . . . . dălz.
Dall' Ongaro . . . . . däl ŏng'-gä-rō.
Dalmatia . . . . . . däl-mä'-shǐ-à.
Dalmores . . . . . . dăl-mō-rěz'.
Dalou, Jules . . . . . zhül dä-lōō'.
Dalrymple . . . . . dăl-rǐm'-pl.
Daman, see Damaun . . dä-män'.
Damaraland . . . . . dä-mä'-rä-lănd.
Damaris . . . . . . dăm'-à-rǐs.
Damascene . . . . . dăm'-ă-sēn.
Damasus . . . . . . dăm'-à-sŭs.
Damaun, see Daman . . dä-môn'.
Dame aux Camélias, La . lä däm ō kä-mä-lē=ä'.
Damiano . . . . . . dä-mē-ä'-nō.
Damien . . . . . . dä-mē=ěn'.
Damis . . . . dä-mēs'.
Damnation de Faust . . däm-nä-sē=ôn' dŭ fowst.
Damoclean . . . . . dăm-ō-klē'-àn.
Damocles . . . . . . dăm'-ō-klēz.
Damon . . . . . . dā'-mŏn.
Dampier . . . . . . dăm'-pēr.
Dampt . . . . dämpt.
Damrosch . . . . . däm'-rŏsh.
Danaë . . . . dăn'-ā-ē.
Danai . . . . dăn'-ā-ī.
Danaïdes . . . . . . dă-nā'-ĭ-dēz, dā-nā'-ĭ-dēz.
Danaoi . . . . dăn'-ā-oi.
Dandin, George . . . zhŏrzh dän-dăn'.
Dandolo . . . . . . dän'-dō-lō.
Danegeld . . . . . . dān'-gěld.
Danelagh, Danelaw . . dān'-lô.
Dannecker . . . . . dän'-něk-ěr.
D'Annunzio, Gabriele . . gä-brē-ä'-lä
          dän-nōōn'-dzē-ō.
Danse Macabre . . . . däns mä-kăbr'.

Dante Alighieri . . . . dăn'-tĕ ăl"-ĭ-gĭ=â'-rĭ. *It.*
                       dän'-tā ä"-lē-gē=ā'-rē.
Dantean . . . . . . dăn'-tē-àn.
Dantès . . . . däṅ-tĕs'.
Danton . . . . . . dăn'-tŏn. *Fr.* däṅ-tôṅ'.
Dantsic, Dantzic, or Danzig dănt'-sĭk. *Ger.* dänt'-sĭċh.
Daphne . . . . . . dăf'-nē.
Daphnis . . . . . . dăf'-nĭs.
Darbhangah, see Durbunga dä-băn'-gä.
D'Arblay, Madame . . mä-dăm' där-blä'.
Darc, or D'Arc, Jeanne . zhän därk.
Dardanelles . . . . . där-dà-nĕlz'.
Dardanus . . . . . där'-dà-nŭs.
Dar-es-Salam . . . . där"-ĕs-sä-läm'.
Darfor or Darfur . . . där'-fōr, där'-fōōr.
Dargomijsky . . . . . där-gō-mĭzh'-skĭ.
Darien . . . . dā'-rĭ-ĕn. *Sp.* dä-rē-ĕn'.
Darío, Rubén . . . . rōō-bĕn' dä-rē'-ō.
Darius . . . . dà-rī'-ŭs.
Darjeeling (-jiling) . . . där-jē'-lĭng.
Darwar, see Dharwar . . där'-wär.
D'Aubigné, Merle . . . mĕrl dō-bēn-yä'.
Daubigny . . . . . dō-bēn-yē'.
Daudet, Alphonse . . . ăl-fôṅs' dō-dä'.
Daudet, Léon . . . . lä-ôṅ' dō-dä'.
Daun . . . . down.
Dauphin . . . . . . dō'-fĭn. *Fr.* dōfăṅ'.
Dauphiné . . . . . . dō-fēn-ä'.
Dauphiness . . . . . dô'-fĭ-nĕs.
Dauphiny . . . . . . dô'-fĭ-nĭ.
Daur, or Dauria . . . . dä-ōōr', dä-ōōr'-rē-ä.
Davalos . . . . . . *Sp.* dä-bä'-lŏs.
David, Gheerardt . . . gä-rärt' dä'-vēt.
David, Felicien . . . fä-lē-sē-ĕṅ' dä-vēd.
David, (L. J.) . . . . dä-vēd'.
Davila . . . . . . dä'-vē-lä.
Da Vinci, Leonardo . . lä-ō-när'-dō dä vēn'-chē.

Davoust . . . . . . dä-vōō′.
De Aar . . . . . . dĕ ar.
Deák . . . . dā-äk′.
De Amicis . . . . . . dā ä-mē′-chēs.
De Amicitia . . . . . dē ăm-ĭ-sĭsh′-ĭ=ä.
Débeney . . . . . . dāb-nā′.
Débonnaire, Louis le . . lōō-ē′ lĕ dā-bŏn-ār′.
Deborah . . . . . . dĕb′-ō-rȧ.
Debreczin . . . . . . dā-brĕt′-sĭn, or
 dā-brĕt′-sĭn.
De Bruycker, Jules . . zhül dẽ broi′-kẽr.
Debussy, Claude . . . klōd dẽ-büs-ē′.
Decameron . . . . . dē-kăm′-ẽr-ŏn.
Decamerone . . . . . dā-kä-mä-rō′-nä.
Decamps . . . . . . dẽ-käṅ′.
Decazes . . . . . . dŭ-kăz′.
Deccan, see Dekkan . . dĕk′-ȧn.
Decelean . . . . . . dĕs-ē-lē′-ȧn.
Deffand, Marquise du . mär-kēz′-dü dĕf-fäṅ′.
Defregger . . . . . . dā-frĕg′-ẽr.
Degas . . . . dẽ-gä′.
Delhi, see Delhi . . . dā′-lē.
Dehra Dun . . . . . dĕh′-rä dōōn.
Deianira, see Dejanira. . dē-yȧ-nī′-rȧ.
De Imitatione Christi . . dē ĭm″-ĭ-tā-shĭ-ō′-nĕ
 krĭs′-tĭ.
Deiphobus . . . . . dē-ĭf′-ō-bŭs.
Dejanira, see Deianira . dĕj-ȧ-nī′-rȧ.
Dejean . . . . dŭ-zhôṅ′.
Dekkan, see Deccan . . dĕk′-ȧn.
De Koven . . . . . . dē ko′-vĕn.
Delacroix . . . . . . dŭ-lä-krwä′.
Delagoa . . . . . . dĕl-ȧ-gō′-ȧ.
Delambre . . . . . . dŭ-läṅbr′.
Deland (Margaret) . . dē-lănd′.
De la Ramée . . . . dŭ lä rä-mā′.
Delaroche . . . . . . dŭ-lä-rŏsh′.

Delaunay	dĕ-lō-nā'.
Delavigne	dŭ lä-vēn'=yŭ.
Declassé	dĕl-kăs-ā'.
Deledda, Grazia . . .	grätz'-ē-à dā-lād'-dä.
Delegorgue	dĕ=lē-gōrg'.
Delft	dĕlft.
Delgado	dĕl-gä'-dō.
Delhi, see Dehli . . .	dĕl'-hī.
Delian	dē'-lī-àn.
Délibes	dā-lēb'.
Délila	Fr. dā-lē-lä'.
Delilah	dē-lī'-lä.
Della Cruscan . . .	dĕl'-là krŭs'-kàn.
Delorme, Marion . . .	mä-rē-ôṅ' dŭ lôrm'.
Delos	dē'-lŏs.
Delphi	dĕl'-fī.
Delphic	dĕl'-fĭk.
Delphine	Fr. dĕl-fēn'.
Del Pino	dĕl pē'-nō.
Delsarte	dĕl-särt'.
Del Sarto, Andrea . .	än-drā'-ä dāl sär'-to.
De Lussan, Zélie . . .	zā-lē' dŭ lüs-sän'.
Delyannis	dĕl-ĭ-ăn'-ĭs.
Demange, Maître . . .	mātr dŭ-mäṅzh'.
Demerara, or Demerary .	dĕm-ē-rä'-rà, dĕm-ēr-rä'-rĭ.
Demeter	dĕ-mē'-tēr.
Demetrius	dĕ-mē'-trĭ-us.
Demidoff, Demidov . .	dĕm'-ē-dŏf.
Democritus	dē-mŏk'-rĭ-tŭs.
Demogorgon	dē-mō-gôr'-gŏn.
Demos	dē'-mŏs.
Demosthenes	dē-mŏs'-thĕ-nēz.
Denderah	dĕn'-dēr-ä.
Deneb	dē'-nĕb, dĕn'-ĕb.
Den Haag	dĕn häch.
Denikin	dyĕ-nē'-kĭn.
Denis, St., see Denys . .	sānt dĕn'-is. Fr. säṅ dē-nē.

Dent du Midi . . . . dŏṅ dü mē-dē'.
Denys, St., see Denis . . sānt dĕn'-ĭs. *Fr.* sän dŭ-nē'
D'Épinay . . . . . . dā-pē-nā'.
Dépit Amoureux, Le . . lĕ dā-pē' tä-mōō-rē'.
De Prés, Josquin, see
   Desprez . . . . . . zhŏs-kăṅ' dŭ prā'.
De Profundis . . . . . dē prō-fŭn'-dĭs.
Deptford . . . . . . dĕt'-fŭrd.
De Quincey . . . . . dŭ kwĭn'-zĭ.
Derajat . . . . . . dĕr-à-jăt'.
Derby . . . . dĕr'-bĭ, där'-bĭ.
Dercetas . . . . . . dĕr'-sĕ-tàs.
Der Fliegende Holländer . dĕr flē'-gĕn-dà hŏl'-ĕn-dĕr.
Dernburg . . . . . . dĕrn'-bōōrch.
Dernier Chouan, Le . . lŭ dĕr-nē=ā' shōō-äṅ'.
Déroulède . . . . . . dā-rōō-lĕd'.
De Ruyter . . . . . . dē rī'-tēr. *D.* dŭ roi'-tĕr.
Dervis, Dervise, or Dervish dĕr'-vĭs, dĕr'-vĭsh.
Desaix de Veygoux . . . dŭ-sā' dŭ vā-gōō'.
Descartes . . . . . . dā-kärt'.
Deschamps . . . . . dā-shäṅ'.
Desdemona . . . . . dĕz-dĕ-mō'-nä.
Desdichado . . . . . dĕs-dĭ-chä'-dō.
Deseada . . . . . . dĕs-ĕ-ä'-dä.
Des Grieux . . . . . dā grē-ē'.
Désirade . . . . . . dā-zē-răd'.
Des Lys, Gaby . . . . gă-bē' dā lēs'.
Des Moines . . . . . dĕ-moin.
Desmoulins . . . . . dā-mōō-lăṅ'.
Despenser . . . . . . dĕ-spĕn'-sēr.
Desprez, Josquin, see De
   Prés . . . . zhŏs-kăṅ' dā-prā'.
Dessalines . . . . . dĕs-ä-lēn'.
Dessau . . . . dĕs'-sow.
Dessauer, ... dĕs'-sow-ēr.
De Staël-Holstein . . . dŭ stä'-ēl-hŏl'-stīn.
                       Fr. dŭ stä-ĕl-ōl-stăn'.

D'Este	dās'-tĕ.
De Stendhal	dŭ stŏṅ-däl'.
Destinn (Emmy). . .	dĕs'-tĭn.
Destouches	dā-tōōsh'.
Detaille	dŭ-tä'=yŭ.
De Tocqueville . . .	dŭ tŏk'-vĭl. *Fr.*
	dŭ tōk-vēl'.
Deucalion	dū-kā'-lĭ-ŏn.
Deutsch	doich.
Deutsche Tages-Zeitung .	doich'-ŭ tä'-gĕs tsī'-tōŏng.
Deux-Ponts	dē pôṅ.
Deux-Sèvres	dē sĕvr.
Deventer	dā-vĕn'-tēr.
Devereux	dĕv'-ēr-ōō, dĕv'-ēr-ŭ.
De Vigny	dŭ vēn-yē'.
Devizes	dē-vī'-zĕz.
D'Ewes	dūz.
De Wet	dā-vĕt'.
Dewetsdorp	dā-vĕts'-dŏrp.
De Wette	dĕ wĕt'-tĕ. *D.* dĕ vĕt'-tĕ.
De Witt	dĕ wĭt. *D.* de vĭt.
Dhaka, see Dacca . .	dhä'-kä.
Dhar	dhär.
Dharwar, see Darwar .	där'-wär.
Dhawalaghiri	dhȧ-wäl''-ä-ghēr'-ē. ·
Dolphur	dhŏl-pōōr'.
Diabelli	dē-ä-bĕl'-lē.
Diable, Robert le . .	rō-bâr' lĕ dē=ăbl'.
Diadochi	dī-ăd'-ō-kī.
Diane de Poitiers . .	dē-ăn dŭ pwä-tē=ā'.
Diarbekir, or Diarbekr .	dē-är''-bĕ-kēr', dē-är-bĕkr'
Dias	dē'-äs.
Diavolo, Fra	frä dē-ä'-vō-lō.
Diaz	*It.* dē'-ätz. *Mex.* dē'-äs.
	Sp. dē'-äth.
Diderot	dēd-rō'.
Didot	dē-dō'.

Dïdymus . . . . . dĭd'-ĭ-mŭs.
Diederichs, von . . . . fŏn dē'-dā-rĭks.
Diego . . . . dē-ā'-gō.
Dieppe . . . . dē-ĕp'.
Dies Irae . . . . . . dī'-ēz ī'-rē.
Dieskau . . . . . dēs'-kow.
Dietrich von Bern . . . dē'-trĭċh fŏn bĕrn.
Dijon . . . . dē-zhôṅ'.
Dilke . . . . dĭlk.
Dimitri . . . . dē-mē'-trē.
Dinan . . . . dē-näṅ'.
Dinant . . . . dē-nänt'. *Fr.* dē-näṅ'.
Dingaan . . . . . . dĭn-gän', *or* dĭng-gän'.
Diodorus Siculus . . . dī-ō-dō'-rŭs sĭk'-ŭ-lŭs.
Diogenes . . . . . . dī-ŏj'-ĕ-nēz.
Diomedes . . . . . . dī-ō-mē'-dēz.
Dionysia . . . . . . dī-ō-nĭsh'-ĭ-à.
Dionysius . . . . . . dī-ō-nĭsh'-ĭ-ŭs.
Dionysus . . . . . . dī-ō-nī'-sŭs.
Dioscuri . . . . . . dī-ŏs-kū'-rī.
Dippel . . . . dĭp'-pĕl.
Dirce . . . . dĕr'-sē.
Discobolus. . . . . . dĭs-kŏb'-ō-lŭs.
Disraeli . . . . . . dĭs-rā'-li, diz-rē'-li.
Dives . . . . dī'-vēz.
Divina Commedia . . . dē-vē'-nä kōm-mä'-dē-ä.
Dixmude . . . . . . dē-müd'.
Dmitri . . . . d-mē'-trē.
Dnieper, or Dniepr . . . nē'-pĕr. *Russ.* dy̆nĕp'-ĕr.
Dniester, or Dniestr . . nēs'-tĕr. *Russ.* dnyĕs'-tĕr.
Dobrudja . . . . . . dō-brōō'-jä.
Dodona . . . . . . dō-dō'-nä.
Dogali . . . . dō-gä'-lē.
Doiran . . . . doi'-rän.
Dolce . . . . dŏl'-chĕ. *It.* dŏl'-chä.
Dolci . . . . dŏlchĭ. *It.* dŏl'-chē.
Dolgorouki, or Dolgoruki . dŏl-gŏ-rōō'-kē.

Döllinger . . . . . . děl'-ĭng-ĕr.
Dolomite . . . . . . dŏl'-ō-mīt.
Dolores . . . . . . dō-lō'-rĕs.
Domenichino. . . . . dō"-mä-nē-kē'-nō.
Domingue. . . . . . dŏ-mǎng'.
Dominguez . . . . *Mex.* dō-mĭn'-gĕs. *Sp.* dō-mĭn'-gĕth.
Dominica . . . . . . dŏm-ĭn-ē'-kȧ.
Dominical . . . . . dō-mĭn'-ĭ-kȧl.
Dominique, La . . . . lä dōm-ē-nēk'.
Domitian . . . . . . dō-mĭsh'-ĭ=ȧn.
Domo d'Ossola . . . . dō'-mō dŏs'-sō-lä.
Dom Pedro . . . . . dōm pä'-drō. *Pg.* dōṅ.
Domremy-la-Pucelle . . dôṅ-rä-mē'-lä-pü-sĕl'.
Doña . . . . dōn'-yä.
Donalbain. . . . . . dōn'-ǎl-bān.
Donatello . . . . . . dōn-ä-tĕl'-lō.
Donati . . . . dō-nä'-tē.
Donauwörth . . . . . dō'-now-vĕrt.
Don César de Bazan . . dôn sä-zär' dŭ bä-zäṅ'.
Donegal . . . . . . dŏn'-ē-gôl.
Don Giovanni . . . . dŏn jō-vän'-nē.
Dongola . . . . . . dŏng'-gō-lä.
Donizetti . . . . . . dō-nē-dzĕt'-tē.
Don Juan . . . . . . dŏnjū'-ȧn.*Sp.*dōn 'hōō-än'.
Donna . . . . . . dŏn'-nä.
Donnay . . . . . . dŏn-ā'.
Donne (John) . . . . dŭn.
Don Pasquale . . . . dōn päs-kwä'-lä.
Don Pedro de Alcántara . dōn pä'-drō dä äl-kän'-tä-rä.
Don Quixote. Sp. Quijote dŏn kwĭks'-ŏt.
                        Sp. dōnkē-ċhō'-tä.
Dorado, El . . . . . äl dō-rä'-dō.
Dordogne. . . . . . dôr-dōn'. *Fr.* dōr-dōn'=yŭ.
Dordrecht . . . . . dôr'-drĕċht.
Doré . . . . dō-rä'.

Dorgelès . . . . . . dōr-zhĕ-lĕz'.
Doria . . . . dō'-rē-ä.
Dorian . . . . dō'-rĭ-àn.
Doric . . . . dôr'-ĭk, dŏr'-ĭk.
D'Orleans . . . . . . dōr-lā-äṅ'.
Dorothea . . . . . . dŏr-ō-thē'-à.
                 Ger. dō-rō-tä'-ä.
Dorothée . . . . . . dō-rō-tä'.
D'Orsay, Quai . . . . kä dôr-sä'.
Dort . . . . dôrt.
D'Orthez, see Orthez . . dŏr-tĕss' *or* -tāz'.
Dossi, Dosso . . . . . dŏs'-sō dŏs'-sē.
Dossier, The . . . . . dŏs-sē-ā'.
Dostoievsky, or Dostoyevsky dŏs-tō-yĕf'-skĭ.
Dotheboys Hall . . . . dō'-thē-boiz hôl.
Douai, or Douay . . . dōō-ā'.
Douaumont . . . . . dōō-ō-mŏṅ'.
Doubs . . . . dōō.
Doulton . . . . . . dōl'-tŏn.
Douma, see Duma . . . dōō'-mä.
Douro . . . . dōō'-rō.
Douw, or Dow . . . . dow.
Drachenfels . . . . . drăk'-ĕn-fĕlz.
                 Ger. drä'-ċhen-fĕlz.
Draconian . . . . . . drà-kō'-nĭ-àn.
Draconic . . . . . . drā-kŏn'-ĭk.
Drakenberg (Mts.) . . . drä'-kĕn-bĕrċh.
Drave . . . . drä'-vĕ.
Drdla . . . . dērd'-lä.
Dreibund . . . . . . drī'-bŏŏnt.
Dreiser . . . . drī'-sēr.
Dreux . . . . drē.
Dreyfus . . . . drā-füs'.
Drina . . . . drē'-nä.
Drogheda . . . . . . drŏċh'-ĕ-dä, drŏ'-'hĕd-à.
Dromio . . . . drō'-mĭ-ō.
Drouet . . . . drōō-ā'.

Droz . . . . drō.
Druid . . . . drū′-ĭd.
Druidian . . . . . . drū-ĭd′-ĭ-àn.
Druidic . . . . drū-ĭd′-ĭk.
Druses . . . . drōoz′-ĕz.
Dryburgh . . . . . drī′-bŭr-ŭ.
Dryope . . . . drī′-ō-pē.
Dry Tortugas . . . . drī tôr-tōō′-gȧz.
Du Barry . . . . . . dü băr-ē′.
Dubois . . . . *Fr.* dü-bwä′.
Du Bois-Reymond . . . dü bwä-rā-môṅ′.
Duc . . . . *Fr.* dük.
Duca . . . . dōō′-kä.
Ducange, or Du Cange . dü-känzh′.
Duccio di Buoninsegna . dōōch′-ō dē
                        bōō=ōn″-ēn-sän′-yä
Du Chaillu . . . . . dü shä-yü′.
Du Châtelet . . . . . dü shät-lä′.
Duchesne . . . . . . dü-shän′.
Duchessa . . . . . . *It.* dōō-kĕs′-sä.
Duchesse . . . . . . *Fr.* dü-shĕs′.
Ducrot . . . . dü-krō′.
Dudevant . . . . . . düd-väṅ′.
Duero . . . . dōō-ā′-rō
Du Guesclin, or Duguesclin dü gä-klăṅ′.
Dukas . . . . dü-kä′.
Dukhobori . . . . . dōō-ċhō-bō′-rē.
Dulcamara . . . . dŏŏl-kä-mä′-rä.
Dulcinea del Toboso . . dŭl-sĭn′-ē-ä dĕl tō-bō′-sō
                        Sp. dōōl-thē-nā′-ä däl
                        tō-bō′-sō.
Dulwich . . . . . . dŭl′-ĭch.
Duma, see Douma . . . dōō′-mä.
Dumas . . . . dūmä. *Fr.* dü-mä′.
Du Maurier . . . . . dü mō rē=ā′.
Dumbarton . . . . . dŭm-bär′-tŏn.
Dumfries . . . . . . dŭm-frēz′.

Dumouriez.	dü-mōō-rē=ā'.
Dünaburg	dü'-nä-bōōrċh.
Dunajecs	dōō-nä-yĕts'.
Dunbar	dŭn-bär'.
Dundee	dŭn-dē'.
Dunedin	dŭn-ē'-dĭn, dŭn-ĕd'-ĭn.
Dunes	dūnz.
Dunfermline	dŭn-fērm'-lĭn.
Dunkeld	dŭn-kĕld'.
Dunois	dü-nwä'.
Dunsany	dŭn-sā'-nĭ.
Dunsinane.	dŭn'-sĭ-nān, dŭn-sĭn'-ān.
Duomo	dōō=ō'-mō.
Dupaty	dü-pä-tē'.
Du Paty de Clam . . .	dü pä-tē' dŭ klàṅ'.
Duplessis	dü-plĕ-sē'.
Duplessis-Mornay . . .	düplĕ-sē'-mōr-nā'.
Duprat	dü-prä'.
Dupré	dü-prā'.
Duprétis	dōō-prā-tēs'.
Dupuy	dü-pwē'.
Duquesne	dü-kān'.
Duquesnoy	dü-kā-nwä'.
Duran, Carolus	kä-rō-lüs' dü-räṅ'.
Durandarte	dōō-rän-där'-tä.
Durango	dōō-rän'-gō.
Durazzo	dōō-rät'-sō.
Durban, or D'Urban . .	dēr'-bǎn.
Durbar	dŭr'-bär.
Durbunga, see Darbhangah	dŭr-bŭn'-gä.
Dürer	dü'-rĕr.
Durham	dŭr'-àm.
Duroc	dü-rōk'.
Duruy	dü-rü=ē'.
Durward	dēr'-wàrd.
Duse	dōō'-sĕ, dōō'-sā. It. dōō'-zā.
Dussek	dōō'-shĕk.

Düsseldorf . . . . . düs'-ĕl-dôrf.
Dvinsk . . . . dvĭnsk.
Dvořák, Anton . . . . än'-tōn dvōr-zhäk'.
Dyak . . . . dī'-ăk.
Dyea . . . . dī'-ā.
Dynow . . . . dē'-nŏv.

E

Eadred . . . . ĕd'-rĕd.
Eadric (Edric) . . . . ĕd'-rĭk.
Eames (Emma) . . . . āmz.
Eau de Cologne . . . . ō dŭ kō-lōn'.
                  Fr. kō-lōn'=yŭ.
Ebal . . . . ē'-băl.
Eberhard . . . . . . ā'-bĕr-härt.
Ebers, Georg . . . . gā=ōrch' ā'-bĕrs.
Ebert . . . . ā'-bârt.
Eblis, see Iblis . . . . ĕb'-lĭs.
Eboli . . . . ā'-bō-lē.
Eboracum, see Eburacum. ē-bŏr'-à-kŭm,
                  ĕb-ō-rā'-kŭm.
Ebro . . . . ē'-bro. Sp. ā'-brō.
Eburacum, see Eboracum ē-bŭr'-à-kŭm,
                  ĕb-ōō-rā'-kŭm.
Ecbatana . . . . . . ĕk-băt'-à-nà.
Ecce Homo . . . . . ĕk'-sē hō'-mō.
Eccelino da Romano, see
  Ezzelino . . . . . ĕch-ā-lē'-nō dä rō-mä'-nō.
Ecclefechan . . . . . ĕk-l-fĕċh'-ăn, ĕk-l-fĕk'-ăn.
Ecclesiastes . . . . . ĕk-klē"-zĭ-ăs'-tēz.
Echague . . . . . . ā-chä'-gā.
Echegaray . . . . . ā"-chä-gä-rä'=ē.
Echeverría . . . . . ā-chä-vĕr-ē'-ä.
Echo . . . . ĕk'-ō, ē'-kō.
École des Beaux Arts, L' . lä-kōl' dä bō-zär'.
École des Femmes, L' . . lä-kōl' dä făm'.

École des Maris, L' . . lā-kōl' dā mă-rē'.
École Polytechnique . . . ā-kōl' pō-lē-tĕk-nēk'.
Écorcheurs, Les . . . lā zā-kŏr-shēr'.
Ecuador . . . . . . ĕk-wȧ-dōr'. *Sp.* ā-kwä-dōr'.
Edam . . . . ē'-dăm. *D.* ā-dăm'.
Eden . . . . ē'-dn.
Edfu . . . . ĕd-fōō'.
Edgecote . . . . . ĕdj'-kōt.
Edinburgh . . . . . ĕd'-ĭn-bŭr''-ō,
 ĕd'-ĭn-bŭr''-ŭ.
Edmond . . . . . . *Fr.* ĕd-môṅ'.
Edom . . . . ē'-dŏm.
Édouard . . . . . . ā-dōō-är'.
Edrei . . . . ĕd'-rē-ī.
Eckhoud Georges . . . zhôrzh āk'-howt.
Eecloo . . . . ā-klō'.
Égalité, Philippe . . . fē-lēp' ā-găl-ē-tā'.
Egean, see Aegean . . ē-jē'-ȧn.
Eger . . . . ā'-gĕr.
Egeria, see Aegeria . . ē-jē'-rĭ-ȧ.
Egeus . . . . ē-jē'-ŭs.
Eginhard, see Einhard . ā'-gĭn-härt.
Eglamour . . . . . . ĕg'-lȧ-mōōr.
Eglantine . . . . . ĕg'-lȧn-tīn.
Eguren, José . . . . . hō-sā' ā-gōō'-rĕn.
Ehrenbreitstein . . . . ā-rĕn-brīt'-stīn.
Ehrenfels . . . . . . ā'-rĕn-fĕlz.
Eichberg . . . . . . īċh'-bĕrċh.
Eiffel . . . . ī'-fĕl. *Fr.* ĕ-fĕl'.
Eikon Basilike . . . . ī'-kōn bă-sĭl'-ĭ-kē.
Eikonoclastes . . . . ī-kŏn''-ō-klăs'-tēz.
Eimbeck, or Einbeck . . īm'-bĕk, īn'-bĕk.
Einhard, see Eginhard . īn'-härt.
Einstein . . . . . . īn'-stīn.
Eisenach . . . . . . ī'-zā-näċh.
Eisleben . . . . . . īs'-lā-bĕn.
Eisner, Kurt . . . . . kōōrt īs'-nĕr.

Eisteddfod	ī-stĕth'-vōd.
Eitel	ī'-tĕl.
Ekaterinburg, see Yekaterinburg	ĕ-kä"-tĕ-rēn-bōōrg'.
Ekber, see Akbar . . .	ĕk'-bēr. *Hind.* ŭk'-bĕr.
Elagabalus, see Heliogabalus	ē-là-găb'-à-lŭs, ĕl"-à-găb'-à-lŭs, ĕl"-ā-gā-bā'-lŭs.
Elamite	ē'-làm'-īt.
Elandslaagte	ā-lănts-läċh'-tĕ.
Elbe	ĕlb. *Ger.* ĕl'-bŭ.
Elberfeld	ĕl'-bĕr-fĕlt.
Elbrooz, Elbruz	ĕl-brōōz'.
El Camino Real	ĕl kä"-mē'-no rā-äl'
El Campeador	āl käm"-pā-ä-dōr'.
El Caney	āl kä-nā'=ē.
Elchingen	ĕlċh'-ĭng-ĕn.
El Dorado	ĕl dō-rā'-dō. *Sp.* ĕl dō-rä'-dō
Eleanor	ĕl'-ē-ā-nôr", ĕl'-à-nēr.
Eleanora d'Este . . .	ā"-lā-ō-nō'-rä dās'-tĕ.
Eleatic	ĕl-ē-ăt'-ĭk.
Eleazar	ĕl-ē'-zàr, ē-lē'-ā-zär.
Eleusinia	ĕl ū-sĭn'-ĭ-à.
Eleusis	ĕ-lū'-sĭs.
Eleuthera	ĕ-lū'-thĕ-rà.
Elgin	ĕl'-jĭn.
Elia	ē'-lĭ-à.
Eliab	ē-lī'-ăb.
Eliakim	ē-lī'-à-kĭm.
Elias	ĕ-lī'-às.
Elidure	ĕl'-ĭ-dūr.
Élie de Beaumont . . .	ā-lē' dŭ bō-môṅ'.
Eliezer	ĕl-ĭ-ē'-zēr.
Elihu	ĕ-lī'-hū.
Elihu (Root)	ĕl'-ĭ-hū.
Elimelech	ĕ-lim'-ĕ-lĕk.

Elío (Gen.) . . . . . ā-lē′-ō.
Eliodoro . . . . . . ā″-lē-ō-dō′-rō.
Eliphalet . . . . . . ĕ-lĭf′-à-lĕt.
Élise . . . . ā-lēz′.
Elisir d'amore, L' . . . lā-lē-zēr′ dä-mō′-rā.
Elizabethan . . . . . ē-lĭz′-ā-bĕth″-ăn, or
    ē-lĭz″-ā-bĕth′-àn.
Elkanah . . . . . . ĕl-kā′-nä, ĕl′-kā-nä.
Ellichpur . . . . . . ĕl-ĭch-pōor′.
El Mahdi, see Mahdi . . āl mä′-dē.
Elmire . . . . ĕl-mēr′.
Elman, Mischa . . . . mĭsh′-ä ĕl′-män.
El Obeid . . . . . . ĕl ŏb-ād′.
Elohim . . . . ē-lō′-hĭm, ĕl′-ō-hĭm.
El Paso del Norte . . . ĕl pă′-sō dĕl nōr′-tĕ.
El Puerto . . . . . . āl pwârt′-tō, pōō=âr′-tō.
Elsass . . . . āl′-zäs.
Elsass-Lothringen . . . āl′-zäs-lōt′-rĭng-ĕn.
Elsinore . . . . . . ĕl-sĭ-nōr′.
Elssler . . . . ĕls′-lēr.
Eltekeh . . . . . . ĕl′-tĕ-kē.
Elul . . . . ē′-lŭl.
Élysée . . . . ā-lē-zā′.
Elysian . . . . . . ē-lĭz′-ĭ-ăn, ē-lĭzh′-ē-an,
    ē-lĭzh′-ăn.
Elysium . . . . . . ē-lĭz′-ĭ-ŭm, ē-lĭzh′-ĭ=ŭm,
    ē-lizh′-ŭm.
Elzevir . . . . ĕl′-zĕ-vēr, ĕl′-zē-vēr.
Emanuele, Vittorio . . vēt-tō′-rē-ō ā-mä-nōō-ā′lā.
Emeer, see Emir . . . ē-mēr′.
Émigrés, Les . . . . . lā zā-mē-grā′.
Emil . . . . ā′-mēl.
Émile . . . . ā-mēl′.
Emilian . . . . . . ē-mĭl′-ĭ-an.
Éminence Grise, L' . . lā-mē-nŏns′ grēz.
Emin Pacha (or Bey) . . ā′-mēn păsh-ô′ (bā),
    pä-shä′, päsh′-à.

Emir, see Emeer . . . ē-mẽr, ē-mẽr'.
Emmaus . . . . . . ĕ-mä'-ŭs, ĕm'-mä-ŭs.
Empedocles . . . . . ĕm-pĕd'-ō-klēz.
Ems . . . . ĕms.
Énault (Louis) . . . . ä-nō'.
Enceladus . . . . . ĕn-sĕl'-à-dŭs.
Encina . . . . ĕn-sē'-nà. *Sp.* än-thē'-nà.
Encke . . . . ĕng'-kŭ.
Encyclopédie . . . . . ŏṅ-sē-klō-pä-dē'.
Endymion . . . . . ĕn-dĭm'-ĭ-ŏn.
Eneas, see Aeneas . . . ē-nē'-às.
Eneid . . . . ē-nē'-ĭd, ē'-nē-ĭd.
Enemessar . . . . . ĕn-ē-mĕs'-sàr.
Enfant Prodigue, L' . . lôn-fäṅ' prō-dēg'.
Engadine . . . . . . ĕn-gä-dēn'.
Engaño. . . . . . . ĕn-gän'-yō.
Engedi . . . . ĕn-gē'-dĭ, ĕn'-gē-dī.
Enghien, Duc d' . . . . dük dän-gē=ăṅ', däṅ-găṅ'.
England . . . . . . ĭng'-glànd.
English . . . . . . ĭng'-glĭsh.
Enid . . . . ē'-nĭd.
Enobarbus . . . . . ĕn-ō-bär'-bŭs.
Enseñada . . . . . ĕn-sĕn-yä'-dà.
Entente . . . . . . ôṅ-tôṅt'.
Entraigues, Henrietta d',
    see Antraigues . . . ŏn-rē-ĕt' dôṅ-trāg'.
Eolian, see Aeolian . . ē-ō'-lĭ-àn.
Eolic, see Aeolic . . . ē-ŏl'-ĭk.
Eolis, see Aeolis . . . ē'-ō-lĭs.
Eothen . . . . ē-ō'-thĕn.
Epaminondas . . . . . ē-păm"-ĭn-ŏn'-dăs.
Epaphroditus . . . . . ē-păf"-rō-dī'-tŭs.
Epeiros, see Epirus . . ē-pī'-rŭs.
Épernay . . . . . . ä-pĕr-nä'.
Épernon, d' . . . . . dä-pĕr-nŏṅ'.
Epes . . . . ĕps.
Ephesians . . . . . . ē-fē'-zhànz.

Ephesus	ĕf′-ĕ-sŭs.
Ephraim	ē′-frā-ĭm.
Ephrata	ĕf′-rā-tä, ĕf′-rȧ-tȧ.
Epicœne	ĕp′-ĭ-sēn.
Epictetus	ĕp-ĭk-tē′-tŭs.
Epicurean	ĕp″-ĭ-kū-rē′-ȧn,
	ĕp-ĭ-kū′-rē-ȧn.
Epicureanism	ĕp″-ĭ-kū-rē′-ăn-ĭzm,
	ĕp-ĭ-kū′-rē-ăn-ĭzm″.
Epicurus	ĕp-ĭ-kū′-rŭs.
Épidaurus	ĕp-ĭ-dôr′-ŭs.
Épinay, d'	dā-pē-nā′.
Epipsychidion	ĕp″-ĭ-sī-kĭd′-ĭ-ŏn.
Epirot	ĕ-pī′-rŏt.
Epirote	ĕ-pī′-rōt.
Epirus, see Epeiros	ē-pī′-rŭs.
Epithalamium	ĕp″-ĭ-thā-lā′-mĭ-ŭm.
Érard	ā-rär′.
Erasmus	ē-răz′-mŭs.
Eraste	ā-răst′.
Erastianism	ē-răst′-yăn-ĭzm.
Erato	ĕr′-ā-tō.
Erastosthenes	ĕr-ā-tŏs′-thē-nēz.
Ercilla	ĕr-sēl′-yȧ.
Erckmann-Chatrian	ĕrk′-män-shä-trē-äṅ′.
Erebus	ĕr′-ē-bŭs.
Erechtheum	ĕr-ĕk-thē′-ŭm,
	ē-rĕk-thē′-ŭm.
Eretria	ĕ-rē′-trĭ-ȧ.
Eretrian	ĕ-rē′-trĭ-an.
Erfurt	ĕr′-fōōrt.
Eric, see Erik	ĕr′-ĭk, ē′-rĭk.
Ericsson	ĕr′-ĭk-sŏn.
Erigena	ĕ-rĭj′-ē-nä, ĕr-ĭj′-ĕ-nȧ,
	ĕr-ĭ-jē′-nȧ.
Erik, see Eric	ĕr′-ik, ē′-rĭk. Sw. ā′-rĭk.
Erin	ē′-rĭn.

Erinnyes, or Erinyes, or
Erinnys . . . . . ĕr-ĭn'-ĭ-ēz, ē-rĭn'-ĭ-ēz,
                   ĕr-ĭn'-ēz, ē-rĭn'-ēz.
Erivan . . . . . . ĕr-ĭ-vän'.
Erlangen . . . . . . ĕr'-läng-ĕn.
Erl-King, or Ger. Erl-König ērl'-kĭng. *Ger.* ĕrl kē'-nĭch.
Ernani . . . . âr-nä'-nē.
Eroica . . . . . . ā-rō'-ē-kä.
Eros . . . . ē'-rŏs.
Erostratus . . . . . ē-rŏs'-trā-tŭs.
Erskine . . . . . . ērs'-kĭn.
Ervine, St. John . . . sĭn'-jŭn ēr'-vīn.
Erzerum . . . . . . ĕrz-rōōm'.
Esaias . . . . ē-zā'-yȧs.
Escadrille, Lafayette . . lä-fȧ-yĕt' ĕs-kä-drē'=yŭ.
Escalus . . . . . . ĕs'-kȧ-lŭs.
Escamillo . . . . . . ĕs-kä-mēl'-yō
Eschenbach, Wolfram von vŏlf'-räm fŏn ēsh'-ĕn-bäch.
Escholier . . . . . . ĕs-kŏl-ē=ā'.
Escholtzia . . . . . . ĕsh-ŏltz'-ē-ȧ.
Escorial, or . . . . . ĕs-kō'-rĭ-ȧl.*Sp.*ĕs-kō-rē-äl'.
Escurial . . . . . . ĕs-kū'-rĭ-ȧl.
Esdraelon . . . . . . ĕs-drā-ē'-lŏn, ĕs-drā'-e-lŏn.
Eskimo, see Esquimaux . ĕs'-kĭ-mō.
Esneh . . . . ĕs'-nĕ.
Esop, see Aesop . . . ē'-sŏp.
España . . . . ĕs-pän'-yä.
Española . . . . . . ĕs-pän-yō'-lä.
Esperey, Franchet d' . . frän-shä' dĕs-pĕ-rä'.
Espinasse, de l', see Les-
pinasse . . . . . . dŭ lä-pē-näs'.
Espiritu Santo . . . . ās-pē'-rē-tōō sän'-tō.
Esprémesnil, or Éprémenil ā-prä-mä-nēl'.
Esquiline . . . . . . ĕs-kē-lēn', ĕs'-kwĭ-līn.
Esquimaux, or Eskimo . ĕs-kē-mō'.
Esquirol . . . . . . ĕs-kē-rōl'.
Essenes . . . . . . ĕs-sēnz', ĕs'-sē-nēz.

Essipoff	ĕs-ē-pŏf'.
Estaing, d'	dĕs-tăṅ'.
Estaires	ĕs-târ'.
Estaunié	ĕs-tōn-yā'.
Estcourt	ĕst'-kōrt.
Este	ās'-tĕ.
Esterhazy, see Estzerházy	ĕs'-tĕr-hä-zĭ, ĕstĕr-hä'-zē.
	Fr. ās-târ-ä-zē'.
Esther	ĕs'-tēr.
Esthonia	ĕs-thō'-nĭ-à.
Estienne, see Étienne	ā-tē=ĕn'.
Estrées, Gabrielle d'	gä-brē-ĕl' dā-trā'.
Estrella, La	lä ĕs-trāl'-yä.
Estramadura	ĕsh″-trā-mä-dōō'-rä.
Estzerházy, see Esterhazy	ĕs'-ter-hä-zĭ, ĕs-tĕr-hä'-zē.
	Fr. ās-târ-ä-zē'.
Etah	ē'-tà.
Etampes	ā-täṅp'.
Etesian	ē-tē'-zhĭ-àn, ē-tē'-zhàn.
Ethelbert, see Aethelberht	ĕth'-ĕl-bērt.
Ethiopic	ĕ-thĭ-ŏp'-ĭk, ē-thĭ-ō'-pĭk.
Étienne, see Estienne	ā-tē=ĕn'.
Eu	ē.
Eubœa	ū-bē'-ä.
Eucken	oi'-kĕn.
Eudes	ēd.
Eudoxia	ū-dŏk'-sĭ-à.
Euergetes	ū-ēr'-jĕ-tēz.
Eugen	*Ger.* oi-gān'.
Eugene	ū-jēn'.
Eugène	*Fr.* ē-zhĕn'.
Eugène de Beauharnais	ē-zhĕn' dŭ bō-är-nā'.
Eugénie de Montijo	ē-zhā-nē' dŭ môn-tē-ċhō'.
	Sp. dā môn-tē'-ċhō.
Eugénie Grandet	ē-zhā-nē' gräṅ-dā'.
Eulalia	ā=ōō-lä'-lē-ä.
Eulalie	ē-lä-lē'.

Eulate	ā=ōō-lä'-tā.
Eulenspiegel	oi'-lĕn-shpē"-gĕl.
Euler	oi'-lĕr.
Eumenes	ū'-mē-nēz.
Eumenidæ	ū-mĕn'-ĭ-dē.
Eumenides	ū-mĕn'-ĭ-dēz.
Eunice	ū'-nĭs, ū-nī'-sē.
Euphrates	ū-frā'-tēz.
Euphrosyne	ū-frŏs'-ĭn-ē.
Euphues	ū'-fū-ez.
Eurasia	ū-rā'-shĭ-à, ū-rā'-zhĭ-à.
Eurasian	ū-rā'-shĭ=àn, ū-rā'-zhĭ=àn.
Eure	ēr.
Eure-et-Loire	ēr-ā-lwär'.
Euridice	Fr. ēr-ē-dēs'.
	It. ā=ōō-rē'-dē-chē.
Euripides	ū-rĭp'-ĭ-dēz.
Euroclydon	ū-rŏk'-lĭ-dŏn.
Europa, or	ū-rō'-pä.
Europe	ū'-rŏp, Class. ū-rō'-pē.
European	ū-rō-pē'-àn.
Euryanthe	ū-rĭ-ăn'-thē.
Eurydice	ū-rĭd'-ĭs-ē.
Eusenada Honda	ā"=ōō-sā-nä'-dä ōn'-dä.
Eustache, St.	săṅ-tēs-tăsh'.
Eustachian	ūs-tā'-kĭ-àn.
Eustachio	ā=ōōs-tä'-kē-o.
Eustachius	ūs-tā'-kĭ-ŭs.
Euterpe	ū-tēr'-pē.
Euterpean	ū-tĕr'-pē-àn.
Euxine	yūks'-ĭn.
Evangeline	ē-văn'-jĕ-līn, ē-văn'-jĕ-lēn.
Evelina	ĕv-ē-lī'-nà, ĕv-ĕ-lē'-nà.
Evesham	ēvz'- hăm, ēvz'-ăm,
	ĕv'-shăm.
Évreux	āv-rē'.
Ewart	ū'-àrt.

Excalibar (—bur) . . . ĕks-kăl′-ĭ-bár.
Exeter . . . . ĕks′-ĕ-tẽr.
Eyck, van . . . . . . văn īk.
Eylau . . . . ī′-low.
Eyre . . . . âr.
Eytinge . . . . ĕt′-tĭng.
Ezekias . . . . . . ĕz-ĕ-kī′-ás.
Ezekiel . . . . ē-zē′-kĭ-ĕl.
Ezra . . . . ĕz′-rä.
Ezzelino da Romano, see
  Eccelino . . . . . ĕt-zā-lē′-nō dä rō-mä′-nō.

F

Fabian . . . . fā′-bĭ-àn.
Fabliau . . . . fă-blē-ō′.
Fabliaux . . . . . . fă-blē-ō′.
Fabre . . . . făbr.
Fabriano . . . . . . fä-brē-ä′-nō.
Faenza . . . . fä-ĕn′-dzä.
Fagin . . . . fā′-gĭn.
Fahrenheit . . . . . fä′-rĕn-hīt.
Faidherbe . . . . . . fā-dârb′.
Failly . . . . fä-yē′.
Fainéants, Les Rois . . lä rwä fä-nä-äṅ′.
Faizabad, see Fyzabad . fī-zä-bäd′.
Fajardo, see Faxardo . . *Sp.* fä-ċhär′-dō.
Falaise . . . . fä-lĕz′.
Falconbridge . . . . . fók′-àn-brĭj.
Falernian . . . . . . fà-lẽr′-nĭ-àn.
Falieri . . . . fä-lē-ä′-rē.
Falkenhayn . . . . . fäl′-kĕn-hīn.
Falkland . . . . . . fók′-lánd.
Faneuil . . . . făn′-ĕl. *pop.* fŭn′-ĕl.
Fantine . . . . fäṅ-tēn′.
Fantin-Latour . . . . fän-tăṅ′ lä-tōōr′.
Faraday . . . . . . făr′-à-dā.

Farallones	fä-räl-yō'-nĕs.
Faridpur, see Furidpur .	fŭr-ēd-pōōr'.
Farnese	fär-nēz'. *It.* fär-nä'-zĕ.
Faro, or Faroe	fä'-rō, fä'-rōō=ĕ.
Farquhar	fär'-kwär, fär'-kär.
Farrakhabad, see Farruk-	
habad	fŭr-rŭk-ä-bäd'.
Farrar (Canon)	fär'-àr.
Farrar (Geraldine) . . .	fàr-är'.
Farrukhabad, see Farrak-	
habad	fŭr-rŭk-ä-bäd'.
Fascisti	fä-shēs'-tē.
Fashoda	fä-shō'-dä.
Fata Morgana	fä'-tà môr-gä'-nà,
	fä'-tä môr-gä'-nä.
Fathipur, see Futtehpur .	fŭt-ē-pōōr'.
Fatima	fä'-tē-mä. *pop.* făt'-ĭ-mà.
Fatimites	făt'-ĭ-mīts.
Faubourg St. Antoine . .	fō-bōōr' sǎn-tän-twän'.
Foubourg St. Germain .	fō-bōōr' sǎn zhâr-mǎn'.
Fauntleroy	fônt'-lēr-oi.
Faure, Félix	fä-lēks' fōr'.
Fauresmith	fôr'-smĭth.
Faust	fowst.
Faustina	fôs-tī'-nà.
Faustus	fôs'-tŭs. *Ger.* fows'-tŏŏs.
Favre	făvr.
Faxardo, see Fajardo . .	fä-ċhär'-dō.
Fayal	fī-ôl'. *Port.* fī-äl'.
Fayoum, Fayum . . .	fī-ōōm'.
February	fĕb'-rōō-ā″-rĭ.
Fechter	fĕċh'-tĕr, fĕsh'-tĕr.
Fédora	fä-dō'-rä.
Fedotoff (—ov)	fĕ-dŏ'-tŏf.
Feejee, see Fiji	fē'-jē.
Feejeean, see Fijian . .	fē-jē'-àn.
Felahie	fä-lä-hē'.

Felice . . . . *It.* fā-lē′-chā.
Félice . . . . *Fr.* fā-lēs′.
Félicité . . . . fā-lēs-ē-tā′.
Felipe . . . . fā-lē′-pā.
Felix . . . . fē′-lĭks.
Félix . . . . *Fr.* fā‐lēks′.
Femme de Trente Ans . făm dŭ trŏṅt äṅ.
Fénelon . . . . . . fĕn′-ĕ-lŭn. *Fr.* fā=nŭ-lôṅ′.
Fenian . . . . fēn′-yȧn.
Feodor . . . . fā′-ō-dōr.
Feodosia . . . . . . fā-ō-dŏ′-sē-ȧ.
Fère-en-Tardenois . . . fĕr-ôṅ-tärd-nwä′.
Ferichta, Feirshta, Fer-
   ischta, see Firishtah . fĕr′-ĭsh-tä.
Fernandez . . . . . fĕr-năn′-dēz. *Sp.*
       fĕr-nän′-dĕth.
Fernandina . . . . . fĕr-năn-dē′-nȧ.
       Sp. fĕr-nän-dē′-nä
Fernando, San . . . . săn fĕr-năn′-dō, sän
       fĕr-nän′-dō.
Ferney or Fernex . . . fâr-nā′.
Ferozepore, see Firozpur fē-rōz-pōr′.
Ferrand . . . . . . fĕ-räṅ′.
Ferrara . . . . fĕr-rä′-rä.
Ferrero, Guglielmo . . gōōl-yäl′-mō fär-rā′-rō.
Ferrières . . . . . . fĕr-ē=âr′.
Ferrol, El . . . . . . äl fĕr-rōl′.
Ferronnière, La Belle . . lä bĕl fĕr-rŏn-ē=âr′.
Ferry, Jules . . . . . zhül fĕ-rē′.
Fesole, see Fiesole . . . fā′-zō-lā.
Festubert . . . . . . fĕs-ü-bĕr′.
Fétis . . . . fā-tēs′.
Feuerbach . . . . . foi′-ĕr-bäċh.
Feuillet, Octave . . . . ōk-täv′ fĕ-yā′.
Feydeau . . . . . . fā-dō′.
Feyjoo y Montenegro . . fā=ē-hō′ ē mōn-tā-nä′-grō.
Fezzan . . . . fĕz-zän′.

Ffrangcon-Davies . . . frăng'-kŏn-dā'-vēz.
Fichte . . . . fĭċh'-tŭ.
Fidelio . . . . fē-dā'-lē-o.
Fierabras . . . . . . fē=ā-rä-brä'.
Fiesole . . . . fē=ā'-zō-lä.
Figaro . . . . fē-gä-rō'.
Figueroa . . . . . . fĭg-ĕr-ō'-à.
Fiji, see Feejee . . . . fē'-jē.
Fijian, see Feejeean . . fē-jē'-àn.
Filarete . . . . . . fē-lä-rā'-tĕ.
Filipina . . . . . fĭl-ĭ-pē'-nà, *Sp.* fē-lē-pē'-nä
Filipino . . . . . fĭl-ĭ-pē'-nō. *Sp.* fē-lē-pē'-nō
Filippo . . . . fē-lēp'-pō.
Fille du Régiment, La . . lä fē dü rä-zhē-môṅ'.
Filomena (St.) . . . . fĭl-ō-mē'-nà.
Finistère (—terre) . . . fĭn-ĭs-tĕr'.
Fiorentino . . . . . fē-ō-rän-tē'-nō.
Firenze . . . . . . fē-rän'-dzä.
Firishtah, see Ferichta . fē'-rēsh-tä.
Firmin Didot . . . . . fēr-măṅ' dē-dō'.
Firozpur, see Ferozepore . fē-rōz-pōōr'.
Fismettes . . . . . . fē-mĕt'.
Fiume . . . . fē-ōō'-mä.
Flagellants . . . . . flăj'-ĕl-ànts.
Flameng . . . . . . flă-môṅ'.
Flaminian . . . . . . flà-mĭn'-ĭ-àn.
Flammarion . . . . . flä-mä-rē-ôṅ'.
Flandrin . . . . . . fläṅ-drăṅ'.
Flaubert . . . . . . flō-bâr'.
Fleance . . . . . . flē'-àns.
Fleurus . . . . . . flē-rüs'.
Fleury . . . . flē-rē'.
Fliegende Holländer, Der dĕr flē'-gĕn-dŭ hŏl'-ēn-dĕr.
Flodden . . . . . . flŏd'-ĕn.
Flonzaley . . . . . flôṅ-ză'-lä.
Floréal . . . . flō-rä-ăl'.
Florentine . . . . . . flŏr'-ĕn-tĭn, flŏr'-ĕn-tīn.

Flores . . . . flō'-rĕs.
Florizel. . . . . . . flŏr'-ĭzĕl.
Flotow, von . . . . . fŏn flō'-tō, *Ger.* flō'-tōv.
Flourens . . . . . . flōō-rŏṅ'.
Foch . . . . fŏsh.
Focsani . . . . . fŏk'-shä-nē.
Fogazzaro . . . . . . fō-gäts-sä'-rō.
Foggia . . . . fŏd'-jä.
Foix . . . . fwä.
Fokien, see Fu-kien . . fō-kē-ĕn'.
Folies Bergères, Les . . lä fŏ-lē' bĕr-zhĕr'.
Foligno, see Fuligno . . fō-lēn'-yō.
Folkestone. . . . . . fōk'-stŭn.
Folkething . . . . . fōl'-kē-tĭng.
Fomalhaut . . . . . fō-măl-ō'.
Fond du Lac . . . . . fŏn dŭ lăk.
Fonseca . . . . . . fōn-sä'-kä.
Fontainebleau . . . . foṅ-tān-blō'.
Fontenoy . . . . . . fŏnt'-ĕ-noi. *Fr.* fôṅt-nwä'.
Fontevrault . . . . . fôṅ=tĕ-vrō'.
Foochow, see Fu-chau . fōō-chow'.
Forlì . . . . fŏr-lē'.
Formosa . . . . . . fôr-mō'-sä.
Formosan . . . . . . fôr-mō'-saṅ.
Fornarina, La . . . . lä fôr-nä-rē'-nä,
Forres . . . . fŏr'-ĕs.
Fors Clavigera . . . . fôrz klă-vĭj'-ēr-à.
Fort de France . . . . fōr dŭ fräṅs.
Fortescue . . . . . . fôr'-tĕs-kū.
Fortinbras . . . . . . fŏr'-tĭn-brăs.
Fortunatus . . . . fŏr-tū-nā'-tūs.
Fortuny . . . . . . fŏr-tōō'-nē.
Forza del Destino, La . . lä fōr-dzä däl däs-tē'-nō.
Foscari . . . . fŏs'-kä-rē.
Foscarini . . . . . . fōs-kä-rē'-nē.
Foscolo . . . . fŏs'-kō-lō.
Fotheringay . . . . . fŏth'-ēr-ĭn-gā.

Foucault	foo-kō'.
Fouché	foo-shā'.
Foucquet	foo-kä'.
Foulques	fook.
Fouqué	foo-kä'.
Fourier	foo-rē=ā'.
Fourierism	foo'-rĭ-ēr-ĭzm''.
Fournet, du	dü foor-nä'.
Fournier	foor-nē=ā'.
Fra Angelico	frä än-jäl'-ē-ko.
Fra Bartolommeo . . .	frä bär-to-lōm-mä'-ō.
Fracasse, Capitaine . .	kä-pē-těn' frä-kăs'.
Fra Diavolo	frä dē=ä'-vō-lō.
Fraermann	frâr'-män.
Fragiacomo, Pietro . . .	pē-ä'-trō frä-jä'-kō-mō.
Fragonard	fră-gō-när'.
France	frăns. *Fr.* fräns.
France, Anatole	ä-nä-tōl' fräns.
France, Île de	ēl dŭ fräns'.
Francesca da Rimini . .	frăn-sěs'-kȧ dä rē'-mē-nē.
	It. frän-chěs'-kä
	dä-rē'-mē-nē.
Francesco	frăn-sěs'-kō. *It.*
	frän-chěs'-kō.
Franche-Comté	fränsh kôṅ-tā'.
Francia	frän'-chä.
Francisco	frăn-sĭs'-kō.
	Sp. frän-thēs'-kō.
Francis de Sales	frăn'-sĭs dŭ sälz. *Fr.* săl.
Franck, César	sä-zär' fräṅk.
François	fräṅ-swä'.
Françoise	fräṅ-swäz'.
Franconian	frăng-kō'-nĭ-ȧn.
Frangipani	frăn-jĭ-păn'-ĭ. *It.*
	frän-jě-pä'-nē.
Franz	fränts.
Franz-Josef	fränts' yō'-zěf.

Frari	frä'-rē.
Frascati	fräs-kä'-tē.
Fraunhofer	frown'-hō-fĕr.
Frédégonde	frä-dä-gōṅd'.
Freiberg	frī'-bĕrċh.
Freiburg, see Fribourg	frī'-bōōrċh.
Freiligrath	frī'-lĭg-rät.
Freischütz, Der	dĕr frī'-shüts.
Freitag, see Freytag	frī'-täċh.
Frelinghuysen	frē'-lĭng-hī"-zĕn.
Frémiet	frä-mē=ā'.
Fréminet	frä-mē-nā'.
Frémont (Gen.)	frä-mŏnt'. *pop.* frē'-mŏnt.
Fremont (Ohio)	frē-mŏnt', frē'-mŏnt.
Fremstad	frĕm'-städ.
Freneau	frĕ-nō'.
Frere	frēr.
Frère	frâr.
Frescobaldi	frĕs-kō-bäl'-dē.
Freud	froit.
Freudian	froi'-dĭ-an.
Frey	frī.
Freya	frī'-ä.
Freycinet	frä-sē-nā'.
Freytag, see Freitag	frī'-täċh.
Friant	frē-äṅ'.
Fribourg, see Freiburg	frē-bōōr'.
Fridthiof, see Frithjof	frēt'-yŏf.
Friedland	frēd'-länt.
Friedrichsbau	frēd'-rĭċhs-bow.
Friedrichshafen	frēd'-rĭċhs-hä'-fĕn.
Friesian, see Frisian	frez'-yan, frēzh'-yan.
Frimaire	frē-mâr'.
Frisian, see Friesian	frĭz'-ĭ=an, frĭzh'-yan.
Frithjof, see Fridthiof	frēt'-yŏf.
Fritz, Der Alte	dĕr äl'-tŭ frĭts.
Fritz, Unser	ōōn'-zĕr frĭts.

Friuli	frē'-ōō-lē.
Fröbel, or Froebel	frē'-bĕl.
Frobisher	frō'-bĭsh-ẽr.
Froissart	froi'-särt. *Fr.* frwä-sär'.
Frollo, Claude	clōd frō-lō'.
Fromentin	frō-mŏn̈-tăn̈'.
Fronde	frŏnd. *Fr.* frôn̈d.
Front de Bœuf	frôn̈ dŭ bēf.
Frontenac	frôn̈t-näk'.
Frossard	frŏs-sär'.
Froude	frōōd.
Frou-Frou	frōō'-frōō'.
Fructidor	frük-tē-dōr'.
Frydek	frē'-dĕk.
Fu-chau, see Foochow	fōō-chow'.
Fuji-san, or	fōō'-jē-sän'.
Fuji-yama	fōō'-jē-yä'-mä.
Fu-kien, see Fokien	fōō-kē-ĕn'.
Fulc, see Fulk	fōōlk.
Fulda	fōōl'-dä.
Fulham	fŭl'-ȧm.
Fuligno, see Foligno	fōō-lĕn'-yō.
Fulk, see Fulc	fōōlk.
Furidpur, see Faridpur	fŭr-ēd-pōōr'.
Furca (-ka)	fōōr'-kä.
Furness	fẽr'-nĕs.
Furor	fū'-rôr'. *Sp.* fōō-rōr'.
Fürst	fürst.
Fürstin	fürst'-ĭn.
Fusan	fōō-sän'.
Fust	fōōst.
Fuszki	fōōs'-kē.
Futtehpur, see Fathipur	fŭt-tĕ-pōōr'.
Fyne, Loch	lŏċh fīn.
Fyt, Jan	yăn fīt.
Fyzabad, see Faizabad	fī-zä-bäd'.

G

Gabael	găb'-ā-ĕl, gā'-bā-ĕl.
Gaberones	găb-ĕ-rō'-nĕs.
Gaboriau, Émile . . .	ā-mĕl' gä-bō-rē=ō'.
Gabriel	gā'-brĭ-ĕl.
Gabriele . . . . . · .	gä-brē-ā'-lĕ.
Gabrielle	Fr. gă-brē-ĕl'.
Gabrielli	gä-brē-ĕl'-lē.
Gabrilowitch	gä-brĭl-ō'-vĭch.
Gaby DesLys	gă-bē' dä-lēs'.
Gadarenes	găd-ā-rēnz'.
Gaddi, Gaddo	gäd'dō gäd'-dē.
Gade	gä'-dĕ.
Gadeira, or	gă-dī'-rä.
Gades	gā'-dēz.
Gadhelic	găd-ĕl'-ĭk, găd'-ĕl-ĭk.
Gadite	gā'-dīt.
Gæa, see Ge	jē'-ȧ.
Gaekwar, see Gaikwar .	gīk'-wär.
Gael	gāl.
Gaelic	gā'-lĭk.
Gaeta	gä-ā'-tä.
Gaikwar, see Gaekwar .	gīk'-wär.
Gainsborough	gānz'-bŭr-ŭ, gānz'-bŭr-ō,
	gānz'-brō.
Gaiseric	gī'-zēr-ĭk.
Gakutei	gä-kōō-tā'-ē.
Galahad	găl'-ȧ-hăd.
Galapagos (Is.)	găl-ȧ-pā'-gōs.
	Sp. gä-lä'-pä-gōs.
Galashiels	găl-ȧ-shēlz'.
Galatea	găl-ȧ-tē'-ȧ.
Galatians	gȧ-lā'-shĭ=ȧns.
Galdos, Pérez	pā'-rĕth gäl'-dōs.
Galen	gā'-lĕn.
Galignani	gä-lĕn-yä'-nē.

Galilean	găl-ĭ-lē'-ăn.
Galilee	găl'-ĭ-lē.
Galilei, Galileo	gä-lē-lä'-o gä-lē-lä'-ē.
Galitzin, see Gallitzin	gä-lēts'-ēn.
Gallait	gäl-lä'.
Gallatin	găl'-à-tĭn.
Gallaudet	găl-ô-dĕt'.
Gallegos	gäl-yä'-gŏs.
Gallicism	găl'-ĭ-sĭzm.
Galli-Curci	găl'-lē kōōr'-chē.
Gallinéi	găl-yä-nē'.
Gallienus	găl-ĭ-ē'-nŭs.
Gallifet, de	dŭ gäl-ē-fä'.
Gallipoli	găl-lĭp'-ō-lĭ. It. gäl-lēp'-ō-lē.
Gallitzin, see Galitzin	gä-lēts'-ēn.
Galsworthy	gôlz-wēr-t̄hĭ.
Galuppi	gä-lōōp'-pē.
Galvani	gäl-vä'-nē.
Galveston	găl'-vĕs-tŭn.
Galway	gôl'-wä.
Gama, da	dä gä'-mä.
Gamaliel	gă-mä'-lĭ-ĕl..
Gambetta	găm-bĕt'-tä.
	Fr. gäṅ-bĕt-tä'.
Gambia	găm'-bĭ-ä.
Gananoque	gä-nä-nōk'.
Gand, see Ghent	gäṅ.
Gandercleugh	găn'-dēr-klūċh.
Gandhi	gänd'-hē.
Gando	găn'-dō.
Ganga, or	Hind. gŭng'-gä.
Ganges	găn'-jēz.
Ganjam	gän-jäm'.
Ganymede	găn'-ĭ-mēd.
Ganymedes	găn-ĭ-mē'-dēz.
Garagantua, see Gargantua	gär-à-găn'-tū-ä.
	Fr. gär-ä-gäṅ-tü-ä'.

Garay . . . . gä-rä′=ē.
Garbieh, see Gharbieh . gär-bē′-yĕ.
García, or . . . . . . gär′-shĭ=a. *Sp.* gär-thē′-ä.
Garcías, see Garzía . . gär-thē′-äs.
Garcilaso . . . . . . gär-thē-lä′-sō.
Gard . . . . gär.
Gardafui, see Guardafui . gär-dä-fwē′.
Gargantua, see Garagantua gär-găn′tū-ä.
     Fr. gär-gän-tü-ä′.
Garguille . . . . . . gär-gē′=yŭ.
Garhwal, see Gurhwal . gŭr-wäl′.
Garibaldi . . . . . . găr-ĭ-bàl′-dĭ.
     It. gä-rē-bäl′-dē.
Garigliano . . . . . . gä-rēl-yä′-nō.
Garnier . . . . . . gär-nē=ā′.
Garnier-Pagès . . . gär-nē=ā′-pä-zhĕz′.
Garofalo . . . . . . gä-rō′-fä-lō.
Garonne . . . . . . gä-rŏn′. *Fr.* gä-rŏn′.
Garshin . . . . . . gär′-shēn.
Garzía, see García . . gär-thē′-ä.
Gascogne . . . . . . gäs-kōn′=yŭ.
Gascony . . . . . . găs′-kō-nĭ.
Gassend . . . . . . gäs-sŏn′.
Gassendi . . . . . . gäs-sen′-dē. *Fr.* gä-săn-dē′.
Gastein . . . . . . gäs′-tīn.
Gaston de Foix . . . găs-tôn′ dŭ fwä.
Gaston d'Orléans . . găs-tôn′ dōr-lā-än′.
Gatacre . . . . . . găt′-à-kĕr.
Gatshina . . . . . . gä′-chē-nä.
Gatti-Casazza . . . găt′-tē-kä-zäts′-sä.
Gatun . . . . . . gä-tōōn′.
Gauchet . . . . . . gō-shä′.
Gaudenzio . . . . . gow-dĕn′-dzē-ō.
Gaudissart . . . . . gō-dē-sär′.
Gauguin . . . . . . gō-găn′.
Gautama, see Gotama . gô′-tà-má.
     Hind. gow′-tä-mä.

Gautier, Théophile . . tä-ō-fēl′ gō-tē=ā′.
Gavan . . . . găv′-àn.
Gaveston . . . . . găv′-ĕs-tŭn. *Fr.* gă-vĕs-tŏṅ′
Gavin . . . . găv′-ĭn.
Gaviota . . . . . gä-vē-ō′-tà.
Gavroche . . . . . gä-vrŏsh′.
Gawain, or Gawayne . . gä′-wān.
Gay-Lussac . . . . gā-lüs-săk′.
Gaza . . . . gā′-zà.
Gazaland . . . . . gä′-zä-länd.
Ge, see Gæa . . . . . gē.
Geber . . . . . . gā′-bĕr.
Gebir . . . . . . gā′-bēr.
Geddes . . . . . . gĕd′-ĕs.
Gefleborg . . . . . yāf′-lĕ-bōrg.
Gehenna . . . . . gē-hĕn′-ä.
Geierstein . . . . . gī′-ĕr-stīn.
Geikie . . . . . . gē′-kĭ.
Gelée, Claude . . . klōd zhē-lā′.
Gellert . . . . . . gĕl′-lĕrt.
Gemini . . . . . . jĕm′-ĭ-nī.
Geminiani . . . . . jām″-ē-nē-ä′-nē.
Gemmi . . . . . . gĕm′-ē.
Genée . . . . . . zhē-nā′.
Genesareth, see Gennesa-
 ret . . . . gĕ-nĕs′-à-rĕth.
Genesis . . . . . jĕn′-ĕ-sĭs.
Geneva . . . . . jĕ-nē′-vä.
Geneviève, Ste. . . . sȧṅt zhĕn-vē=ĕv′.
Genevra . . . . . jĕn-ĕv′-rà.
Genghis Khan, see Jenghiz jĕn′-gĭs khän.
Genlis, de . . . . . dŭ zhŏṅ-lēs′.
Gennesaret, see Genesa-
 reth . . . . gĕn-nĕs′-à-rĕt, jĕ-nĕs′-à-rĕt
Genoa . . . . . . jĕn′-ō-ä.
Genoese . . . . . jĕn-ō-ēz′, jĕn-ō-ēs′.
Genova . . . . . . jän′-ō-vä.

Genovefa	gā-nō-fā′-fä.
Genseric	jĕn′-sĕr-ĭk.
Gentiles	jĕn′-tīlz.
Geoffrey	jĕf′-rĭ.
Geoffrin	zhō-frăṅ′.
Geoffroy	zhō-frwä′.
Georg	Ger. gā=ōrch′. Sw.
	yā-ôrch′.
Georges	zhôrzh.
Georgics	jôr′-jĭks.
Georgievsk	gē=ôr′-gē-ĕfsk,
	dyôr′-dyĕfsk.
Geraint	gĕ-rānt′.
Gérard	Fr. zhā-rär′.
Gerardy (Jean)	zhĕ-rär-dē′.
Gergesenes	gĕr-gē-sēnz′.
Gerhardt	Fr. zhā-rär′. Ger. gâr′-härt.
Géricault	zhā-rē-kō′.
Gericke	gâr′-ĭ-kŭ.
Gerizim	gĕr′-ĭż-ĭm.
Germain	jĕr-mān′. Fr. zhâr-măṅ′.
Germania	jĕr-mā′-nĭ-à.
	Ger. gĕr-mä′-nē-ä.
Germanicus	jĕr-măn′-ĭ-kŭs.
Germinal	zhâr-mē-năl′.
Gernszheim	gĕrns′-hīm.
Gérôme	zhā-rōm′.
Gerona, see Jerona, Xerona	Sp. chā-rō′-nä.
Geronimo, Chief	jĕ-rŏn′-ĭ-mō.
	Sp. chā-rŏn′-ē-mō.
Géronte	zhā-rôṅt′.
Gerould (Mrs. K. F.)	jĕr-ō′.
Gerry	gĕr′-ĭ.
Gers	zhâr.
Gerster	gĕrs′-tĕr.
Gervais	zhĕr-vā′.
Gervaise	zhĕr-vĕz′.

Gervase . . . . . . jĕr'-vās, jĕr-vāz'.
Gervex . . . . zhâr-vā'.
Gerville-Réache . . . . zhâr-vēl'-rā-äsh'.
Gervinus . . . . . . gĕr-vē'-nōŏs.
Geryon . . . . jĕ'-rĭ-ŏn.
Geryones . . . . . . jē-rī'-ō-nēz.
Gesenius . . . . . . gĕ-sē'-nĭ-ŭs. Ger.
                      gā-zā'-nē-ōŏs.
Gessart, see Gossaert . . gĕs'-ärt.
Gesta Romanorum . . jĕs'-tä rō-mā-nō'-rŭm.
Gethsemane . . . . . gĕth-sĕm'-à-nē.
Geulincx . . . . . . chē'-lĭnks. Fr. zhē-lăṅks'.
Gezer . . . . gē'-zĕr.
Gharbieh, see Garbieh . gär-bē'-yĕ.
Ghats, Ghaunts . . . . gôts.
Ghazipur . . . . . . gä-zē-pōōr'.
Ghent, see Gand . . . gĕnt.
Gherardesca, Ugolina della ōō-gō-lē'-nō dĕl'-lä
                      gā-rär-dĕs'-kä.
Ghetto . . . . gĕt'-tō.
Ghibellines . . . . . gĭb'-ĕ-lĭnz.
Ghiberti . . . . . . gē-bĕr'-tē.
Ghil, René . . . . . rĕ-nā'gĕl.
Ghirlandajo . . . . . gĕr-län-dä'-yō.
Ghizeh, see Gizeh . . . gē'-zĕ.
Ghoorkas, see Goorkhas,
   or Ghurkas . . . . gōōr'-käs.
Giacomo . . . . . . jä'-kō-mō.
Gian Galeazzo Visconti . jän gä-lā-ätz'-ō vĭs-kōn'-tē.
Gibara . . . . ċhē-bä'-rä.
Gibeah . . . . gĭb'-ē-ä.
Gibra . . . . ċhē'-brä.
Gibraltar . . . . . . jĭb-rôl'-tàr.
Giers . . . . gērs.
Giessbach . . . . . gēs'-bäċk
Gil . . . . Fr. zhēl. Sp. 'hēl.
Gila . . . . hē'-lä. Sp. ċhē'-lä.

Gil Blas de Santillane,   *Fr.* zhēl blăs dŭ säntēl-ăn'.
   Sp. Santillana   *Sp.* 'hēl bläs dā
                      sän-tēl-yä'-nȧ.

Gilboa . . . .   gĭl-bō'-ä, gĭl'-bō-ä.
Gilda . . . .   *Fr.* zhēl-dä', *It.* jēl'-dä.
Gilead . . . . . .   gĭl'-ē-ăd.
Giles . . . .   jīlz.
Gilgal . . . . . .   gĭl'-găl.
Gilibert . . . . .   zhēl-ē-bĕr'.
Ginchy . . . .   zhăṅ-shē'.
Ginevra . . . . . .   gĭ-nĕv'-rä, jē-nĕv'-rȧ.
Gioconda, La . . . .   lä jŏ-kōn'-dä.
Giocondo . . . . .   jō-kŏn'-dō.
Gioja del Colle, or Gioia .   jō'-yä dāl kŏl'-lĕ.
Giordano Bruno . . . .   jōr-dä'-nō broō'-nō.
Giorgio . . . . . .   jŏr'-jō.
Giorgione . . . . .   jŏr-jō'-nĕ.
Giotto . . . . . .   jŏt'-tō.
Giovanni . . . . .   jō-vän'-nē.
Girardin . . . . .   zhē-rär-dăṅ'.
Giraudoux . . . . .   zhē-rō-doō'.
Girgeh . . . . . .   jēr'-jĕ.
Girgenti . . . . .   jēr-jĕn'-tē.
Girolamo . . . . .   jē-rō'-lä-mō.
Gironde . . . . . .   jĭ-rŏnd'. *Fr.* zhē-rôṅd'.
Girondins . . . . .   jĭ-rŏṅ'-dĭnz.
                      Fr. zhē-rôṅ-dăṅ'.
Girondists . . . . .   jĭ-rŏn'-dĭsts.
Gisors . . . . . .   zhē-zŏr'.
Gittite . . . . . .   gĭt'-īt.
Giulia . . . . . .   joōl'-yä.
Giuliano . . . . .   joō-lē=ä'-nō.
Giulietta . . . . .   joō-lē-āt'-tä.
Giulio di Pietro di Filippo   joō'-lē=ō dē
                   pē=ä'-trō dē fē-lēp'-pō.
Giulio Romano . . . .   joō'-lē=ō rō-mä'-nō.
Giuseppe . . . . .   joō-sĕp'-pĕ.

Giustiniani	jōōs″-tē-nē-ä′-nē.
Givenchy	zhē-vôṅ-shē′.
Gizeh, see Ghizeh . .	gē′-zŭ.
Gladstone	glăd′-stŭn, glăd′-stōn.
Glamis, or Glammis . .	glämz.
Glamorgan	glă-môr′-găn
Glasgow	glăs′-gō.
Glaucus	glô′-kŭs.
Glazounoff (-ow), or	
Glazunov (-ow) . . .	glă-zōō-nŏf′.
Glendower	glĕn-dow′-ĕr, glĕn′-dōōr.
Glière	glē-ĕr′.
Godard, Benjamin. . .	bŏṅ-zhă-maṅ′ gō-där′.
Gloriana	glō-rĭ-ä′-nä.
Gloster, or Gloucester .	glŏs′-tēr.
Glück	glük.
Glumdalclitch	glŭm-dăl′-klĭch.
Glycera	glĭs′-ĕ-rä.
Glyptotheca	glĭp-tō-thē′-kȧ.
Glyptothek	glĭp-tō-tāk′.
Gneist	g=nīst.
Gnostics	nŏs′-tĭks.
Goa	gō′-ä.
Goajira, see Guajira . .	gō=ä-'hē′-rä, gwä-'hē′-rä.
Goalpara	gō-äl-pä′-rä.
Gobelin	gōb-lăṅ′.
Gobi, see Cobi	gō′-bē.
Gobseck	gŏb-sĕk′.
Godavari	gō-dä′-vä-rē.
Godebski	gō-dĕb′-skĭ.
Godefroy de Bouillon . .	Fr. gō=dŭ-frwä′ dŭ
	bōō-yôṅ′.
Godfrey of Bouillon . .	gŏd′-frĭ ov bōō-yôṅ′.
Godiva	gō-dī′-vȧ.
Godolphin	gŏ-dŏl′-fĭn.
Godowsky	gō-dŏf′-skĭ.
Godoy	gō′-doi. Sp. gō-dō′=ē.

Godounoff   (Godunov),
Boris . . . . bō-rēs' gō-dōō-nŏf'.
Goebel (Wm.) . . . . gō'-bĕl.
Goeben . . . . . . gē'-bĕn.
Goessler, see Gössler . . gēs'-lĕr.
Goethals . . . . . . gō'-thålz.
Goethe, see Göthe . . gē'-tŭ.
Goetz von Berlichingen,
see Götz . . . . . gētz fŏn bâr'-lĭċh-ĭng"-ĕn.
Gogol . . . . gŏ-gŏl'.
Goldoni . . . . . . gōl-dō'-nē.
Golgotha . . . . . . gŏl'-gō-thå.
Goliath . . . . gō-lī'-ăth.
Golitzin . . . . . . gō-lĭts'-ĭn.
Gomara . . . . . . gō-mä'-rä.
Gomez . . . . gō'-mĕz. Sp. gō'-mĕth.
Gomorrah . . . . . . gŏ-mŏr'-ä.
Gompers . . . . . . gŏm'-pērs.
Gonaive, La . . . . . lä gō-nä-ēv'.
Gonaives, Les . . . . lā gō-nä-ēv'.
Goncharoff (-ov) . . . gŏn-chär'-ŏf.
Goncourt, de . . . . . dŭ gôn-kōōr'.
Gonda . . . . gŏn'-dä.
Goneril . . . . gŏn'-ēr-ĭl.
Gonfaloniere . . . . . gōn"-fä-lō-nē-ä'-rĕ.
Góngora . . . . . . gŏn'-gō-rå.
Gonsalvo de Cordova . . gōn-säl'-vō dĕ kŏr'-dō-vä.
Gonse . . . . gōn'-sĕ.
Gonzaga . . . . . . gŏn-zä'-gä.Sp.gōn-thä'-gä.
                         It. gōn-dzä'-gä.
Gonzales . . . . . . Sp. gōn-thä'-lĕs.
Gonzalez . . . . . . gōn-thä'-lĕth.
Gonzalo de Córdoba . . gōn-thä'-lō dä kŏr'-dō-bä.
Goorkhas, see Ghoorkas . gōōr'-käz.
Gorakhpur, see Goruckpur gŏ-rŭk-pōōr'.
Gorboduc . . . . . . gôr'-bō-dŭk.
Gordian, or Gordianus . . gôr'-dĭ-ån, gôr-dĭ-ā'-nŭs.

Görgei, or Görgey . . . gēr′-gĕ-ĭ.
Gorgias . . . . . . gôr′-jĭ-ȧs.
Goriot, Père . . . . . pâr gō-rē-ō′.
Gorizia . . . . gō-rēdz′-ē-ä.
Gorki (-ky) . . . . . gôr′-kĭ.
Görlitz . . . . gēr′-lĭts.
Gortchakoff, or -kow, or
    -kov . . . . gŏr-chä-kŏf′.
Goruckpur, see Gorakhpur gŏ-rŭk-pōōr′.
Görz . . . . gērts.
Goshenland . . . . . gō′-shĕn-lănd.
Gossaert, see Gessart . . gŏs′-ärt.
Gossé, or Gossec . . . gŏs-sā′, gŏ-sĕk′.
Gössler, see Goessler . . gēs′-lĕr.
Got . . . . gō.
Gotama, see Gautama . gô′-tȧ-má.
Göteborg, see Gothenburg yē′-tĕ-bŏrċh.
Goth . . . . gŏth.
Gotha (duchy) . . . . gō′-thä. *Ger.* gō′-tä.
Götha (canal) . . . . gē′-tä. *Sw.* yē′-tä
Gotham . . . . . . gō′-thȧm.
Göthe, see Goethe . . . gē′-tŭ.
Gothenburg, see Gotten-
    burg, Göteborg . . . gōt′-ĕn-bōōrċh.
Gothic . . . . gŏth′-ĭk.
Gothland, or . . . . . gŏth′-lȧnd.
Gotland, Sw. . . . . . gōt′-länd.
Gotland (I.) . . . . . gōt′-länd.
Gottenburg, see Gothen-
    burg . . . . gŏt′-ĕn-bōōrċh.
Götterdämmerung, Die . dē gĕt-tĕr-dȧm′-mĕ-rōōng.
Göttingen . . . . . . gĕt′-tĭng-ĕn.
Gottschalk . . . . . gŏt′-shälk.
Götz von Berlichingen, see
    Goetz . . . . . . gĕts fŏn bâr′-lĭch-ĭng″-ĕn.
Gough . . . . gôf.
Goujon . . . . gōō-zhôṅ′.

Gounod . . . . . . gōō-nō'.
Gouraud . . . . . . gōō-rō'.
Gouverneur . . . . . gōōv'-ẽr-nẽr.
      Fr. gōō-vẽr-nẽr'.
Gouvion- Saint-Cyr . . gōō-vĭ=ôṅ'-săṅ-sẽr'.
Gower . . . . gow'-ẽr.
Goya y Lucientes . . . gō'-yä ē lōō-thē=ĕn'-tĕs.
Goyaz . . . . gō-yäz'.
Gozo, or Gozzo . . . . gŏd'-zō, gŏt'-sō.
Gozzoli, Benozzo . . . bä-nŏt'-sō gŏts'-ō-lē.
Graal, see Grail, Grael . grāl.
Gracias á Dios . . . . grä'-thē=äs ä dē-ōs'.
Gradiska . . . . . . grä-dĭs'-kä.
Graefe, Gräfe, von . . . fōn grâ'-fŭ.
Grael, see Grail, Graal . grāl.
Graeme . . . . . . grām.
Graf . . . . gräf.
Gräfin . . . . grâ'-fĭn.
Graham . . . . . . grä-àm, grām.
Grail, see Grael, Graal . grāl.
Gramont . . . . . . grä-môṅ'.
Granada . . . . . . grǎ-nä'-dä.
Grande Anse du Diamante gräṅ däṅs dü dē-ä-mäṅt'.
Grande Mademoiselle, La lä gräṅd mäd-mwä-zĕl'-ŭ.
Grande-Terre . . . . gräṅd-târ'.
Grandet, Eugénie . . . ē-zhä-nē' gräṅ-dā'.
Grand Monarque, Le . . lē gräṅ mō-närk'.
Grandpré . . . . . . gräṅ-prā'.
Grand Prix, Le . . . . lē gräṅ prē.
Granier de Cassagnac . . grä-nē=ā' dŭ käs-sän-yăk'.
Gratiano . . . . . . grä-shĭ-ä'-nō.
      It. grä-tē=ä'-nō.
Gratz, see Graz . . . . gräts.
Gravelines, or . . . . grăv-lēn'.
Gravelingen, or . . . . *Ger.* grä'-vĕ=lĭng″-ĕn.
Gravelinghe . . . . . *Fl.* grä'-vĕ-lĭng″-ĕ.
Gravelotte . . . . . . gräv-lōt'.

Graveure . . . . . . gră-vēr'.
Graz, see Gratz . . . . gräts.
Grechaninoff (-ov) . . grĕch-ä-nē'-nŏf.
Greenough . . . . . grēn'-ō.
Greenwich . . . . . *Eng.* grĭn'-ĭj.
Gregory Nazianzen . . grĕg'-ō-rĭ năz-ĭ-ăn'-zĕn.
Greig . . . . grĕg.
Gremio . . . . grē'-mĭ-ō.
Grenada . . . . . . grĕn-ā'-dä.
Grenoble . . . . . . grĕ-nō'-bl.
Greta . . . . grē'-tȧ.
Gretchen . . . . . . grĕch'-ĕn. *Ger.* grāt'-ċhĕn.
Gretel . . . . grā'-tĕl.
Grétry . . . . . . grā-trē'.
Greuze . . . . . . grēz.
Grève . . . . grĕv.
Greville . . . . . . grĕv'-ĭl.
Gréville . . . . . . *Fr.* grā-vēl'.
Grévy . . . . grā-vē'.
Griboyédoff . . . . grē-bō-yä'-dŏf.
Gridley . . . . . . grĭd'-lĭ.
Grieg . . . . grēg.
Grillparzer . . . . . grĭl'-pärt-zĕr.
Grindelwald . . . . . grĭn'-dĕl-vält.
Griqualand . . . . . grē'-kwȧ-lănd.
Grisi . . . . grē'-zē.
Grisons . . . . . . grē-zôṅ'.
Grodno . . . . grŏd'-nō.
Grolier . . . . . . grō'-lē꞊ā. *Fr.* grō-lē꞊ā'.
Groningen, or . . . . *D.* ċhrō'-nĭng-ċhĕn.
Gröningen, Ger.. . . . grē'-nĭng-ĕn.
Groot . . . . grōt.
Groote Kerke . . . . grō'-tĕ kĕr'-kĕ.
Gros . . . . grō.
Grossi . . . . grŏs'-sē.
Grosvenor . . . . . grōv'-nĕr, grō'-vĕ-nĕr.
Grote . . . . grōt.

Grotius . . . . grō'-shǐ-ǔs.
Grouchy, de . . . . . dǔ grōō-shē'.
Grütli, see Rütli . . . grüt'-lǐ.
Gruyère, Gruyères . . grü-yâr'.
Guadalajara . . . . . gwä"-dä-lä-ċhä'-rä.
Guadalquivir . . . . . gô-dăl-kwǐv'-ēr.
     Sp. gwä"-däl-kē-vēr'.
Guadalupe . . . . . gô-dä-lōōp'.
     Sp. gwä-dä-lōō'-pä.
Guadeloupe . . . . . gô-dĕ-lōōp'. *Fr.* gäd-lōōp'.
Guahan, Sp. Guajan . . gwä-hän'.
Guaira, La, see La Guayra lä gwī'-rȧ, lä gī'-rȧ.
     Sp. lä gwä'=ē-rä.
Guajan, see Guahan . . *Sp.* gwä-'hän'.
Guajira, see Goajira . . gwä-'hē'-rä.
Gualfonda . . . . . . gwäl-fŏn'-dä.
Guam . . . . gwăm. *Sp.* gwäm.
Guanabacoa . . . . . gwä"-nä-bä-kō'-ä.
Guanahani . . . . . gwä-nä-ä-nē'.
Guanaja . . . . . . gwä-nä'-'hä.
Guanajay . . . . . . gwä-nä-ċhä'=ē.
Guanica . . . . . . gwä-nē'-kä.
Guantanamo . . . . gwän-tä-nä'-mō.
Guap, see Yap . . . . gwäp.
Guardafui, see Gardafui . gwär-dä-fōō=ē'.
Guarico . . . . . . gwä'-rē-kō.
Guarneri, or . . . . . gwär-nä'-rē.
Guarnerius . . . . . gwär-nē'-rǐ-ǔs.
Guatemala . . . . . gô-tē-mä'-lä.
     Sp. gwä-tä-mä'-lä.
Guayaquil . . . . . . gī-ȧ-kēl'. *Sp.* gwī-ä-kēl'.
Guaymas . . . . . . gwī'-mäs. *Mex.* wī'-mȧs.
Guayra, La, see La Guaira lä gwī'rä, lä gī'rȧ.
     Sp. lä gwä'=ē-rä.
Gudrun . . . . . . gōō-drōōn'.
Guébriant . . . . . . gä-brē-äṅ'.
Guelfs, Guelphs . . . gwĕlfs.

Guendolen	gwĕn'-dŏ-lĕn.
Guenevere	gwĕn'-ĕ-vēr.
Guercino	gwĕr-chē'-nō.
Guérin	gā răn'.
Guernsey	gĕrn'-zĭ.
Guerrero	gĕr-âr'-ō.
Guerrière, La	lä gâr-rē=âr'.
Gueux	gē.
Guglielmo	gōōl-ē=ĕl'-mo.
Gui, see Guy	Fr. gē.
Guiana, see Guyana . .	gē-ä'-nä.
Guicciardini	gwē-chär-dē'-nē.
Guiccioli	gwē'-chō-lē.
Guichard	gē-shär'.
Guiderius	gwĭ-dē'-rĭ-ŭs.
Guidi, Casa	kä'-zä gwē'-dē.
Guido Aretino	gwē'-dō ä-rä-tē'-nō.
Guido d'Arezzo	gwē'-dō dä-rĕt'-sō.
Guido Franceschini . .	gwē'-dō frän-chĕs-kē'-nē.
Guido of Lusignan, see	
Guy de	gwē'-dō ŭv lü-zēn-yän'.
Guido Reni	gwē'-dō rā'-nē.
Guilbert, Yvette	ē-vĕt' gēl-bĕr'.
Guillaume	gē-yom'=ŭ.
Guillaumet	gē-yŏ-mä'.
Guillemont	gēl-môn'.
Guillotin	gē-yō-tăn'.
Guilmant	gēl-män'.
Guimarás	gē-mä-räs'.
Guines	gēn.
Guinever, Guinevere . .	gwĭn-ĕ-vēr'.
Guion	gī'-ŏn. Fr. gē-ôn'.
Guiscard	gēs-kär'.
Guise, de	dŭ gēz.
Guitry, Sacha	săsh-ä' gē-trē'.
Guizot	gē-zō'.
Gujranwala	gŭzh-ràn-wä'-lä.

Gujrat . . . . gŭzh-rät′.
Gula . . . . gōō′-lä.
Gulistan . . . . . . gōō-lĭs-tän′.
Günther, Guenther . . gün′-tĕr.
Gurdaspur . . . . . gōō-däs-pōōr′.
Gurhwal, see Garhwal . gŭr-wäl′.
Gurkhas, see Ghoorkas . gōōr′-käz.
Gustavus Adolphus . . gŭs-tä′-vŭs ä-dŏl′-fŭs.
        Ger. gŏŏs-tä′-vōōs
        ä-dōl-fŏŏs. [vä′-sä.
Gustavus Vasa . . . . gŭs-tä′-vŭs, gŏŏs-tä′-vŏŏs
Gutenberg . . . . . gōō′-tĕn-bērg.
        Ger. gōō′-tĕn-bĕrċh.
Gutiérrez Nájera . . . gōō-tē-ĕr′-ĕs näċh′-ä-rä.
Gutzkow . . . . . . gōōts′-kō.
Guy, see Gui . . . . . gī. Fr. gē.
Guyana, see Guiana . . gē-ä′-nä.
Guyandotte . . . . . gī-ăn-dŏt′.
Guy de Lusignan, see Guido
 of Lusignan . . . . gē dŭ lü-zēn-yäṅ′.
Guyon . . . . gī′-ŏn. Fr. gē-ôṅ′.
Guyot . . . . gē-ō′.
Guzman . . . . . . gōōth-män′.
Gwalior . . . . . . gwä′-lē-ôr.
Gyges . . . . gī′-jēz.

H

Haag, Den, see The Hague dĕn häċh.
Haakon . . . . hô′-kŏn.
Haas . . . . häs.
Habakkuk . . . . . . hă-băk′-ŭk, hăb′-à-kŭk.
Habana, see Havana . . ä-bä′-nä.
Habsburg, see Hapsburg . häps′-bōōrċh.
Hadad . . . . hä′-dăd.
Haden . . . . hä′-dn.
Hades . . . . hä′-dēz.

Hading (Jane) . . . . ă-dăṅ'.
Hadrian, see Adrian . . hā'-drĭ-àn.
Haeckel . . . . . . hĕk'-l. *Ger.* hâk'ĕl.
Hafiz . . . . *Pers.* hô-fĭz'.
Hagar . . . . hā'-gär.
Hagedorn, von . . . . fōn hä'-gā-dôrn.
Hagen . . . . *Ger.* hä'-gĕn.
Haggai, or Haggi . . . hăg'-i.
Hagiographa . . . . . hā-jĭ-ŏg'-rà-fà,
 hăg-ĭ-ŏg'-rä-fä.
Hague (The), see Den
 Haag, La Haye . . . hāg.
Hahnemann . . . . . hä'-nā-män.
Haidarabad, see Hydera-
 bad . . . . hĭ″-dä-rà-bäd'.
Haidar-Ali, see Hyder Ali hĭ'-där ä'-lē.
Haidee . . . . hĭ-dē'.
Haiduks, see Hayduks . hĭ'-dōōks.
Hainan . . . . hĭ-nän'.
Hainault, or Hainaut . . hā-nō'. *Fr.* ā-nō'.
Haiti, see Hayti . . . . hā'-tĭ. *Fr.* ä-ē-tē'.
Hakluyt . . . . . . hăk'-lōōt.
Hakodate . . . . . hä-kō-dä'-tä.
Halberstadt . . . . . häl'-bĕr-stät.
Halcyone, see Alcyone . hăl-sĭ'-ō-nē.
Haldane . . . . . . hăl'-dān.
Haldeman . . . . . hôl'-dĕ-măn.
Halévy . . . . ă-lā-vē'.
Halicarnassus . . . . häl'-ĭ-kär-năs'-ŭs.
Halicz . . . . hä'-lĭch.
Halle . . . . häl'-lŭ.
Haller, von . . . . . fŏn häl'-lĕr.
Hals . . . . häls.
Ham (Fort) . . . . . äm.
Hamah, or Hamath . . hä'-mä, hā'-măth.
Hamburg . . . . . . hăm'-bĕrg.
 Ger. häm'-bōōrch.

Hamelin, or Hameln . . hä'-mŭ-lĭn, hä'-mĕln.
Hamerling . . . . . hä'-mĕr-lĭng.
Hamerton . . . . . . hăm'-ēr-tŭn.
Hamilcar Barca . . . . hă-mĭl'-kär bär'-ka.
Hamitic . . . . . . hăm-ĭt'-ĭk.
Hamsun, Knut . . . . knüt häm'-so͞on.
Hanabusa . . . . . hä'-nä'-bo͞o'-sä'.
Hanau . . . . hä'-now.
Händel, Handel . . . . hăn'-dĕl. *Ger.* hân'-dĕl.
Hang-chau, or Hangchow häng'-chow.
Hangshan . . . . . . häng'-shän.
Han Hok . . . . . . hän' hōk.
Han-Kow, or Hankow, or
  Han-kau . . . . . hän-kow'.
Hannover, see Hanover . hän-nō'-vĕr.
Hanoi . . . . hä-no'-ĭ.
Hanover, see Hannover . hăn'-ō-vēr.
Hanotaux . . . . . . än-ō-tō'.
Hans . . . . hänts.
Hansa . . . . hän'-sä.
Hanseatic . . . . . . hăn-sē-ăt'-ĭk.
Hänsel and Gretel . . . hĕn'-zĕl o͞ont grä'-tĕl.
Hanyang . . . . . . hän-yäng'.
Hapsburg, see Habsburg . hăps'-bĕrg.
                          Ger. häps'-bo͞orċh.
Harbin . . . . här'-bēn.
Hardanger Fjord . . . här'-däng-ĕr fyôrd.
Hardecourt . . . . . ärd-ko͞or'.
Hardelot, Guy d' . . . gē där=dē-lō'.
Harderwijk . . . . . här'-dĕr-wīk.
Hardicanute . . . . . här''-dĭ-kā-nūt'.
Hardoi . . . . hŭr'-dō-ē.
Harfleur . . . . . . är-flēr'.
Harleian . . . . . . här'-lē-ȧn.
Harlequin . . . . . . här'-lē-kwĭn, här'-lē-kĭn.
Haro, Luis de . . . . lo͞o-ēs' dä ä'-rō.

Haroun al Raschid, see
Harun . . . . . . hä-rōōn′ äl răsh′-ĭd,
                    hä-rōōn′ äl rä-shēd′.
Harpagon . . . . . . är-pä-gôṅ′.
Harpagus . . . . . . här′-pā-gŭs.
Harpignies . . . . är-pēn-yē′.
Harpocrates . . . . här-pŏk′-rȧ-tēz.
Hartmann von Aue . . härt′-män fŏn ow′-ŭ.
Harun al Rashid, see
Haroun . . . . . . hä-rōōn′ äl răsh′-ĭd, *or*
                    rä-shēd′.
Harwich . . . . . . hăr′-ĭch, hăr′-ĭj.
Harz . . . . härts.
Hasan, see Hassan . . hä′-sȧn.
Hasdrubal, see Asdrubal . hăs′-drōō-băl.
Hassan, see Hasan . . häs′-sȧn.
Hauch, (J. C.), von . . . fŏn howċh.
Hauck (Minnie) . . . hôk.
Haupt . . . . howpt.
Hauptmann, Gerhart . . gâr′-härt howpt′-män.
Hauser, Caspar . . . . käs′-pär how′-zĕr.
Haussman (Baron) . . . ōs-män′.
Haute-Garonne . . . . ōt-gä-rŏn′.
Haute-Loire . . . . . ōt-lwär′.
Haute-Marne . . . . ōt-märn′.
Hautes-Alpes . . . . ōt-zälp′.
Haute-Saône . . . . ōt-sōn′.
Haute-Savoie . . . . ōt-sä-vwä′.
Hautes-Pyrénées . . . ōt-pē-rä-nä′.
Haute-Vienne . . . . ōt-vē-ĕn′.
Haüy, Abbé . . . . . äb-ā′ ä-wē′, ä-ü=ē′.
Havana, see Habana . . hă-văn′-ȧ.
Havel . . . . hä′-fĕl.
Haverhill . . . . . . *Am.* hā′-vĕr-ĭl.
                    Eng. hăv′ĕr-ĭl.
Havilah . . . . . . hăv′-ĭl-ȧ.
Havre-de-Grace . . . ä′-vr-dŭ-grăs′.

Hawaii	hä-wĭ'-ē.
Hawaiian	hä-wī'-yän.
Hawarden	hôr'-dn, här'-děn.
Haweis	hois.
Hayakawa, Sessue . .	sās'-ōō'-ä hä'-yä'-kä'-wä'.
Haydée	ā-dä'.
Haydn	hā'-dn. *Ger.* hī'-dn.
Hayduks, see Haiduks .	hī'-dōōks.
Haye, La, see The Hague,	
Den Haag	lä ä.
Hayti, see Haiti . . .	hā'-tĭ. *Fr.* ä-ē-tē'.
Hazael	hăz'-ā- lĕ hā'-zā-ĕl.
Hazaribagh	hä-zä-rē-bô'.
Hazebrouck	ăz'-brŏŏk.
Hazlitt	hăz'-lĭt.
Hebe	hē'-bē.
Hébert	ā-bâr'.
Hebraist	hē'-brā- sĭ.
Hebrides	hĕb'-rĭ-dēz.
Hebron	hē'-brŏn.
Hecate	hĕk'-ā-tē, hĕk'-āt.
Hecuba	hĕk'-yū-bà.
Hedin, Sven	svĭn hĭ-dēn'.
Hedone	hĕd'-ō-nē.
Hédouin	ā-dōō-ăṅ'.
Hegel	hā'-gĕl.
Hegelian	hē-gē'-lĭ-àn.
Hegira, see Hejira . . .	hē-jī'-rà, hĕj'-ĭ-rà.
Heidelberg	hī'-dĕl-bērg.
	Ger. hī'-dĕl-bĕrċh.
Heidenmauer	hī'-dĕn-mow"-ĕr.
Heijn (Admiral)	hīn.
Heilbronn	hĭl'-brŏn.
Heimskringla	hīms'-krĭng-lä.
Heine	hī'-nŭ.
Heinrich	hīn'-rĭċh.
Hejira, see Hegira . . .	hē-jī'-rà, hĕj'-ĭr-à.

Helen . . . . hĕl'-ĕn.
Helena . . . . hĕl'-ĕ-nȧ.
Helena (Montana) . . . hĕl'-ĕ-nȧ.
Helena, St. (I.) . . . . sĕnt hĕl-ē'-nȧ.
Helenus . . . . . . hĕl'-ĕ-nŭs.
Helgoland, see Heligo-
    land . . . . hĕl'-gō-länd.
Helicanus . . . . . . hĕl-ĭ-kā'-nŭs.
Helicon . . . . . . hĕl'-ĭ-kŏn.
Heligoland, see Helgo-
    land . . . . . . hĕl'-ĭ-gō-länd″.
Heliodorus . . . . . . hē″-lĭ-ō-dō'-rŭs.
Heliogabalus, see Elagaba-
    lus . . . . hē″-lĭ-ō-găb'-ā-lŭs,
                      hē″-lĭ-ō-gā-bā'-lŭs.
Heliopolis . . . . . . hē-lĭ-ŏp'-ō-lĭs.
Helios . . . . hē'-lĭ-ŏs.
Hellas . . . . hĕl'-ȧs.
Hellenes . . . . . . hĕl-lē'-nēz, hĕl'-ēnz,
Hellenic . . . . . . hĕl-lē'-nĭk, hĕl-lĕn'-ĭk.
Hellespont . . . . . hĕl'-lĕs-pŏnt.
Hellevoetsluis, see Hel-
    voetsluis . . . . . hĕl-lĕ-vōōt-slois'.
Héloïse . . . . . . ā-lō-ēz'.
Helots . . . . hĕl'-ŏts, hē'-lŏts.
Helsingfors . . . . . hĕl'-sĭng-fŏrs.
Helsinki . . . . . . hĕl'-sĭnk-kĭ.
Helvetia . . . . . . hĕl-vē'-shĭ=ȧ.
Helvétius . . . . . . hĕl-vē'-shĭ-ŭs.
                      Fr. ĕl-vā-sē-üs'.
Helvoetsluis . . . . . hĕl-vōōt-slois'.
Hemans (Mrs.) . . . . hĕm'-ȧnz. pop. hē'-mȧnz.
Hengist . . . . . . hĕng'-gĭst.
Hengstenberg . . . . hĕng'-stĕn-bĕrch.
Henlopen . . . . . . hĕn-lō'-pĕn.
Hennepin . . . . . . hĕn'-ĕ-pĭn. Fr. ĕn-păn'.
Hennequin . . . . . hĕn'-nĕ-kwĭn. Fr. ĕn-kăn'.

Henri	ŏn-rē'.
Henriade	ŏn-rē-yăd'.
Henrici	hān-rēt'-sē.
Henri de Bourbon. . .	ŏn-rē' dŭ bōōr-bôn'.
Henriette	hĕn-rĭ-ĕt'. *Fr.* ôn-rē-ĕt'.
Henri Quatre	ôn-rē' kätr'.
Henriquez	ān-rē'-kĕth.
Henry (Col.)	ôn-rē'.
Hephæstion	hē-fĕs'-tĭ-ŏn.
Hephæstus, or	hĕ-fĕs'-tŭs.
Hephaistos	hē-fīs'-tŏs.
Heptameron	hēp-tăm'-ĕ-rŏn.
Heptarchy	hĕp'-tär-kĭ.
Heptateuch	hĕp'-tȧ-tūk.
Hera	hē'-rä.
Heraclean	hĕr-ȧ-klē'-ȧn.
Heracles	hĕr'-ȧ-klēz.
Heraclidæ	hĕr-ā-klī'-dē.
Heraclitus	hĕr-ā-klī'-tŭs.
Herat	hĕr-ät'.
Hérault	ā-rō'.
Herculaneum . . .	hĕr-kū-lā'-nē-ŭm.
Herculean	hĕr-kū'-lē-ȧn.
Hercules	hĕr'-kū-lēz.
Here	hē'-rē.
Heredia	*Sp.* ā-rā'-dē-ä.
Hérédia	*Fr.* ā-rä-dē-ä'.
Hereford	hĕr'-ĕ-fŭrd.
Hereward	hĕr'-ĕ-wȧrd.
Hergesheimer	hĕr'-gĕs-hī-mēr.
Héricourt	ā-rē-kōōr'.
Heristal, or Heristall, see	
Herstal	hĕr'-ĭs-täl.
Hermann	hĕr'-män.
Hermant	âr-män'.
Hermaphroditus	hĕr-măf″-rō-dī'-tŭs.
Hermes	hĕr'-mĕz.

Hermione	hẽer-mī'-ō-nē.
Hermogenes	hẽr-moj'-ĕ-nēz.
Hermosillo	hĕr-mō-sēl'-yō.
Hernandez	ār-nän'-dĕth.
Hernani	ār-nä'-nē.
Herod	hĕr'-ŏd.
Hérodiade	ā-rō-dē-ăd'.
Herodian	hē-rō'-dĭ-àn.
Herodias	hē-rō'-dĭ-às.
Herodotus	hē-rŏd'-ō-tŭs.
Hérold	ā-rŏld'.
Herrera	ār-rā'-rä.
Herreros	ār-rā'-rōs.
Herschel	hẽr'-shĕl.
Herstal, see Heristal . .	hĕr'-stäl.
Hertford	hẽrt'-fôrd, här'-fôrd.
Heruli	hĕr'-ōō-lī
Hervé Riel	âr-vā' rē-ĕl'.
Hervieu, Paul	pōl âr-vē=ē'.
Herzegovina	hĕrt"-sĕ-gō-vē'-nä.
Herzog	hĕrt'-zōċh.
Herzogin	hĕrt'-zō-gĭn.
Heshvan, see Hesvan . .	hĕsh'-văn.
Hesiod	hē'-sĭ-ŏd, hē'-shĭ-ŏd.
Hesiodus	hē-sī'-ō-dŭs.
Hesione	hē-sī-ō-nē.
Hesperides	hĕs-pĕr'-ĭ-dēz.
Hesse	hĕs.
Hesse-Cassel	hĕs-kăs'-ĕl.
Hessen	hĕs'-sĕn.
Hesse-Nassau	hĕs-năs'-ô.
Hessian	hĕsh'-ĭ-àn.
Hestia	hĕs'-tĭ-à.
Hesvan, see Heshvan . .	hĕs'-văn.
Heureaux, Ulisse . . .	ü-lēs' ĕr-ō'.
Heyne	hī'-nŭ.
Heyse	hī'-zŭ.

Hexö . . . . hĕx′-ē.
Hiawatha . . . . . . hī-à-wô′-thà, hĭ-à-wô′-tà.
Hibernia . . . . . . hī-bẽr′-nĭ=à.
Hidalgo . . . . . . ē-däl′-gō.
Hiero . . . . hī′-ĕ-rō.
Hieron . . . . hī′-ĕ-rŏn.
Hieronymus . . . . . hĭ-ē-rŏn′-Ĭ-mŭs.
Hilary . . . . hĭl′-à-rĭ.
Hildebrandslied . . . . hĭl′-dä-bränts-lēt.
Hilo . . . . hē′-lō.
Himalaya . . . . . . hĭm-ä′-lä-yà, hĭm-ä-lä′-yä.
Himilco . . . . . . hĭ-mĭl′-kō.
Hindenburg . . . . . hĭn′-dĕn-bo͞orċh.
Hindoo, see Hindu . . hĭn′-do͞o, hĭn-do͞o′.
Hindoostan, see Hindustan hĭn-do͞o-stän′.
Hindoostanee, see Hindu-
stani . . . . hĭn-do͞o-stăn′-ē.
Hindostan, see Hindoo-
stan, Hindustan . . . hĭn-dō-stän′, hĭn-dŏ-stăn′.
Hindu, see Hindoo . . hĭn′-do͞o, hĭn-do͞o′.
Hindu Kush . . . . . hĭn′-do͞o ko͞osh.
Hindustan, see Hindoostan hĭn-do͞o-stän′.
Hindustani, see Hindoo-
stanee . . . . . . hĭn-do͞o-stăn′-ē.
Hiogo . . . . hē-ō′-gō.
Hippocrates . . . . . hĭp-pŏk′-rä-tēz.
Hippocrene . . . . . hĭp′-ō-krēn, hĭp-ō-krē′-nē.
Hippolita, or Hippolyta . hĭ-pol′-Ĭ-tä. ˙
Hippolyte . . . . . . hĭ-pŏl′-Ĭ-tē. *Fr.* ē-pō-lēt′.
Hippolytus . . . . . hĭ-pŏl′-Ĭ·tŭs.
Hiren . . . . hī′-rĕn.
Hiroshige . . . . . . hē′-rō′-shē′-gä′.
Hiroshima . . . . . . hē′-rō′-shē′-mä′.
Hirsch . . . . hẽrsh.
Hishikawa Moronobu . . hē′-shē′-kä′-wä′
                        mō′-rō′-nō′-bŭ′.
Hispania . . . . . . hĭs-pā′-nĭ=à.

Hispaniola . . . . . hĭs″-păn-ĭ=ō′-là.
               Sp. ēs″-pä-nē=ōō′-lä.
Hissar . . . . hĭs-sär′.
Hittite . . . . hĭt′-īt.
Hivite . . . . hī′-vīt.
Hlangwane (Hill) . . . hlăng-wä′-nŭ.
Hoang-ho, see Hwang-ho hwäng′-hō.
Hobbema . . . . . . hŏb′-bĕ-mä.
Hobbes . . . . hŏbz.
Hobbesian . . . . . hŏb′-zĭ-àn.
Hobbididence . . . . hŏb′-ĭ-dĭ″-dĕns.
Hoboken . . . . . . hō′-bō-kĕn, hō-bō′-kĕn.
Hoche (Gen.) . . . . ŏsh.
Hochkirch . . . . . . hōċh′-kērċh.
Höchst . . . . hēċhst.
Höchstädt . . . . . . hēċh′-stĕt.
Hogolen, or Hogolin . . hō′-gō-lĕn, hō′-gō-lĭn.
Hogolu, or Hogolou . . hō′-gō-lōō.
Hohenlinden . . . . . hō-ĕn-lĭn′-dĕn.
Hohenlohe . . . . . hō-ĕn-lō′-ŭ.
Hohenlohe-Schillingsfürst hō-ĕn-lō′-ŭ shĭl′-lĭngs-fürst
Hohenstaufen, or -stauffen hō′-ĕn-stow-fĕn.
Hohenzollern . . . . . hō′-ĕn-tsŏl-ĕrn.
Hohenzollern-Sigmaringen hō′-ĕn-tsŏl-lĕrn
               zēg′-mä-rĭng″-ĕn.
Hokkaido . . . . . . hŏk′-kī′-dō′.
Hokusai . . . . . . ho′-kōō′-sä′=ē′.
Holbein . . . . . . hōl′-bīn, hŏl′-bīn.
Holberg . . . . . . hŏl′-bĕrċh.
Holborn . . . . . . hō′-bŭrn.
Holger Danske . . . . hōl′-gĕr däns′-kĕ.
Holguin . . . . . . hŏl-gēn′, ŏl-gēn′.
Holinshed . . . . . . hŏl′-ĭnz-hĕd.
Holmes . . . . hōmz
Holmès (Augusta) . . ōl-mĕs′.
Holofernes . . . . . hŏl-ō-fēr′-nēz.
Holstein . . . . . . hōl′-stīn.

Holyhead	hŏl-ĭ-hĕd′, hŏl′-ĭ-hĕd.
Holyoke	hōl′-yōk.
Holyrood	hŏl′-ĭ-rōōd, hōl′-ĭ-rōōd.
Hombourg, or	ōm-bōōrg′.
Homburg	hŏm-bōōrċh.
Homer	hō′-mĕr.
Homeric	hō-mĕr′-ĭk.
Homildon Hill	hŏm′-l-dŏn hĭl.
Hondekoeter	hŏn′-dĕ-kōō″-tĕr.
Honduras	hŏn-dōō′-ràs.
Hong-Kong	hŏng′-kŏng′.
Honiton	hŭn′-ĭ-tŭn.
Honolulu	hō-nō-lōō′-lōō.
Honoré	ō-nō-rā′.
Hooge	D. hô′-ghĕ. Fr. ŏzh.
Hooghly, see Hugli . .	hōōg′-lē.
Hoogvliet	hōċh′-vlēt.
Hoopstad	hōp′-stăt.
Hoorn (Count), see Horn	hōrn.
Hoozier	hōō′-zhĕr.
Horace	hŏr′-às.
Horæ	hō′-rē.
Horatii	hō-rā′-shĭ-ī.
Horatio	hō-rā′-shĭ-ō.
Horatius Cocles	hō-rā′-shĭ-ŭs kō′-klēz.
Horn (Count), see Hoorn	hōrn.
Horsa	hôr′-sà.
Hortense	ôr-täṅs′.
Hortensio	hôr-tĕn′-shĭ-ō.
Hortensius	hôr-tĕn′-shĭ-ŭs.
Hortus Inclusus	hôr′-tŭs ĭn-klū′-sŭs.
Hosea, see Hoshea . .	hō-zē′-à.
Hoshangabad, see Hu-	
shangabad	hō-shŭng′-ä-bäd.
Hoshea, see Hosea . .	hō-shē′-à.
Hôtel de Cluny	ō-tĕl′ dŭ klü-nē′.
Hôtel de Rambouillet . .	ō-tĕl′ dŭ räṅ-bōō-ē̇=ā′.

Hôtel des Invalides . . .	ō-tĕl′ dā zăn̈-vä-lēd′.
Hôtel de Ville	ō-tĕl′ dŭ vēl.
Hôtel Dieu	ō-tĕl′ dē-ē′.
Hötzendorf	hētz′-ĕn-dŏrf.
Houdin	ōō-dăn̈′.
Houdon	ōō-dôn̈′.
Houssain, see Hussain, and Hussein	'hōō′-sīn, 'hōō-sīn′, 'hōō′-sän.
Houssaye, Arsène . . .	är-sĕn′ ōō-sä′.
Houston (Tex.)	hūs′-tŏn.
Houyhnhnms . . .	hōō′-ĭn-ĭn-mz.
Hsüan-tung	shü′-än-tōōng′.
Hubert de Burgh . . .	hū′-bērt dŭ bērg, bōōrg.
Hudibras	hū′-dĭ-brăs.
Hué, or	hōō-ā′, hwā.
Hué-fu	hōō-ā′-fōō′.
Huerta, Victoriano . . .	vĭk-tō-rē-ä′-nō wĕr′-tȧ.
Hugh Capet	hū kā′-pĕt. Fr. üg kä-pä′.
Hugli, see Hooghly . .	hōōg′-lē.
Hugo, Victor	hū′-gō. Fr. ü-gō′.
Huguenots	hū′-gĕ-nŏts.
Huguenots, Les	lä üg=ŭ-nō′.
Huis ten Bosch	hois tĕn bŏsċh′.
Humacao	ōō-mä-kä′-ō.
Humboldt	hŭm′-bōlt. Ger. hōŏm′-bōlt.
Humperdinck	hoom′-pĕr-dĭnk.
Humphrey	hŭm′-frĭ.
Huneker	hŭn′-ĕ-kēr.
Hungarian	hŭng-gȧ′-rĭ-ȧn.
Hungary	hŭng′-gā-rĭ.
Hunyady János	hōōn′-yä-dē yä′-nōsh.
Hus, see Huss	hŭs. Ger. hōŏs.
Hushangabad, see Hoshangabad	hŭsh-ŭng′-ä-bäd.
Huss, see Hus	hŭs. Ger. hōŏs.

Hussain, see Houssain, or
Hussein . . . . . . 'hōō'-sīn, 'hōō-sīn',
'hōō'-sän.

Hussan . . . . . . 'hōō'-sän.

Huygens, or Huyghens . hī'-gĕnz. *D.* hoi'-chĕns.

Huysmans . . . . . *D.* hois'-mäns.
Fr. wēs-män.

Huysmans, J. K. . . . wēs-mäns'.

Huysum, Jan van . . . yăn văn hoi'-sŭm.

Hwang-ho, see Hoang-ho hwăn'-hō.

Hyacinthe, Père . . . . pâr ē-ä-sănt'.

Hyacinthus . . . . . hī-à-sĭn'-thŭs.

Hyades . . . . . . hī'-ā-dēz.

Hybla . . . . hī'-blä.

Hyblæan (-blean) . . . hī-blē'-àn.

Hyderabad, see Haidara-
bad . . . . hī''-dĕr-à-bäd'.

Hyder Ali, see Haidar Ali . hī'-dĕr ä'-lē.

Hydra . . . . hī'-drà.

Hyères . . . . ē-âr'.

Hygeia . . . . hī-jē'-à.

Hyksos . . . . hĭk'-sŏs, hĭk'-sōz.

Hymen . . . . hī -mĕn.

Hymettos (-tus) . . . . hī-mĕt'-ŭs.

Hypatia . . . . . . hī-pā'-shĭ=à.

Hyperboreans . . . . hī-pĕr-bō'-rē-ànz.

Hypereides, Hyperides . hī-pĕr-ī'-dēz.

Hyperion . . . . . . hī-pē'-rĭ-ŏn, hī-pĕr-ī'-ŏn.

Hyppolite . . . . . . ē-pō-lēt'.

Hyrcanian . . . . . . hĕr-kā'-nĭ-àn.

Hyrcanus . . . . . . hĕr-kā'-nŭs.

I

Iachimo	yăk'-ĭm-ō, ĭ-ăk'-ĭ-mō.
Iago	ē=ä'-gō.
Ian	ī'-ȧn *or* ē'-ȧn.
Iapetus	ī-ăp'-ē-tŭs.
Ibañez, Vicente Blasco	vē-thĕn'-tĕ bläs'-kō ē-bän'-yĕth.
Ibea	ī-bē'-ȧ.
Iberia	ī-hē'-rĭ-ȧ.
Ibiza, see Iviça . . .	ē'-bē-thä.
Iblis, see Eblis . . .	ĭb'-lĭs.
Ibo, see Igbo	ē'-bō. *Port.* ē'-boō.
Ibrahim Pasha . . .	ĭb-rä-hēm' păsh-ô', pȧ-shä', päsh'-ȧ.
Ibsen	ĭb'-sĕn.
Icarian	ī-kā'-rĭ-ȧn.
Icarus	ĭk'-ȧ-rŭs, ĭk'-ā-rŭs.
Ichabod	ĭk'-ȧ-bŏd.
Ichang	ē-chäng'.
Icolmkill	ī-kōm-kĭl'.
Ictinus	ĭk-tī'-nŭs.
Ides	īdz.
Iditarod	ī-dĭt'-ȧ-rŏd.
Idumæa, Idumea . . .	ī-dū-mē'-ȧ, ĭd-ū-mē'-ȧ.
Idumæan, Idumean . .	ī-dū-mē'-ȧn.
Idzo	ēd'-zō.
If, Château d'	shä-tō' dēf'.
Ifugao	ēf-oō-gä'=o.
Igbo, see Ibo	ēg'-bō.
Igdrasil, see Yggdrasil	ĭg'-drȧ-sĭl.
Igerna, or	ĭ-gēr'-nȧ.
Igerne, see Yguerne . .	ĭ-gērn'.
I Gioelli della Madonna	ē jō-yāl'-lē dĕl'-lä mä-dŏn'-nä.
Ignatieff	ĭg-nät'-yĕf.
Ignatius	ĭg-nā'-shĭ=ŭs.

Igorrote . . . . . . ē-gōr-rō'-tā.
Ik Marvel . . . . . . ĭk mär'-vĕl.
Il Barbiere di Seviglia . ĕl bär-bē-ä'-rā dē sä-vēl'-yä.
Ile-de-France . . . . ēl-dŭ-fräns'.
Ile de la Tortue . . . . ēl dŭ lä tôr-tü'.
Il Flauto Magico . . . ēl flä'=ōō-tō mä'-jē-kō.
Illinois . . . . ĭl-ĭ-noi', ĭl-ĭ-noĭz'.
Illuminati . . . . . . ēl-lōō-mē-nä'-tē.
Illusions Perdues, Les . lā zē-lü-zē=ôṅ' pâr-dü'.
Ilocos . . . . ē-lō'-kōs.
Iloilo . . . . ĭ'-lō-ĭ'-lō. Sp. ē-lō-ē'-lō.
Ilori, or Ilorin . . . . ē-lō'-rē, ē-lō'-rēn.
Il Penseroso . . . . . ĭl pĕn-sĕ-rō'-sō.
Il Pensiero . . . . . ēl pān-sē=ä'-rō.
Il Segreto di Susanna . . ēl sā-grä'-tō dē sōō-zän'-nä.
Imber . . . . ăṅ-bâr'.
Imbert de Saint-Amand . ăṅ-bâr' dŭ săṅ-tä-män'.
Immelmann . . . . . ĭm'-ĕl-män.
Imogen. . . . . . . ĭm'-ō-jĕn.
Imola . . . . ē'-mō-lä.
Imus . . . . ē'-mōōs.
Inca . . . . ĭng'-kä.
Indy, d' . . . . . . däṅ-dē'.
Indore . . . . ĭn'-dōr.
Indre-et-Loire . . . . ăṅdr-ä-lwär'.
Ines . . . . ē-nĕs'.
Inez . . . . ĭ'-nĕz. Port. ē-nĕs'.
Iñez . . . . Sp. ēn'-yeth.
Infanta . . . . ĭn-făn'-tȧ. Sp. ĭn-fän'-tä.
Infante . . . . ĭn-făn'-tĕ.   Sp. ĭn-fän'-tä.
Inferno . . . . ĭn-fĕr'-nō. It. ēn-fĕr'-nō.
Ingelow, Jean . . . . jēn ĭn'-jĕ-lō.
Ingres . . . . ăṅg'-r.
Inigo . . . . ĭn'-ĭ-gō.
Injalbert . . . . . . ăṅ-zhäl-bĕr'.
Inkerman . . . . . . ĭnk'-ĕr-mȧn.
                       Russ. ĭngk-ĕr-män'.

In Montibus Sanctis . . ĭn mŏn'-tĭ-bŭs sănk'-tĭs.
Innsbruck, or Innspruck . ĭns'-brŏŏk, ĭns'-prŏŏk.
Intelligentsia . . . . . ĭn-tĕl-ĭ-gĕnt'-sĭ-à.
Interlachen, or . . . . ĭn'-tĕr-läċh-ĕn.
Interlaken . . . . . ĭn'-tĕr-lä-kĕn.
Intombi . . . . . . ĭn-tŏm'-bĭ.
Invalides, Hôtel des . . ō-tĕl' dä-zăṅ-văl-ĕd'.
Inverness . . . . . . ĭn-vēr-nĕs'.
Io . . . . ī'-ō.
Iolanthe . . . . . . ī-ō-lăn'-thē.
Ion . . . . ī'-ŏn.
Iona . . . . ī-ō'-nä.
Ionia . . . . ī-ō'-nĭ=à.
Ionian . . . . ī-ō'-nĭ=àn.
Ionic . . . . ī-ŏn'-ĭk.
Iowa . . . . ī'-ō-wä.
I Pagliacci . . . . . ē päl-yä'-chē.
Iphigeneia, or Iphigenia . ĭf"-ĭ-jē-nī'-à.
Iphigenie auf Tauris . . ĭf-ē'-gä'-nē-ŭ owf tow'-rĭs.
Iphigénie en Aulide . . ĭf-ē-zhä-nē' ôn=nō-lēd'.
Ippolitoff-Ivanoff . . . ĭp-ō-lē'-tŏf-ē-vä'-nŏf.
Ipswich . . . . ĭps'-wĭch.
I Puritani . . . . . . ē pōō-rē-tä'-nē.
Iquique . . . . ē-kē'-kä.
Iran . . . . ē-rän'.
Iras . . . . ī'-ràs.
Irawadi, see Irrawaddy . ĭr-à-wăd'-ĭ.
Irenæus . . . . . . ī-rē-nē'-ŭs.
Irene . . . . ī-rē'-nē. pop. ī-rēn'.
Irène . . . . Fr. ē-rĕ'n'.
Iriarte, see Yriarte . . . ē-rē-är'-tä.
Irigoyen . . . . . . ē-rē-gō'-yĕn.
Iris . . . . ī'-rĭs.
Irkutsk, Irkootsk, Irkoutsk ĭr-kōōtsk'.
Iroquois . . . . . ĭr-ō-kwoī'. Fr. ĭr-o-kwä'.
Irrawaddy, see Irawadi . ĭr-à-wăd'-ĭ.
Isaacs, Jorge . . . . ċhōr'-ċhä ē-zäk'.

Isabela . . . . ēs-ä-bā'-lä.
Isabey . . . . ēz-ä-bā'.
Isaiah . . . . ī-zā'-yä, ī-zä'=ī-à.
Isandlana, or Isandula . ē-sänd-lä'-nä, ē-sän-dōō'-lä
Isar (R.) . . . . . . ē'-zär.
Ischia . . . . ēs'-kē-ä.
Ischl. . . . . ēshl.
Isengrim . . . . . . ĭs'-ĕn-grĭm.
Iser . . . . ē'-zēr.
Iseult, see Isolde, Yseult . ī-sōōlt', ē-sēlt'.
Isfahan, see Ispahan . . ĭs-fä-hän'.
Isham . . . . ī'-shăm.
Ishbosheth . . . . . ĭsh-bō'-shĕth.
Ishii . . . . ēsh'-ē-ē.
Ishmael . . . . . . ĭsh'-mā-ĕl.
Ishmaelite . . . . . ĭsh'-mā-ĕl-īt".
Isis . . . . ī'-sĭs.
Isla, see Islay . . . . *Sp.* ēs'-lä. *Sc.* ī'-lä.
Isla de Pinos . . . . . ēs'-lä dā pē'-nōs.
Islam . . . . ĭs'-lăm.
Islamic . . . . ĭs-lăm'-ĭk.
Islamite . . . . . . ĭs' lám-īt.
Islas Filipinas . . . . ēs'-läs fē-lē-pē'-näs.
Islay, see Isla . . . . ī'-lā.
Islington . . . . . . ĭs'-lĭng-tŭn.
Islip . . . . ĭs'-lĭp.
Ismail Pasha . . . . . ĭs-mä-ēl' păsh-ô', pà-shä',
          päsh'-ä.
Ismailia . . . . . . ĭs-mā'-lĭ=à.
          Turk. ĭs-mä-ē'-lē-ä.
Isocrates . . . . . . ī-sŏk'-rà-tēz.
Isola Bella . . . . . ē'-zō-lä bĕl'-lä.
Isolde, see Iseult, Yseult . ī-sōld'. *Ger.* ē-zōl'-dŭ.
Isonzo . . . . ē-zōn'-dzō.
Isoude, see Ysoude . . ē-sōōd'.
Ispahan, see Isfahan . . ĭs-pà-hän'.
Israel . . . . ĭs'-rā-ĕl.

Israelitic . . . . . . ĭz″rā-ĕl-ĭt′-ĭk.
Israelitish . . . . . . ĭz″-rā-ĕl-īt′-ĭsh.
Israels, Josef . . . . . yō′-sĕf ĭz′-rä-ĕls.
         D. ēz-rä-āls′.
Israfil, Israfel, Israfeel . ĭz-rä-fēl′, ĭs′-rä-fēl,
         ĭz′-rä-fēl.
Issachar . . . . . . ĭs′-à-kär.
Istamboul, or Istambul . ēs-täm-bōōl′.
Isthmian . . . . . . ĭs′-mĭ-àn.
Istria . . . . . . ĭs′-trĭ-à.
Italia Irredenta . . . . ē-tä′-lē-ä ēr-rä-dän′-tä.
Italian . . . . ĭ-tăl′-yàn.
Italianate . . . . . . ĭ-tăl′-yăn-āt.
Italiens, Boulevard des . bōōl-vär′ dä zē-tăl-yĕṅ′
Ithaca . . . . ĭth′-à-kà.
Ithuriel . . . . ĭ-thōō′-rĭ-ĕl.
Ito . . . . ē′-tō.
Ituræa . . . . ĭ-tū-rē′-ä.
Iturbide . . . . . . ē-tōōr-bē′-dä.
Iulus . . . . ī-ū′-lŭs.
Ivan . . . . ī-văn. *Russ.* ē-vän′.
Ivanhoe . . . . . . ī′-văn-hō.
Ivan Ivanovitch . . . . ē-vän′ ē-vän′-ō-vĭch.
Iviça, or Iviza, see Ibiza . ē′-bē-thä.
Ivry-la-Bataille . . . . ēv-rē′-lä-bä-tä′=yŭ.
Ivry-sur-Seine . . . . ēv-rē′-sür-sĕn′.
Ixion . . . . ĭks-ī′-ŏn.
Ixtaccihuatl, see Iztacci-
 huatl . . . . ēs-täk-sē′-hwätl.
Ixtlilxochitl . . . . . ĭst-tlĭl-shō′-chĭtl.
Iyar . . . . ē′-är.
Izdubar . . . . . . ĭz-dōō-bär′.
Iztaccihuatl, see Ixtacci-
 huatl . . . . ēs-täk-sē′-hwätl.

J

Jabalpur, see Jubbulpore . jŭb-ăl-po͞or'.
Jablonica . . . . . . yä-blō-nē'-kä.
Jablunka (Pass) . . . yäb-lo͞on'-kä.
Jacmel . . . . zhäk-mĕl'.
Jacob . . . . jā'-kŏb. *Ger.* yä'-kōp.
Jacobean, Jacobian . . jăk-ō-bē'-àn, jà-kō'-bē-àn.
Jacobi . . . . jă-kō'-bĭ. *Ger.* yä-kō'-bē.
Jacobins . . . . . . jăk'-ō-bĭnz.
Jacobites . . . . . . jăk'-ō-bīts.
Jacòbo . . . . 'hä-kō'-bō.
Jacobsdal . . . . . yä'-kŏps-dăl.
Jacopo . . . . yä'-kō-pō.
Jacquard . . . . . . jäk'-ärd. *Fr.* zhä-kär'.
Jacqueline . . . . . zhäk-lēn'.
Jacquerie . . . . . . zhäk-rē', zhäk=ēr-ē'.
Jacques . . . . . . zhäk.
Jael . . . . jā'-ĕl.
Jaëll . . . . yä'-ĕl.
Jaen . . . . 'hä-ĕn'.
Jaffa, see Yafa, Japho, Heb. jäf'-fä, yäf'-fä.
Jagellons . . . . . . yä-gĕl'-ŏnz.
Jagow . . . . yä'-gŏf.
Jagua . . . . 'hä'-gwä.
Jah . . . . yä.
Jahveh . . . . yä'-vā, yä'-vĕ.
Jaime (Don.) . . . . . 'hä'-ē-mä.
Jain . . . . jīn.
Jaipur, see Jeypore . . jī-po͞or'.
Jairus . . . . jī'-rus *in New Testament.*
jā'-ĭr-ŭs *in Apocrypha.*
Jakobäa . . . . . . yä-kō-bā'-ä.
Jakutsk, see Yakutsk . . yä-ko͞otsk'.
Jalabert . . . . . . zhä-lä-bâr'.
Jalalabad, see Jalalabad . jăl-à-lä-bäd'.
Jalandhar, see Jullunder . jŭl'-àn-dhär.

Jalapa, see Xalaps . . . 'hä-lä'-pä.
Jalisco, see Xalisco . . . 'hä-lēs'-kō.
Jamaica . . . . . . jà-mā'-kà.
Jamblichus . . . . . jăm'-blĭk-ŭs.
Jameson . . . . . . jā'-mĕ-sŭn.
Jammersberg . . . yăm'-ĕrs-bĕrċh.
Jammes, François . . . frän-swä' zhăm.
Jamont . . . . zhä-môṅ'.
Jan . . . . D. yăn.
Janauschek . . . . yä'-now-shĕk.
Jane Eyre . . . . . . jān âr.
Janet, Paul . . . . . pōl zhä-nā'.
Janiculum . . . . . . jăn-ĭk'-yū-lŭm.
Janin, Jules . . . . . zhül zhä-năṅ'.
Janina, see Yanina . . . yä'-nē-nä.
Jansen . . . . jăn'-sĕn. D. yän'-sĕn.
Jansenist . . . . . . jăn'-sĕn-ĭst.
Jansenius . . . . . . jăn-sē'-nĭ=ŭs.
January . . . . . . jăn'-ū-ā-rĭ.
Janus . . . . jā'-nŭs.
Japanese . . . . . . jăp-ăn-ēz' or -ēs'.
Japapa . . . . hä-pä'-pä.
Japheth, or Japhet . . . jā'-fĕth, jā'-fĕt.
Japho, Heb., see Jaffa, Yafa jä'-fō.
Jaquenetta . . . . . jăk-ĕ-nĕt'-tä.
Jaques . . . . jāks, jäks. Shakespeare,
                              jā'-kwēz.
Jardar . . . . yär-där'.
Jardin des Plantes . . . zhär-dăṅ' dā pläṅt.
Jardine . . . . jär-dēn'.
Jardines . . . . . . Sp. 'här-dē'-nĕs.
Jardinière, La Belle . . lä bĕl zhär-dēn-ē=âr'.
Jardinillos . . . . . . 'här-dē-nēl'-yōs.
Jared . . . . jā'-rĕd.
Jarnac . . . . zhär-näk'.
Jarndyce . . . . . . järn'-dĭs.
Jaroslaff, see Yaroslaff . yä-rō-släf'.

Jaruco . . . . 'hä-rōō'-kō.
Jasher . . . . jā'-shẽr.
Jason . . . . jā'-sŭn.
Jaudenes . . . . . . 'hä=ōō-dä'-nĕs.
Jauja, see Xauxa . . . 'how'-ċhä.
Jaunpur, see Jounpoor . jown-pōōr'.
Jaurès . . . . zhŏ-rĕz'.
Java . . . . jä'-vä.
Javan . . . . adj. jä'-vȧn. *Bib.* jā'-vȧn.
Javert . . . . zhȧ-vâr'.
Jean de Meun . . . . zhŏṅ dŭ mŭṅ'.
Jean Jacques Rousseau . zhŏṅ zhäk rōō-sō'.
Jeanne d'Albret . . . . zhän däl-brā'.
Jeanne d'Arc, or Darc . . zhän därk'.
Jean Paul . . . . . . zhŏṅ pōl.
Jebusite . . . . jĕb'-ū-zīt.
Jedburgh . . . . . . jĕd'-bŭr-ŭ.
Jeddo, see Yeddo . . . yĕd'-dō.
Jehoahaz . . . . . . jē-hō'-ȧ-hăz.
Jehoiachin . . . . . . jē-hoi'-ȧ-kĭn.
Jehoiada . . . . . . jē-hoi'-ȧ-dä.
Jehoiakim . . . . . . jē-hoi'-ȧ-kĭm.
Jehoram, see Joram . . jĕ-hō'-rȧm.
Jehoshaphat . . . . . jē-hŏsh'-ȧ-făt.
Jeisk, see Yeisk . . . . yā'-ĭsk.
Jekyll . . . . jē'-kĭl.
Jelalabad, see Jalalabad . jĕl″-ȧ-lä-bäd'.
Jellicoe . . . . jĕl'-ĭ-kō.
Jellyby . . . . jĕl'-ĭ-bĭ.
Jemappes, see Jemmapes. zhĕ-mäp'.
Jemima . . . . jē-mī'-mȧ. *Bib.* jē-mī'-mȧ,
jĕm'-ĭm-ȧ.
Jemmapes, see Jemappes zhĕ-mäp'.
Jena . . . . jĕn'-ȧ. *Ger.* yā'-nä.
Jenghiz Khan, see Genghis
Khan, or Jinghis Khan . jĕn'-gĭs khän.
Jenner . . . . jĕn'-ẽr.

Jephthah . . . . . . jĕf'-thä.
Jeremiah . . . . . . jĕr-ĕ-mī'-à.
Jeremy . . . . jĕr'-ĕ-mĭ
Jeres, see Xeres, or . . ʽhā'-rĕs.
Jerex de la Frontera, see
  Xerez de la Frontera . ʽhā-rĕth' dā lä frŏn-tā'-rä.
Jerome . . . . jĕ-rōm', jĕr'-ōm.
Jérôme Bonaparte . . . zhā-rŏm' bō-nä-pärt'.
Jerona, see Gerona, Xerona ʽhā-rō'-nä.
Jerrold . . . . jĕr'-ŏld.
Jerusalem . . . . . . jĕ-rōō'-sà-lĕm.
Jessica . . . . jĕs'-ĭ-kà.
Jesso, see Yesso . . . yĕs'-sō.
Jessor, or Jessore . . . jĕs-sōr'.
Jesu . . . . jē'-zōō, yä -sōō.
Jesuit . . . . jĕs'-yū-ĭt.
Jesus . . . . jē'-zŭs. *Sp.* ʽhā-sōōs.
Jethro . . . . jĕth'-rō, jē'-thro.
Jeunesse Dorée . . . . zhē-nĕs' dō-rä'.
Jevons . . . . jĕv'-ŏnz.
Jeypore, see Jaipur . . jī-pōr'.
Jezebel . . . . jĕz'-ĕ-bĕl.
Jezreel . . . . jĕz'-rē-ĕl.
Jhansi . . . . jän'-sē.
Jiguani . . . . ʽhē-gwä'-nē.
Jimena, see Ximena . . ʽhē-mĕn'-ä.
Jimenez, see Ximenez . ʽhē-mĕn'-ĕth.
Jinghis Khan, see Jenghiz
  Khan, Genghis Khan . jĭn'-gĭs khän.
Jitomir, see Zhitomir . . zhĭt-ōm'-ēr.
Joachim . . . . . . jō'-à-kĭm.
                Ger. yō'-äċh'-ĭm.
Joan of Arc . . . . . jōn, *or* jō-ăn', *or* jō'-àn ŏv
                ärk.
João . . . . *Port.* zhō-owṅ'.
Joaquin . . . . . . ʽhō=ä-kēn'.
Jodhpur . . . . . . jŏd-pōōr'.

Joffre . . . . zhŏfr.
Johann . . . . yō'-hän.
Johannes . . . . . jō-hăn'-ēz.
      Ger. yō-hän'-nĕs.
Johannisberg . . . . jō-hăn'-nĭs-bĕrg.
      D. yō-hăn'-nĭs-bĕrċh.
John o' Groat's . . . . jŏn ō grôts.
Joinville . . . . . . zhwăṅ-vēl'.
Jókai . . . . yō'-kä=ĭ.
Joló, see Sooloo . . . . 'hō-lō'.
Jomelli, see Jommelli . . yō-mĕl'-lē.
Jomini . . . . zhō-mē-nē'.
Jommelli, see Jomelli . . yŏm-mĕl'-lē.
Jonescu, Take . . . . tä'-kē yō-nĕs'-kŭ.
Jongleur . . . . . . zhôṅ-glĕr'.
Joram, see Jehoram . . jō'-rȧm.
Jordaens . . . . . . yŏr'-däns.
Jordanes, or . . . . . jôr-dā'-nēz.
Jordanis, see Jornandes . jôr-dā'-nĭs.
Jorge . . . . *Sp.* 'hōr'-ċhä.
Jorilla . . . . 'hō-rēl'-yä.
Jornandes, see Jordanes . jôr-năn'-dēz.
Jorullo, see Xorullo . . 'hō-rōōl'-yō.
José . . . . *Sp.* 'hō-sä'. *Port.* zhō-zhä'.
Joseffy . . . . . . yō-sĕf'-ĭ.
Josephus . . . . . jō-sē'-fŭs.
Josiah . . . . . . jō-sī'-ä.
Josquin Desprez . . . zhŏs-kăṅ' dā-prä'.
Jost . . . . yōst.
Jotham . . . . . . jō'-thȧm.
Jötunheim . . . . . yē'-tōōn-hīm.
Jouaust . . . . . . zhōō-ō'.
Joubert, Fr. . . . . . zhōō-bâr'.
Joubert, D. . . . . . yow'-bĕrt.
Joule . . . . jowl.
Jounpoor, see Jaunpur . jown-pōōr'.
Jourdain . . . . . . zhōōr-dăṅ'.

Jourdan . . . . zhōōr-däṅ'.
Journal des Débats . . zhōōr-năl' dä dä-bä'.
Jouvenet, Jean . . . . zhäṅ zhōōv-nä'.
Jouy . . . . zhōō-ē'.
Jowett . . . . jow'-ĕt.
Joyeuse Garde, La . . . lä zhwä-yēz' gärd.
Juan . . . . 'hōō=än'.
Juana, see Juanna . . . 'hōō-ä'-nä.
Juan Diaz . . . . . . 'hōō-än' dē'-äth.
Juan Fernandez . . . . jōō'-ȧn fēr-nän'-dēz.
                        Sp. 'hōō-än'
                        fĕr-nän'-dĕth.
Juanna, see Juana . . . 'hōō-än'-nä.
Juarez . . . . 'hōō-ä'-rĕth.
Juba . . . . jōō'-bä.
Jubbulpore, see Jubalpur. jŭb-bŭl-pōr'.
Jubilate . . . . . . jū-bĭl-ä'-tē, jū-bĭl-ä'-tē.
Júcar, see Xúcar . . . 'hōō'-kär.
Júcaro . . . . 'hōō'-kä-rō.
Judaic . . . . jū-dä'-ĭk.
Judas Maccabeus . . . jōō'-dȧs măk-ȧ-bē'-ŭs.
Judic . . . . zhü-dēk'.
Juggernaut . . . . . jŭg'-ēr-nȯt.
Jugurtha . . . . . . jōō-gēr'-thä.
Juif Errant, Le . . . . lē zhü=ēf' "r-räṅ'.
Juillard . . . . . . zhwē-yär'.
Jules . . . . zhül.
Jülich, see Juliers . . yü'-lĭċh.
Julie . . . . Fr. zhü-lē'.
Julien . . . . Fr. zhü-lē=ĕn'.
Juliers, see Jülich . . . Fr. zhü-lē=ä'.
Juliet . . . . jū'-lĭ=ĕt.
Julliot . . . . zhü-lĭ-ō'.
Jullunder, see Jalandhar . jŭl'-lŭn-dēr.
Jumel . . . . zhū-mĕl'.
Jumièges . . . . . . zhü-mē=ĕzh'.
Juneau . . . . jū-nō'.

Jungfrau . . . . . . yŏong'-frow.
Juniata (R.) . . . . . jōō-nĭ-ăt'-ä.
Junkers . . . . . . yŏong'-kĕrz.
Junot . . . . zhü-nō'.
Junta . . . . jŭn'-tä.
Jupiter . . . . jōō'-pĭ-tĕr.
Jura (I. and Mts.) . . . jōō'-rä.
Jura . . . . Fr. zhü-rä'.
Jurassic . . . . . . jū-răs'-ĭk.
Jurgensen. . . . . . yōōr'-gĕn-sĕn.
Jusserand . . . . . . zhüs-räṅ'.
Jussieu, de . . . . . dŭ jŭs-sū'.
                        Fr. dŭ zhü-sē=ē'.
Justine . . . . jŭs-tēn'.   Fr. zhüs-tēn'.
Justinian . . . . . . jŭs-tĭn-ĭ-àn.
Jutes . . . . jōōts.
Juvenal . . . . . . jōō'-vĕ-nàl.

K

Kaaba, see Caaba . . . kä'-bä, kā'-à-bà.
Kaaterskill . . . . . kä'-tĕrs-kĭl.
Kabail, see Kabyle . . kà-bīl'.
Kabbala, see Cabala . . kăb'-à-lä.
Kabul, see Cabul . . . kä-bōōl'.
Kabyle, see Kabail . . . kà-bīl'.
Kadapa, see Cuddapah . kŭd'-ä-pä.
Kadesh Barnea . . . . kā'-dĕsh bär'-nē-ä.
Kaffa . . . . käf'-fä.
Kaffir, see Kafir, Caffre,
    Kaffre . . . . . . käf'-ĕr.
Kaffraria . . . . . . kăf-frâr'-ĭ-à.
Kaffre, see Kafir, Caffre . kăf'-ĕr.
Kafir, see Kaffir, Caffre,
    Kaffre . . . . . . kăf'-ĕr.
Kaifeng, or . . . . . kī-fĕng'.
Kai-fung . . . . . . kī-fŭng'.

Kaiser . . . . kī'-zĕr.
Kaiser Friedrich . . . kī'-zĕr frēd'-rĭch.
Kaiserin . . . . . . kī'-zĕr-ĭn.
Kaiserin Augusta . . . kī'-zĕr-ĭn ow-gŏ͞os'-tä.
Kaiser Wilhelm . . . . kī'-zĕr vĭl'-hĕlm.
Kalakaua . . . . . . kăl-à-kow'-ä.
Kalevala, or Kalewala . . kä-lĕ-vä'-lä.
Kalid Bahr . . . . . kä'-lēd bär.
Kalidasa . . . . . . kä-lĭ-dä'-sà.
Kalmar, see Calmar . . käl'-mär.
Kálnoky . . . . . . käl'-nŏ-kĭ.
Kaluga . . . . kä-lō͞o'-gä.
Kamchatka, see Kamt-
chatka . . . . . . käm-chät'-kä.
Kamehameha . . . . kä-mä"-hä-mä'-hä.
Kamerun, see Cameroon. kä-mĕ-rō͞on'.
Kamimura . . . . . kä'-mē'-mō͞o'-rä'.
Kamtchatka, Fr., see Kam-
chatka . . . . . . käm-chät'-kä.
Kanakas . . . . . . kă-năk'-àz.
Kanaris, see Canaris . . kä-nä'-rĭs.
Kanawha . . . . . . kà-nô'-wà.
Kanazawa . . . . . . kä-nä-zä'-wä.
Kanchanjanga, see Kun-
chainjunga, Kinchinjinga kän-chän-jäng'-gä.
Kandahar, Candahar, or . kän-dä-här', kăn-dà-här'.
Kandehar . . . . . . kän-dĕ-här', kăn-dĕ-här'.
Kang-Kao, see Cancao . käng-kow'.
Kang-Wu-Wei . . . . käng'-wō͞o-wä'.
Kano Masanobu . . . kä'-nō' mä'-sä'-nō'-bŭ'.
Kansas . . . . kăn'-zàs.
Kan-su . . . . kän-sō͞o'.
Kant . . . . känt.
Kantian . . . . . . kăn'-tĭ-àn.
Kanuck, see Canuck . . kă-nŭk'.
Kara Bagh, or Karabagh,
see Carabagh . . . . kä-rä-bäg'.

Kara-Hissar . . . . . kä"-rä-hĭs-sär'.

Kara Mustapah, see Cara
   Mustafa . . . . . kä'-rä mōŏs'-tä-fä, kä'-rä'
                mōŏs'-tä-fä.

Karénina, Anna . . . . än'-nä kä-rä'-nē-nä.

Karnak . . . . kär'-năk.

Karlovingian, see Carlo-
   vingian . . . . . . kär-lo-vĭn'-jĭ-an.

Karlowitz, see Carlowitz . kär'-lō-vĭts.

Karlsbad, see Carlsbad . kärlz'-bät.

Karlsruhe, see Carlsruhe . kärlz'-rōō-ū.

Kartoum, Kartum, see
   Khartoum . . . . . kär-tōōm', ċhär-tōōm'.

Karwina . . . . . . kär-vē'-nä.

Kasan, see Kazan . . . kä-zän'.

Kashgar . . . . . . kăsh'-gär. *Turk.* käsh-gär'.

Kashmere, Kashmir, see
   Cashmere . . . . . kăsh-mēr'.

Kassai, (R.) . . . . . kä-sī'.

Katahdin, see Ktaadn . . ká-tä'-dĭn.

Katak, see Cattack, Cuttack ká-täk'.

Kathiawar, see Kattywar kät"-ē-ä-wär'.

Kathlamba, see Quath-
   lamba . . . . . . kät-läm'-bä.

Katrine, Loch . . . . lŏċh kăt'-rĭn.

Kattegat, see Cattegat . kăt'ĕ-găt.

Kattywar, see Kathiawar . kät-ē-wär'.

Kauai (I.) . . . . . . kow-ī'.

Kauffman . . . . . . kowf'-män.

Kaulbach . . . . . . kowl'-bäċh.

Kaun . . . . kown.

Kaunitz . . . . . . kow'-nĭts.

Kavanagh . . . . . . kăv'-ă-nä.

Kay . . . . kā. *Ger.* kī.

Kayor, see Cayor . . . kī-ōr'.

Kazak . . . . kä-zäk'.

Kazan, see Kasan . . . kä-zän'.

Keang-Se, see Kiang-si . kē=äng'-sē'.
Keang-Soo, see Kiang-su . kē-äng'-sōō'.
Kearney . . . . . . kär'-nĭ.
Kearsarge . . . . . kēr'-särj.
Keble . . . . kē'-bl.
Kedleston . . . . . . kĕd'-l-stŭn, kĕl'-sŭn.
Kedron, see Cedron, Kid-
 ron . . . . kĕ'-drŏn.
Kehama . . . . . . kē-hä'-mä.
Kei (R.) . . . . . . kā.
Keighley, or Keithley . . kēth'-lĭ.
Kekrops, see Cecrops . . kē'-krŏps.
Kelat, see Khelat . . . kĕ-lät'.
Kelts, see Celts . . . . kĕlts.
Kempis, (Thomas) à . . ä kĕm'-pĭs.
Kenai . . . . kē'-ni.
Kenelm Chillingly . . kĕn'-ĕlm chĭl -ĭng-lĭ.
Kenilworth . . . . . kĕn'-l-wĕrth.
Kennebec . . . . . . kĕn-ē-bĕk'.
Kensington . . . . . kĕn'-zĭng-tŭn.
Keokuk . . . . . . kē'-ō-kŭk.
Kerensky . . . . . . kēr-ĕn'-skĭ.
Kerguelen . . . . . kēr'-gĕl-ĕn. *Fr.*
 kĕr-gä-lôn'.
Kerman, see Kirman . . kēr-män'.
Kéroualle, see Quérouaille kä-rōō-äl'.
Keshab Chandra Sen . . kĕ-shŭb' chăn'-drà sän.
Kesho . . . . kĕsh'-ō.
Keswick . . . . . . kĕz'-ĭk.
Ketshwayo, see Cettiwayo kāch-wä'-yō.
Khafra . . . . khăf'-rä.
Khalif, see Calif, Caliph kä-lēf', kā'-lĭf.
Khalifa, or . . . . . kä-lē'-fä.
Khaliff . . . . kä-lēf'.
Khan . . . . kôn, kän, kăn.
Khandesh, see Candeish . khän-dĕsh'.
Khania, see Canea . . . kä-nē'-ä.

Khartoum, or Khartum,
  see Kartoum . . . . kär-tōōm', char-tōōm'.
Khedive . . . . . . kä-dēv', kē'-dĭv, kĕ-dēv',
  kä-dē'-vä.
Khelat, see Kelat . . . kĕ-lät'.
Kherson . . . . . . ċhĕr-sōn'.
Khiva . . . . kē'-vä, chē'-vä.
Khorasan, or Khorassan . ċhō-rä-sän'.
Khorsabad . . . . . khōr-sä-bäd'.
Khosru, or . . . . . kŏs-rōō'.
Khusrau . . . . . . khŭs-row'.
Khyber . . . . ċhĭ'-bĕr.
Kiang-si, see Keang-Se . kē-äng'-sē'.
Kiang-su, see Keang-Soo. kē-äng'-sōō'.
Kiao-chau . . . . . . kĭ-ä'=ō-chow'.
Kichinef, Kichenev, see
  Kishineff . . . . . kĭsh-ĭ-nĕf'.
Kidron, see Cedron . . kĭd'-rŏn.
Kieff, see Kiev . . . . kē'-ĕf, kē-ĕf'.
Kiel . . . . kēl.
Kiev, or Kiew, see Kieff . kē'-ĕv, kē-ĕf'.
Kilauea . . . . . . kē-low-ä'-ä.
Kilimane, see Quilimane . kē-lē-mä'-nä.
Kimry, Kymry, see Cymry kĭm'-rĭ.
Kincardine . . . . . kĭn-kär'-dĭn.
Kinchinjinga, see Kanchan-
  janga, Kunchain-Junga kĭn-chĭn-jĭng'-gä.
King-te-chen . . . . . kĭng-tĕ-chĕn'.
Kioto, see Kyoto . . . kē-ō'-tō.
Kirchhoff . . . . . . kērċh'-hŏf.
Kirchner . . . . . . kērċh'-nĕr.
Kirghiz . . . . kĭr-gēz'.
Kirkcaldy . . . . . . kĕr-kô'-dĭ.
Kirkcudbright . . . . kĕr-kōō'-brĭ.
Kirman, see Kerman . kēr-män'.
Kishineff, Kichenev, Kis-
  chenew, see Kichinef . kēsh-ē-nĕf'.

Kishlangov, or	kēsh-län-gŏv'.
Kishlanou	kēsh-lä-nō'.
Kiskelim	kĭs-kē'-lĭm.
Kissingen	kĭs'-sĭng-ĕn.
Kittim, see Chittim . .	kĭt'-ĭm.
Kiung-chau	kē-ōōng'-chow.
Kiusiu	kyōō'-syōō'.
Kiyomine	kē'-yō'-mē'-nā'.
Kiyonaga	kē'-yo'-nä'-gä'.
Kizil-Irmak (R.) . . .	kĭz'-ĭl ĭr-mäk'.
Klamath	klä'-măt.
Klaus	klows.
Kléber	klē'-bĕr, klä'-bâr.
	Fr. klä-bâr'.
Klephts	klĕfts.
Klindworth	klĭnt'-vŏrt.
Kluck, von	fŏn klŏŏk.
Knaus	k=nows'.
Knecht Ruprecht . . .	k=nĕcht rōō'-prĕcht.
Kneisel	k=nī'-zĕl.
Kneller	nĕl'-ēr.
Knollys	nōlz.
Knut, see Canute . . .	k=nōōt. Dan. künt.
Kobe	kō'-bĕ.
Koch	kŏċh.
Kochanowski	kō-chän-ŏf'-skĭ.
Kochian	kōċh'-ē-än.
Koedoesberg, see Koo-	
doesberg	kōō-dōōs'-bĕrch.
Koedoes Rand, see Koo-	
doos Rand	kōō-dōōs' rănt.
Koerner, see Körner . .	kēr'-nĕr.
Koffyfontein . . .	kŏf"-fī-fŏn'-tīn.
Koh-i-nur, Kohinoor . .	kō-ē-nōōr'.
Köhler	kē'-lĕr.
Koimbatur, see Coimbatore	kō-ĭm"-bȧ-tōōr'.
Kokstadt	kŏk'-stăt.

Kolapoor, Kolapur, Kol-
  hapur, see Colapur . . kō-lä-pōōr'.
Kolchak . . . . . . kōl-chäk'.
Kolmar, see Colmar . . kōl-mär'.
Köln . . . . kēln.
Kolokol . . . . . . kŏl-ō-kŏl'.
Komorn . . . . . . kō'-mŏrn.
Koniah, or . . . . . kō'-nē-ä.
Konieh . . . . kō'-nē-ĕ.
König . . . . kē'-nĭćh.
Königgrätz . . . . . kē'-nēg-grâtz.
Königin . . . . . . kē'-nē-gĭn. [kē'-nĭćhs-bĕrch
Königsberg . . . . . kēn'-ĭgz-bērg. *Ger.*
Koodoesberg, see Koe-
  doesberg . . . . . kōō-dōōs'-bĕrch.
Koodoes Rand, see Koe-
  does Rand . . . . . kōō-dōōs' rănt.
Koordistan, see Kurdistan kōōr-dĭs-tän'.
Koords, see Kurds . . kōōrdz.
Kooril, see Kurile . . . kōō'-rĭl.
Koran . . . . kō'-răn, kō-rän'.
Kordofan . . . . . . kŏr-dō-fän'.
Korea, see Corea . . . kō-rē'-ä.
Korean, see Corean . . kō-rē'-ȧn.
Körner, see Koerner . . kēr'-nĕr.
Korn Spruit . . . . . kŏrn sproit.
Korniloff . . . . . . kôr-nē'-lŏf.
Korolenko . . . . . . kō-rō-lĕn'-kō.
Korsakoff . . . . . . kōr-sä'-kŏf.
Kosciusko, or . . . . kŏs-sĭ-ŭs'-kō.
Kosciuszko . . . . . kōsh-chōō'-skō. [kŏsh'-ōōt.
Kossuth . . . . . . kŏs-sōōth'. *Hung.*
Kotzebue (von) . . . . kŏt'-sĕ-bōō, kŏt'-sē-bōō.
Koutouzof, see Kutusoff . kōō-tōō'-zŏf.
Kouyunjik . . . . . . kōō'-ŭn-jĭk.
Kraaft, or Krafft, or Kraft kräft.
Krag-Jörgensen . . , . . kräg'-yēr'-gĕn-sĕn.

Kragujevatz . . . . . krä'-gwē-yā-väts.
Krakau, or . . . . . krä'-kō, krä'-kow, *or*
Krakow, see Cracow . . *Pol.* krä'-kŏf.
Kramskoy . . . . . . kräm-skō'-ē.
Kranach, see Cranach . . krăn'-àk. *Ger.* krä'-näċh.
Krapf . . . . kräpf.
Krapotkin . . . . . . krä-pŏt'-kĭn.
Krasnik . . . . . . kräs'-nēk.
Krasnoi, or . . . . . kräs-noi'.
Krasnyi Jar . . . . kräs-noi' yär.
Kraszewki . . . . . . krä-shĕf'-skĭ.
Krause . . . . krow'-zŭ.
Kreisler . . . . . krīs'-lĕr.
Kremlin . . . . . . krĕm'-lĭn.
Kreutzer, Kreuzer . . . kroit'-zĕr.
Kriemhild, see Chriemhild krēm'-hĭlt.
Kronos, see Cronus . . krŏn'-ŏs. [krōn'-stät.
Kronstadt, see Cronstadt. krŏn'-stăt. *Russ.*
Kroonstad . . . . . krōn'-stăt.
Kruger . . . . krü'-gĕr.
Krugersdorp . . . . . krü'-gĕrs-dŏrp.
Krupp . . . . krŏŏp.
Ktaadn, see Katahdin . . k=tä'-dn.
Kuanza, see Coanza,
Quanza . . . . . . kwän'-zä.
Kubelik . . . . . . kōō'-bā-lēk.
Kubla Khan, or . . . . kōōb'-lä khän.
Kublai Khan . . . . . kōōb'-lī khän.
Ku-Klux-Klan . . . . kū'-klŭks-klăn.
Kuku-Khoto . . . . . kōō'-kōō-kō'-tō.
Kuli Khan . . . . . . kōō'-lē khän.
Kulmbach, see Culmbach kŏŏlm'-bäċh.
Kumassi, see Coomassie . kōō-mäs'-sē.
Kunchain-Junga, or . . kŭn-chīn-jŭng'-gà.
Kunchin-Ginga, or . . . kōōn-chĭn-jĭng'-gà.
Kunchin-Junga, see Kan-
chanjanga . . . . . kōōn-chĭn-jŭng'-gà.

Kunersdorf . . . . . kōō'-nĕrs-dŏrf.
Kunisada . . . . . . kōō'-nē'-säd'-t͡hä'.
Kuniyoshi . . . . . . kōō'-nē'-yō'-shē'.
Kurdistan, see Koordistan kōōr-dĭs-tän'.
Kurds, see Koords . . . kōōrdz.
Kurfürst . . . . . . kōōr'-fürst.
Kurile, see Kooril . . . kōō'-rĭl.
Kuroki . . . . kōō'-rō'-kē'.
Kuropatkin . . . . . kōō-rō-pät'-kēn.
Kursk . . . . kōōrsk.
Kurukshetra . . . . . kōō-rōōk-shä'-trȧ.
Kurwenal . . . . . . kōōr'-vä-näl.
Küstrin, see Cüstrin . . küs-trēn'.
Kutais . . . . kōō-tīs'.
Kut-el-Amara . . . . kōōt-ĕl-ä-mä'-rä.
Kutusoff, or Kutuzoff, see
　Koutouzof . . . . . kōō-tōō'-zŏf.
Kuychau, see Kweichow . kwī-chow'.
Kuyp, see Cuyp . . . . koip.
Kwangsi, see Quangsi . . kwäng-sē'.
Kwang Su . . . . . . kwäng-sōō'.
Kwangtung, see Quang-
　tong . . . . kwäng-tōōng'.
Kweichow, see Kuy-chau kwī-chow'.
Kwhichpak . . . . . kwĭk-päk'.
Kymry, see Cymry . . . kĭm'-rĭ.
Kyoto, see Kioto . . . kē-ō'-tō.
Kyrie eleïson . . . . . kĭr'-ĭ-ĕ ĕ-lā'-ĭ-sŏn.

L

La Antigua . . . . . lä än-tē'-gwä.
Labanoff de Rostoff . . lä-bä'-nŏf dŭ rŏs'-tŏf.
La Bassée . . . . . . lä băs-sā'.
Labienus . . . . . . lä-bĭ-ē'-nŭs.
Lablache, Luigi . . . . lōō-ē'-jē lä-bläsh'.
La Bohème . . . . . lä bō-ĕm'.

Labori, Maître . . . . mātr lä-bō-rē'.
Labouchere . . . . . lä-bōō-shâr'.
Laboulaye . . . . . . lä-bōō-lä'.
Labrador . . . . . . lăb-rȧ-dôr'.
La Bruyère . . . . . lä brü-yâr'.
Labuan . . . . lä-bōō-än'.
La Cabaña . . . . . lä-kä-bän'-yä.
La Caille, or Lacaille . . lä kä'-yŭ.
La Caimanera . . . . lä kä"=ē-mä-nä'-rä.
Laccadive, see Lakkadiv . lăk'-ȧ-dīv.
Lacedæmon . . . . . lăs-ē-dē'-mŏn.
Lacépède . . . . . . lä-sä-pĕd'.
Lachaise, or La Chaise . lä shĕz'.
Lachesis . . . . . . lăk'-ē-sĭs.
Lachine . . . . . . lä-shēn'.
Lachme, see Lakme . . lăk'-mē.
La Cieca . . . . . . lä chē-ä'-kä.
Laconia . . . . . . lā-kō'-nĭ-ȧ.
Lacroix . . . . lä-krwä'.
Ladikieh, see Latakia . . lä-dē-kē'-ĕ.
Ladislaus . . . . . . lăd'-ĭs-lôs.
Ladoga . . . . lä'-dō-gä.
Ladrone (Is.) . . . . . lä-drōn'.
Ladrones . . . . . . lä-drōnz'. *Sp.* lä-drō'-nĕs.
Ladybrand . . . . . lā'-dĭ-brănd.
Laeken . . . . lä'-kĕn.
Laennec . . . . . . lĕn-nĕk'.
Laertes . . . . lā-ēr'-tēz.
La Estrella . . . . . lä ĕs-träl'-yä.
La Farge . . . . . . lä färj. *Fr.* färzh.
La Favorita . . . . . lä fä-vō-rē'-tä.
Lafayette, De . . . . dŭ lä-fā-ĕt'.
La Fère . . . . lä fâr.
La Ferrière . . . . . lä fĕr-rē=âr'.
Lafeu . . . . lä-fē'.
Laffitte . . . . lä-fēt'.   [dŭ lä fŏṅ-tĕn'.
La Fontaine, de . . . . dŭ lä fŏn'-tän. *Fr.*

La Forêt Bleu . . . . lä fō-rĕ' blē.
La Fourche . . . . . lä foōrsh'.
L'Africaine . . . . . lä-frē-kĕn'.
Lagado . . . . lä-gā'-dō.
La Gazza Ladra . . . lä gät'-zä lä'-drä.
Lagerlöf . . . . . . lä'-gĕr-lēv.
La Gioconda . . . . . lä jō-kŏn'-dä.
La Gloire . . . . . . lä glwär'.
Lagos . . . . *Af.* lä'-gŏs. *Port.* lä'-goōs.
Lagrange, de . . . . . dŭ lä gränzh'.
La Granja . . . . . . lä grän'-ċhä.
Lagthing . . . . . . läg'-tĭng.
La Guaira, or La Guayra . lä gwī' -rä *or* gī'-rä.
                        Sp. lä gwä'=ē=rä.
Laguna de Bay . . . . lä-goō'-nä dä bä'=ē.
La Habanera . . . . . lä ä-bä-nä'-rȧ.
La Haye, see The Hague lä ā'.
Lahor, or Lahore . . . lä-hōr'.
Laibach, see Laybach . . lī'-bäċh.
L'Aiglon . . . . . . lä-glôṅ'.
Laing's Nek . . . . . lāngz nĕk.
Lajeunesse . . . . . lä-zhēn-ĕs'.
La Jolla . . . . . . lä hō'-yȧ.
La Juive . . . . . . lä zhwēv.
Lakhimpur, see Luckimpur lŭk-ĭm-poōr'.
Lakhnau, see Lucknow . lŭk'-now. *pop.* lŭk'-nō.
Lakkadiv, see Laccadive . lăk'-ȧ-dīv.
Lakme, see Lachmi . . lăk'-mē.
Lakshmi, or Lakchmi . . lăksh'-mē.
Lalage . . . . läl'-ā-jē.
La Liberté . . . . . lä lē-bĕr-tā'.
Lalitpur, see Lullitpur . . lŭl-lĭt-poōr'
Lalla Rookh . . . . . lä'-lä-roōk.
L'Allegro . . . . . . lä-lā'-grō.
Lamartine . . . . . . lä-mär-tēn'.
Lamballe, Princesse du . prăṅ-sĕs' dŭ läṅ-bäl'.
Lambert, Louis . . . . loō-ē' läṅ-bâr'.

Lamech	lā'-mĕk.
Lamennais	lä-mĕ=nâ'.
Lamia	lā'-mĭ-à.
La Miranao	lä mē-rä-nä'-ō.
Lammermoor, or . . .	lăm-mēr-mōōr'.
Lammermuir	lăm-mēr-mūr'.
L'Amore di tre Re . . .	lä-mō'-rä dē-trä rä.
Lamoricière	lä-mō-rē-sē=âr'.
La Motte-Fouqué . . .	lä mŏt'-fōō-kā'.
Lamoureux	lä-mōō-rē'.
Lanark	lăn'-ärk.
La Navidad	lä nä-vē-däd'.
Lancaster	lăng'-kăs-tēr.
Lancelot du Lac . . .	lăn'-sē-lŏt dū lăk.
Lan-chau	län-chow'.
Lanciani	län-chä'-nē.
Lancret	län-krĕ'.
Landes (The)	länd.
Landgraf	länt'-gräf.
Landgravine	länt'-grä-vēn.
Landsthing	läns'-tĭng.
Landtag	länt'-täċh.
Landwehr	länt'-vâr.
Lanfranc	lăn'-frăngk. Fr. län-fräṅ'.
Lange	läng'-ŭ.
Langres	längr.
Languedoc, or Langue d'Oc	lăng'-gwē-dŏk.
	Fr. läṅ=gŭ-dŏk'.
Langue d'Oil	läṅ dō=ēl'.
Lanier	lă-nēr'.
Lanjuinais	läṅ-zhwē-nä'.
Lannes	lăn. Fr. län.
La Noue	lä nōō'.
Lanson, Gustave . . .	güs-tăv' läṅ-sôṅ'.
Laocoön	lā-ŏk'-ō-ŏn.
Laodameia, or Laodamia .	lā''-ŏd-ā-mī'-à.
Laodicea	lā''-ŏd-ĭs-ē'-à.

Laomedon . . . . . . lā-ŏm'-ē-dŏn.
Laon . . . . lŏṅ.
Laos . . . . lä'-ōs.
Lao-tsze . . . . . . lä'-ō-tsĕ'.
La Paloma . . . . . lä pä-lō'-må.
La Patrie . . . . . . lä pä-trē'.
La Paz . . . . lä päz. *Sp.* lä päth.
Lapham . . . . . . lăp'-åm.
Lapithæ . . . . . . lăp'-ĭ-thē.
La Place, de . . . . . dŭ lä plăs.
La Plata . . . . . . lä plä'-tä.
La Princesse Lointaine . lä prăṅ-sĕs' lwăṅ-tĕn'.
Laputa . . . . lå-pū'-tå.
Lara . . . . lä'-rä.
La Rábida . . . . . lä rä'-bē-dä.
Laramie . . . . . . lăr'-å-mĭ.
La Reine de Saba . . . lä rĕn dē sä-bä'.
Lares . . . . lā'-rēz.
Largellière . . . . . lär-zhĕl-yâr'.
Larisa, or Larissa . . . lä-rēs'-å.
L'Arlésienne . . . . . lär-lä-zē=ĕn'.
La Rochefoucault . . . lä rōsh-fōō-kō'.
La Rochejacquelein . . lä rōsh-zhäk-lăṅ'.
La Rochelle . . . . . lä rō-shĕl'.
Larrey . . . . lä-rä'.
Larroumet . . . . . . lär-rōō-mä'.
La Saisiaz . . . . . . lä så-zē-äss'.
La Salle . . . . . . lä săl. *Fr.* lä säl.
La Scala . . . . . . lä skä'-lä.
Lascaris . . . . . . läs'-kä-rĭs.
Las Casas, de . . . . dā läs kä'-säs.
Las Cases, de . . . . *Fr.* dŭ läs käz.
Las Guasimas . . . . läs gwä-sē'-mäs.
La Socapa . . . . . lä sō-kä'-pä.
La Sorbonne . . . . . lä sōr-bŏn'.
Laspiñas . . . . . . läs-pēn'-yäs.
Lassalle . . . . . . lä-säl'.

Lassen	läs'-sĕn.
Lassigny	lăs-ēn-yē'.
Latakia, or Latakiyah, see	
Ladikieh	lä-tä-kē'-à.
Lateran	lăt'-ēr-ăn.
Latium	lā'-shŭm.
Latour d'Auvergne . . .	lä-tōōr' dō-vârn'=yŭ.
La Trappe	lä träp.
Latreille	lä-trā'=yŭ.
Laud	lôd.
Laudon, see Loudon . .	low'-dŏn.
Lauenburg	low'-ĕn-bōōrċh.
Launfal	lôn'-fàl.
Laura	lô'-rà. It. lä'=ōō-rä.
Laurent	lō-rôṅ'.
Laurier	lō'-rē=ā.
Lausanne	lō-zän'.
La Vallière	lä väl-lē=âr'.
Lavater	lä'-vä-tĕr. Ger. lä-fä'-tĕr.
	Fr. lä-vä-târ'.
Lavedan	lä=vŭ-däṅ'.
Laveleye	läv-lā'.
La Vendée	lä vôṅ-dā'.
Lavengro	lăv-en'-grō.
Lavigerie	lä-vēzh-rē'.
Lavoisier	lä-vwä-zē=ā'.
Laweman, or	lô'-mǎn.
Layamon	lä'-yà-mŏn.
Layard	lā'-àrd.
Laybach, see Laibach . .	lī'-bäċh.
Leah	lē'-ä.
Leamington Spa	lĕm'-ĭng-tŏn spä.
Leander	lē-ăn'-dēr
Léandre	lā-äṅdr'.
Le Cateau	lē kă-tō'.
Lebbaeus, or Lebbeus . .	lĕl-bē'-ŭs.
Leboeuf	lē-bēf'.

Lebrun, see Vigée-Lebrun lĕ-brŭṅ'.
Lecce . . . . lĕch'-ĕ.
Leclerc, or Le Clerc . . lĕ-klâr'.
Leconte de Lisle . . . lĕ-kôṅt' dŭ lēl'.
Lecouvreur, Adrienne . . ä-drē-ĕn' lĕ-kōōv-rēr'.
Le Creusot . . . . . lĕ krē-so'.
Leda . . . . lē'-dȧ.
Lederer . . . . . . lā'-dĕr-ĕr.
Ledru-Rollin . . . . . lĕ-drü'-rōl-lăṅ'.
Leeds . . . . lēdz.
Leeuwarden . . . . . lā'-vär-dĕn.
Leeuwenhoek, see Leuwen-
  hoek . . . . lā'-vĕn-hōōk.
Leeward . . . . . . lē'-wȧrd, lē'-ärd, lū'-ärd.
Lefebre, or Lefèvre . . lĕ-fĕvr'.
Legaré (H. S.) . . . lŭ-grē'.
Legaspi, or . . . . . lā-gäs'-pē.
Legazpe . . . . . . lā-gäth'-pā.
Legendre . . . . . . lĕ-zhŏṅdr'.
Leghorn . . . . . . lĕg'-hôrn, lĕg-ôrn'.
Legnago . . . . . . län-yä'-gō.
Legouvé . . . . . . lĕ-gōō-vā'.
Le Grand Monarque . . lĕ gräṅ mō-närk'.
Lehar . . . . lĕ-är'.
Lehman, Lisa . . . lē'-zȧ lā'-män.
Leibl . . . . lībl.
Leibnitz, or Leibniz . . līb'-nĭtz.
Leicester . . . . . . lĕs'-tĕr.
Leiden, see Leyden . . lī'-dĕn.
Leigh . . . . lē.
Leighton . . . . . . lā'-tŭn.
Leila . . . . lē'-lȧ.
Leilah . . . . lā-lä'.
Leinster . . . . . . lēn'-stĕr, lĭn'-stĕr.
Leipsic, or . . . . . . līp'-sĭk.
Leipzig . . . . līp'-tsĭch.
Leith . . . . lēth.

Le Jongleur de Notre Dame	lĕ zhŏṅ-glēr' dē Nōtr dăm.
Le Journal des Débats .	lĕ zhōōr-näl' dā dā-bä'.
Lely (Sir Peter)	lē'-lĭ.
Lemaître	lĕ-mĕtr'.
Léman	lā-män'.
Le Mans	lĕ män.
Lemberg	lĕm'-bĕrch.
Lemercier	lĕ-mâr-sē=ā'.
Lemerre	lĕ-mĕr.'
Lemonnier, Camille . .	kä-mēl'lĕ-mŏn-ē=ā'.
Le Moyne	lĕ moin'. *Fr.* lĕ mwăn'.
Lemprière	lĕm-prēr', lĕm'-prē-ēr.
	Fr. lŏṅ-prē-âr'.
Lena (R.)	lyĕ'-nȧ.
Lenape	lĕn'-ȧ-pē.
Lenbach	lĕn'-bäch.
Lenclos, Ninon de, or L'Enclos	nē-nôṅ' dŭ lŏṅ-klō.'
L'Enfant Prodigue . . .	lôṅ-fäṅ' prō-dēg'.
Lenglen, Suzanne . . .	sü-zăṅ' lôṅ-glôṅ'.
Lenin	lĕ-nēn'.
Lenni-Lenape	lĕn'-nĭ-lĕn'-ȧ-pē.
Lenore	lĕ-nōr'.
Lenôtre	lĕ-nŏtr'.
Lens	läṅ.
Leo	lē'-ō. *It.* lā'-ō.
Leofric	lĕ-ŏf'-rĭk.
Leofwine	lĕ-ŏf'-wĭn-ĕ.
Leominster	lĕm'-ĭn-stēr.
Leon	lē'-ōn. *Sp.* lā-ōn'.
Léon	*Fr.* lā-ôṅ'.
Leonardo da Vinci . . .	lä-ō-när'-dō dä vēn'-chē.
Leonato	lē-ō-nä'-tō.
Leoncavallo, Ruggiero .	roŏdzh'-ā-rō lä"-ōn-kä-väl'-lō.
Leonidas	lē-ŏn'-ĭ-dăs.

Leonora . . . . . . *It.* lā-ō-nō'-rä.
Léonore . . . . . . lā-ō-nōr'.
Leontes . . . . . . lē-ŏn'-tēz.
Leopardi . . . . . . lā-ō-pär'-dē.
Lepage, Bastien . . . bäs-tē-ĕṅ'-lē-păzh'.
Lepando . . . . . . lā-pän'-dō.
Lepanto . . . . . . lĕ-păn'-tō, lā-pän'-tō.
Le Prophète . . . . . lē prō-fĕt'.
Le Nozze di Figaro . . lā nŏts-sä. dē fē'-gä-rō.
Lérida . . . . lĕr'-ē-dä.
Lérins, Îles de . . . . ēl dē lā-răn'.
Lermontoff, Lermontov . lĕr'-mŏn-tŏf.
Leroux . . . . lē-rōō'.
Leroy-Beaulieu . . . . lē-rwä'-bō-lē=ē'.
Le Sage, or Lesage . . lē săzh'.
Leschetizki . . . . . lĕsh-ĕ-tĭts'-kĭ.
Les Contes d'Hoffman . lā-kōṅt dŏf-män'.
Lesdiguières . . , . . lā-dē-gē=âr'.
Les Huguenots . . . . lā üg-nō'.
Les Italiens . . . . . lā zē-tä-lē=ĕṅ'.
Lespinasse, de, see Espi-
nasse . . . . . . dŭ lā-pē-näs'.
Les Rougon-Macquart . lā rōō-gôṅ'-mäk-är'.
Lesseps, de . . . . . dŭ lĕs'-ĕps.
                 Fr. dŭ lē-sĕps'.
Lessing . . . . lĕs'-sĭng.
Le Sueur, or Lesueur . . lē-sü-ēr'.
Leszczynski, Stanislaus . stăn'-ĭs-läs lĕsh-chĭn'-skē.
Le Temps . . . . . . lē tôṅ.
Lethe . . . . lē'-thē.
Lethean . . . . . . lē-thē'-ȧn.
Letitia . . . . lē-tĭsh'-ȧ.
L'Étoile . . . . . . lā-twäl'.
Leucophryne . . . . . lū-kō-frī'-nē.
Leucothea . . . . . . lū-kō'-thē-ä.
Leuctra . . . . lūk'-trä.
Leuk . . . . loik.

Leuthen . . . . . . loi′-tĕn.
Leutze . . . . loit′-zŭ.
Leuwenhoek, see Leeu-
  wenhoek . . . . . lē′-vĕn-hōōk.
Lévan . . . . lä-väṅ′.
Levant . . . . lĕ-vänt′, lē-vănt′.
Levantine . . . . . . lĕ-văn′-tĭn.
Leven, Loch . . . . . lŏch lēvn.
Lever, Chas. . . . . . lē′-vēr.
Leverrier, or Le Verrier . lŭ-vĕr′-ĭ-ēr. *Fr.* lē-vĕ-rē=ā′.
Leveson-Gower . . . . lū′-sŭn-gōr′.
Levitan . . . . lä-vē′-tän.
Levite . . . . lē′-vīt.
Levitic . . . . lē-vĭt′-ĭk.
Leviticus . . . . . . lĕ-vĭt′-ĭ-kŭs.
Lévy (Émile) . . . . . lä-vē′.
Lewes . . . . lū′-ĕs.
Leyden, see Leiden . . lī′-dĕn.
Leyds . . . . līts.
Leyra (Antonio), de . . dā lā′=ē-rä.
Leys . . . . līs, lā.
Leyte . . . . lā′-tā. *Sp.* lā′-ē-tā.
L'hermitte . . . . . lĕr-mēt′.
L'Hôpital, or L'Hospital . lō-pē-tăl′.
Liadow . . . . lē-ä′-dŏf.
Liaotung, Liantung . . lē=ow-tŏṅ′.
Liapounoff (-ov) . . . lē-ä-pōō′-nŏf.
Libanius . . . . . . lĭ-bā′-nĭ=ŭs.
Libanus . . . . . . lĭb′-ā-nŭs.
Libau . . . . lē′-bow.
Liber . . . . lī′-bēr.
Liberi . . . . lē′-bā-rē.
Liberia . . . . lĭ-bē′-rī-à.
Libra . . . . lī′-brä.
Libya . . . . lĭb′-ĭ-à.
Lichas . . . . lī′-kås.
Lichnowsky . . . . . lĭċh-nŏv′-skĭ.

Lichtenstein	lĭċh′-tĕn-stīn.
Licinian	lĭ-sĭn′-ĭ-àn.
Liddell	lĭd′-ĕl.
Lie (Jonas)	lē.
Lieber	lē′-bĕr.
Liebig	lē′-bĭċh.
Lieder ohne Worte . .	lē′-dĕr ō′-nŭ vŏr′-tŭ.
Liège	*Fr.* lē-ĕzh′.
Liegnitz	lēg′-nĭtz. *Ger.* lēċh′-nĭtz.
Ligea, or Ligeia	lĭ-jē′-ä.
Ligne, de	dŭ lēn′=yŭ.
Ligny	lēn′-yĭ. *Fr.* lēn-yē′.
Ligonier	lĭg-ō-nēr′.
Liguori	lē-gwō′-rē.
Li Hung Chang	lē hōōng chông.
Lilis	lĭ′-lĭs.
Lilith	lĭ′-lĭth, lĭl′-ĭth.
Liliuokalani	lē″-lē-wō-kä-lä′-nē.
Lille	lēl.
Lillibullero	lĭl″-lĭ-bŏŏl-lâ′-rō.
Lima	lĭ′-mȧ. *Sp.* lē′-mä.
Limerick	lĭm′-ĕ-rĭk.
Limoges, see Lymoges .	lē-mŏzh′.
Limousin	lē-mōō-zȧṅ′.
Limpopo	lĭm-pō′-pō.
Linares	lē-nä′-rĕs.
Lincoln	lĭng′-kŭn.
Lingayen	lēn-gä-yĕn′.
Linlithgow	lĭn-lĭth′-gō.
Linnankoski	lĭn-än-kŏs′-kĭ.
Linnæan, see Linnean .	lĭn-nē′-àn.
Linnæus	lĭn-nē′-ŭs.
Linnean, see Linnæan .	lĭn-nē′-àn.
Linz	lĭnts.
Liotard	lē=ō-tär′.
Lipari	lĭp′-ä-rē.
Lippe	lĭp′-pŭ.

Lippi, Lippo	lēp'-pō lēp'-pē.
Lisboa, or	*Port. and Sp.* lēs-bō'-ä.
Lisbon	lĭz'-bŏn.
Lisieux	lē-zē=ē'.
Lisle, Leconte de . . .	lē-kōṅt' dĕ lēl'.
L'Isle, Rouget de . . .	rōō-zhä' dĕ lēl'.
Liszt	lĭst.
Littorale	lēt-tō-rä'-lä.
Littré	lē-trä'.
Litvinof	lĭt-vē'-nŏf.
Liu Kiu, see Loo Choo,	
Lieou Khieou, and . .	lē-ōō' kē-ōō'.
Liu Tchou	lē-ōō' chōō.
Liutprand, see Luitprand .	lĭ-ōōt'-prănd.
Livenza	lē-vän'-dzä.
Livonia	lĭ-vō'-nĭ=à.
Livorna, see Leghorn . .	lē-vōr'-nō.
Li Yuan-Lung	lē-yōō-än-hôṅ'.
Llanberis	ċhlăn-bĕr'-ĭs.
Llandaff	ċhlăn-dăf'.
Llangollen	ċhlăn-gŏċh'-lĕn.
Llanos	*Sp.* l-yä'-nōs.
Llewelyn ap Gruffydd, or	
Llywelyn ap Gruffydd .	ċhlōō-ĕl'-ĭn ăp grü'-fĕth.
Loanda	lō-än'-dä.
Loanda, São Paulo de . .	säṅ pow'-lōō dĕ lō-än'-dä.
Loango	lō-äng'-gō.
Loangwa	lō-ăng'-wä.
Lobengula	lō-bĕng-gōō'-lä.
Lochaber	lŏċh-ä'-bēr.
Loches	lŏsh.
Lochiel	lŏċh-ēl'.
Lochinvar	lŏċh-ĭn-vär'.
Loch Katrine	lŏċh kăt'-rĭn.
Lochleven	lŏċh-lĕv'-n, lŏċh-lē'-vn.
Loch Lomond	lŏċh lō'-mŭnd.
Lockroy	*Fr.* lōk-rwä'.

Lodi . . . . lō'-dē.
Lodovico . . . . . lō-dō-vē'-kō.
Lódz . . . . lōdz.
Loew . . . . lēv.
Loffoden, or Lofoden, or . lŏf-fō'-dĕn.
Lofoten . . . . . lō-fō'-tĕn.
Loggia dei Lanzi . . . lōj'-jä dä'-ē länd'-zē.
Logroño . . . . . lō-grōn'-yō.
Lohardaga, or . . . lō-här-dä'-gä.
Lohardugga . . . . lō-här-dŭg'-gä.
Lohengrin . . . . . lō'-ĕn-grĭn.
Loire . . . . . . lwär.
Loire, Haute . . . . ōt-lwär'.
Loire-Inférieure . . . lwär'-ăṅ-fä-rē=ēr'.
Loiret . . . . . . lwä-rä'.
Loir-et-Cher . . . . lwär'-ā-shâr'.
Lokal-Anzeiger . . . lō-käl'-än'-tsī-gĕr.
Loke, or Loki . . . . lō'-kĕ.
Lola Montez . . . . lō'-lä mŏn'-tĕz.
Lombard's Kop . . . lŏm'-bärts kŏp.
Lombardy . . . . . lŏm'-bär-dĭ.
Lombroso . . . . . lōm-brō'-zō.
Lome . . . . lō'-mä.
Lomonosoff . . . . lō-mō-nō'-sŏf.
Lomza . . . . . . lŏm'-zhä.
Longchamp . . . . . lôṅ-shäṅ'.
Longimanus . . . . lŏn-jĭm'-ā-nŭs.
Longinus . . . . . lŏn-jī'-nŭs.
Longjumeau . . . . lôṅ-zhü-mō'.
Longueville, de . . . . dŭ lôṅg-vēl'.
Longwy . . . . . . lŏṅ-vē'.
Loo Choo, Liu Tchou, see
  Liu Kiu, and Lieou
  Khieou . . . . . . loo chōo.   ˟
Loos . . . . lŏ-ŏs'.
Lope de Vega . . . . lō'-pä dä vä'-gä.
Lopez . . . . lō'-pĕth.

Lopez (C. A., Pres. Para-
guay) . . . . . . lō'-pĕth, *locally* lō'-pĕz.
Lorbrulgrud . . . . . lôr-brŭl'-grŭd.
Lorelei, or Loreley, see
Lurlei . . . . . . lō'-rä-lī.
Lorenzetti . . . . . lō-rĕnd-zĕt'-tē.
Lorenzo . . . . . . lō-rĕn'-zō. *It.* lō-rĕnd'-zō.
Sp. lō-rĕn'-thō.
Lorenzo de' Medici . . lō-rĕnd'-zō dä mä'-dē-chē.
Lorenzo Marques, see
Lourenço Marques . . lō-ren'-sō mär'-kĕs.
Port. lō-răṅ'-sōō
mär'-kĕs.
Loreto, or . . . . . . lō-rä'-tō.
Loretto . . . . lō-rĕt'-tō.
Lorraine . . . . . . lŏr-rän'. *Fr.* lō-rĕn'.
Los Angeles . . . . . lōs ăn'-gĕl-ĕs.
Sp. lōs äng'-ċhä-läs.
Lot-et-Garonne . . . . lō-tä-gä-rŏn'.
Lothario . . . . . . lō-thä'-rē-ō.
Lothringen . . . . . lōt'-rĭng-ĕn.
Loti, Pierre . . . . . pē=âr' lō-tē'.
Lotophagi . . . . . . lō-tŏf'-ā-jī.
Lotto, Lorenzo . . . . lō-rĕnd'-zō lŏt'-tō.
Lotze . . . . lŏt'-sŭ.
Loubet . . . . lōō-bä'.
Loucheur . . . . . . lōō-shĕr'.
Loudon, see Laudon . . low'-dŏn.
Loudun . . . . . . lōō-dŭṅ'.
Louis . . . . lōō'-ĭs. *Fr.* lōō-ē'.
Louisiana . . . . . . lōō"-ē-zē-ä'-nä,
lōō"-ē-zē-ăn'-ä.
Louis Lambert . . . . lōō-ē' läṅ-bâr'.
Louis Philippe . . . . lōō-ē' fē-lēp'.
Louis Quatorze . . . . lōō-ē' kă-tôrz'.
Louis Quinze . . . . . lōō-ē' kăṅz.
Louis Seize . . . . . lōō-ē' sĕz.

Louis Treize . . . . . lōō-ē′ trĕz.
Louisville . . . . . . lōō′-ĭ-vĭl, lōō′-ĭs-vĭl.
Lourdes . . . . . . lōōrd.
Lourenço Marques,   see
  Lorenzo Marques . . lō-rĕn′-sō mär′-kĕs.
                    Port. lōō-räṅ′-sōō
                    mär′-kĕs.
Louvain . . . . . . lōō-văṅ′.
Louverture, Toussaint, or
  L'Ouverture . . . . tōō-săṅ′ lōō-vĕr-tür′.
Louvre . . . . lōōvr.
Louÿs, Pierre . . . . pē=âr′ lōō-ēs′.
Lowestoft . . . . . . lō′-stŏft, lō′-ĕ-stŏft.
Loyola . . . . loi-ō′-lä. Sp. lō-yō′-lä.
Lozère . . . . lō-zâr′.
Lo Zingaro . . . . . lō dzēn′-gä-rō.
Lualaba . . . . . . lōō-ä-lä′-bä.
Luapula . . . . . . lōō-ä-pōō′-lä.
Lübeck . . . . lü′-bĕk.
Lübke . . . . lüb′-kŭ.
Lublin . . . . lōō′-blĭn.
Lucan . . . . lū′-kȧn.
Lucania . . . . . . lū-kā′-nĭ=ȧ.
Lucaya . . . . lōō-kī′-ä.
Lucayos . . . . . . lōō-kī′-ōs.
Lucca, Bagni di . . . bän′-yē dē lōōk′-ä.
Lucchese . . . . . . lŭk-ēz′, lŭk-ēs′.
Lucerne, see Luzern . . lū-sērn′. Fr. lü-sârn′
Lucia di Lammermoor . lōō-chē′-ä dē
                    läm-mĕr-mōōr′
Lucian . . . . lū′-shĭ-ăn.
Luciana . . . . . . lōō-shi-ā′-nä.
Lucina . . . . lū-sī′-nä.
Lucinda . . . . . lū-sĭn′-dȧ.
Lucinde . . . . . . lü-săṅd′.
Luckimpur, see Lakhimpur lŭk-ĭm-pōōr′.
Lucknow, see Lakhnau . lŭk′-now. pop. lŭk-nō.

Luçon, see Luzon . . . lōo-zōn′.   *Sp.* lōo-thōn′.
Lucrece . . . . . . lū′-krēs, lū-krēs′.
Lucretius . . . . . . lū-krē′-shĭ-ūs.
Lucrezia Borgia . . . . lōo-krād′-zē-ä bōr′-jä.
Lucullus . . . . . . lū-kŭl′-ŭs.
Ludendorf . . . . . . lōo′-dĕn-dŏrf.
Ludhiana . . . . . . lōo-dē-ä′-nä.
Ludovisi Ares . . . . lōo-dō-vē′-zē ä′-rēz.
Ludwig . . . . . . lōod′-vĭċh.
Lugano . . . . lōo-gä′-nō.
Lugo . . . . lōo′-gō.
Luigi . . . . lōo-ē′-jē.
Luini . . . . lōo-ē′-nē.
Luis . . . . lōo-ēs′.
Luise . . . . *Ger.* lōo′-ē′-zŭ.
Luitpold . . . . . . lōo′-ĭt-pōlt.
Luitprand, see Liutprand . lōo-ĭt′-prănd.
Luiz . . . . *Port.* lōo-ēth′.
Lulli . . . . lŏol′-lē.
Lullitpur, see Lalitpur . . lŭl-lĭt-pōor′.
Lüneburg . . . . . . lü′-nĕ-bōorċh.
Lunéville . . . . . . lü-nä-vēl′.
Lupercal . . . . . . lū′-pêr-kăl, lū-pēr′-kăl.
Lupercalia . . . . . . lū-pêr-kā′-lĭ=à.
Luria . . . . lōo′-rē-ä.
Luristan . . . . . . lōo-rĭs-tän′.
Lurlei, see Lorelei . . . lōor′-lī.
Lusiad . . . . lū′-sĭ-ăd.
Lusignan . . . . . . lü-zēn-yän′.
Lusitania . . . . . . lū-sĭ-tā′-nĭ-à.
Lutetia . . . . lū-tē′-shĭ-à.
Luther . . . . lū′-thêr.   *Ger.* lōo′-tĕr.
Lützen . . . . lüt′-zĕn.
Luxembourg . . . . . lüks-än-bōor′.
Luxemburg . . . . . lŭk′-sĕm-bêrg.
                       D. lük′-sĕm-bŭrċh.
Luxor . . . . lŭks′-ôr, lŏoks′-ôr.

Luynes, de . . . . . dŭ lü=ēn'.
Luzern, see Lucerne . . lōō-tsĕrn'.
Luzon, see Luçon . . . lōō-zōn'. *Sp.* lōō-thōn'.
Lvoff . . . . l-vŏf'.
Lyautey . . . . . . lē-ō-tā'.
Lycaon . . . . lī-kā'-ŏn.
Lycaonia . . . . . . lĭk-ä-ō'-nĭ=à.
Lyceum . . . . . . lī-sē'-ŭm.
Lycidas . . . . lĭs'-ĭ-dàs.
Lydenburg . . . . . lī'dĕn-bŭrċh.
Lyell . . . . lī'-ĕl.
Lyly (John) . . . . . lĭl'-ĭ.
Lymoges, see Limoges . lē-mŏzh'.
Lyonesse . . . . . . lī-ŏn-ĕs'.
Lyonnais . . . . . . lĕ-ŏn-â'.
Lyonnaise . . . . . . lē-ŏn-ĕz'.
Lyons . . . . lī'-ŏnz. *Fr.* lē-ôṅ'.
Lys dans la Vallée, Le . lē lēs däṅ lä väl-ā'.
Lysias . . . . lĭs'-ĭ-ăs.
Lysimachus . . . . . lī-sĭm'-à-kŭs.
Lysippus . . . . . . lī-sĭp'-ŭs.
Lystra . . . . lĭs'-trà.
Lytton . . . . lĭt'-ŭn.

M

Maartens, Maarten . . mär'-tĕn mär'-tĕnz.
Maas, see Meuse . . . mäs.
Maastricht, see Maestricht,
   Mastricht . . . . . mäs'-trĭċht.
Mabillon . . . . . . mä-bē-yôṅ'.
Mabinogion (The) . . . măb-ĭ-nō'-gĭ-ŏn.
Mabuse, see Maubeuge . mä-büz'.
Macao . . . . mä-kä'=ō, mä-kow'.
Macbeth . . . . . . măk-bĕth'.
Maccabaeus . . . . . măk-à-bē'-ŭs.
Maccabean . . . . . măk-à-bē'-àn.

Maccabees . . . . . măk'-à-bēz.
Macchiavelli, see Machia-
velli . . . . măk"-ĭ-à-vĕl'-lĭ.
    It. mä"-kē-ä-vāl'-lē.
Macedonia . . . . . măs-ē-dō'-nĭ-à.
Maceo . . . . mä-thä'-ō.
Macerata . . . . . . mä-chä-rä'-tä.
Machado . . . . . . mä-chäd-ŧhō.
Machiavel . . . . . . măk'-ĭ-à-vĕl".
Machiavelian . . . . măk"-ĭ-à-vēl'-yàn,
    măk"-ĭ-à-vē'-lĭ-àn.
Machiavelism . . . . măk'-ĭ-à-vel-ĭz"-m.
Machiavelli, see Macchia-
velli . . . . măk"-ĭ-à-vĕl'-lĭ.
    It. mä"-kē-ä-vāl'-lē.
Machpelah . . . . . măk-pē'-lä.
Macias . . . . mä-thē'-äs.
MacIvor . . . . . . măk-ē'-vôr.
Mackay (Charles) . . . măk-ī', măk-ā', măk'-ĭ.
Mackaye (Percy) . . . mă-kī'.
Mackensen . . . . . mäk-ĕn'-zĕn.
Maclaren, Ian . . . . ē'-àn, ī'-àn mà-klă'-rĕn,
    măk-lä'-rĕn.
Maclise . . . . . . mà-klēs', măk-lēs'.
MacMahon . . . . . măk-mä'-ŏn.
    Fr. mäk-mä-ôṅ'.
MacMonnies . . . . . măk-mŭn'-ĭz.
Mâcon . . . . *Fr.* mä-kôṅ'.
Macon (Ga.) . . . . . mā'-kŏn.
Macready . . . . . . mà-krē'-dĭ, măk-rē'-dĭ.
Mactan . . . . mäk-tän'.
Madame Bovary . . . mă-dăm' bō-vä-rē'.
Madeira (R.) . . . . mä-dā'=ē-rä.
Madeira (I.) . . . . . mă-dē'-rä.
    Port. mä-dā'=ē-rä.
Madeleine (Church) . . mäd-lĕn'.
Mademoiselle de Maupin. mäd-mwä-zĕl' dŭ mō-păṅ'.

Mademoiselle, La Grande   lä gränd mäd-mwä-zĕl'.
Madonna . . . . . . mă-dŏn'-à. *It.* mä-dōn'-nä.
Madras . . . . . . mă'-drås, măd-răs'.
Madrazo . . . . . . mä-drä'-thō.
Madrid . . . . mà-drĭd'. *Sp.* mä-drēd'.
Madruga . . . . . . mä-drōō'-gä.
Madura . . . . . . mä-dōō'-rä.
Mæcenas . . . . . . mē-sē'-nàs.
Mænad . . . . . . mē'-năd.
Maestricht, see Maas-
  tricht, Mastricht . . . mäs'-trĭċht.
Maeterlinck . . . . . mĕt'-ēr-lĭngk.
              D. mä'-tĕr-lĭngk.
Mafeking . . . . . . mä-fā-kĭng'.
Maffei . . . . . . mäf-fā'-ē.
Maffia, or Mafia . . . mä-fē'-ä.
Magalhães, see Magellan *Port.* mä-gäl-yä'=ĕns
Magaliesberg . . . . măg'-ă-lēs-bĕrċh.
Magallanes, see Magellan mä-gäl-yä'-nĕs.
Magdala . . . . . . (Abyssinia) mäg-dä'-là
             Bib. măg'-dà-lä.
Magdalen . . . . . . măg'-dà-lĕn. *Eng. college,*
             môd'-lĭn.
Magdalene . . . . . măg-dä-lē'-nĕ,măg'-dā-lēn.
Magdeburg . . . . . măg'-dĕ-bŭrg.
             Ger. mäċh'-dā-bōōrċh.
Magellan, see Magalhães,
  Maghellanes . . . . mà-jĕl'-àn.
             Sp. mä-gĕl-yän'.
Magellanic . . . . . măj-ĕl-lăn'-ĭk.
Magendie . . . . . . mà-jĕn'-dĭ.
             Fr. mä-zhŏṅ-dē'.
Magenta . . . . . . mä-jĕn'-tä.
Magersfontein . . . . mä"-ċhĕrs-fŏn'-tīn.
Maggiore . . . . . . mäd-jō'-rĕ.
Maghellanes, see Magel-
  lan . . . . mä-gĕl-lä'-nās.

Magi . . . . mā'-jī.
Magian . . . . . . mā'-jĭ-ản.
Magna Carta, or Magna
    Charta . . . . . . măg'-nä kär'-tä.
                  pop. ċhär'-tả.
Magnard . . . . . . măn-yär'.
Magnusson . . . . . mäg'-nōōs-sŏn.
Maguindanao, see Min-
    danao . . . . . . mä-gēn″-dä-nä'-ō.
Magog . . . . mā'-gŏg.
Magyar . . . . . . mŏd'-yŏr, mă-jär'.
Mahabarata, or Mahabha-
    rata . . . . mä″-hä-bä'-rä-tä.
Mahableshwur . . . . mä″-hä-blĕsh-wŭr'.
Mahalaleel . . . . . mả-hä'-lả-lē″-ĕl,
                  mả-hăl'-ả-lē″-ĕl.
Mahan . . . . mả-hăn'.
Maharajah . . . . . mä-hä-rä'-jä.
Mahdi, see El Mahdi . . mä-dē.
Mahdist . . . . . . mä'-dĭst.
Mahican, see Mohican . mä-hĭk'-ản.
Mahmud . . . . . . mä-mōōd'.
Mahomet, see Mohammed mā-hŏm'-ĕt, mā'-hō-mĕt,
                  mä'-hō-mĕt.
Mahon . . . . mả-hōn'.
Mahony . . . . . . mả-hō'-nĭ, mä'-hŏ-nĭ.
Mahopac . . . . . . mā'-ō-păk.
Mahound . . . . . . mă-hownd', mä'-hownd.
Mahrattas, see Marhattas mă-răt'-äz, mä-rä'-tảz.
Mahu . . . . mä'-hōō, mả-hōō'.
Maia . . . . mā'-yả.
Mailand, *Ger.* for Milan . mī'-länt.
Maillol . . . . mä=ē-yŏl'.
Maimansinh, see My-
    mensing . . . . . mī-män-sĭn'.
Maimonides . . . . . mĭ-mŏn'-ĭ-dēz.
Main (R.) . . . . . . mān. *Ger.* mīn.

Maindron . . . . . . măṅ-drôṅ'.
Maine-et-Loire . . . . mān'-ā-lwär'.
Mainpuri, see Mynpuri . mīn-pōō'-rē.
Maintenon, de . . . . dŭ măṅ=tŭ-nôṅ'.
Mainz, see Mayence . . mīnts.
Maison Vauquer . . . mā-zôṅ' vō-kā'.
Maistre, Xavier de . . zăv'-ĭ-ēr. Fr. zăv-ē-ā'
　　　　　　　　　　　　dŭ mā=tr.
Maisur, see Mysore . . mī-sōōr'.
Maiwand . . . . . . mī-wänd'.
Majano . . . . . . mä-yä'-nō.
Majorca, see Mallorca . mȧ-jôr'-kä.
Majuba . . . . . . mä-jōō'-bä.
Makart . . . . mäk'-ärt, mä-kärt'.
Makua . . . . . . mä-kōō'-ä.
Malabar . . . . . . măl-ȧ-bär'.
Malacca . . . . . . mȧ-lăk'-ä.
Malachi . . . . . . măl'-ȧ-kī.
Malaga . . . . măl'ȧ-gȧ. Sp. mä'-lä-gä.
Malate . . . . mä-lä'-tä.
Malay . . . . mä-lā'.
Malayan . . . . . . mä-lā'-ȧn.
Malaysia . . . . . mä-lā'-shĭ=ȧ.
　　　　　　　　　　　　mä-lā'-zhĭ=ȧ.
Malaprop (Mrs.) . . . măl'-ȧ-prŏp.
Malbrook, or . . . . . măl-brŏŏk'.
Malbrough . . . . . mäl-brōōk'.
Malczewski . . . . . măl-chĕf'-skĭ.
Maldive . . . . . . măl'-dīv.
Male-bolge . . . . . mä-lĕ-bōl'-jĕ.
Malebranche . . . . măl-bräṅsh'.
Malesherbes, de . . . dŭ măl-zârb'.
Malet, Lucas . . . . . lū'-kȧs măl-ā'.
Malherbe . . . . . . măl-ârb'.
Malibon . . . . . . mä-lē-bōn'.
Malibran . . . . . . mä-lē-bräṅ'.
Malignants . . . . . mȧ-lĭg'-nȧnts.

Malines, see Mechlin . mă-lēn'.
Mallarmé, Stéphane . . stā-făn' măl-är-mā'.
Mallorca, see Majorca . mäl-yŏr'-kä.
Mallory, see Malory . . măl'-lŏ-rĭ.
Malmaison . . . . . mäl-mā-zŏṅ'.
Malmesbury . . . . . mämz'-bĕr-ĭ.
Malmö . . . . mäl'-mē.
Malmsey . . . . . . mäm'-zĭ.
Malolos . . . . . . mä-lō'-lōs.
Malory, see Mallory . . măl'-ō-rĭ.
Malot, Hector . . . . ĕk-tōr' mä-lō'.
Malpighi . . . . . . mäl-pē'-gē.
Malpighian . . . . . mäl-pē'-gĭ=àn,
                   măl-pĭg'-ĭ-àn.
Malplaquet . . . . . măl-plă-kā'.
Malta, or . . . . . . môl'-tà.   It. mäl'-tä.
Malte, Fr. . . . . . . mält='ŭ.
Maltese . . . . . . môl-tēz', môl-tēs'.
Malthus . . . . . . măl'-thŭs.
Malthusianism . . . măl-thū'-sĭ-ăn-ĭzm", or
                   măl-thū'-zhăn-ĭzm.
Malvern (Ark.) . . . . măl'-vērn.
Malvern (Eng.) . . . . mô'-vērn.
Malvoisy . . . . . . măl-vwä-zē'.
Malvolio . . . . . . măl-vō'-lĭ-ō.
Malyavin . . . . . . mäl-yä-vĭn'.
Mambrino . . . . . mäm-brē'-nō.
Mambrinus . . . . . măm-brī'-nŭs.
Mambulao . . . . . mäm-bōō-lä'-ō.
Mamelukes . . . . . măm'-ĕ-lūks.
Mamertine . . . . . măm'-ēr-tĭn, măm'-ēr-tēn.
Mamertines, or . . . . măm-ēr-tīnz.
Mamertini . . . . . măm-ēr-tī'-nĭ.
Mamiani della Rovere . mä-mē-ä'-nē dĕl'-lä
                   rō'-vä-rā.
Mamre . . . . măm'-rē.
Manaos . . . . . . mä-nä'-ōs.

Manasseh . . . . . . măn-ăs'-ŭ.
Manbhoom, Manbhum . män'-bhōōm.
Mancha, La . . . . . lä män'-chä.
Manchester . . . . . măn'-chĕs-tēr.
Manchoos, see Manchus . măn-chōōz'.
Manchuria, see Mantchuria măn-chōō'-rĭ-à.
Manchus, see Manchoos . măn-chōōz'.
Mancinelli . . . . . män-chē-nāl'-lē.
Mancini . . . . . . män-chē'-nē.
      Fr. män-sē-nē'.
Mandalay, or . . . . măn'-dà-lā.
Mandelay . . . . . . măn'-dĕ-lā.
Manet . . . . mä-nā'.
Manetho . . . . . . măn'-ĕ-thō.
Mangalore, or . . . . măng-gà-lōr'.
Mangalur . . . . . . măng-gà-lōōr'.
Mangin . . . . . . män-zhăn'.
Manichæans, or Mani-
   cheans . . . . . . măn-ĭ-kē'-ànz.
Manichee . . . . . . măn'-ĭ-kē.
Manila, Manilla . . . mà-nĭl'-à. *Sp.* mä-nē'-lä.
Manin . . . . mä-nēn'.
Manipur, see Mannipur . măn-ĭ-pōōr'.
Manito, see Manitou . . măn'-ĭ-tō.
Manitoba . . . . . măn-ĭ-tō-bä', măn-ĭ-tō'-bà.
Manitou, see Manito . . măn'-ĭ-tōō.
Mannheim . . . . . män'-hīm.
Mannipur, see Manipur . măn-ĭ-pōōr'.
Manoah . . . . . . mà-nō'-ä.
Manon Lescaut . . . mä-nôn' lĕs-kō'.
Manrico . . . . . . män-rē'-kō.
Manrique, Gómez . . . gō-mĕth män-rē'-kā.
Mans, Le . . . . . . lē män.
Mansard, or Mansart . . män-sär'.
      Anglicized, măn'-särd.
Mansfeld . . . . . . mäns'-fĕlt.
Mansour, or Mansur, Al . äl män-sōͧr'.

Mantalini . . . . . . măn-tȧ-lē'-nē.
Mantchuria, see Manchuria măn-choō'-rĭ-ȧ.
Mantegna . . . . . . män-tān'-yä.
Mantelli . . . . . . măn-tāl'-lē.
Manteuffel . . . . . män'-toif-fĕl.
Mantinea, or . . . . . măn-tĭ-nē'-ȧ.
Mantineia . . . . . . măn-tĭ-nī'-ä.
Mantova, or . . . . . *It.* män'-tō-vä.
Mantua . . . . . . măn'-tū-ȧ.
Mantuan . . . . . . măn'-tū-ȧn.
Manutius . . . . . . mă-nū'-shĭ=ŭs.
Manzanares . . . . . män-thä-nä'-rĕs.
Manzanilla . . . . . män-thä-nēl'-yä.
Manzanillo . . . . . män-thä-nēl'-yō.
Manzoni . . . . . . män-dzō'-nē.
Maori . . . . mä'=ō-rĭ, mow'-rĭ.
Maoris . . . . mä'-ō-rĭz, mow'-rĭz.
Map (Walter), or . . . măp.
Mapes (Walter) . . . . māps.
Maracaibo, or Maracaybo mä-rä-kī'-bō.
Marah . . . . mā'-rä.
Marais, Le . . . . . lē mă-rā'.
Maran, René . . . . . rē-nā' mă-räṅ'.
Marat . . . . mä-rä'.
Marathon . . . . . . măr'-ȧ-thŏn.
Maratta, or . . . . . mä-rät'-tä.
Maratti . . . . mä-rät'-tē.
Marceau . . . . . . mär-sō'.
Marchesa . . . . . . mär-kä'-zä.
Marchese . . . . . . mär-kä'-zĕ.
Marchesi . . . . . . mär-kä'-zē.
Marcke, von . . . . . fŏn mär'-kŭ.
Marconi . . . . . . mär-kō'-nē.
Marcus Aurelius Antoninus mär'-kŭs'- ô-rē'-lĭ=ŭs
ăn-tō-nī'-nŭs.
Mardi Gras . . . . . mär'-dē grä'.
Marengo . . . . . . mä-rĕng'-gō.

Mareotis . . . . . . mä-rē-ō'-tĭs, mä-rē-ō'-tĭs.
Mareuil, Villebois- . . . vēl-bwä'-mä-rē'=yŭ.
Margarethe . . . . . mär-gä-rā'-tŭ.
Margot, La Reine . . . lä rĕn mär-gō'.
Margrave . . . . . . mär'-grāv.
Margravine . . . . . mär'-grä-vēn.
Marguérite . . . . . mär-gä-rēt'.
Margueritte, Paul . . . pōl mär-gē-rĭt'.
Marhattas, see Mahrattas mä-rä'-tàz, mă-răt'-äz.
Maria de' Medici, see
  Marie de Médicis . . mä-rē'-ä dä mā'-dē-chē.
Maria Feodorovna . . . mä-rē'-ä fä-ō-dōr'-ŏv-nä.
Maria-Hérédia, José de . ċhō-sä' dä mä-rē'-ä-
                            ä-rä-dē-ä'.
Mariamne . . . . . . mä-rĭ-ăm'-nē.
Marian (Maid) . . . . mâr'-ĭ-àn.
Mariana (Is.) . . . . mä-rē-ä'-nä.
Mariana (Mason's) . . mä-rĭ-ā'-nȧ.
Mariana (Shak.) . . . mä-rĭ-ăn'-ȧ, mă-rē-ä'-nä.
Marianao . . . . . . mä"-rē-ä-nä'-ō.
Marianne, La . . . . lä mär-ē=än'.
Maria Theresa . . . . mä-rĭ'-ȧ tē-rē'-sȧ.
                        Ger. mä-rē'-ä tä-rä'-zä.
Mariazell . . . . . . mä-re"-ä-tsĕl'.
Marie Amélie . . . . mä-rē' ă-mä-lē'.
Marie Antoinnette . . . măr'-ĭ ăn-toi-nĕt'.
                        Fr. mă-rē' äntwä-nĕt'.
Marie de Médicis, see
  Maria de' Medici . . mä-rē' dŭ mä-dē-sēs'.
Marie Galante . . . . mä-rē' gä-länt'.
Marienburg . . . . . mä'-rē-ĕn-bōōrċh".
Marignano, see Melegnano mä-rēn-yä'-nō.
Marilhat . . . . . . mär-ē-lä'.   [mä-rē'-nä.
Marina . . . . Shak. mȧ-rī'-nȧ. Sp.
Marinduque . . . . . mä-rēn-dōō'-kä.
Marini, or . . . . . . mä-rē'-nē.
Marino . . . . mä-rē'-nō.

Marino Faliero . . . .   mä-rē'-nō fä-lē=ā'-rō.
Mario . . . .   mä'-rē-ō.
Mariolatry . . . . .   mâr'-ĭ-ŏl'-à-trĭ.
Marion Delorme . . .   mă-rē-ôṅ' dŭ-lôrm'.
Mariotte . . . . . .   mă-rē=ŏt'.
Maris . . . .   mär'-ēs.
Maritzburg . . . . .   mär'-ĭts-bōōrċh.
Marius . . . .   mā'-rĭ-ŭs.
Marivaux . . . . . .   mä-rē-vō'.
Mariveles . . . . . .   mä-rē-vā'-lĕs.
Marjoribanks . . .   märsh'-bănks.
Markgraf . . . . . .   märk'-gräf.
Marlboro, or Marlborough   Am. märl'-bŭr-ō, môl'-brō.
Marlborough (Duke) . .   môl'-brō, môl'-bŭr-ŭ.
Mármaros-Sziget . . .   mär'-mŏ-rŏsh-sĭg'-ĕt.
Marmont . . . . . .   mär-môṅ'.
Marmontel . . . . .   mär-môṅ-tĕl'.
Marmora (Sea) . . . .   mär'-mō-rà.
Marne . . . .   märn.
Marni . . . .   mär-nē'.
Marochetti . . . . .   mä-rō-kät'-tē.
Maronite . . . . . .   măr'-ō-nīt.
Marot, Clément . . . .   klä-mŏṅ' mă-rō'.
Marquesas (Is.) . . . .   mär-kā'-säs.
Marquette . . . . . .   mär-kĕt'.
Marquis . . . . . .   mär'-kwĭs. *orig.* mär'-kis.
                         Fr. mär-kē'.
Marquise . . . . . .   mär-kēz'.
Marryat . . . . . .   măr'-ĭ-ăt.
Marseillaise, La . . . .   lä mär-sĕl-āz'. *Fr.* lä
                         mär-sā-yĕz'.
Marseille, *Fr.* or . . .   mär-sā'-yŭ.
Marseilles . . . . . .   mär-sālz'.
Marshalsea . . . . .   mär'-shăl-sē.
Mars-la-Tour . . . .   märs-lä-tōōr'.
Marsyas . . . . . .   mär'-sĭ-às.
Marszalkowska . . . .   mär-shäl-kŏv'-skä.

Martel de Janville . . .	mär-tĕl′ dŭ zhŏṅ-vēl′.
Martin, Henri	ôṅ-rē′ mär-tăṅ′.
Martineau	mär′-tĭ-nō.
Martinez Campos . . .	mär-tē′-nĕth käm′-pōs.
Martini-Henry . . .	mär-tē′-nē-hĕn′-rĭ.
Martini, Simone . . .	sē-mō′-nä mär-tē′-nē.
Martinique	mär-tĭ-nēk′.
Martinist	mär′-tĭn-ĭst.
Martius	mär′-shĭ-ŭs.
Marullus	mä-rŭl′-ŭs.
Marylebone	mā′-rĭ-lĕ-bōn″, mär′-lĕ-bŭn,
	mär′-ĭ-bŭn.
Masaccio	mä-sät′-chō.
Masaniello	mä-sä-nē=äl′-lō.
Masaryk	mä′-sä-rīk.
Masbate	mäs-bä′-tä.
Mascagni	mäs-kän′-yē.
Mascarene	mäs-kȧ-rēn′.
Mascarille	mäs-kä-rēl′.
Masefield	māz′-fēld.
Maseru	măz′-ēr-ōō.
Mashonaland	mă-shō′-nä-lănd,
	mä-shō′-nä-lănd.
Maskelyne	măs′-kĕ-lĭn, măs′-kĕ-līn.
Masolino da Panicale . .	mä-zō-lē′-nō dä
	pä-nē-kä′-lĕ.
Maspéro	măs-pä-rō′.
Massada	mäs-sä′-dä.
Massasoit	măs′-ȧ-soit.
Masséna	mä-sä′-nä. *Fr.* mä-sā-nä′.
Massenet	măs-nā′.
Massillon	*U. S.* măs′-ĭl-ŏn.
	Fr. mă-sē-yôṅ′.
Massimo	mäs′-ē-mō.
Massinger	măs′-ĭn-jēr.
Masso	mäs′-sō.
Massuccio, see Masuccio	mä-sōōt′-chō.

Massys, see Matsys and
   Metsys . . . . . . mäs-sīs'.
Mastricht, see Maastricht
   and Maestricht . . . mäs'-trĭcht.
Masuccio di Salerno, see
   Massuccio . . . . . mä-zŏŏt'-chō dē sä-lĕr'-nō.
Masurenland . . . . . mä-zōō'-rĕn-länt.
Masurian, see Mazurian . mă-sŭ'-rĭ-àn.
Mataafa . . . . . . mà-tä'-fà.
Matabele, see Matabeli
   and Matebeli . . . . mä-tä-bā'-lĕ.
Matabeleland . . . . mä-tä-bā'-lĕ-lănd.
Matabeli, see Matabele
   and Matebele . . . . mä-tä-bā'-lē.
Matanzas . . . . . . mă-tăn'-zàs.
                    Sp. mä-tän'-thäs.
Matapan (Cape) . . . . mà-tä-pän'.
                    pop. măt-à-păn'.
Matebele, see Matabele . mä-tĕ-bā'-lĕ.
Matejko . . . . . . mä-tä'-kō.
Mater Dolorosa . . . . mā'-tēr dŏl-ō-rō'-sä,
                    mä'-tĕr dō-lō-rō'-zä.
Materna . . . . . . mà-tēr'-nä.
                    Ger. mä-tĕr'-nä.
Mather (Cotton) . . . măth'-ēr.
Mathieu . . . . . . mä-tē=ē'.
Mathilde . . . . . . mä-tēld'.
Matisse . . . . . . mă-tēs'.
Matsys, Quentin, see
   Massys and Metsys . kwĕn'-tĭn mät-sīs'.
Mattei, Tito . . . . . tē'-tō mät-tā'-ē.
Matthias . . . . . . mà-thī'-às. *Ger.* mät-tē'-äs.
Matthias Corvinus . . . mà-thī'-às kôr-vī'-nŭs.
Maturin . . . . . . măt'-ū-rĭn.
Matzenauer . . . . . mäts'-ĕn-ow-ĕr.
Maubeuge, see Mabuse . mō-bēzh'.
Mauch Chunk . . . . môk chŭngk'.

Maugham . . . . . . môm.
Maui (I.) . . . . . . mow'-ē.
Mauna Kea . . . . . mow'-nä kā'-ä.
Mauna Loa . . . . . mow'-nä lō'-ä.
Maundy . . . . . . môn'-dĭ.
Maupassant . . . . . mō-pä-säṅ'.
Maupertuis . . . . . mō-pâr-twē'.
Maupin, Mlle. de . . . mäd-mwä-zĕl' dŭ mō-pǎṅ'.
Mauprat . . . . . . mō-prä'.
Maurel . . . . mō-rĕl'.
Maurepas . . . . . . mō̄=rĕ-pä'.
Maurice . . . . . . Fr. mō-rēs'.
Mauritius . . . . . . mô-rĭsh'-ĭ=ŭs.
Maurocordatos, see Mav-
  rocordatos . . . . . mäv″-rō-kŏr-dä'-tŏs.
Mauser . . . . . . mow'-zĕr.
Mausolus . . . . . . mô-sō'-lŭs.
Mauve . . . . mōv.
Mavrocordatos, see Mau-
  rocordatos . . . . . mäv″-rō-kŏr-dä'-tŏs.
Maximilian . . . . . mǎks-ĭ-mĭl'-yȧn.
                         Ger. mäks-ē-mē'-lē-än.
Maximin . . . . . . mǎks'-ĭ-mĭn.
Maya . . . . mä'-yä, mī'-ä.
Mayaguez . . . . . . mī-ä-gwĕth'.
Maybun . . . . . . mä=ē-bō̄on'.
Mayence, see Mainz . . Fr. mä-yŏṅs'.
Mayenne . . . . . . mī-ĕn', mä-yĕn'.
Mayer . . . . mā'-ēr. Ger. mī'-ĕr.
Maysi . . . . mä-ē'-sē.
Maytsouye . . . . . mät-sō̄o'-yĕ.
Mazagan . . . . . . mȧz-ȧ-gän'.
Mazanderan . . . . . mä″-zȧn-dĕ-rän'.
Mazarin . . . . . . mǎz'-ȧ-rĭn, mǎz-ȧr-ēn'.
                         Fr. mȧ-zä-rǎṅ'.
Mazarini . . . . . . mäd-zär-ē'-nē.
Mazurian, see Masurian . mä-tsō̄o-rē'-än.

Mazzini . . . . . . mät-sē'-nē.
Mazzuola . . . . . . mät-zo͞o-ō'-lä.
Meagher . . . . . . mä'-ċhēr, mä'-'hēr.
Meaux . . . . mō.
Mechlin, see Malines . . měk'-lĭn. D. měċh'-lĭn.
Mechoacan, see Michoacan mä-chō"-ä-kän'.
Mecklenburg-Schwerin . měk-lĕn-bo͞orċh-shvä-rēn'.
Mecklenburg-Strelitz . . měk'-lĕn-bo͞orċh-strä'-lĭts.
Medea . . . . mē-dē'-ä.
Médée . . . . mä-dä'.
Media . . . . mē'-dĭ-à.
Medici, de' . . . . . dä mä'-dē-chē.
Médicis, de . . . . . dŭ mä-dē-sēs'.
Medina . . . . . . Sp. mä-dē'-nä.
                        U. S. mē-dī'-nà.
Medina-Celi . . . . . mä-dē'-nä-thä'-lē.
Medina-Sidonia . . . mä-dē'-nä-sē-dō'-nē-ä.
Medjidi . . . . . . měj-jēd'-ē.
Médoc . . . . mä-dŏk'.
Medusa . . . . . . mě-dū'-sä.
Meerkatsfontein . . . mâr'-kăts-fŏn'-tīn.
Meerut, see Mirat . . . mē'-rŭt.
Mefistofele . . . . . mä-fēs-tō'-fä-lä.
Megæra . . . . . . mě-gē'-rä.
Megara . . . . . . měg'-à-rä.
Megiddo . . . . . . mě-gĭd'-ō.
Mehemet Ali, see Moham-
   med Ali . . . . . . mä'-hě-mět ä'-lē.
Méhul . . . . mä-ül'.
Meilhac . . . . . . mä-yäk'.
Meissen . . . . . . mī'-sĕn.
Meissonier . . . . . mä-sō-nē=ā'.
Meistersinger von Nürn-
   berg, Die . . . . . dē mīs'-tĕr-zĭng"-ĕr fŏn
                        nürn'-bĕrċh.
Mejnoun . . . . . . měj-no͞on'.
Mekhong, or Mekong . . mä-kŏng'.

Melanchthon, or . . . mē-lăngk'-thŏn.
　　　　　　　　　　 Ger. mā-längċh'-tōn.
Melanthon . . . . . mĕ-lăn'-thŏn.
Melba . . . . mĕl'-bä.
Melchisedec, or Melchize-
　　dek . . . . mĕl-kĭz'-ĕ-dĕk.
Meleager . . . . . . mĕl-ē-ā'-jĕr, mē-lē-ā'-jĕr,
　　　　　　　　　　 mē-lē'-ä-jĕr.
Melegnano, see Marignano mā-lān-yä'-nō.
Melibœus . . . . . . mĕl-ĭ-bē'-ŭs.
Melilla . . . . *Sp. Af.* mā-lēl'-yȧ.
Méline . . . . mā-lēn'.
Melita . . . . mĕl'-ĭt-ȧ.
Mello (José de) . . . . mā'-lōō.
Melos, see Milo . . . mē'-lŏs.
Melozzo da Forlì . . . mā-lŏt'-zō dä fŏr-lē'.
Melpomene . . . . . mĕl-pŏm'-ĕ-nē.
Melton Mowbray . . . mĕl'-tŭn mō'-brā, mō'-brĕ.
Melusina . . . . . mĕl-ōō-sī'-nä.
Mélusine, *Fr.* . . . . mā-lü-zēn'.
Memling . . . . . . mĕm'-lĭng.
Menabrea . . . . . . mā-nä-brā'-ä.
Menahem . . . . . . mĕn'-ȧ-hĕm.
Menai . . . . mĕn'-ī. *pop.* mĕn'-ā *or*
　　　　　　　　　　 mĕn'-ĕ.
Ménard, René . . . . rē-nā' mā-när'.
Mencayan . . . . . . mān-kä-yän'.
Menchikoff, see Menshi-
　　koff . . . . mĕn'-shē-kŏf.
Mencius . . . . . . mĕn'-shĭ-ŭs.
Mendelssohn-Bartholdy . mĕn'-dĕl-sōn-bär-tōl'-dē.
Mendès, Catulle . . . . kä-tül' mŏṅ-dĕz'.
Mendocino . . . . . mĕn-dō-sē'-nō.
Mendoza . . . . . . mĕn-dō'-thä.
Menelaus . . . . . . mĕn-ĕ-lā'-ŭs.
Menendez de Aviles . . mā-nän'-dĕth dä äbē'-lĕs.
Ménippée, Satire . . . sä-tēr' mā-nē-pā'.

Menocal	mä-nō-käl'.
Menorca, *Sp.* for Minorca	mä-nōr'-kä.
Menpes, Mortimer . .	mĕm'-pĕs.
Menshikoff, see Menchi-	
koff	mĕn'-shē-kŏf.
Menton, or	môṅ-tŏṅ'.
Mentone	mĕn-tō'-nĕ.
Menzel	mĕnt'·zĕl.
Mephibosheth	mĕ-fīb'-ō-shĕth.
	Heb. mĕf-ĭ-bō'-shĕth.
Mephistophelean . . .	mĕf″-ĭs-tō-fē'-lē-àn.
Mephistopheles	mĕf-ĭs-tŏf'-ĕ-lēz.
Mercator	mĕr-kā'-tĕr.
	D. mĕr-kä'-tŏr.
Mercédes	mĕr-thä'-dĕs.
Mercia	mĕr'-shĭ=à.
Mercié	mĕr-sē=ā'.
Mercier	mâr-sē=ā'.
Mercurius	mĕr-kū'-rĭ-ŭs.
Mercutio	mĕr-kū'-shĭ=ō.
Merejkowski	mĕr-ĕzh-kŏv'-skē.
Mergui	mĕr-gē'.
Mérimée	mä-rē-mä'.
Merindol	mĕ-răṅ'-dōl'.
Merle (Maj.)	mĕrl.
Merle d'Aubigné . . .	mĕrl dō-bēn-yä'.
Merlin	mĕr'-lĭn.
Merodach	mĕr'-ō-dăk.
Meroë	mĕr'-ō-ē.
Merom	mē'-rŏm.
Merope	mĕr'-ō-pē.
Merovingians	mĕr-ō-vĭn'-jĭ-ànz.
Merowig, see Merwig . .	mĕr'-ō-wĭg.
Merrilies	mĕr'-ĭ-lēz.
Merry del Val	mĕr-ē' dĕl väl.
Mersey	mĕr'-sĭ.
Merwig, see Merowig . .	mĕr'-wĭg.

Méry . . . . mä-rē'.
Mesa, or . . . . . . mē'-zä. *Sp.* mā'-sä.
Mesha . . . . mē'-shä.
Meshach . . . . . . mē'-shăk.
Mesmer . . . . . . měs'-mēr.
Mesolonghi, see Misso-
   longhi . . . . . . mä-sō-lŏng'-gē.
Mesolongion, *mod. Gr.* . mä-zō-lŏng'-gē-ŏn.
Mesopotamia . . . . . měs″-ō-pō-tä'-mĭ-á.
Messalina, or Messallina . měs-ă-lī'-nä.
Messianic . . . . . měs-sĭ-ăn'-ĭk.
Messidor . . . . . . měs-ē-dōr'.
Messina, Antonello da . än-tō-näl'-lō dä měs-sē'-nä.
Messines . . . . . . měs-ēn'.
Mestrovich . . . . . měs'-trō-vĭch.
Mesurado (Cape) . . . mä-sōō-rä'-dō.
Metastasio . . . . . mä-täs-tä'-zē-ō.
Météren . . . . . . mä-tä-rôṅ'.
Methuen (Gen.) . . . měth'-ŭ-ĕn.
Methuen (U. S.) . . . mě-thū'-ĕn.
Methuselah . . . . . mě-thū'-sĕ-lä.
Metsu, see Metzu . . . mět'-sü.
Metsys, see Massys and
   Matsys . . . . . . mět-sīs'.
Metternich-Winneburg . mět-těr-nĭch-
                        vĭn'-nĕ-bōōrch.
Metz . . . . *Fr.* měz. *Ger.* měts.
Metzu, see Metsu . . . mět'-zü.
Meudon . . . . . . mě-dŏṅ'.
Meung, Jean de . . . zhäṅ dū mŭṅ.
Meunier . . . . . . mē-nē=ā'.
Meurthe-et-Moselle . . mērt'-ä-mō-zĕl'.
Meuse, see D. Maas . . mūz. *Fr.* měz.
Mexicali . . . . . . měks-ĭ-kä'-lĭ.
Meyerbeer . . . . . mī'-ĕr-bār.
Meynell . . . . . . mā'-nĕl.
Meyrick . . . . . . mī'-rĭk.

Mézières . . . . . . mā-zē=âr'.
Mezzofanti . . . . . mĕt-zō-fän'-tē.
Miako . . . . mē-ä'-kō.
Miami . . . . mī-äm'-ē, mī-äm'-ĭ.
Miantonomoh . . . . mĭ-ăn″-tō-nō'-mō.
Micaela . . . . . . mĭ-kä'-ā-lä.
Micah . . . . mī'-kä.
Mi-Carême . . . . . mē-kă-rĕm'.
Micawber . . . . . . mĭ-kô'-bĕr.
Michael . . . . . . mī'-kĕl, mī'-kā=ēl.
Michael Angelo . . . . mī'-kā=ĕl ăn'-jē-lō.
Michaelis . . . . . . mē-kā'-lēs.
Michael Nicolaevitch
   (Grand Duke) . . . mī'-kĕl nē-kō-lä'-ĕ-vĭch.
Michaelmas . . . . . mĭk'-ĕl-más.
Michal . . . . mī'-kál.
Michel . . . . Fr. mē-shĕl'.
Michelagnolo, or . . . mē-kĕl-än'-yō-lō.
Michelangelo . . . . mī-kĕl-án'-jĕ-lō.
                     It. mē-kĕl-än'-jä-lō.
Michelet . . . . . . mēsh-lā'.
Michelis . . . . . . mē-ċhā'-lĭs.
Michelozzo Michelozzi . mē-kĕ-lŏt'-zō mē-kĕ-lŏt'-zē.
Michetti, Paolo . . . . pä'-ō-lō mē-kāt'-tē.
Michoacan, see Mechoacan mē-chō-ä-kän'.
Mickiewicz . . . . . mĭts-kē-ĕv'-ĭch.
Micronesia . . . . . mī-krō-nē'-shĭ-á.
Micronesian . . . . . mĭ-krō-nē'-shĭ=án,
                     mĭk-rō-nē'-shĭ=án.
Midas . . . . mī'-dás.
Midgard . . . . . . mĭd'-gärd.
Midianites . . . . . mĭd'-ĭ-ăn-īts″.
Midnapur . . . . . . mĭd-ná-pōōr'.
Mierevelt . . . . . . mē'-rĕ-vĕlt.
Mieris . . . . mē'-rĭs.
Mieroslawski . . . . . mē=ā-rō-släv'-skē.
Mignard . . . . . . mēn-yär'.

Mignet . . . . . . mēn-yā'.
Mignon . . . . . . mēn-yôṅ'.
Miguel . . . . mē-gĕl'.
Mikado . . . . . . mĭ-kä'-dō.
Milan (City) . . . . mĭl'-ăn, mĭ-lăn'.
Milan (King of Servia) . mĭl'-än.
Milanese . . . . . . mĭl-ăn-ēz', or ēs'.
Milano, see Milan . . . mē-lä'-nō.
Milazzo . . . . . . mē-läts'-sō.
Milesian (Irish) . . . . mĭ-lē'-shĭ=àn, mĭ-lē'-zhàn.
Miliukoff (-kow, -kov) . mĭl'-yū-kŏf.
Millais . . . . mĭl-lā'.
Millerand . . . . . mēl-räṅ'.
Millet . . . . Eng. mĭl'-lĕt. Fr. mē-yā'.
                         pop. mē-lā'.
Millevoye . . . . . mēl-vwä'.
Millot . . . . mē-yō'.
Milne-Edwards . . . mĭln-ĕd'-wàrdz.
                         Fr. mēl-nā-dōō-är', or
                         mēl-nā-dōō-ärs'.
Milnes . . . . mĭlnz.
Milo, see Melos . . . mē-lō'.
Miloradovitch . . . mē-lō-rä'-dō-vĭch.
Miltiades . . . . . . mĭl-tī'-ă-dēz.
Mimi . . . . mē-mē'.
Mimir . . . . mē'-mĭr.
Mincio . . . . mĭn'-chō.
Mindanao, see Maguin-
   danao . . . . . . mĭn-dä-nä'-ō.
Mindoro . . . . . . mĭn-dō'-rō.
Minerva . . . . . . mĭn-ēr'-và.
Ming . . . . mēng.
Minho, Port., see Miño . mēn'-yōō.
Minié . . . . mĭn'-ĕ. Fr. mē-nē=ā'.
Minna von Barnhelm . . mĭn'-ä fŏn bärn'-hĕlm.
Minnegerode . . . . mĭn'-ĕ-gā-rōd.
Minnewit, see Minnuit . mĭn'-ĕ-wĭt.

Miño, *Sp.*, see Minho . .	mēn′-yō.
Mino da Fiesole . . .	mē′-nō dä fē-ä′-zō-lä.
Minorca, see Menorca .	mĭ-nōr′-kä.
Minos	mī′-nŏs.
Minotaur	mĭn′-ō-tôr.
Minnuit, see Minnewit .	mĭn′-ū-ĭt.
Mir	mēr.
Mirabeau	mĭr′-ă-bō. *Fr.* mē-rä-bō′.
Miraflores	mē-rà-flō′-rĕs.
Miragoane	mĭ-rà-gōn′.
	Fr. mē-rä-gwän′.
Miramon	mē-rä-mōn′.
Miranao, La	lä mē-rä-nä′-ō.
Miranda	*Shak.* mĭ-răn′-dà.
	Sp. mē-rän′-dä.
Mirandola, Pico della . .	pē′-kō dāl′-lä mē-rän′-dō-lä.
Mirat, or	mē′-ràt.
Mirath, see Meerut . .	mē′-räth.
Mirbeau, Octave . . .	ōk-tăv′ mer-bō′.
Mirbel	mĕr-bĕl′.
Mirebalais	mē=rĕ-bä-lä′.
Mirecourt	mĕr-koōr′.
Miron, Diaz	dē′-äs mē-rōn′.
Mirouét, Ursule . . .	ür-sül′ mē-roō-ä′.
Mirs (Bay)	mērs.
Mirzapur	mēr-zä-poōr′.
Mirza-Schaffy . . .	mēr′-zä-shäf-fē′.
Misamis	mē-säm′-ēs.
Misanthrope, Le . .	lē mē-zäṅ-trŏp′. [äm-ē-ôṅ′.
Mise of Amiens . .	mīz ŏv ăm′-ĭ-ĕns. *Fr.*
Misérables, Les . . .	lä mē-zä-rä′-bl.
Miserere	mē-zä-rā′-rä.
Misericordia	mē″-zä-rē-kōr′-dē-ä.
Miskólcz	mĭsh-kŏlts.
Missolonghi, see Mesolonghi, mod. Gr. Mesolongion	mĭs-sō-lŏng′-gē.

Missouri . . . . . . mĭs-sōō'-rĭ, mĭ-zōō'-rĭ.
       pop. mĭz-ōō'-rȧ.
Misterosa . . . . . . mēs-tā-rō'-sȧ.
Mistral . . . . mēs-träl'.
Mitau . . . . mē'-tow.
Mithradates, see Mithri-
 dates . . . . mĭth-rȧ-dā'-tēz.
Mithridate . . . . . *Fr.* mēt-rē-dät'.
Mithridates, see Mithra-
 dates . . . . mĭth-rĭ-dā'-tēz.
Mithridatic . . . . . mĭth-rĭ-dăt'-ĭk.
Mitre, Bartolomé . . . bär-tō-lō-mä' mē'-trä.
Mitsuoki . . . . . . mēts'-ōō'-ō'-kē'.
Mitylene, see Mytilene . mĭt-ĭ-lē'-nē.
Mivart . . . . mĭv'-ärt.
Mizraim . . . . . . mĭz-rā'-ĭm, mĭz'-rā-ĭm.
Mlava . . . . mlä'-vä.
Mnemosyne . . . . . nē-mŏs'-ĭn-ē.
Moa . . . . mō'-ä.
Moab . . . . mō'-ăb.
Mobangi . . . . . . mō-bäng'-gē.
Mobile . . . . mō-bēl'.
Mocenigo . . . . . . mō-chā-nē'-gō.
Mocha . . . . mō'-kä. *Arab.* mō'-ċhä.
Modder . . . . . . mŏd'-ĕr.
Modder's Spruit . . . mŏd'-ĕrs sproit.
Modena . . . . . . mō'-dĕ-nä. *It.* mō'-dā-nä.
Modeste Mignon . . . mō-dĕst' mēn-yôṅ'.
Modjeska . . . . . . mŏd-jĕs'-kȧ.
Modred, see Mordred . mō'-drĕd, mŏd'-rĕd.
Moeris (L.) . . . . . mē'-rĭs.
Moewe . . . . mē'-vŭ.
Mogador . . . . . . mŏg-ȧ-dōr'.
Mogilef, see Mohileff . mō-gē-lĕf'.
Moguls, see Mughals . . mō-gŭlz'.
Mohács . . . . . . mō-häch'.
Mohammed, see Mahomet mō-hăm'-ĕd.

Mohammed Ali, see Me-
    hemet Ali . . . . . . mō-hăm′-ĕd ä′-lē.
Mohave, see Mojave . . mō-hä′-vā.
Mohican, see Mahican . mō-hĭk′-ȧn.
Mohileff, see Mogilef . . mō-ċhē-lĕf′.
Mohun . . . . mō′-hŭn.
Moiseiwitsch . . . . . mō-ē-sē′-vĭch.
Moldavia . . . . . . mōl-dä′-vĭ-ȧ.
Moivre . . . . mwävr.
Mojave, see Mohave . . mō-ʻhä′-vā.
Moldau . . . . . . mŏl′-dow.
Molech, see Moloch . . mō′-lĕk.
Molenbeek-Saint-Jean . mŏ-lŏṅ-bāk′-săṅ-zhäṅ′.
Molière . . . . . . mō-lē=âr′.
Molina . . . . mō-lē′-nä.
Molinists . . . . . . mō′-lĭ-nĭsts.
Molinos . . . . . . mō-lē′-nōs.
Mollwitz, see Molwitz . mŏl′-vĭts.
Moloch, see Molech . . mō′-lŏk.
Molokai . . . . . . mō-lō-kī′.
Molokani . . . . . . mō-lō-kä′-nē.
Moltke, von . . . . . fŏn mŏlt′-kŭ.
             Ger. mŏlt′-kŭ.
Moluccas . . . . . . mō-lŭk′-ȧz.
Molwitz, see Mollwitz . mŏl′-vĭts.
Molyneux . . . . . . mŭl′-ĭ-nŏŏks, —nū.
Mombas, or . . . . . mŏm-bäs′.
Mombasa, or . . . . . mŏm-bä′-sä.
Mombaz . . . . . . mŏm-bäs′.
Mombuttu, see Monbuttu mŏm-bōōt′-tōō.
Mommsen . . . . . mŏm′-zĕn.
Momus . . . . mō′-mŭs.
Monaco . . . . . . mŏn′-ä-kō.
Mona Lisa . . . . . mō′-nä lē′-zä.
Monarque, Le Grand . . lē gräṅ mō-närk′.
Monastir . . . . . . mō-näs-tēr′.
Monbuttu, see Mombuttu mŏn-bōōt′-tōō.

Moncey . . . . . . môṅ-sā'.
Mondidier . . . . . . mŏṅ-dē-dē=ā'.
Monet . . . . mō-nā'.
Monfalcone . . . . . mōn-fäl-kō'-nä.
Monge . . . . mŏṅzh.
Monghir, or Monghyr, see
　Mungir . . . . . . mŏn-gēr'.
Mongol . . . . mŏng'-gŏl, mŏn'-gŏl.
Mongolian . . . . . mŏn-gō'-lĭ-àn.
Monmouth . . . . . mŏn'-mŭth, mŭn'-mŭth.
Monna Vanna . . . . mōn'-nä vän'-nä.
Monreale . . . . . . mŏn-rä-ä'-lĕ.
Monroe . . . . . . mŭn'-rō.
Mons . . . . môṅs.
Monseigneur . . . . . môṅ-sān-yēr'.
Mons-en-Pévêle . . . . môṅs'-ŏṅ-pā-vĕl'.
Monserrat, see Montserrat mōn-sĕr-rät'.
Monsieur . . . . . . mŏ-sē=ē'.
Monson . . . . . . mŭn'-sŭn.
Montagu, or Montague . mŏnt'-à-gū.
Montaigne . . . . . mŏn-tān'.
　　　　　　　　Fr. môṅ-tān'=yŭ.
Montalembert . . . . môṅ-tä-lŏṅ-bâr'.
Montalvan . . . . . mōn-täl-bän'.
Montana . . . . . . mŏn-tä'-nä.
Montargis . . . . . . môṅt-är-zhē'.
Montauban . . . . . môṅ-tō-bäṅ'.
Montauk (Point) . . . mŏn-tôk'.
Mont Blanc, see Mount
　Blanc . . . . . . Fr. môṅ bläṅ.
Montcalm Gozon de Saint-
　Véran . . . . . . mŏnt-käm'.
　　　　　Fr. môṅ-kälm' gōzôṅ'
　　　　　dŭ säṅ-vā-räṅ'.
Mont Cenis . . . . . môṅ sĕ-nē'.
Montebello . . . . mōn-tā-bāl'-lō.
Monte Cristo . . . . . mŏn'-tĕ krĭs'-tō.

Montecucoli, or . . . . mŏn-tĕ-kōō'-kō-lē.
Montecuculi . . . . . mŏn-tĕ-kōō'-kōō-lē.
Montefiore . . . . . mŏn-tĕ-fē=ō'-rĕ.
Montego (Bay) . . . . mŏṅ-tē'-gō.
Monte Grappa . . . . mōn'-tā gräp'-pä.
Montejo . . . . . . mōn-tā'-ċhō.
Montemezze . . . . . mōn-tā-māts'-sā.
Montenegro . . . . . pop. mŏn-tĕ-nē'-gro.
                It. mōn-tā-nā'-grō.
Montereau . . . . . môṅ=tĕ-rō'.
Monterey (Cal.) . . . . mŏn-tĕ-rā'.
Monterey (Mexico) . . mōn-tā-rā'=ē.
Montero Rios . . . . mōn-tā'-rō rē'-ōs.
Montes, Lola, see Montez lō'-lä mōn'-tĕs.
Montespan . . . . . mŏn-tĕs-păn'.
                Fr. môṅ-tĕs-päṅ'.
Montesquieu . . . . . mŏn-tĕs-kū'.
                Fr. môṅ-tĕs-kē=ē'.
Montessori . . . . . mōn-tās-sō'-rē.
Monte Testaccio . . . mōn'-tĕ tĕs-tä'-chō.
Monteverde . . . . . It. mōn-tĕ-vâr'-dĕ.
                Sp. mōn-tā-vĕr'-t̄hā.
Montevideo . . . . . mŏn-tĕ-vĭd'-ē-ō.
                Sp. mōn''-tā-vē-ā'-t̄hō.
Montez, Lola, see Montes lō'-lä mōn'-tĕs.
Montfaucon . . . . . mŏṅ-fō-kŏṅ'.
Montfleury . . . . . môṅ-flē-rē'.
Montfort . . . . . . mŏnt'-fôrt. Fr. môṅ-fōr'.
Montgolfier . . . . . mŏnt-gŏl'-fĭ-ēr.
                Fr. môṅ-gōl-fē=ā'.
Montholon . . . . . môṅ-tō-lôṅ'.
Monti, Vincenzo . . . vēn-chānd'-zō mŏn'-tē.
Monticello . . . . . mŏn-tē-sĕl'-lō.
                It. mōn-tē-chāl'-lō.
Montijo . . . . . . Sp. mōn-tē'-ċhō.
Montijo, Eugénie de . . Fr. ē-zhā-nē' dŭ
                môṅ-tē-zhō'.

Montjoie . . . . . . môṅ-zhwä'.
Montluc . . . . . . môṅ-lük'.
Montmartre . . . . . môṅ-mär'=tr.
Montmirail . . . . . môṅ-mē-rä'=yŭ.
Montmorenci, or . . . mŏnt-mō-rĕn'-sē.
Montmorency . . . . Fr. môṅ-mō-rôṅ-sē'.
Montojo . . . . . . mōnt-ō'-ċhō.
Montpelier . . . . . mŏnt-pēl'-yĕr.
Montpellier . . . . . Fr. môṅ-pĕl-lē=ā'.
Montpensier . . . . . môṅ-pôṅ-sē=ā'.
Montreal . . . . . . mŏn-trē-äl'.
                     Fr. môṅ-rā-äl'.
Montreuil-sous-Bois . . môṅ-trē'=yŭ-sōō-bwä'.
Montserrat, see Monserrat mônt-sĕr-rät',
                     mônt-sĕ-rȧt'.
Montserrat (I.) . . . . mŏnt-sĕ-rȧt'.
Monza . . . . mōn'-zä.
Moodkee, see Mudki . . mōōd'-kē.
Mooi . . . . mō'-ē.
Mooltan, see Multan . . mōōl-tän'.
Moore (Thomas) . . . mōōr, mōr.
Moorshedabad, see Mur-
    shidabad . . . . . mōōr"-shĕ-dä-bäd'.
Moraczewski . . . . . mō-rä-chĕv'-skĭ.
Moradabad, see Murad-
    abad . . . . mō"-räd-ä-bäd'.
Morales . . . . . . mō-rä'-lĕs.
Moran (Thomas) . . . mō-răn'.
Moray . . . . mŭr'-ĭ, mŭr'-ā.
Mordecai . . . . . . môr'-dĕ-kī, môr'-dē-kā.
Mordred, see Modred . môr'-drĕd.
Morea . . . . mō-rē'-ä.
Moreau . . . . . . mō-rō'.
Morelos . . . . . . mō-rä'-lŏs.
Moren . . . . mō-rän'.
Morghen . . . . . . mōr'-gĕn.
Morgue . . . . . . môrg. Fr. mōrg.

Moriah	mō-rī'-ä.
Morillo	mō-rēl'-yō.
Morisot, Berthe	bĕrt mō-rē-sō'.
Moritz	mō'-rĭts.
Mornay, Duplessis . .	dü-plä-sē' mōr-nā'.
Morny	mōr-nē'.
Moro (Castle), see Morro	mŏr'-rō. *Sp.* mōr'-rō.
Moroko	mō-rō'-kō.
Moron de la Frontera . .	mō-rōn' dā lä fron-tā'-rä.
Morosini	mō-rō-zē'-nē.
Morpheus	môr'-fē-ŭs, môr'-fūs.
Morrisania	mŏr-rĭs-ā'-nĭ=à.
Morro (Castle), see Moro	mŏr'-rō. *Sp.* mōr'-rō.
Morte d'Arthur	môrt där-tür'.
Mort Homme	mōr-tŏm'.
Mortier	mōr-tē=ā'.
Mosaic	mō-zā'-ĭk.
Mosby	mōz'-bĭ.
Moscheles	mōsh'-ĕ-lĕs.
Moscow	mŏs'-kō.
Mosel, or	mō-zĕl'.
Moselle	mō-zĕl'.
Mosenthal	mō'-zĕn-täl.
Mosheim	mōs'-hīm.
Moskva	mŏsk-vä'.
Moslem	mŏs'-lĕm.
Mosquitia, or	mōs-kē-tē'-ä.
Mosquito	mōs-kē'-tō.
Mossoul, Mosul, see Mousul	mō'-sŭl.
Moszkowski	mōs-kŏv'-skĭ.
Moukden, see Mukden .	mōōk-dĕn'.
Moulin Rouge	mōō-lăṅ' rōōzh. [mōō'-trĭ.
Moultrie	mōl'-trĭ, mōōl'-trĭ,
Mounet Sully	mōō-nā' sü-lē'.
Mount Blanc, see Mont Blanc	mownt blăngk.

Mount Desert . . . . mownt dĕ-zẽrt′

Mouquet . . . . . . mōō-kā′.

Mousqueton . . . . . mōōsk=ŭ=tôn′.

Moussorgsky . . . . . mōō-sôrg′-skĭ.

Mousul, see Mossoul . . mōō′-sŭl.

Mouton . . . . . . mōō-tôn′.

Mowbray . . . . . . mō′-brā.

Mozambique . . . . . mō-zăm-bēk′.

Mozarab . . . . . . mōz-âr′-ăb, mō-zä′-răb.

Mozart . . . . . . mō′-zärt. *Ger.* mō′-tsärt.

Mozuffergurh, see Mu-
zaffargarh . . . . . mŭz-ŭf-ȧr-gōōr′.

Mozuffernugger, see Mu-
zaffarnagar . . . . mŏz-ŭf-ẽr-nŭg′-gẽr.

Mozufferpore, see Muzaff-
arpur . . . . . . mŏs-ŭf-ẽr-pōr′.

Msta . . . . mstä.

Mtesa . . . . mtā′-sä.

Mucha, Alphonse . . . mōōċh′-ȧ.

Mudie . . . . mōō′-dē.

Mudki, see Moodkee . . mōōd′-kē.

Muette de Portici, La . . lä mü-ĕt′ dŭ pōr′-tē-chē.

Mughals, see Moguls . . mōō′-gȧlz.

Mühlbach . . . . . . mül′-bäċh.

Mühlhausen . . . . . mül′-how-zĕn.

Muir . . . . mūr.

Mukden, see Moukden . mōōk-dĕn′.

Müller (Max) . . . . mül′-ẽr.

Multan, see Mooltan . . mōōl-tän′. [mōōn′-kä-chē.

Muncaczy, see Munkácsy mōōn-kä′-chē,

Münchausen, see Münch-
hausen . . . . . . *Eng.* mŭn-chô′-zĕn.
Ger. münċh-how′-zĕn.

München, see Munich . mün′-ċhĕn.

- Münchhausen, see Mün-
chausen . . . . . . *Eng.* mŭn-ċhô′-zĕn.
Ger. münċh-how′-zĕn.

Mungir, see Monghir . .   mŭn-gēr'.
Munich, see München .   mū'-nĭk.
Munkácsy, see Muncaczy   mōōn-kä'-chē,
           mōōn'-kä-chē.
Muñoz . . . .   mōōn-yōth'.
Münster . . . . . .   mün'-ster.
Murad . . . .   mōō'-räd.
Muradabad, see Morada-
   bad . . . .   mōō"-räd-ä-bäd'.
Murano . . . . . .   mōō-rä'-nō.
Murat . . . .   mū-răt'.   Fr. mü-rä'.
Muratore, Lucien . . .   lü-sē-ĕn' mü-rȧ-tōr'.
Muratori . . . . . .   mōō-rä-tō'-rē.
Muravieff . . . . .   mōō-rä-vē=ĕf'.
Murcia . . . .   mēr'-shĭ-ȧ.
           Sp. mōōr'-thē-ä.
Murfreesboro, or Mur-
   freesborough . . . .   mēr'-frēz-bŭr"-ō.
Murger . . . .   mür-zhâr'.
Murillo . . . .   mū-rĭl'-ō.   Sp. mōō-rēl'-yō.
Muroy Salazar . . . .   mōō'-rō-ē sä-lä-thär'.
Murshidabad, see Moor-
   shedabad . . . . .   mōōr"-shĭ-dä-bäd'.
Muscovite . . . . . .   mŭs'-kō-vīt.
Muscovy . . . . . .   mŭs'-kō-vĭ.
Musée des Thermes . .   mü-zā dā târm'.
Musée du Louvre . . .   mü-zā' dü lōōvr'.
Musée du Luxembourg .   mü-zā' dü lük-sŏn-bōōr'.
Muskingum . . . . .   mŭs-kĭng'-gŭm.
Musset . . . .   müs-ā'.
Mussulman . . . . .   mŭs'-sŭl-mȧn.
Mustafa, or Mustapha .   mŏŏs'-tä-fä.
Mustapha Kemal . . .   mŏŏs'-tä-fä kā-mäl'.
Mutra . . . .   mŭt'-rä.
Mutsuhito . . . . . .   mōōt'-sōōsh-tō.
Muzaffargarh, see Mozuff-
   ergurh . . . . . .   mŭz-ăf-ȧr-gär'.

Muzaffarnagar, see Mo-
zuffernugger . . . .   mŭz-ăf-ȧr-năg′-är.
Muzaffarpur, see Mozuff-
erpore . . . . .   mŭz-ăf-ȧr-pōōr′.
Muziano . . . . .   mōōd-zē-ä′-nō.
Mycale . . . . . .   mĭk′-ä-lē.
Mycenæ . . . . . .   mī-sē′-nē, mĭ-kĕn′-ĭ.
Mymensing, see Mai-
mansinh . . . . .   mī-mĕn-sĭng′.
Mynpuri, see Mainpuri .   mīn-pōō′-rē.
Myrmidons . . . . .   mēr′-mĭ-dŏnz.
Myron . . . .   mī′-rŏn.
Mysia . . . . . .   mĭsh′-ĭ=ä.
Mysore, see Maisur . .   mī-sōr′.
Mytilene, see Mitylene .   mĭt-ĭ-lē′-nē.

N

Naaman . . . . . .   nā′-ȧ-mȧn.
Naauw Poort . . . . .   nä′=üv-pōrt.
Nabonidus . . . . .   năb-ō-nī′-dŭs.
Nadelman, Elie . . . .   ĕl-yĕ′ nä′-dĕl-män.
Nadir Shah . . . . .   nä′-dēr shä.
Nadiya, see Nuddea . .   nŭd′-ē-yä.
Nador . . . .   nä-dōr′.
Nagasaki, see Nangasaki   nä-gä-sä′-kē.
Nägeli . . . .   nâ′-gĕ-lē.
Nagny-Várad . . . . .   nŏd′-yŭ-vä-räd.
Nagoya . . . .   nä-gō′-yä.
Nagpore, or . . . . .   näg-pōr′.
Nagpur . . . . . .   näg-pōōr′.
Nahant . . . .   nȧ-hänt′, nȧ-hănt′.
Naiad . . . .   nā′-yȧd.
Nain . . . .   nā′-ĭn.
Nájara . . . .   nä′-ċhä-rä.
Nájera, Gutiérrez . . .   gōō-tē-ĕr′-ĕs näċh′-ä-rȧ.
Namaqualand . . . .   nä-mä′-kwä-länd.

Namur . . . . nā'-mōōr. *Fr.* nä-mür'.
Nana . . . . nä-nä'.
Nana Sahib . . . . . nä'-nä sä'-hĭb.
Nan-chang . . . . . nän-chäng'.
Nancy (France) . . . . năn'-sĭ. *Fr.* näṅ-sē'.
Nangasaki, see Nagasaki nän-gä-sä'-kē.
Nanking . . . . . . nän-kĭng'.
Nansen . . . . nän'-sĕn.
Nantes . . . . nănts. *Fr.* näṅt.
Nanteuil . . . . . . näṅ-tē'-yŭ.
Naomi . . . . nā-ō'-mī, nā'-ō-mē.
Naonabu . . . . . nä'-ō'-nō'-bē'.
Naphtali . . . . . . năf'-tȧ-lī, năf'-tā-lī.
Napier . . . . nā'-pĭ-ēr.
Napoleon . . . . . . nȧ-pō'-lē-ŏn.
Napoléon . . . . . . *Fr.* nä-pō-lä-ôṅ'.
Napoleone . . . . . . nä-pō-lä-ō'-nä.
Napravnik . . . . . . nä-präv'-nĭk.
Narbada, see Nerbudda . när-bä'-dä.
Narciso Lopez . . . . när-thē'-sō lō'-pĕs, *or*
lō'-pĕth.
Narcissus . . . . . . när-sĭs'-ŭs.
Narvaez . . . . . . när-bä'-ĕth.
Naseby . . . . nāz'-bĭ.
Nasik, see Nassick . . . nä'-sĭk.
Nasmyth . . . . . . nā'-smith.
Nasr-ed-Din, see Nassr-
ed-Din . . . . . . näs'=r-ĕd-dēn'. [nä-sō'.
Nassau . . . . năs'-ô. *Ger.* näs'-ow. *Fr.*
Nassau (Is.) . . . . . năs'-ô.
Nassick, see Nasik . . . nä'-sĭk.
Nassr-ed-Din, see Nasr-
ed-Din . . . . . . näs'=r-ĕd-dēn'.
Natal . . . . nȧ-tăl'. *Port.* nä-täl'.
Natalie, see Nathalie . . năt'-ȧ-lē. *Fr.* nä-tä-lē'.
Natchitoches . . . . năk-ē-tŏsh',
năch-ĭ-tŏch'-ĕs.

Nathalie, see Natalie . . năth'-à-lē.
National Zeitung . . . nät"-zē-ō-näl' tzī'-tŏŏng.
Naucydes . . . . . . nô-sī'-dēz.
Nauplia . . . . . . nô'-plĭ-à.
Nausicaa . . . . . . nô-sĭk'-ä-ä, nô-sĭ-kä'-ä.
Nautch . . . . nôch.
Navajo . . . . năv'-ă-'hō.
Navarete, see Navarrette nä-vär-rä'-tä.
Navarino . . . . . . nä-vär-rē'-nō.
Navarra, *Sp.*, or . . . . nä-vär'-rä.
Navarre . . . . . . nà-vär'. *Fr.* nä-vär'.
Navarrette, see Navarete nä-vär-rä'-tä.
Navarro . . . . . . nä-vär'-rō.
Nazarene . . . . . . năz-à-rēn', năz'-ä-rēn.
Nazarite . . . . . . năz'-à-rīt.
Naze . . . . *Eng.* nāz. *Norw.* nä'-zĕ.
Nazianzen . . . . . . nä"-zĭ-ăn'-zĕn.
Nazimof . . . . . . nä-zē'-mŏf.
Nazimova . . . . . . nä-zē'-mō-vä.
Nebuchadnezzar, or . . nĕb"-ū-kăd-nĕz'-är.
Nebuchadrezzar . . . . nĕb"-ū-kăd-rĕz'-är.
Nebushazban . . . . nĕb-ū-shăz'-băn.
Neckar (R.) . . . . . nĕk'-kär.
Necker (Jacques) . . . nĕk'-ēr. *Fr.* nä-kâr'.
Neerwinden . . . . . nâr'-vĭn-dĕn.
Negri, Ada . . . . . ä'-dä' nä'-grē.
Négrier . . . . nä-grē=ā'.
Negritos . . . . . . nĕ-grē'-tōs.
                          Sp. nä-grē'-tōs.
Negropont . . . . . . nĕg'-rō-pŏnt.
Negros (Philippine I.) . . nä'-grōs.
Nekrasoff, or Nekrassoff . nĕk-rä'-sŏf.
Nellore, or . . . . . nĕ-lōr'.
Nellur . . . . nĕ-lōōr'.
Nemea (City) . . . . nē'-mē-à, nĕ-mē'-à.
Nemea (Games) . . . nĕ-mē'-à, nē'-mē-à,
                          nĕm'-ē-à.

Nemean . . . . . . ně-mē'-ȧn, nē'-mē-ȧn.
Nemesis . . . . . . něm'-ě-sĭs.
Némours . . . . . . nā-mōōr'.
Neoptolemus . . . . nē-ŏp-tŏl'-ē-mŭs.
Nepal, or Nepaul, see Nipal ně-pôl'.
Nepissing, see Nipissing . něp'-ĭs-ĭng.
Nepomuk . . . . . . nā'-pō-mōōk.
Nepos . . . . nē'-pŏs.
Neptune . . . . . . něp'-tūn.
Nerbudda, or Nerbuddah,
    see Narbada . . . . něr-bŭd'-dä.
Nereids . . . . . . nē'-rē-ĭdz.
Nereus . . . . nē'-rē-ŭs, nē'-rūs.
Nergalsharezer . . . . něr''-gäl-shă-rē'-zēr.
Neri . . . . nā'-rē.
Nerissa . . . . . . nē-rĭs'-sä.
Néron . . . . nā-rŏṅ'.
Néry . . . . nā-rē'.
Nesle . . . . nāl.
Neuchâtel . . . . . ně-shä-těl'.
Neueste Nachrichten . . noi'-ěs-tŭ nȧċh'-rĭċh-těn.
Neuilly-sur-Seine . . . ně-yē''-sür-sěn'.
Neumann . . . . . . nū'-mȧn. Ger. noĭ'-män.
Neuss . . . . nois.
Neuve Chapelle . . . . něv shă-pěl'.
Neuvillette, Christian de . krĭs-tē=äṅ' dŭ ně-věl-ět'.
Neuwied . . . . . . noĭ'-vēt.
Neva . . . . nē'-vȧ. Russ. nyě'-vä.
Nevada . . . . ně-vä'-dä.
Nevers . . . . ně-vâr'.
Nevis . . . . něv'-ĭs.
Nevskii Prospekt . . . něf'-skĭ=ĭ prŏs-pěkt'.
New-Chwang, see Niu-
    chuang . . . . . . nū-chwäng'.
Newfoundland . . . . *pop.* nū-fownd'-lȧnd,
                    loc. nū'-fŭnd-lănd,
                    nū-fŭnd-lănd'.

Newnham . . . . . . nūn'-ȧm.
New Orleans . . . . . nū ôr'-lē-ȧnz.
     loc. nū ōr-lā-äṅ'.
Nexö . . . . něks'-ē.
Ney . . . . nā.
Nez Percé . . . . . . nā pěr-sā'.
Ngan-hui, see Anhwei . . n-gän-hwē'.
Niam-Niam, see Nyam-
  Nyam . . . . . . nǐ=ăm'-nǐ=ăm'.
Niassa, see Nyassa . . nē=äs'-sä.
Nibelungenlied, or Nibe-
  lungen Lied . . . . nē'-bě-lŏŏng''-ěn-lēt.
Nicæa . . . . nǐ-sē'-ä.
Nicaragua . . . . . nǐk-ȧr-ä'-gwä.
     Sp. nē-kä-rä'-gwä.
Niccola Pisano, see Nicola nēk'-ō-lä pē-zä'-nō.
Niccolini . . . . . . nēk-kō-lē'-nē.
Niccolò, see Nicolò . . . nē-kō-lō'.
Nice . . . . nēs.
Nicene . . . . nǐ'-sēn.
Nicias . . . . nǐs'-ǐ-ȧs, nǐsh'-ǐ-ȧs.
Nicola, Niccola . . . . *It.* nē-kō'-lä.
Nicolai . . . . nē'-kō-lī.
Nicolette . . . . . . nē-kō-lět.'
Nicolò de' Lapi, see Niccolò nē-kō-lō' dä lä'-pē.
Nicot . . . . nē-kō'.
Nictheroy, see Nitherohi . nē-tā-rō'-ē.
Niebuhr . . . . . . nē'-bōōr.
Niemen . . . . . . nē'-měn. *Pol.* nyěm'-ěn.
Niepce . . . . nyěps.
Nietzsche . . . . . . nēt'-shŭ.
Nieuport, see Nieuwport . nē=ē-pōr'.
Nieuwe Kerke . . . nē-ēv'-ě kěrk'-ě.
Nieuwport, see Nieuport . nē=ēv'-pōrt.
Nieuwveld . . . . . nē=ēv'-fělt.
Nièvre . . . . nē-ěvr'.
Niflheim . . . . . . něf'-l-hīm.

Nigel	nĭ′-jĕl.
Niger	nĭ′-jẽr.
Nigra	nē′-grä.
Niigata	nē-ē-gä′-tä.
Nijni-Novgorod, or Nijniy-Novgorod, see Nizhni-Novgorod	nēsh′-nĭ-nŏv′-gŏ-rŏd.
Nike Apteros	nĭ′-kē ăp′-tĕ-rŏs.
Nikisch	nē′-kĭsh.
Nikita	nē-kē′-tä.
Nikko	nēk′-kō.
Nikola	nē′-kō-lä.
Nilsson (Christine) . . .	nĭl′-sŏn.
Nimar	nē-mär′.
Nimeguen, see Nimwegen	nĭm′-ä-gĕn.
Nîmes, see Nimes . . .	nēm.
Nimwegen, see Nimeguen and Nymegen	nĭm′-wä-gĕn.
Niña, La	lä nēn′-yä.
Nineveh	nĭn′-ĕ-vŭ.
Ningpo, or	nĭng′-pō′.
Ningpo-fu	nĭng′-pō′-fōō′.
Niño	nēn′-yō.
Ninon de Lenclos, or L'Enclos	nē-nôn′ dŭ lŏn-klō′.
Niobe	nĭ′-ō-bē.
Nipal, see Nepal . . .	nĭ-pôl′.
Niphon, see Nipon . . .	nĭf-ŏn′.
Nipissing, see Nepissing .	nĭp′-ĭs-sĭng.
Nipon, or	nĭp-ŏn′.
Nippon, see Niphon . .	nĭp-ŏn′.
Nirvana	nĭr-vä′-nä.
Nisan	nĭ′-săn.
Nisard	nē-zär′.
Nisch, or Nish, see Nissa	nēsh.
Nismes, see Nîmes . .	nēm.
Nissa, see Nisch . . .	nēs′-sä.

Nitherohi, see Nictheroy . nē-tä-rō′-ē.

Nitocris . . . . . . nĭ-to′-krĭs.

Nitti . . . . nēt′-tē.

Niu-chuang, see New-
  Chwang . . . . . nū-chwăṅ′.

Nivelle . . . . nē-vĕl′.

Nivernais . . . . . . nē-vĕr-nĕ′.

Nivernaise . . . . . nē-vĕr-nĕz′.

Nivôse . . . . nē-vŏz′.

Nizam . . . . nĭ-zăm′, nī′-zăm.

Nizhni-Novgorod, see Nij-
  ni-Novgorod . . . . nēzh′-nĭ-nŏv′-gŏ-rŏd.

Noachian . . . . . . nō-ā′-kĭ-àn.

Noacolly, see Noakhali . nō-ă-kŏl′-ĭ.

Noailles . . . . . . nō-ī′, nō-ä′=yŭ.

Noakhali, see Noacolly . nō-äk-hä′-lē.

Nobel . . . . nō-bĕl′.

Noctes Ambrosianae . . nŏk′-tēz ămbrō″-zĭ-ā′-nē.

Nodier . . . . nō-dē=ā′.

Noël . . . . nō-ĕl′.

Nogi . . . . nō′-gē′.

Noir Fainéant . . . . nwär fā-nā-äṅ′.

Noli me tangere . . . nō′-lī mē tăn′-jĕ-rē.

Noll . . . . nŏl.

Nombre de Dios . . . nōm′-brä dä dē′-ōs.

Nome . . . . nōm.

Nord . . . . *Fr.* nōr.

Nordau . . . . nōr′-dow.

Nordenskjöld . . . . nōō′-dĕn-shĕlt.

Nordica . . . . . . nôr′-dĭ-kä.

Nördlingen . . . . . nērd′-lĭng-ĕn.

Norn . . . . nôrn.

Northanger (Abbey) . . nôrth′-än-jĕr.

Norumbega . . . . . nō-rŭm-bē′-gä.

Norwich . . . . . . *Eng.* nŏr′-ĭch, nŏr′-ĭj.
  Am. nôr′-wĭch.

Nôtre Dame . . . . . nō′-tr dăm.

Nottingham . . . . . nŏt'-ĭng-ảm.
Nourmahal . . . . . nōōr-mả-häl'.
Novaes, Guiomar . . . gē-ō'-mär nō-vä'-ĕs.
Novalis . . . . nō-vä-'lĭs.
Novara . . . . nō-vä'-rä.
Nova Scotia . . . . . nō'-vả skŏ'-shĭ=ả.
Novaya Zemlya, or . . *Russ.*, nō'-vä-yä zĕm-lĭ=ä'.
Nova Zembla . . . . nō'-vả zĕm'-blả.
Novgorod . . . . . . nŏv'-gŏ-rŏd.
Novikoff . . . . . . nŏv'-ĭ-kŏf.
Novó Bazar . . . . . nō-'vō' bä-zär'.
Novo Georgievsk . . . nō-vō' gē-ôr'-gē-efsk.
Nowanagar, or . . . . nō"-wä-nä-gär'.
Nowanuggur . . . . . nō"-wä-nŭ-gŭr'.
Noyes . . . . noiz.
Noyon . . . . nwä-yōṅ'.
Nozze di Figaro, Le . . lä nŏt'-sĕ dē fē'-gä-rō.
Nuchingen, La Maison . lä mä-zôṅ' nü-säṅ-zhôṅ'.
Nuddea, see Nadiya . . nŭd'-ē-ä.
Nueva Andalucía . . . nōō=ä'-vä
　　　　　　　　　　 än"-dä-lōō-thē'-ä.
Nueva Ecija . . . . . nōō=ä'-vä ä'-thē-ćhä.
Nueva Galicia . . . . nōō=ä'-vä gä-lē'-thē-ä.
Nueva Vizcaya . . . . nōō='-vä bēth-kī'-ä.
Nuevitas . . . . . . nōō=ä"-vē-täs'.
Nuevo Leon . . . . . nōō=ä'-vō lä-ōn'.
Nuggur . . . . nŭg'-ŭr.
Nunce Dimittis . . . . noŏnk dĭ-mĭt'tĭs.
Nundydroog . . . . . nŭn-dĭ-drōōg'.
Nuneaton . . . . . . nŭn'-ē-tŭn.
Nuñez . . . . nōōn'-yĕth.
Nuova Antologia . . . nōō=ō'-vä än-tō-lō'-jä.
Nu-Pieds, Nu-pieds . . nü-pē-ä'.
Nyam-Nyam . . . . . n-yäm'-n-yäm'.
Nyanza . . . . n-yăn'-zä.
Nyassa, see Niassa . . nē=äs'-sä.
Nyassaland . . . . . nē=äs'-ä-lănd.

Nydia . . . . nĭd'-ĭ-ä.
Nyland . . . . nü'-länd.
Nymegan, see Nimwegen nĭm'-ā-gĕn.
Nyoro . . . . n-yō'-rō.
Nystad . . . . nü'-städ.

O

Oahu . . . . ō-ä'-hō͞o, wä'-hō͞o.
Ob, see Obi . . . . . ōb.
Obeid, El . . . . . . ĕl ō-bād', ĕl ō-bä'-ēd.
Ober Ammergau . . . ō'-bĕr äm'-mĕr-gow.
Oberland . . . . . . ō'-bĕr-länt.
Obermann. . . . . . ō-bĕr-män'.
Oberon . . . . ō'-bĕ-rŏn, ŏb'-ēr-ŏn.
Oberpfalz . . . . . . ō'-bĕr-pfälts.
Obi, see Ob . . . . . ō'-bē.
Obidicut . . . . . . ō-bĭd'-ĭ-cŭt.
Obispo, Calle . . . . käl'-yā ō-bĭs'-pō.
Obiter dicta . . . . . ō'-bĭ-tēr dĭk'-tä.
Obregon . . . . . . ō-brä-gōn'.
Obrenovitch . . . . . ō-brĕn'-ō-vĭch.
Ocaña . . . . ō-kän'-yä.
Ocantos . . . . . . ō-kän'-tōs.
Oceana. . . . . . . ō-sē'-à-nä, ō-shē-ä'-nà,
 ō-shē-ä'-nà.
Oceania, or . . . . . ō-sē-ä'-nĭ-à, ō-shē-ä'-nĭ-à.
Oceanica . . . . . . ō-sē-ăn'-ĭ-kà,
 ō-shē-ăn'-ĭk-à.
Oceanides . . . . . . ō-sē-ăn'-ĭ-dēz.
Oceanus . . . . . . ō-sē'-à-nŭs.
Ochiltree . . . . . . ōċh'-l-trē.
Ochoa y Acuña . . . . ō-chō'-à ē ä-kō͞on'-yà.
Ocklawaha . . . . . ŏk-lä-wä'-hä.
Oconomowoc . . . . . ō-kō-nŏm'-ō-wŏk.
Octavian . . . . . . ŏk-tā'-vĭ-àn.
Odelsthing . . . . . ō'-dĕlz-tĭng.

Odéon . . . . ō-dē'-ŏn.   *Fr.* ō-dā-ôṅ'.
Odessa . . . . ō-dĕs'-ä.
Odoacer, see Ottokar, or . ō-dō-ā'-sēr.
Odovaker . . . . . . ō-dō-vä'-kär.
Odysseus . . . . . . ō-dĭs'-ē-ŭs, ō-dĭs'-sūs.
Odyssey . . . . ŏd'-ĭs-ē.
Œdipe . . . . *Fr.* ē-dēp'.
Œdipus Coloneus . . . ĕd'-ĭ-pŭs kō-lō-nē'-ŭs,
        kō-lō'-nūs.
Œdipus Tyrannus . . . ĕd'-ĭ-pŭs tĭr-ăn'-ŭs.
Oehlenschläger, see Öhlen-
    schläger . . . . . ē'-lĕn-shlā"-gĕr.
Oenone . . . . . . ē-nō'-nĕ.
Oersted, see Örsted . . ēr'-stĕd.
Oesterreich, see Österreich ēs'-tĕr-rīċh.
Offenbach, Jacques . . zhäk ŏf-ĕn-bäk'.
        Ger. ŏf-ĕn-bäċh'.
Ofterdingen . . . . . ŏf'-tĕr-dĭng"-ĕn.
Oggione, see Uggione . . ōj-jō'-nĕ.
Ogier . . . . ō'-jĭ-ēr.
Ogier de Danemarcke . . ō-zhē̄=ā' dŭ dăn-märk'.
Ogier le Danois . . . . ō-zhē̄=ä' lĕ dä-nwä'.
Ogoway, or Ogowé . . . ō-gō-wä'.
O'Higgins . . . . . . ō-hĭg'-ĭnz.   *Sp.* ō-ē'-gēns.
Öhlenschläger, see Oehlen-
    schläger . . . . . . ē'-lĕn-shlā"-gĕr.
Ohnet, Georges . . . . zhŏrzh zō-nā'.
Ohod, or . . . . . . ō-hōd'.
Ohud . . . . ō-hōōd'.
Oileus . . . . ō-ĭl'-ē-ŭs, ō-ī'-lūs.
Oise . . . . wäz.
Ojeda . . . . ō-ċhā'-dä.
Ojetti . . . . ō-yāt'-tē.
Okayama . . . . . . ō'-kä'-yä'-mä'.
Okefinokee . . . . . ō"-kē-fĭ-nō'-kē.
Okhotsk Sea . . . . . ō-ċhtōsk', ō-hōtsk'.
Okinawa . . . . . . ō-kē-nä'-wä.

Oklahoma . . . . . . ŏk-lä-hō'-mä.
Okuma . . . . ō'-kōō'-mä'.
Okumura . . . . . . ō'-kōō'-mōō'-rä'.
Olaf . . . . ō'-läf.
Olaus (St.) . . . . . ō-lä'-ŭs.
Oldenbarneveldt, van . . fän ōl"-dĕn-bär'-nĕ-vĕlt.
Ole . . . . ō'-lä.
Oléron . . . . ō-lä-rŏṅ'.
Olifaunt . . . . . . ŏl'-ĭ-fȧnt.
Oliphant . . . . . . ŏl'-ĭ-fȧnt.
Olitzka . . . . ō'-lĭts-kä.
Oliva (Peace of) . . . . ō-lē'-fä.
Olivarez . . . . . . ō-lē-vä'-rĕth.
Olivia . . . . ō-lĭv'-ĭ-ä.
Ollivier, Émile . . . . ä-mēl' ō-lē-vē=ā'.
Olmütz . . . . ŏl'-mütz.
Olympe . . . . . . Fr. ō-lăṅp'.
Olympiad . . . . . . ō-lĭm'-pĭ-ăd.
Olympus . . . . . . ō-lĭm'-pŭs.
Omaha . . . . ō'-mȧ-hä.
Oman . . . . ō-män'.
Omar Khayyam, see Umar
   Khaiyâm . . . . . ō'-mär khī-yäm'.
Omar Pasha, see Omer
   Pasha . . . . . . ō'-mär pȧsh-ô', pȧ-shä',
               päsh'-ȧ.
Omega . . . . ō'-mĕg-ä, ō-mĕg'-ȧ.
Omer Pasha, see Omar
   Pasha . . . . . ō-mĕr pash-ô', pȧ-shä',
               päsh'-ȧ.
Omeyyades, see Ommiads ō-mä'-yădz.
Ommaya . . . . . . ŏm-mä'-yä.
Ommiads, see Omeyyades ō-mī'-ădz.
Omphale . . . . . . ŏm'-fȧ-lē.
Omsk . . . . ŏmsk.
Oñate . . . . ōn-yä'-tä.
Onega (L.) . . . . . ō-nē'-gȧ. Russ. ōn-yĕ'-gä.

Oneida	ō-nī′-dä.
Onesimus	ō-nĕs′-ĭ-mŭs.
Onesiphorus	ō-nē″-sĭf′-ō-rŭs.
Ongaro, Dall' . . .	däl ōng′-gä-rō.
Onias	ō-nī′-ȧs.
Onions (Oliver) . . .	ō-nī′-ŭnz.
Onondaga	ŏn-ŏn-dô′-gȧ.
Oodeypoor, see Udaipur .	ōō-dī-pōōr′.
Oonalaska, see Unalaska	ōō-nȧ-lăs′-kȧ.
Ophelia	ō-fē′-lĭ-ȧ, ō-fēl′-yȧ.
Ophir	ō′-fēr.
Ophiucus	ō-fī-yū′-kŭs, ŏf-ĭ-ū′-kŭs.
Opie	ō′-pĭ.
Opigena	ō-pĭj′-ē-nȧ.
Oporto, Port, o. Porto . .	ō-pōr′-tō.
	Port. ōō-pōr′-tōō.
Oppenheim	ŏp′-ĕn-hīm.
Ops	ŏps.
Oran	ō-rän′. Fr. ō-räṅ′.
Orcagna	ōr-kän′-yä.
Oread	ō′-rē-ăd.
Orel	ō-rĕl′.
Orellana	ō-rāl-yä′-nä.
Orense	ō-rĕn′-sā.
Orestes	ō-rĕs′-tēz.
Orfeo ed Euridice . . .	ŏr-fā′-ō ĕd ā=ōō-rē-dē′-chĕ.
Oriana	ō-rĭ-ȧn′-ȧ.
Origen, or	ŏr′-ĭ-jĕn.
Origenes	ō-rĭj′-ĕ-nēz.
Orinoco	ō-rĭ-nō′-kō.
Orion	ō-rī′-ŏn.
Orissa	ō-rĭs′-ä.
Orizaba	ō-rē-thä′-bä.
Orlando	ôr-lăn′-dō. It. ōr-län′-dō.
Orlando Furioso . . .	ŏr-län′-dō fōō-rē-ō′-sō.
Orlando Innamorato . .	ŏr-län′-dō ēn-nä″-mō-rä′-to.

Orléanais, see Orléannais   ôr-lā-ä-nĕ'.
Orleanists . . . . . .   ôr'-lē-àn-ĭsts".
Orléannais, see Orléanais   ôr-lā-ä-nĕ'.
Orléans (Maid of) . . .   ôr'-lē-ànz. *Fr.* ôr-lā-äṅ'.
Orloff . . . .   ŏr-lŏf'.
Ormulum . . . . . .   ôr'-mū-lŭm.
Ormuzd . . . . . .   ôr'-mŭzd, ôr'-mŏŏzd.
Orne . . . .   ôrn.
Oronte . . . .   ō-rôṅt'.
Orontes . . . . . .   ō-rŏn'-tēz.
Orphée et Euridice . .   ôr-fā' ā ē-rē-dēs'.
Orphéon . . . . . .   ôr-fā-ôṅ'.
Orpheus . . . . . .   ôr'-fē-ŭs, ôr'-fūs.
Or San Michele . . . .   ōr sän mē-kā'-lā.
Orsay . . . .   ŏr-sā'.
Orsini . . . .   ōr-sē'-nē.
Orsino . . . .   ôr-sē'-nō. *It.* ōr-sē'-nō.
Orsova . . . .   ōr'-shō-và.
Örsted, see Oersted . .   ēr'-stĕd.
Ortega . . . .   ōr-tā'-gä.
Orthez, see D'Orthez . .   ōr-tĕss', ŏr-tĕz'.
Ortrud . . . .   ōr'-trōōt.
Oruba . . . .   ō-rōō'-bä.
Orvieto . . . .   ōr-vē=ā'-tō.
Osage . . . .   ō-sāj', ō'-sàj. *Fr.* ō-zäzh'.
Osaka, see Ozaka . .   ō-sä'-kä.
Osbaldistone . . . . .   ŏs-bôl'-dĭs-tŭn.
Osceola . . . . . .   ŏs-ē-ō'-lä.
Osiris . . . .   ō-sī'-rĭs.
Osman Digna . . . .   ŏs'-măn dĭg'-nä.
Osmanli . . . . . .   ŏs-măn'-lĭ.
Osnabrück . . . . .   ŏs'-nä-brük.
Ospedale degli Innocenti .   ōs-pā-dä'-lĕ dāl'-yē
                              ēn-nō-shān'-tē.
Osrick . . . .   ŏz'-rĭk.
Ossa . . . .   ŏs'-à.
Osserwatore Romano . .   ōs"-sĕr-vä-tō'-rä rō-mä'-nō.

Ossian . . . . ŏsh'-àn, ŏsh'-ē=àn
Ossoli . . . . ōs'-sō-lē.
Ostade . . . . ŏs'-tä-dĕ.
Ostend . . . . ŏs-tĕnd'.
Osterode (in Harz) . . ŏs'-tĕ-rō"-dŭ.
Österreich, see Oesterreich ēs'-tĕr-rĭċh.
Ostrogoths . . . . . ŏs'-trō-gŏths.
Otaheite, or Otaheiti . . ō-tä-hē'-tē.
Othello . . . . ō-thĕl'-ō.
Othman . . . . . . ŏth-män'.
Otho . . . . ō'-thō.
Otranto . . . . . . ō-trän'-tō.
Otricoli . . . . ō-trē'-kō-lē.
Ottawa (Canada) . . . ŏt'-à-wä.
Ottawa (Ohio) . . . . ŏt'-à-wä.
Ottilie . . . . ŏt'-tēl-yŭ.
Otto . . . . ŏt'-tō.
Ottokar, see Odoacer . . ŏt'-tō-kär.
Oude, see Oudh, Audh . owd.
Oudenaarde, or Ouden-
    arde, see Audenarde . ow'-dĕn-är"-dĕ.
Oudh, see Oude, Audh . owd.
Oudinot . . . . . . ōō-dē-nō'.
Ouida . . . . ōō=ē'-dä, wē'-dä
Ourcq . . . . ōōrk.
Ouse . . . . ōōz.
Outram . . . . . . ōō'-tràm.
Ovalle (Alfonso) de . . dä ō-väl'-yä.
Overijssel, or Overyssel . ō'-vĕr-īs"-sĕl.
Ovid . . . . ŏv'-ĭd.
Oviedo . . . . ō-vē-ä'-dō.
Owhyhee, or Owyhee . . ō-wī'-hē.
Oxenstiern, or . . . . ŏks'-ĕn-stērn.
Oxenstierna, or Oxen-
    stjerna, Sw. . . . . ŏks'-ĕn-shâr"-nä.
Oxon . . . . ŏks'-ŭn.
Oxonian . . . . . . ŏks-ō'-nĭ=àn.

Oyama . . . . ō-yä'-mä.
Oyer . . . . ō'-yĕr.
Ozaka, see Osaka . . . ŏ-zä'-kä.
Ozaki . . . . ō'-zä'-kē'.
Ozias . . . . ō-zĭ'-às.

P

Paardeberg . . . . . pär'-dĕ-bĕrċh.
Pablo . . . . *Sp.* päb'-lō.
Pabna . . . . päb'-nä.
Pacchiarotto . . . . päk″-kē-är-ōt'-tō.
Pacha, see Pasha . . . pǎsh-ô', pà-shä', päsh'-à.
Pacheco . . . . . . pä-chä'-kō.
Pachmann. . . . . . päċh'-män.
Pachuca . . . . . . pä-chōō'-kä.
Pactolus . . . . . . pǎk-tō'-lŭs.
Padan-aram . . . . . pä-dàn-âr'-àm.
Paderewski . . . . . pä-dä-rĕv'-skē.
Padilla, Juan Lopez de . ċhōō=än' lō'-päth dä
　　　　　　　　　　pä-dēl'-yä.
Padishah . . . . . . pä-dē-shä'.
Padoue, *Fr.,* or . . . . pä-dōō'.
Padova, *It.,* or . . . . pä'-dō-vä.
Padua . . . . pǎd'-yū-à.
Paedobaptist, see Pedo-
　baptist . . . . . . pē-dō-bǎp'-tĭst.
Paesiello, see Paissiello . pä″=ā-zē=ĕl'-lō.
Paestum . . . . . . pĕs'-tŭm.
Páez . . . . pä'-ĕs.
Paganini . . . . . . pä-gà-nĭn'-i.
　　　　　　　　　It. pä-gä-nē'-nē.
Paget . . . . pǎj'-ĕt. *Fr.* pä-zhä'.
Pagliacci, I. . . . . . ē päl-yä'-chē.
Pago-Pago, see Pango-
　Pango . . . . . . pän'-gō-pän'-gō.
Pailleron . . . . . . pä-yĕ-rôṅ'.

Painlevé	păṅ-lē-vā'.
Paissiello, see Paesiello .	pä"=ē-zē=äl'-lō.
Paiwar, see Peiwar . .	pī-wär'.
Paix des Dames . . .	pā dā dăm'.
Pajou	pä-zhōō'.
Pakenham	păk'-ĕn-àm.
Pakhoi, see Peihai . . .	päk-hoi'.
Pala d'Oro	pä'-lă dō'-rō.
Palaemon	pà-lē'-mŏn, pă-lē'-mŏn.
Palaeologus	pä-lē-ŏl'-ō-gŭs.
Palais Bourbon	pä-lā' bōōr-bôṅ'.
Palais de Justice . . .	pä-lā' dē zhüs-tēs'.
Palais du Trocadéro . .	pä-lā' dü trō-kä-dä-rō'.
Palais Royal	pä-lā' rwä-yăl'.
Palamedes	păl-ā-mē'-dēz.
Palamon and Arcite . .	păl'-à-mŏn and är'-sīt.
Palaos	pä-lä-ōs'.
Palatinate	pă-lăt'-ĭ-nāt.
Palatine	păl'-à-tīn, păl'-à-tĭn.
Palatinus	păl-ā-tī'-nŭs.
Palau, see Pellew, Pelew	pä-low'.
Paláwan	pä-lä'-wän.
Palazzo Borghese . . .	pä-lät'-sō bōr-gä'-zĕ.
Palazzo della Cancelleria	pä-lät'-sō dĕl'-lä kän"-chĕl-lä-rē'-ä.
Palazzo Doria	pä-lät'-sō dō'-rĭ-ä.
Palazzo Farnese. . . .	It. pä-lät'-sō fär-nä'-zĕ.
Palazzo Pandolfini . . .	pä-lät'-sō pän-dōl-fē'-nē.
Palazzo Pitti	pä-lät'-sō pēt'-tē.
Palazzo Pubblico . . .	pä-lät'-sō pōōb'-lē-kō.
Palazzo Reale	pä-lät'-sō rä-ä'-lĕ.
Palazzo Vecchio . . .	pä-lät'-sō vĕk'-kē-ō.
Palencia	pä-län'-thē-ä.
Palenque	pä-län'-kä.
Paleologus	pä-lē-ŏl'-ō-gŭs.
Palermo	pà-lĕr'-mō. It. pä-lĕr'-mō.
Palestine	păl'-ĕs-tīn.

Palestrina . . . . . . pä-lĕs-trē'-nä.
Palfrey . . . . pôl'-frĭ.
Palgrave . . . . . . pôl'-grāv.
Pali, see Pallee . . . . pä'-lē, pä'-lĭ.
Palikao . . . . pä-lē-kä'=ō.
Palinurus . . . . . . păl-ĭ-nū'-rŭs.
Palissy . . . . păl'-ĭs-ĭ.   Fr. pä-lē-sē'.
Palitana . . . . . . pä-lē-tä'-nä.
Palladio . . . . . . päl-lä'-dē-ō.
Pallas . . . . păl'-ȧs.
Pallee, see Pali . . . pä'-lē.
Pall Mall . . . . . . pĕl mĕl.
Palma Giovine . . . . päl'-mä jō'-vē-nĕ.
Palma Vecchio . . . . päl'-mä vĕk'-kē-ō.
Palmerston . . . . . päm'-ēr-stŭn.
Palmyra . . . . . . păl-mī'-rȧ.
Palo Alto . . . . . . pä'-lō äl'-tō.
Palos . . . . pä-lōs', pä'-lōs.
Pameer, see Pamir . . pä-mēr'.
Pamela . . . . pȧ-mē'-lȧ, păm'-ē-lȧ.
Pamir, see Pameer . . pä-mēr'.
Pamlico . . . . . . păm'-lĭ-kō.
Pampanga . . . . . . päm-pän'-gä.
Pampeluna, or . . . . päm-pä-loo'-nä.
Pampelune, Fr., or . . pŏṅp-lün'.
Pamplona . . . . . . päm-plō'-nä.
Panama . . . . . . păn-ȧ-mä'. Sp. pä-nä-mä'.
Panathenæa . . . . . păn''-ăth-ē-nē'-ȧ.
Panay . . . . pä-nä'=ē.
Panch Mahalz . . . . pȧnch mȧ-hälz'.
Pandæan, see Pandean . păn-dē'-ȧn.
Pandarus . . . . . . păn'-dȧ-rŭs.
Pandean, see Pandæan . păn-dē'-ȧn.
Pando . . . . păn'-dō.
Pandoor, see Pandour . păn-door', păn'-door.
Pandora . . . . . . păn-dō'-rä.
Pandour, see Pandoor . păn-door', păn'-door.

Pangani . . . . . . päng-gä'-nē.
Pangasinan . . . . . pän″-gä-sē-nän'.
Pango-Pango, see Pago-
    Pago . . . . . . pän'-gō-pän'-gō.
Panhard . . . . . . păn-är'.
Panizzi . . . . pä-nēt'-sē.
Panjab, see Punjab, Pen-
    jab . . . . păn-jäb'.
Panna, see Punnah . . păn'-ä.
Panslavic . . . . . . păn-släv'-ĭk.
Pantagruel . . . . . păn-tăg'-rōō-ĕl.
                Fr. pän-tä-grü-ĕl'.
Pantalon, or . . . . . păn'-tȧ-lŏn.
Pantalone . . . . . . pän-tä-lō'-nĕ.
Pantheon . . . . . . păn'-thē-ŏn, păn-thē'-ŏn.
Panthéon . . . . . . *Fr.* pän-tä-ôṅ'.
Panurge . . . . . . păn-ērj'. *Fr.* pä-nürzh'.
Panza, Sancho . . . săn'-kō păn'-zä.
                Sp. sän'-chō pän'-thä.
Paola (Fra.) . . . . . pä'=ō-lä.
Paoli, di . . . . . . dē pä'=ō-lē.
Paolo Veronese . . . pä'=ō-lō vä-rō-nä'-zĕ.
Pao-ting, see Pauting . . pä-ō-tĭng'.
Paphian . . . . . . pā'-fĭ-ȧn.
Paphos . . . . pā'-fŏs.
Papin . . . . pä-păṅ'.
Pappenheim . . . . . päp'-ĕn-hīm.
Papua . . . . păp'-ōō-ȧ, pä'-pōō-ȧ.
Pará . . . . pä-rä'.
Paracali, see Parakale . pä-rä-kä'-lē.
Paracelsus . . . . . păr-ȧ-sĕl'-sŭs,
                păr-ā-sĕl'-sŭs.
Paraclet . . . . . . *Fr.* pä-rä-klĕ'.
Paraclete . . . . . . păr'-ȧ-klēt.
Paradiso . . . . . . pä-rä-dē'-zō.
Paragoa . . . . . . pä-rä-gō'-ä.
Paragua . . . . . . pä-rä'-gwä.

Paraguay, or . . . . . pär-à-gwī', pä-rä-gwā', p̆ar'-à-gwī.
Paraguaya, *Sp.* and *Port.* pär-ä-gwī'-ä.
Parahiba, or Parahyba . pä-rä-ē'-bä.
Parakale, see Paracali . pä-rä-kä'-lä.
Paramaribo . . . . . p̆ar-à-m̆ar'-ĭ-bō.
Paran . . . . pā'-ràn.
Paraná . . . . pä-rä-nä'.
Parañaque . . . . . pär-än-yä'-kä.
Parcae . . . . pär'-sē, pär'-kē.
Parc-aux-Cerfs . . . . pär-kō-sâr'.
Paré . . . . pä-rä'.
Paredes . . . . . pä-rä'-dĕs.
Parepa-Rosa . . . . pä-rä'-pä-rō'-zä.
Paria . . . . . . pä-rē-ä', pä'-rē-ä.
Parian . . . . . . pā'-rĭ-àn.
Paris . . . . . . p̆ar'-ĭs. *Fr.* p̆ar-ē'.
Paris, Comte de . . . kōṅt dŭ p̆ar-ē'.
Parisian . . . . . p̆a-rĭz'-ĭ=àn, pā-rĭzh'-àn.
Parisien . . . . . p̆ar-ēz-ē-ĕṅ'.
Parisienne . . . . . p̆ar-ēz-ē=ĕn'.
Parmegiano, see Parmigiano . . . . . . pär-mä-jä'-nō.
Parmenides . . . . . pär-mĕn'-ĭ-dēz.
Parmesan . . . . . . pär-mē-zăn'.
Parmigiano, see Parmegiano . . . . . pär-mē-jä'-nō.
Parnassian . . . . . pär-năs'-ĭ=àn.
Parnassus . . . . . pär-năs'-ŭs.
Parnell . . . . pär'-nĕl.
Parolles . . . . . . pä-rŏl'-ĕs.
Paros . . . . pā'-rŏs.
Parral . . . . pär-räl'.
Parrhasius . . . . p̆a-rä'-shĭ=ŭs.
Parsee, or Parsi . . . . pär'-sē.
Parsifal, or Parsival, see *Ger.* Parzival . . . . pär'-sē-fäl.

Partabgarh, see Pertab-
gurh . . . . pŭr-täb-gŭr'.
Parthenon. . . . . . pär'-thĕ-nŏn.
Parthenope . . . . . pär-thĕn'-ō-pē.
Parthenopean . . . . pär-thĕn"-ō-pē'-àn.
Parzival, see Parsifal . . pärt'-sē-fäl.
Pascal . . . . păs'-kăl. *Fr.* păs-kăl'.
Pasha, see Pacha . . . păsh-ô', pà-shä', päsh'-à.
Pasig . . . . pä-sēg'.
Pasini . . . . pä-sē'-nē.
Pasiphaë . . . . . . pä-sĭf'-ā-ē.
Pasquier . . . . . . päs-kē═ā'.
Passarowitz . . . . . päs-sä'-rō-vĭts.
Passau . . . . päs'-sow.
Passchendaele . . . . päs'-chĕn-dä-lĕ.
Passignano . . . . . päs-sēn-yä'-nō.
Passy . . . . pä-sē'.
Pasteur . . . . . . päs-tēr'.
Patchogue . . . . . păt-chōg', păt-chŏg'.
Pater (Walter) . . . . pā'-tēr.
Pater Patriæ . . . . . pā'-tēr pā'-trĭ-ē.
Patiala . . . . pŭt-ē-ä'-lä.
Patna . . . . păt'-nä.
Paton . . . . pāt'-n.
Patrae, or . . . . . . pā'-trē.
Patras . . . . pä-träs'.
Patroclus . . . . . . pä-trō'-klŭs, pă-trō'-klŭs.
Patti (Adelina) . . . . păt'-ē.
Paty de Clam, du . . . dü pä-tē' dŭ-kläm.
Pau . . . . pō.
Pauer . . . . pow'-ĕr.
Paul . . . . pôl. *Fr.* pōl. *Ger.* powl.
Paulina . . . . . . pô-lē'-nà, pô-lī'-nä.
Pauline, adj. . . . . . pô'-lĭn, pô'-lĭn.
Pauline, n. . . . . . pôl-lēn'. *Fr.* pō-lēn'.
Paulo, see Polo . . . pō'-lō. *It.* pä'═ōō-lō.
Pauncefote . . . . . pôns'-fŭt.

Paur . . . . powr.
Pausanias . . . . . pô-sā′-nĭ-ás.
Pausilipo, see Posilipo . pow-zē-lē′-pŏ.
Pauting, see Paoting . . pä=ō-tĭng′.
Pavia . . . . pä-vē′-ä.
Pavlowa . . . . . . päv′-lō-vä.
Pavlovsk . . . . . . päv-lŏvsk′.
Pawnee . . . . . . pô′-nē.
Paz, La . . . . . . *loc.* lä-päz′. *Sp.* lä päth.
Pazzi . . . . pät′-sē.
Peary (Robert E.) . . . pē′-rĭ.
Pecci, Gioachimo . . . jō-ä′-kē-mō pĕch′-ē.
Pe-chi-li, see Petchili . . pĕ-chē-lē′.
Pedobaptist, see Paedo-
    baptist . . . . . . pē-dō-băp′-tĭst.
Pedro . . . . pē′-drō. *Sp.* pā′-drō.
Peer Gynt . . . . . . pā′-ĕr günt, yünt.
Pegasean, Pegasian . . pē-gā′-sĭ-án.
Pegasus . . . . . . pĕg′-á-sŭs, pĕg′-ā-sŭs.
Pegu . . . . pē-gōō′, pĕ-gōō′.
Péguy, Charles . . . . shärl pä-gē′.
Peihai, see Peihoi, Pakhoi pī-hī′.
Pei-ho . . . . pā-hŏ′. *pop.* pī-hŏ′.
Peihoi, see Peihai, Pakhoi pī-hoi′.
Peiræus, see Piræus . . pī-rē′-ŭs.
Peirithous, see Pirithous . pī-rĭth′-ō-ŭs.
Peishwa, see Peshwa . . pĕsh′-wä.
Peiwar, see Paiwar . . pī-wär′.
Peixoto or Peixotto . . . pā-shō′-tōō.
Pekin (Ill.) . . . . . pē′-kĭn.
Pekin, or . . . . . . pē-kĭn′.
Peking (China) . . . . pē-kĭng′.
Pelagians . . . . . . pē-lā′-jĭ-ánz.
Pelagius . . . . . . pē-lā′-jĭ-ŭs.
Pelasgi . . . . pē-lăs′-jī.
Pelayo . . . . pā-lä′-yō.
Pele, or . . . . . . pē′-lē.

Pelee, or	pē'-lē.
Pelée, Pointe	pwănt pĕ=la'.
Peleus	pē'-lē-ŭs, pē'-lŭs.
Pelew, see Pellew, Palau	pĕ-lōō'.
Pelion	pē'-lĭ-ŏn.
Pélissier	pā-lēs-ē=ā'.
Pelleas	pĕl'-ē-ăs.
Pelléas et Mélisande . .	pĕl-ā-ăs' ā mā-lē-sänd'.
Pellew, see Pelew, Palau	pĕ-lōō'.
Pellico, Silvio	sēl'-vē-ŏ pĕl'-lē-kō.
Pellieux (Gen.), Le . .	lĕ pĕl-ē-ē'.
Pelopid	pĕl'-ō-pĭd.
Pelopidas	pĕ-lŏp'-ĭ-dăs.
Peloponnesian	pĕl"-ō-pŏn-nē'-shĭ=ản,
	pĕl"-ō-pŏn-nē'-shản.
Peloponnesus	pĕl"-ō-pŏn-ē'-sŭs.
Pelops	pē'-lŏps.
Pemigewasset	pĕm"-ĭj-ē-wŏs'-ĭt.
Penang	pē-năng'.
Peñas	pĕn'-yäs.
Penates	pē-nā'-tēz.
Penelope	pē-nĕl'-ō-pē.
Peniel	pĕ-nī'-ĕl.
Penjab, see Panjab, Pun-	
jab	pĕn-jäb'.
Penrith	pĕn'-rĭth.
Penryn	pĕn-rĭn'.
Penseroso, Il	ĭl pĕn-sĕ-rō'-sō.
Pensiero, Il	ēl pān-sē-ā'-rō.
Pensieroso, Il	ēl pān-sē-ā-rō'-sō.
Pentateuch	pĕn'-tȧ-tūk, pĕn'-tā-tūk.
Pentecost	pĕn'-tē-kŏst, pĕn'-tĕ-kōst.
Pentelic	pĕn-tĕl'-ĭk.
Pentelican	pĕn-tĕl'-ĭ-cản.
Penthesilea	pĕn"-thē-sĭ-lē'-ȧ.
Pentheus	pĕn'-thē-ŭs, pĕn'-thūs.
Penuel	pĕ-nū'-ĕl.

Penza . . . . pĕn'-zä.
Penzance . . . . . . pĕn-zăns'.
Pepe . . . . pā'-pĕ.
Pepin . . . . pĕp'-ĭn.
Pépin le Bref . . . . pā-păṅ' lĕ brĕf.
Pepys . . . . pēps, pĕps, pĭps, pĕp'-ĭs.
Pera . . . . pā'-rä.
Perak . . . . pā-räk'.
Perceval, Percival . . . pĕr'-sĕ-vȧl.
Percheron . . . . . . pĕr=shĕ-rôṅ'.
Perdicaris . . . . . pĕr-dēk'-ä-rĕs.
Perdiccas . . . . . . pĕr-dĭk'-ăs.
Perdita . . . . pĕr'-dĭ-tä.
Pereda, José Maria de . 'hō-sä' mȧ-rē'-ä dā
pā-rād'-thȧ.
Père Goriot . . . . . pâr gō-rē-yō'.
Père Lachaise . . . . pâr lä-shĕz'.
Peremysl . . . . . . pĕr'-ĕ-mĭsl.
Perez (Antonio) . . . . pā'-rāth.
Pergamos . . . . . . pĕr'-gȧ-mŏs.
Pergamum . . . . . pĕr'-gȧ-mŭm.
Pergolese, or . . . . . pĕr-gō-lā'-zĕ.
Pergolesi . . . . . . pĕr-gō-lā'-zē.
Peri . . . . pē'-rĭ.
Peri (It. composer) . . pā'-rē.
Periander . . . . . . pĕr-ĭ-ăn'-dĕr.
Pericles . . . . . . pĕr'-ĭ-klēz.
Périer, Casimir . . . . käz-ē-mēr' pā-rē=ā'.
Périgord . . . . . . pā-rē-gōr'.
Périgueux . . . . . . pā-rē-gē'.
Periœci . . . . . . pĕr-ĭ-ē'-sī.
Perizzites . . . . . . pĕr'-ĭ-zīts.
Pernambuco . . . . . pĕr-nȧm-bū'-kō,
pĕr-näm-boo'-kō.
Port. pĕr-näṅ-boo'-koo.
Péronne . . . . . . pā-rŏn'.
Perosi . . . . pā-rō'-sē.

Perowne . . . . . . pĕ-rown'.
Perpignan . . . . . . pĕr-pēn-yäṅ'.
Persephone . . . . . pĕr-sĕf'-ō-nē.
Perseus . . . . . . pĕr'-sē-ŭs, pĕr'-sūs.
Persia . . . . pĕr'-shĭ=à, pĕr'-shà,
 pĕr'-zhà.
Persian . . . . pĕr'-shàn, pĕr'-zhàn.
Pertabgurh,
 see Partabgarh . . . pĕr-täb-gŭr'.
Peru, or . . . . . . pĕ-rōō'.
Perú, Sp. . . . . . . pā-rōō'.
Perugia . . . . . . pā-rōō'-jä.
Perugino . . . . . . pā-rōō-jĕ'-nō.
Peruzzi, Baldassare . . bäl-däs-sä'-rä pā-rōŏt'-sē.
Pesaro . . . . pā'-zä-rō.
Pescadores . . . . . pĕs-kä-dō'-rĕs.
Pescara . . . . . . pĕs-kä'-rä.
Peschiera . . . . . . pĕs-kē=ä'-rä.
Peshawar, or Peshawur . pĕsh-ow'-ēr.
Peshwa, see Peishwa . . pĕsh'-wä.
Pestalozzi . . . . . . pĕs-tä-lŏt'-sē.
Pesth . . . . pĕst. Hung. pĕsht.
Pétain . . . . pā'-tăṅ'.
Petchili, see Pe-chi-li . . pĕ-chē-lē'.
Petchora . . . . . . pĕt-chō'-rä, pĕt'-chō-rä.
Péthion, or Pétion . . . pā-tē-ôṅ'.
Petit André . . . . . pĕ-tē' täṅ-drä'.
Petöfi . . . . pĕ'-tĕ-fĭ.
Petrarca, It., or . . . . pā-trär'-kä.
Petrarch . . . . . . pē'-trärk.
Petrine . . . . pĕ'-trīn, pē'-trĭn'.
Petrograd . . . . . . pĕt'-rō-gräd.
Petruccio . . . . . . pā-trōŏch'-ō.
Petruchio . . . . . . pē-trū'-chĭ-ō.
 It. pā-trōŏ'-kē-ō.
Petschnikoff . . . . . pĕtsh'-nē-kŏf.
Peyrebrune . . . . . pâr-brün'.

Pfalz . . . . pfälts.
Phæacians . . . . . fē-ā'-shǐ-ȧnz.
Phædo, or . . . . . . fē'-dō.
Phædon . . . . . . fē'-dǒn.
Phædra . . . . . . fē'-drä.
Phædrus . . . . . . fē'-drŭs.
Phæthon . . . . . . fā'-ĕ-thǒn.
Phalaris . . . . . . fǎl'-ȧ-rǐs.
Phanariot . . . . . . fǎ-nǎr'-ǐ-ǒt.
Pharaoh . . . . . . fā'-rō, fā'-rā-ō.
Pharisee . . . . . . fǎr'-ǐ-sē.
Pharos . . . . fā'-rǒs, fä'-rǒs.
Pharpar . . . . . . fär'-pär.
Pharsalus . . . . . . fär-sā'-lŭs.
Phèdre . . . . fĕdr.
Phenice . . . . . . fē-nī'-sē.
Phenicia, see Phœnicia . fĕ-nǐsh'-ǐ=ȧ.
Phidias . . . . . . fǐd'-ǐ-ȧs.
Philae . . . . fī'-lē.
Philemon . . . . . . fǐ-lē'-mǒn, fī-lē'-mǒn.
Philémon et Baucis . . fē-lā-mȯṅ' ā bō-sēs'.
Philinte . . . . . . fē-lǎṅt'.
Philippa . . . . . . fǐl-ǐp'-ȧ.
Philippe Egalité . . . . fē-lēp' ā-gǎl-ē-tā'.
Philippi . . . . . . fǐ-lǐp'-ī.
Philippians . . . . . fǐ-lǐp'-ǐ-ȧnz.
Philippine (Is.) or . . . fǐl'-ǐp-ǐn. pop. fǐl'-ǐ-pīn.
Philippines . . . . . fǐl'-ǐp-ǐnz. pop. fǐl'-ǐ-pīnz.
Philistine . . . . . . fǐl-ǐs'-tǐn, fǐl'-ǐs-tǐn.
Philoctetes . . . . . fǐl-ǒk-tē'-tēz.
Philo Judæus . . . . fī'-lō jōō-dē'-ŭs.
Philomel . . . . . . fǐl'-ō-mĕl.
Philomela . . . . . . fǐl-ō-mē'-lä.
Phineas . . . . . . fǐn'-ē-ȧs.
Phlegethon . . . . . flĕj'-ĕ-thǒn, flĕj'-ē-thǒn.
Phlegyas . . . . . . flē'-jǐ-ȧs.
Phocæa . . . . . . fō-sē'-ȧ.

Phocian . . . . fō'-shǐ=àn.
Phocion . . . . fō'-shǐ-ŏn.
Phocis . . . . fō'-sǐs.
Phœbus . . . . . . fē'-bŭs.
Phœnicia, see Phenicia . fē-nǐsh'-ǐ=à.
Phorcys . . . . . . fôr'-sǐs, fôr'-kǐs.
Phrygia . . . . . . frǐj'-ǐ-à.
Phryne . . . . frī'-nē.
Phthiotis . . . . . . thī-ō'-tǐs.
Piacenza . . . . . . pē-ä-chĕn'-zä.
Piauhí, or Piauhy . . . pē-ow-ē'.
Piave . . . . pē-ä'-vĕ.
Piazza del Gran Duca, or pē-ät'-sä dĕl grän dōō'-kä.
Piazza della Signoria . pē-ät'-sä dĕl'-lä
                         sēn-yō-rē'-ä.
Piazza del Popolo . . . pē-ät'-sä dĕl pō'-pō-lō.
Piazza di Spagna . . . pē-ät'-sä dē spän'-yä.
Picardy . . . . . . pǐk'-är-dǐ.
Picasso . . . . pē-kǎ-sō'.
Piccini . . . . pē-chē'-nē.
Picciola . . . . . . pē'-chō-lä.
Piccolomini . . . . . pēk-ō-lŏ'-mē-nē.
Pichegru . . . . . . pēsh-grōō'.
                      Fr. pēsh-grü'.
Pichincha . . . . . . pē-chēn'-chä.
Pico della Mirandola . . pē'-kō dĕl'-lä
                         mē-rän'-dō-lä.
Pico, Giovanni . . . . jō-vän'-nē pē'-kō.
Picot . . . . pē-kō'.
Picquard . . . . . . pē-kär'.
Picquigny . . . . . . pē-kēn-yĕ'.
Piedmont, see Piémont,
  Piemonte . . . . . pēd'-mŏnt.
Piedres (R.) . . . . . pē-ä'-dräs.
Piémont, *Fr.*, see Piedmont pē=ä-môṅ'.
Piemonte, *It.*, see Piedmont pē-ä-mōn'-tĕ.
Pierian . . . . pī-ē'-rǐ-àn.

Pierné . . . . pēr-nā′.
Pierre . . . . pē=âr′.
Pierrefonds . . . . . pē=âr-fôṅ′.
Pierrette . . . . . . pē=âr-ĕt′.
Pierrot . . . . pē=ĕr-rō′.
Pietà . . . . pē-ā-tä′.
Pietermaritzburg . . . pē-tĕr-mär′-ĭts-bŭrċh.
Pietro . . . . pē=ā′-trō.
Pilate . . . . *Bib.* pī′-lāt. *Fr.* pē-lät′.
Pilatus (Mt.) . . . . . pī-lā′-tŭs. *It.* pē-lä′-to͞os.
Pilatus, Pontius . . . . pŏn′-shĭ-ŭs pī-lā′-tŭs.
Piloty . . . . pē-lō′-tē, pē′-lō-tē.
Pilpay . . . . pĭl′-pī.
Pilsudski . . . . . . pĭl-soŏd′-skĭ.
Pinacotheca . . . . . pĭn″-á-kō-thē′-ká.
Pinacothek . . . . . pĭn′-á-kō-thĕk″.
                        Ger. pē-nä′-kō-tāk.
Pinar del Rio . . . . pē-när′ dĕl rē′-ō.
Pinchot . . . . . . pĭn′-shō.
Pincian (Hill) . . . . pĭn′-shĭ-àn, pĭn′-chàn.
Pincio, Monte . . . . mōn′-tĕ pēn′-chō.
Pindaric . . . . . . pĭn-dăr′-ĭk.
Pindarus . . . . . . pĭn′-dā-rŭs.
Pines, see Pinos, Isla de . pīnz.
Pinos, Isla de, see Pines . ēs′-lä dä pē′-nōs.
Pinta, La . . . . . . lä pēn′-tä.
Pinto, Aníbal . . . . . ä-nē′-bäl pĭn′-tō.
Pinturicchio . . . . . pēn-to͞o-rēk′-kē=ō.
Pinzon . . . . *Sp.* pĭn-thōn′.
Piombo . . . . pē-ŏm′-bō.
Piotrkow . . . . . . pē-yŏtr′-kŏv.
Piozzi . . . . . . pĭ-ŏz′-ĭ. *It.* pē-ŏt′-sē.
Pippa . . . . pĭp′-pä.
Piqua . . . . pĭk′-wä, pĭk′-wā.
Pique-Dame . . . . . pēk-dăm.
Piræeus, or . . . . . pī-rē′-yūs.
Piræus, see Peiræus . . pī-rē′-ŭs.

Pirithous, see Peirithous .   pī-rĭth'-ō-ŭs.
Piron . . . .   pē-rôṅ'.
Pisa . . . .   pī'-sà.   *It.* pē'-zä.
Pisano, Niccolò . . . .   nē-kō-lō' pē-zä'-nō.
Piscataqua . . . . .   pĭs-kăt'-à-kwä.
Pisces . . . .   pĭs'-ēz.
Pisgah . . . .   pĭz'-gä.
Pisistratidæ, or . . . .   pĭs-ĭs-trăt'-ĭ-dē.
Pisistratids . . . . .   pĭs-ĭs'-trà-tĭds.
Pisistratus . . . . .   pĭ-sĭs'-trà-tŭs,
                    pī-sĭs'-trā-tŭs.
Pissarro . . . . . .   pē-sä-rō'.
Pistoia, or Pistoja . . .   pĭs-tō'-yä.
Pitcairn (I.) . . . . .   pĭt'-kârn, pĭt-kârn'.
Pithom . . . .   pī'-thŏm.
Pittacus . . . . . .   pĭt'-à-kŭs.
Pitti . . . .   pĭt'-tē.
Pizarro . . . .   pĭ-zä'-rō.   *Sp.* pē-thär'-rō.
Place de la Bastille . .   plăs dŭ lä bäs-tē'=yŭ.
Place de la Concorde . .   plăs dŭ lä kôṅ-kōrd'.
Place du Carrousel . .   plăs dü kä-rōō-zĕl'.
Place Vendôme . . . .   plăs vŏṅ-dōm'.
Plaideurs, Les . . . .   lä plä-dēr'.
Planche . . . . . .   plänsh.
Planché . . . . . .   plän-shä'.
Planchette . . . . .   plän-shĕt'.
Plançon, Pol . . . .   pōl plän-sôṅ'.
Plantagenet . . . . .   plăn-tăj'-ĕ-nĕt.
Plantin, Musée . . . .   mü-zā' plän-tăṅ'.
Plassey, or Plassi . . .   pläs'-sĭ.
Plata, Rio de la, see Plate   rē'-ō dä lä plä'-tä.
Platæa, or . . . . .   plă-tē'-à, plä-tē'-à.
Platææ . . . .   plă-tē'-ē.
Plate (R.), see Rio de la
  Plata . . . .   plāt, plät.
Platine . . . .   plä'-tĭn.
Plato . . . .   plä'-tō.

Platonic . . . . . . plā-tŏn'-ĭk.
Plautus . . . . . . plô'-tŭs.
Plava . . . . plä'-vä.
Pléiade, La . . . . . lä plā-yăd'.
Pleiades, or . . . . . plī'-à-dēz.
Pleiads . . . . plī'-ădz.
Plessis-les-Tours . . . plĕ-sē'-lä-tōōr'.
Pleyel . . . . plī'-ĕl.
Pliny . . . . plĭn'-ĭ.
Plockhorst . . . . . plŏk'-hŏrst.
Ploërmel . . . . . . plō-ĕr-mĕl'.
Plombières . . . . . plôṅ-bē=âr'.
Plon-Plon . . . . . . plŏṅ-plŏṅ.
Plotinus . . . . . . plō-tī'-nŭs.
Pluto . . . . plū'-tō.
Pluton . . . . *Fr.* plü-tōṅ'.
Plutus . . . . plū'-tŭs.
Pluviose . . . . . . plü-vē-yŏz'.
Pnyx . . . . nĭks.
Pobyedonostsev . . . pŏb"-yĕ-dŏ-nŏs'-tsĕf.
Pocono . . . . pō'-cŏ-nō.
Poděbrad, or Podiebrad . pŏd'-yĕ-bräd.
Podolia . . . . pō-dō'-lĭ-à.
Podolsk . . . . . . pō-dōlsk'.
Poictiers, see Poitiers . . poi-tērz'.   *Fr.* pwä-tē=ā'.
Poincaré . . . . . . pwăṅ-kă-rā'.
Pointe Pelée, or . . . . *Fr.* pwăṅt pĕ-lā'.
(Point) Pelee, or Pele . . pē'-lē.
Poissy . . . . pwä-sē'.
Poitevin . . . . . . pwät-văṅ'.
Poitiers, see Poictiers . . poi-tērz'.   *Fr.* pwä-tē=ā'.
Poitou . . . . pwä-tōō'.
Polaris . . . . pō-lā'-rĭs.
Polavieja, Camilo . . . kä-mē'-lō pō"-lä-vē=ĕ́h'-ä.
Polignac . . . . . . pō-lēn-yäk'.
Polillo . . . . pō-lēl'-yō.
Politian . . . . . . pō-lĭsh'-ĭ-àn.

Polixenes . . . . . . pŏ-lĭks′-ĕ-nēz.
Poliziano, It. . . . . . pō-lēd-zē-ä′-nō.
Polk . . . . pōlk.
Pollaiuolo, or Pollajuolo . pōl″-lä-yōō=ō′-lō.
Pollux . . . . pŏl′-ŭks.
Polo, see Paulo . . . pō′-lō.
Polonius . . . . . . pō-lō′-nĭ-ŭs.
Poltava, see Pultowa . . pŏl-tä′-vä.
Polybius . . . . . pŏ-lĭb′-ĭ-ŭs.
Polycarp . . . . . . pŏl′-ĭ-kärp.
Polycletus, or . . . . pŏl-ĭ-klē′-tŭs.
Polyclitus . . . . . . pŏl-ĭ-klī′-tŭs.
Polycrates . . . . . pŏ-lĭk′-rȧ-tēz,
　　　　　　　pō-lĭk′-rȧ-tēz.
Polyeucte . . . . . . pō-lē-ēkt′.
Polygnotus . . . . . pŏl-ĭg-nō′-tŭs.
Polyhymnia, or . . . . pŏl-ĭ-hĭm′-nĭ-ȧ.
Polymnia . . . . . . pō-lĭm′-nĭ-ȧ.
Polynesia . . . . . . pŏl-ĭ-nē′-shĭ=ȧ.
Polyphemus . . . . pŏl-ĭ-fē′-mŭs.
Pomerania . . . . . pŏm-ĕr-ā′-nĭ-ȧ.
Pomfret, see Pontefract . pŏm′-frĕt.
Pomœrium . . . . . pō-mē′-rĭ-ŭm.
Pomona . . . . . . pō-mō′-nȧ.
Pompadour, de . . . . dŭ pŏm′-pȧ-dōōr.
　　　　　　Fr. dŭ pôṅ′-pä-dōōr′.
Pompeia . . . . . . pŏm-pē′-yȧ.
Pompeian . . . . . . pŏm-pē′-yȧn.
Pompeii . . . . . . pŏm-pā′-yē.
　　　　　　Lat. pŏm-pē′-yī.
Pompeius . . . . . . pŏm-pē′-yŭs.
Pompilia . . . . . . pōm-pē′-lē-ä.
Ponape . . . . pō′-nä-pä.
Ponce . . . . pŏn′-sē. *Sp.* pōn′-thä.
Ponce de Leon . . . . pŏns dŭ lē′-ŏn.
　　　　　　Sp. pōn′-thä dä lä-ōn′.
Ponchielli . . . . . . pōn-kē-ĕl′-lē.

Pondicherri, or
Pondicherry, or . . . . pŏn-dĭ-shĕr'-ĭ.
Pondichéry, Fr. . . . . pôṅ-dē-shā-rē'.
Pondoland . . . . . pŏn'-dō-lănd.
Poniatowski . . . . . pō-nē=ä-tŏv'-skē.
Pont-Aven . . . . . pŏṅ-tä-vôṅ'.
Pontchartrain . . . pŏn-chär-trān'.
          Fr. pôṅ-shär-trăṅ'.
Pontefract, see Pomfret . pŏn'-tĭ-frăkt.
          pop. pŏm'-frĕt.
Ponte Vecchio . . . . pŏn'-tĕ vĕk'-kē=ō.
Pontevedra . . . . . pōn-tä-vā'-drä.
Pontine . . . . . . pŏn'-tĭn, pŏn'-tīn.
Pontius . . . . . . pŏn'-shĭ-ŭs.
Pont Neuf . . . . . . pôṅ nēf.
Pont-Noyelles . . . . pôṅ'-nwä-yĕl'.
Pontoise . . . . . . pŏnt-wäz'.
Poo Choo, see Pou Tchou,
  Pu Chu . . . . . . poō choō'.
Poona, or Poonah . . . poō'-nä.
Pooree, see Puri . . . poō-rē'.
Pooshkin, see Pouschkin,
  Puschkin . . . . . poōsh'-kĭn, poōsh'-kĭn.
Popocatepetl . . . . . pō-pō''-kä-tä-pĕt'-l,
          pō-pō'-kä-tä-pĕt''-l.
Poppæa Sabina . . . . pŏp-pē'-ä să-bī'-nä.
Pordenone . . . . . pōr-dä-nō'-nĕ.
Pornic . . . . pōr-nēk'.
Porpora . . . . . . pōr'-pō-rä.
Porsena, or . . . . . pôr'-sĕ-nȧ.
Porsenna . . . . . . pôr-sĕn'-nȧ.
Port Arthur . . . . . pōrt är'-thĕr.
Port-au-Prince . . . . pōrt'-ō-prĭns'.
          Fr. pōr-tō-prăṅs'.
Porte (The) . . . . . pōrt.
Porteous . . . . . . pōr'-tē-ŭs.
Porte St.-Antoine . . . pōrt săṅ-tŏṅ-twăn'.

Porte St.-Denis . . . .   pōrt săn-dē-nē'.
Porte St.-Martin . . .   pōrt săn-mär-tăn'.
Porthos . . . . . .   pōr-tōs'.
Portia . . . .   pōr'-shĭ-à, pôr'-shĭ=à.
Portici . . . .   pōr'-tē-chē.
Porto Bello, see Puerto
  Bello . . . .   pōr'-tō bĕl'-lō.
                         Port. pōr'-tōō bāl'-yō.
Porto Rico, see Puerto Rico   pōr'-tō rē'-kō.
Port Saïd . . . . . .   pōrt sä-ēd'. *pop.* sād.
Portugal . . . . . .   pōrt'-yū-gàl.
                         Port. pōr-tōō-gäl'.
Portuguese . . . .   pōrt-yū-gēz', pōr'-tū-gēz,
                         or gēs.
Poseidon, or Posidon . .   pō-sī'-dŏn.
Posilipo, see Pausilipo .   pō-zē-lē'-pō.
Posthumus, Leonatus . .   lē-ō-nā'-tŭs pŏst'-hū-mŭs,
                         pŏs'-tū-mŭs.
Potchefstrom . . . .   pŏ'-chĕf-strŏm.
Potemkin . . . . . .   pŏ-tĕm'-kĭn.
                         Russ. pŏt-yŏm'-kĭn.
Potgieter . . . . . .   pŏt'-gē-tĕr.
Potinière, La . . . . .   lä pō-tēn-yâr'.
Potocka . . . . . .   pŏ-tŏt'-skä.
Potocki . . . . . .   pŏ-tŏt'-skē.
Potomac . . . . . .   pō-tō'-màk.
Potosí . . . .   pō-tō'-sē. *Sp.* pō-tō-sē'.
Potsdam . . . . . .   pŏts'-dăm.
                         Ger. pŏts'-däm.
Poughkeepsie . . . .   pō-kĭp'-sĭ.
Pourbus . . . . . .   pōōr-büs'.
Pourceaugnac, de . . .   dŭ pōōr-sōn-yäk'.
Pourtalès . . . . . .   pōōr-tä-lĕz'.
Pouschkin, or Pouchekine,
  see Pushkin, Pooshkin,
  Puschkin . . . . .   pōōsh'-kĭn, pōōsh'-kĭn.
Poussin . . . . . .   pōō-săn'.

Pou Tchou, see Poo Choo,
   Pu Chu . . . . . . po͞o cho͞o'.
Powhatan . . . . . . pō-ăt-än', pow-hăt-ăn'.
Pozières . . . . . . pō-zē=âr'.
Pozzuoli, see Puteoli . . pōt-so͞o-ō'-lē.
Prado . . . . . . prä'-dō.
Praed . . . . . . präd.
Præmunire (Statute of) . prē-mū-nī'-rĕ.
Præterita . . . . . prē-tēr'-ī-tä.
Prag . . . . . . präg.
Prague . . . . . . präg. *Fr.* präg.
Prairial . . . . . . prā-rē-ăl'.
Prairie de Chien . . . prā'-rē dū shēn.
               Fr. prā-rē' dü shē-ĕṅ'.
Prakrit . . . . . . prä'-krĭt, präk'-rĭt.
Prater . . . . . . prä'-tĕr.
Praxiteles . . . . . prăks-ĭt'-ĕ-lēz.
Pré aux Clercs (Le) . . prā ō klâr.
Pré Catalan . . . . prā kä-tä-läṅ'.
Précieuses Ridicules . . prā-sē-ēz' rē-dē-kül'.
Preciosa . . . . . prĕs-ĭ-ō'-sȧ.
               Ger. prät-sē-ō'-zä.
Predis, Ambrogio de . . äm-brō'-jō dä prä'-dēs.
Prelude (The) . . . . prē'-lūd, prĕl'-ūd.
Presbyterian . . . . . prĕz-bĭ-tē'-rĭ-ăn,
            prĕs-bĭ-tē'-rĭ-ăn.
Presidio . . . . . . prä-sē'-dē-ō.
Pressensé . . . . . . prĕs-sŏṅ-sä'.
Pretoria . . . . . . prē-tō'-rĭ-ȧ.
Prévost-Paradol . . . prā-vŏst'-pä-rä-dŏl'.
Priam . . . . . . prī'-ăm.
Priapus . . . . . . prī-ā'-pŭs.
Pribilof (-byloff) . . . prē-bē-lŏf'.
Priene . . . . . . prī-ē'-nē.
Prieska . . . . . . prēs'-kä.
Prigioni, Le Mie . . . lā mē'-ĕ prē-jō'-nē.
Prilep . . . . . . prē'-lĕp.

Prim (General) . . . . prēm.
Prince . . . . *Fr.* prăṅs.
Princesse de Clèves . . prăṅ-sĕs' dŭ klĕv.
Princesse Lointaine, La . lä praṅ-sĕs' lwăṅ-tĕn'.
Principe . . . . . . prēn'-chē-pĕ.
Principessa . . . . . prēn-chē-pĕs'-sä.
Prinz . . . . prĭnts.
Prinzessin . . . . . prĭnts-ĕs'-ĭn.
Prinzivalle . . . . . prĭnts-ē-väl'-lē.
Priscian . . . . . . prĭsh'-ĭ=àn.
Procne, see Progné . . prŏk'-nē.
Procris . . . . prŏk'-rĭs.
Procrustean . . . . . prō-krŭs'-tē-àn.
Proculeius . . . . . . prō-kū-lē'-ŭs.
Procyon . . . . . . prō'-sĭ-ŏn, prŏs'-ĭ-ŏn.
Profeta, Il, see Prophète,
  Le . . . . ēl prō-fā'-tä.
Profillet . . . . . . prō-fē-yā'.
Progné, see Procne . . prŏg-nā'.
Prokofief . . . . . . prō-kō'-fē-ĕf.
Promessi Sposi, I . . . ē prō-mĕs'-sē spō'-zē.
Promethean . . . . . prō-mē'-thē-àn.
Prometheus . . . . . prō-mē'-thē-ŭs,
  prō-mē'-thūs.
Prophète, Le, see Profeta,
  Il . . . . lē prō-fĕt'.
Propylæa . . . . . . prŏp-ĭ-lē'-ä.
Proserpina . . . . . prō-sēr'-pĭ-nà,
  prŏs-ēr-pī'-nä.
Proserpine . . . . . prŏs'-ēr-pĭn, prŏs'-ēr-pĭn.
Protean . . . . . . prō'-tē-àn, prō-tē'-àn.
Protesilaus . . . . . prō-tĕs"-ĭ-lā'-ŭs.
Protestancy . . . . . prŏt'-ĕs-tàn-sī.
Protestant . . . . . . prŏt'-ĕs-tànt.
Proteus . . . . . . prō'-tē-ŭs, prō'-tūs.
Proudhon . . . . . . prōō-dôṅ'.
Proust, Marcel . . . . mär-sĕl' prōōst.

Provençal . . . . . . prō-věn'-săl.
                  Fr. prō-vŏn̄-săJ'₃
Provence . . . . . . prō-vôn̄s̄.
Prudhomme . . . . . prü-dŏm'.
Prud'hon (Pierre Paul) . prü-dôn̄'.
Prussia . . . . prŭsh'-à, prŏŏsh'-ĭ=à.
Prussian . . . . . . prŭsh'-àn, prŭsh'-ĭ-àn,
                  prŏŏsh'-ĭ-àn.
Prytaneum . . . . . prĭt-ā-nĕ'-ŭm.
Przasnysz . . . . . . pshăs'-nĭsh.
Przemysl . . . . . . pshā'-mĭshl.
Psalms . . . . sämz.
Psammetichus . . . . să-mĕt'-ĭ-kŭs.
Psichari . . . . . . psē-shă-rē'.
Pskoff . . . . pskŏf.
Psyche . . . . sī'-kē.
Ptah . . . . ptä.
Ptolemaic . . . . . . tŏl-ē-mā'-ĭk.
Ptolemais . . . . . . tŏl-ē-mā'-ĭs.
Ptolemy . . . . . . tŏl'-ē-mĭ.
Puccini . . . . pōō-chē'-nē.
Puccio . . . . pŏŏch'-ō.
Pucelle, La . . . . . lä pü-sĕl'.
Pu Chu, see Poo Choo,
   Pou Tchou . . . . . pōō chōō'.
Puebla . . . . pōō=ĕb'-lä.
Pueblo . . . . pōō=ĕb'-lō.
                  Sp. pōō=ā'-blō.
Puerto, El . . . . . . äl pōō=âr'-tō.
Puerto Bello, see Porto
   Bello . . . . pōō=âr'-tō bĕl'-lō.
                  Sp. pōō=âr'-tō bĕl'-yō.
Puerto Cabello . . . . pōō=âr'-tō kà-bĕl'-lō.
                  Sp. pōō=âr'-tō kä-bĕl'-yō.
Puerto de Santa Maria . pōō=âr'-tō dä sän'-tä
                  mä-rē'-ä.
Puerto d'España . . . pōō=âr'-tō dä spän'-yä.

Puerto Plata	poo̅=âr′-to̅ plä′-tä.
Puerto Princesa	poo̅=âr′-to̅ prēn-thä′-sä.
Puerto Príncipe	poo̅-âr′-to̅ prēn′-thē-pä.
Puerto Real	poo̅=r′-to̅ rä-äl′.
Puerto Rico, see Porto	
Rico	poo̅=âr′-to̅ rē′-ko̅.
Puget (Pierre)	pü-zhä′.
Puget (Sound)	pū′-jĕt.
Puglia	poo̅l′-yä.
Pugno	poo̅n′-yo̅.
Pujol, de	dē pü-zhŏl′.
Pulci	poŏl′-chē.
Pulcinella, or	poŏl-chē-nĕl′-lä.
Pulcinello	poŏl-chē-nĕl′-lo̅.
Pulkowa	poo̅l′-ko̅-vä.
Pultava, see Poltava, or .	poŏl-tä′-vä.
Pultowa	poŏl-to̅′-vä.
Pultusk	poŏl′-toŏsk, poo̅l′-too̅sk.
Punchinello	pŭn-chĭ-nĕl′-o̅.
Punic	pū′-nĭk.
Punjab, see Panjab, Pen-	
jab	pŭn-jäb′.
Punjaub	pŭn-jôb′.
Punnah, see Panna . .	pŭn′-ä.
Punta Gorda	poŏn′-tä go̅r′-dä.
Puntilla	poo̅n-tēl′-yä.
Purana	poo̅-rä′-na.
Purcell	pŭr′-sĕl.
Purgatorio	poo̅r-gä-to̅′-rē-o̅.
Puri, see Pooree . . .	poo̅-rē′.
Purim	poo̅′-rĭm.
Puritani di Scozia, I . .	ē poo̅-rē-tä′-nē dē sko̅d′-zē-ä.
Purneah, or	pēr′-nĕ-ä.
Purniah	pēr′-nĭ-ä.
Pusey	pū′-zĭ.
Puseyism	pū′-zĭ-ĭzm.

Pushkin, see **Pouschkin,**
  Pooshkin . . . . . poōsh'-kĭn.
Puteoli, see **Pozzuoli** . . pū-tē'-ō-lĭ.
Putnik . . . . poōt-nĭk'.
Puvis de Chavannes . . pü-vēs' dĕ shä-văn'.
Puy-de-Dôme . . . . pü=ē'-dŭ-dōm'.
Pyeshkov . . . . . . p-yĕsh'-kŏf.
Pylades . . . . . . pĭl'-à-dēz.
Pyramus . . . . . . pĭr'-à-mŭs.
Pyrenean . . . . . . pĭr-ē-nē'-àn.
Pyrenees, or . . . . . pĭr'-ē-nēz.
Pyrénées, *Fr.* . . . . pē-rā-nä'.
Pyrrha . . . . pĭr'-à.
Pyrrhic . . . . pĭr'-ĭk.
Pyrrhus . . . . . . pĭr'-ŭs.
Pythagoras . . . . . pĭth-ăg'-ō-ràs.
Pythagorean . . . . . pĭth″-ā-gō'-rē-àn,
           pĭth″-à-gō-rē'-àn.
Pythia . . . . pĭth'-ĭ-à.
Pythian . . . . . . pĭth'-ĭ-àn.
Python . . . . pĭ'-thŏn.
Pythoness . . . . . . pĭth'-ŏn-ĕs.

Q

Quadragesima . . . kwäd-rä-jĕs'-ĭ-mä.
Quai d'Anjou . . . . kā däṅ-zhoō'.
Quai d'Orsay . . . . kā dôr-sä'.
Quangsi, see **Kwangsi** . kwäng-sē'.
Quangtong, see **Kwangtung** kwäng-toōng'.
Quanza, see **Coanza,**
  Kuanza . . . . . . kwän'-zä.
Quasimodo . . . . . kwä-sĭ-mō'-dō.
        Fr. kä-zē-mō-dō'.
Quathlamba, see **Kath-**
  lamba . . . . . . kwät-läm'-bä.
Quatre-Bras . . . . . kă'=tr-brä'.

Quatre-Vingt-Treize . . kă′-tr-văṅ-trĕz′.
Quebec . . . . kwē-bĕk′. *Fr.* kē-bĕk′.
Queenston . . . . . kwēnz′-tŭn.
Queenstown . . . . . kwēnz′-town.
Queiros, see Quiros, de . dā kā-ē-rŏs′.
Quelpaerd, or . . . . kwĕl′-pärd.
Quelpart, or Quelpaert . kwĕl′-pärt.
Quentin . . . . . . kwĕn′-tĭn. *Fr.* kôṅ-tăṅ′.
Quercia, della . . . . dĕl′-lä kwĕr′-chä.
Querétaro . . . . . . kā-rā′-tä-rō.
Querimba . . . . . . kā-rēm′-bä.
Quérouaille (Louise Renée
    de) see Kéroualle . . kā-rōō-ä′=yŭ.
Quesada, Ximenez de . . zĭ-mē′-nēz.
                         Sp. ′hē-mā′nāth dā
                         kā-sä′-dä.

Quesnay . . . . . . kā-nā′.
Quesnel . . . . . . kā-nĕl′.
Quevedo y Villegas . . kā-bā′-dō ē vēl-yā′-gäs.
Quiberon . . . . . . kē-brôṅ′.
Quicherat . . . . . . kē-shē̄=rä′.
Quijote, Don, see Quixote dōn kē-′hō′-tā.
Quilimane, see Kilimane . kē-lē-mä′-nä.
Quiller-Couch . . . . kwĭl′-ēr-kōōch.
Quincy (Mass.) . . . . kwĭn′-zĭ.
Quinet . . . . kē-nā′.
Quiniluban . . . . . kē-nē-lōō-bän′.
Quinquagesima . . . . kwĭn-kwȧ-jĕs′-ĭ-mȧ.
Quintas da Recreo . . . kēn′-täs dä rā-krā′-ō.
Quintilian . . . . . . kwĭn-tĭl′-ĭ-ăn.
Quirinal, or . . . . . kwĭr′-ĭ-năl.
Quirinale . . . . . . kwē-rē-nä′-lä.
Quirinalis, Mons, *Lat.* . mŏnz kwĭr-ĭ-nā′-lĭs.
Quirites . . . . . . kwĭ-rī′-tēz.
Quiros, de, see Queiros . dā kē′-rŏs.
Quito . . . . kē′-tō.
Qui tollis . . . . . . kwī tŏl′-ĭs.

Quixote, Don, see Quijote,
Don . . . . *Eng.* dŏn kwĭks′-ōt.
                   Sp. dōn kē-'hō′-tä.
Quogue . . . . . . kwōg, kwŏg.
Quoniam . . . . . . kwō′-nĭ-ăm.

R

Raamah . . . . . . rā′-à-mä.
Rabelais . . . . . . răb-ĕ-lā′.
Rabelaisian . . . . . răb-ĕ-lā′-zĭ-àn.
Rabutin, Bussy . . . büs-sē′ rä-bü-tăṅ′.
Raca . . . . rā′-kà.
Rachel . . . . . . rā′-chĕl. *Fr.* rä-shĕl′.
Rachmaninoff . . . räċh-mä-nē′-nŏf.
Racine . . . . . . ră-sēn′. *Fr.* ră-sēn′.
Radack, or Radak . . rä′-däk.
Radetzki, or Radetzky . rä-dĕt′-skē.
Radom . . . . . . rä′-dōm.
Raemakers . . . . . rä′-mä-kĕrz.
Raffaelle, or . . . . räf-fä-ĕl′.
Raffaello, see Raphael . räf-fä-ĕl′-lō.
Ragatz, or Ragaz . . . rä′-gäts.
Rages . . . . rā′-jēz.
Ragnar Lodbrok . . . räg′-när lōd′-brōk.
Ragnarök . . . . . . räg′-nä-rēk′.
Ragon, Félix . . . . fä-lēks′ rä-gôṅ′.
Ragusa . . . . rä-gōō′-zä.
Rahab . . . . rā′-hăb.
Rahway . . . . . . rô′-wä.
Rai Bareli, see Roy Ba-
reilly . . . . . . rī bä-rā′-lē.
Raimondi, Marcantonio . märk-än-tō′-nē-ō
                   rä=ē-mōn′-dē.
Rainer . . . . rī′-nĕr.
Rainier (Mount) . . . rā′-nēr.
Raipur, or Raipoor . . rī-pōōr′.

Rais, de, or Raiz . . . dŭ rās.
Raisa . . . . rä-ē'-sä.
Raisuli . . . . rä-ē-soō'-lē.
Rajah, or Raja . . . . rä'-jä.
Rajeshaye, see Rajshahi . rä-jĕ-shä'-ē.
Rajpeepla . . . . . räj-pē'-plä.
Rajpoor . . . . . . räj-poōr'.
Rajpootana, see Rajputana räj-poō-tä'-nä.
Rajpoots, see Rajputs . . räj-poōts'.
Rajputana, see Rajpootana räj-poō-tä'-nä.
Rajputs, see Rajpoots . . räj-poōts'.
Rajshahi, see Rajeshaye . räj-shä'-hē.
Rákóczy . . . . . . rä'-kōt-sē.
Rákos . . . . rä'-kōsh.
Raleigh. . . . . . . rô'-lĭ, rǎl'-ĭ.
Ralick, Ralik. . . . . rä'-lĭk.
Rama . . . . rā'-mȧ, rä'-mä.
Ramah. . . . . . . rā'-mä.
Ramapo . . . . . . rǎm'-ȧ-pō, rǎm-ȧ-pō'.
Ramayana . . . . . rä-mä'-yä-nä,
                      rǎm'-ä-yä''-nä.
Rambaud . . . . . . räṅ-bō'.
Rambouillet, de . . . . dŭ räṅ-boō-yä'.
Rameau . . . . . . rä-mō'.
Ramée, Pierre de la . . pē=âr' dŭ lä rä-mä'.
Ramenghi . . . . . . rä-mĕng'-gē.
Rameses, see Ramses . rǎm'-ē-sēz, rǎ-mē'-sēz,
                      rǎm'-ĕ-sēz.
Ramillies . . . . . . rǎm'-ĭl-ēz. _Fr._ rä-mē-yē'.
Ramiro. . . . . . . rä-mē'-rō.
Rammohun Roy. . . . räm-mō-hŭn' roi.
Ramona . . . . . . rȧ-mō'-nȧ.
Rampur . . . . . . räm-poōr'.
Ramses, see Rameses . rǎm'-sēz.
Ramus . . . . rä-müs'.
Rancé . . . . räṅ-sä'.
Rangoon, see Rangun . . rän-goōn'.

Rangpur, see Rungpoor . rŭng-po͞or'.
Rangun, see Rangoon . . rän-go͞on'.
Ranke, von . . . . . fŏn räng'-kŭ.
Ranz des Vaches . . . räṅ dä väsh.
Raoul . . . . rä=o͞ol'.
Rapallo . . . . rä-päl'-lō.
Raphael, see Raffaelle . răf'-ā-ĕl, rä'-fä-ĕl, rä'-fā-ĕl.
Raphaelesque . . . . răf"-ā-ĕl-ĕsk'.
Raphaelite . . . . . răf'-ā-ĕl-īt".
Raphaelitism . . . . . răf'-ā-ĕl-ī-tizm".
Rapidan . . . . . . răp-ĭ-dăn'.
Ras-el-Abiad . . . . räs-ĕl-ä'-bē-äd.
Rasputin . . . . . . räs-po͞ot'-ēn.
Rasselas . . . . . . răs'-ĕ-lăs.
Rata, see Rota . . . . rä'-tä.
Rathenau . . . . . . rä'-tĕn-ow.
Ratisbon . . . . . . răt'-ĭs-bŏn.
Ratlam, see Rutlam . . rŭt'-làm.
Ratnagiri, see Rutnagherry rŭt-nà-gē'-rē.
Ratti . . . . rät'-tē.
Rauch . . . . rowċh.
Ravaillac . . . . . . rä-vä-yäk'.
Ravel . . . . rä-vĕl'.
Ravenna . . . . . . rà-vĕn'-ä. *It.* rä-vĕn'-nä.
Rawal Pindi, or Rawul
   Pindee . . . . . . rô'-ŭl pĭn'-dē.
Rayo . . . . rä'-yō.
Reay . . . . rā.
Ré, Ile de, see Rhé . . ēl dŭ rā.
Reading . . . . . . rĕd'-ĭng.
Réaumur, de . . . . dŭ-rä-ō-mür'.
Rebikoff . . . . . . rĕ-bē'-kŏf.
Récamier . . . . . . rā-kă-mē=ā'.
Rechab . . . . rē'-kăb.
Rechabites . . . . . rĕk'-à-bīts, rē'-kăb-īts.
Recife . . . . rĕ-sē'-fĕ.
Reclus . . . . rĕ-klü'.

Recollet . . . . rĕk'-ŏl-lĕt.
Reddersburg . . . . . rĕd'-dĕrs-bŭrċh.
Redon . . . . rĕ-dŏṅ'.
Redriff . . . . rĕd'-rĭf.
Regensburg . . . . . rā'-gĕns-bo͠orċh.
Reger . . . . rā'-gĕr.
Reggio . . . . rĕd'-jō.
Regillus (L.) . . . . . rĕ-jĭl'-ŭs.
Regnard . . . . . . rĕn-yär'.
Regnault . . . . . . rĕn-yō'.
Régnier . . . . . . rän-yā'.
Regulus . . . . . . rĕg'-ū-lŭs.
Rehan (Ada) . . . . . rĕ'-àn.
Rehoboam . . . . . rĕ-hō-bō'-àm.
Rehoboth . . . . . . rĕ-hō'-bŏth.
Reichardt . . . . . . rīċh'-ärt.
Reichenbach . . . . . rī-ċhĕn-bäċh.
Reichsrath . . . . . rīċhs'-rät.
Reichstadt . . . . . rīċh'-stät.
Reichstag . . . . . . rīċhs'-täċh.
Reikiavik, see Reykjavik . rī'-kĭ=à-vĭk.
Reims, see Rheims . . rēmz. *Fr.* răṅs.
Reina Mercedes . . . rā-ē'-nä mâr-thā'-dās.
Reine de Saba, La . . . lä rĕn dŭ sä-bä'.
Reine Margot, La . . . lä rĕn mär-gō'.
Reinhold . . . . . . rīn'-hōlt.
Réjane . . . . rā-zhăn'.
Religio Medici . . . . rĕ-lĭj'-ĭ-ō mĕd'-ĭ-sī.
Rembrandt, or . . . . rĕm'-brănt.
Rembrandt van Rijn, or
    Ryn . . . . rĕm'-brănt făn rīn.
Remedios . . . . . . rā-mä'-dē-ōs.
Remedius . . . . . . rĕ-mē'-dĭ-ŭs.
Remenyi . . . . . . rĕ-mān'-yē.
Remi, or . . . . . . rĕ-mē'.
Remigius . . . . . . rĕ-mĭj'-ĭ-ŭs.
Remus . . . . rē'-mŭs.

Rémusat, de . . . . . dŭ rā-mü-zä′.

Renaissance . . . . . rĕ-nā-säṅs′, rĕ-nā′-sȧns.

Renan . . . . *Anglicized,*rē-năn′, rē′-năn.
Fr. rĕ-näṅ′.

Renard, see Reynard . . *Fr.* rĕ-när′.

Renaud . . . . . . rĕ-nō′.

René, Renée . . . . . rĕ-nā′.

Renfrew . . . . . . rĕn′-frōō.

Reni, Guido . . . . . gwē′-dō rā′-nē.

Rennes . . . . rĕn.

Renouvier . . . . . . rĕ-nōō-vē=ā′.

Rensselaer . . . . . rĕn′-sē-lĕr.

Repin . . . . rā-pēn′.

Repnin, Nikolai . . . . nē′-kō-lä=ē rĕp-nēn′.

Repplier . . . . . . rĕp′-lē-ĕr.

Resaca de Guerrero . . rā-sä′-kä dā gā-rā′-rō.

Resaca de la Palma . . rā-sä′-kä dā lä päl′-mä.

Reshid Pasha . . . . rĕ-shēd′ păsh-ô′, pȧ-shä′,
pä′-shȧ.

Restigouche . . . . . rĕs-tē-gōōsh′.

Reske, de . . . . . . dŭ rĕsh′-kĕ.

Rethel . . . . rĕ-tĕl′.

Retté, Adolphe . . . . ä-dŏlf′ rĕt-tā′.

Retz, see Rais, Raiz . . rĕz.

Reuchlin . . . . . . rŏĭċh′-lĭn.

Réunion, Ile de la . . . rē-ūn′-yŭn.
Fr. ēl dŭ lä rā-ü-nē=ôṅ′.

Reuss . . . . rois.

Reuter . . . . roi′-tĕr.

Reutlingen . . . . . roit′-lĭng-ĕn.

Reval, or . . . . . . rĕv′-äl.

Revel . . . . rĕv′-ĕl.

Revue des Deux Mondes . rĕ-vü′ dā dē mŏṅd.

Rewa, or Rewah . . . rā′-wä.

Reykjavik, see Reikiavik . rī′-kĭ=ä-vĭk.

Reynaldo . . . . . . rā-näl′-dō. [*Fr.* rĕ-när′.

Reynard, see Renard . . rĕn′-ȧrd, rā′-närd, rĕn′-ärd.

Reynier . . . . . . rā-nē=ā'.
Reynolds . . . . . . rĕn'-ŭldz.
Rezonville . . . . . . rē-zôṅ-vēl'.
Rhadamanthine, Rhada-
   mantin . . . . . . răd-à-măn'-thĭn, -tĭn.
Rhadamanthus . . . . răd-à-măn'-thŭs.
Rhaetian . . . . . . rē'-shĭ=àn.
Rhé, Ile du, see Ré . . ēl dŭ rā.
Rhea . . . . rē'-ä.
Rheims, see Reims . . rēmz. *Fr.* răṅs.
Rheinberger . . . . . rīn'-bĕr-gĕr.
Rheingold, Das . . . . däs rīn'-gōlt.
Rhenish . . . . . . rĕn'-ĭsh.
Rhodes . . . . rōdz.
Rhodesia . . . . . . rōd'-zhĭ=à, rō-dē'-sĭ=à.
Rhodope . . . . . . rŏd'-ō-pē.
Rhondda . . . . . . rŏnd'-à.
Rhys . . . . rēs.
Rialto . . . . rē-äl'-tō.
Riazan, see Ryazan . . rē-ä-zän'.
Ribault, or Ribaut . . . rē-bō'.
Ribecourt . . . . . . rēb-kōōr'.
Ribera . . . . rē-bā'-rä.
Ribot . . . . rē-bō'.
Ricardo . . . . . . rĭ-kär'-dō, rē-kär'-dō.
Ricasoli . . . . . . rē-kä'-sō-lē.
Ricci . . . . rēt'-chē.
Ricciarelli . . . . . . rēch-är-ĕl'-lē.
Riccio (David), see Rizzio rēt'-chō.
Richelieu, de . . . . . dŭ rĭsh-ĕ-lū'.
              Fr. dŭ rēsh=ŭ-lē=ē'.
Richepin . . . . . . rēsh-păṅ'.
Richier . . . . rē-shē=ā'.
Richter . . . . rĭċh'-tĕr.
Ricimer . . . . . . rĭs'-ĭ-mēr.
Rickenbacker . . . rĭk'-ĕn-băk-ēr.
Rictus, Jehan . . . . zhäṅ rĭk-tüs'.

Ridel . . . . rē'-dĕl.
Riedesel (Gen.), von . . fŏn rēd'-ā"-zĕl.
Riego y Nuñez . . . . rē-ā'-gō ē nōōn'-yĕth.
Rienzi, Cola di, or . . . kō'-lä dē rē-ĕnd'-zē.
Rienzo . . . . rē-ĕnd'-zō.
Riesen-Gebirge . . . . rē'-zĕn-gä-bērg'-ŭ.
Riet (R.) . . . . . . rēt.
Riga . . . . rē'-gä.
Rigaud . . . . rē-gō'.
Rigault . . . . rē-gō'.
Righi, or Rigi . . . . rē'-gĭ.
Rigoletto . . . . . . rē-gō-lāt'-tō.
Rigsdag . . . . . . rĭgs'-dăg.
Rigveda . . . . . . rĭg-vā'-dä.
Riis . . . . rēs.
Rijks (Museum) . . . rīks.
Rijksdag . . . . . . rīks-dăċh.
Rimbault . . . . . . răṅ-bō'.
Rimini . . . . rē'-mē-nē.
Rimsky-Korsakov . . . rĭm"-ski-kōr-sä'-kŏf.
Rinaldo ed Armida . . rē-näl'-dō ād är-mē'-dä.
Rinehart . . . . . . rīn'-härt.
Ring der Nibelungen, Der dĕr rĭng dĕr
                   nē'-bĕ-lōōng"-ĕn.
Ring Strasse . . . . . rĭng'-shträ-sŭ.
Rio Bravo del Norte, see
  Rio Grande del Norte . rē'-ō brä'-vō dĕl nōr'-tā.
Rio de Janeiro . . . . *pop.* rē'-ō jȧ-nēr'-ō,
              jȧ-nī'-rō. *Port.* rē'-ō dä
              zhä-nā'-rō, zhä-nā'=ē-rō.
Rio de la Plata, see Plate . rē'-ō dä lä plä'-tä.
Rio Grande . . . . . rī'-ō grănd.
              Sp. rē'-ō grän'-dä.
Rio Grande de Cagayan . rē'-ō grän'-dä dä
              kä-gä-yän'.
Rio Grande de la Pampanga rē'-ō grän'-dä dä lä
              päm-pän'-gä.

Rio Grande del Norte, see
    Rio Bravo del Norte . rē'-ō grän'-dā děl nōr'-tā.
Rio Grande de Santiago . rē'-ō grän'-dā dā
    sän-tē=ä'-gō.
Rio Grande do Norte . . rē'-ō grän'-dā dōō nŏr'-tĕ.
Rio Grande do Sul . . rē'-ō grän'-dā dōō sōōl.
Rio Negro . . . . . . *Sp.* rē'-ō nā'-grō.
    Port. rē-ōō nā'-grōō.
Rio Negro, São José do . sowń zhō-zā' dōō
    rē'-ōō nā'-grōō.
Riordan . . . . . . rēr'-dàn.
Ripon . . . . rĭp'-ŭn.
Ristori . . . . rē-stō'-rē.
Riviera . . . . rē-vē=ā'-rä.
Rivière, Duc de . . . . dük dŭ rē-vē-âr'.
Rivinus . . . . . rē-vē'-nŭs.
Rivoli, Rue de . . . rü dŭ rē-vō-lē'.
Rizzio, see Riccio . . . rĭt'-sē-ō, rēt'-sē-ō.
Roanoke . . . . . . rō-à-nōk'.
Roatan, see Ruatan . . rō-à-tän'.
Robbia, Luca della . . . lōō'-kä děl'-lä rōb'-bē-ä.
Robert-Fleury . . . rō-bâr'-flĕr-ē'.
Robert Guiscard . . . rŏb'-ērt gēs-kär'.
    Fr. rō-bâr'.
Robert le Diable . . . rō-bâr' lē dē-ä'=bl.
Robespierre, de . . . . dŭ rō'-bĕs-pēr.
    Fr. dŭ rŏbs-pē=âr'.
Robsart (Amy) . . . . rŏb'-särt.
Robusti, Jacopo . . . . yä-kō'-pō rō-bōōs'-tē.
Roch, Saint . . . . . săń rōk.
Rochambeau, de . . . dŭ rō-shäń-bō'.
Rochefort . . . . . . rŏsh-fōr'.
Rochefoucauld, La . . . lä rŏsh-fōō-kō'.
Rochejacquelein, La . . lä rŏsh-zhăk-lăń'.
Rochelle . . . . . rō-shĕl'.
Rochet . . . . . . rō-shā'.
Rochus . . . . . . rō'-kŭs.

Rockefeller	rŏk'-ĕ-fĕl-ẽr.
Rockingham	rŏk'-ĭng-am.
Rocroi	rŏk-rwä'.
Rod, Édouard	ä-dōō-är' rŏd.
Rode, Pierre	rŏd.
Rodenbach, Georges . .	zhŏrzh rō-dĕn-bäċh'.
Roderick Dhu	rŏd'-ẽr-ĭk dū.
Roderigo	rŏd-ẽr-ē'-gō.
Rodin, Auguste	ō-güst' rō-dȧṅ'.
Rodó, José	hō-sä' rō-dō'.
Rodrigo Diaz de Bivar .	rōd-rē'-gō dē'-äth dä bē-bär'.
Rodrigues, or	Fr. rōd-rēg'.
Rodriguez (I.)	rō-drē'-gĕs.
Rodríguez (José Joaquin)	rōd-rē'-gĕth.
Rodzianko	rŏdz-yän'-kō.
Roelas, Juan de las . .	'hōō-än' dä läs rō-ä'-läs.
Roeselare, see Roulers, Rousselaere	rōō-sĕ-lä'-rĕ.
Roeskilde, see Röskilde .	rēs'-kēl-dĕ.
Rofreit	rōf'-rīt.
Rogero, see Ruggiero . .	rō-jä'-rō.
Roget	rō-zhä'.
Rohan, de	dŭ rō-äṅ'.
Rohilcund, or Rohilkhand	rō-hĭl-kŭnd'.
Rohtak	rō-tŭk'.
Roi des Montagnes . .	rwä dä môṅ-tän'-yŭ.
Roi d'Yvetot, Le . . .	lẽ rwä dēv-tō'.
Roi s'Amuse, Le . . .	lẽ rwä sä-müz'.
Rois Fainéants, Les . .	lä rwä fä-nä-äṅ'.
Rojas-Zorilla, or Zorrilla .	rō'-ċhäs-thōr-rēl'-yä.
Rokeby	rŏk'-bĭ.
Roland	rō'-lȧnd. Fr. rō-läṅ'.
Roland, Chanson de . .	shän-sôṅ' dŭ rō-läṅ'.
Roland de la Platière . .	rō-läṅ' dŭ lä plä-tē=âr'.
Roland de Roncevaux . .	rō-län' dŭ rôṅs-vō'.
Roldan	rōl-dän'.

Rolf . . . . rŏlf.
Rolland, Romain . . . rō-mäṅ', rŏl-äṅ'.
Rollin . . . . rŏl'-ĭn. *Fr.* rō-läṅ'.
Rollo . . . . rŏl'-ō.
Romagna . . . . . . rō-män'-yä.
Romaic . . . . rō-mä'-ĭk.
Romance . . . . . . rō-măns'.
Roman de la Rose . . . rō-män' dŭ lä rŏz.
Roman de Rou . . . . rō-män' dŭ roō.
Romanes . . . . . . rō-mä'-nēz.
Romanesque . . . . . rō-män-ĕsk'.
Romano, Ezzelino da . . ĕt-zā-lē'-nō dä rō-mä'-nō.
Romanof, or Romanoff . rō-mä'-nŏf.
Romany, see Rommany . rŏm'-à-nĭ.
Romeo . . . . rō'-mē-ō.
Roméo et Juliette . . . rō-mä-ō' ā zhül-ē=ĕt'.
Romero (Matias) . . . rō-mä'-rō.
Romilly . . . . . . rŏm'-ĭ-lĭ.
Rommany, see Romany . rŏm'-à-nĭ.
Romola . . . . . . rŏm'-ō-lȧ, rō-mō'-lȧ.
Roncesvalles, or . . . rŏn-sē-väl'-lĕs.
      Sp. rōn-thĕs-väl'-yĕs.
Roncevaux . . . . . *Fr.* rôṅs-vō'.
Ronda . . . . rōn-dȧ.
Ronge . . . . rŏng'-ŭ.
Ronsard (Pierre de) . . rôṅ-sär'.
Röntgen . . . . . . rĕnt'-gĕn.
Roodepoort . . . . . rō-dĕ-pōrt'.
Rooidam . . . . . . rō-ē-dăm'.
Roosevelt . . . . . . rōs'-vĕlt, rō'-sĕ-vĕlt.
Roquefort . . . . . . rŏk-fōr'.
Rosa, Salvator . . . . säl-vä'-tōr rō'-zä.
Rosalind . . . . . . rŏz'-à-lĭnd.
Rosaline . . . . . . rŏz'-à-lĭn.
Rosamond, Rosamund . rŏz'-à-mŭnd.
Rosbach, see Rossbach . rŏs'-bäċh.
Roscelin, or . . . . . *Fr.* rŏs=ĕl-äṅ'.

Roscellin, or . . . . . rŏs'-ĕl-ĭn.
Roscellinus, see Rucelinus rŏs-ĕ-lī'-nŭs.
Roscius . . . . . . rŏsh'-ĭ-ŭs.
Roscommon . . . . . rŏs-kŏm'-ŭn.
Rosecrans . . . . . . rō'-zĕ-krănz.
Rosellini . . . . . . rō-zĕl-lē'-nē.
Rosenkranz . . . . . rō'-zĕn-kränts.
Rosetta . . . . . . rō-zĕt'-à.
Rosicrucian . . . . . rŏz-ĭ-krū'-shĭ=àn,
                          rōz-ĭ-krōō'-shĭ=àn.
Rosinante, see Rozinante rŏz-ĭ-năn'-tē.
Röskilde, see Roeskilde . rĕs'-kĕl'-dĕ.
Rosny (Léon de) . . . rŏs-nē'.
Rospigliosi, Palazzo . . pä-läts'-sō rō-spĕl-yō'-sē.
Rossbach, see Rosbach . rŏs'-bäċh.
Rossellino . . . . . . rŏs-sĕl-lē'-nō.
Rossetti . . . . . . rŏs-sĕt'-tē.
Rossi . . . . rŏs'-sē.
Rossini . . . . . . rŏs-sē'-nē.
Rostand, Edmond . . . ĕd-môn' rōs-tän'.
Rostock . . . . . . rŏs'-tŏk.
Rostoff . . . . rŏs-tŏf'.
Rostoptchin . . . . . rŏs'-tŏp-chĭn,
                          rŏs-tŏp-chēn'.
Rota, see Rata . . . . rō'-tä.
Rotherhithe . . . . . rŏth'-ĕr-hīth.
Rothesay . . . . . . rŏth'-sā.
Rothschild . . . . . rŏths'-chīld, rōs'-chīld.
                          Ger. rōt'-shĭlt.
Rotrou . . . . rō-trōō'.
Rotterdam . . . . . . rŏt'-ĕr-dăm.
                          D. rŏt-tĕr-dăm'.
Roubaix . . . . . . rōō-bā'.
Roubillac . . . . . . rōō-bē-yäk'.
Rouen . . . . rōō'-ĕn. Fr. rōō-ôn'.
Rougé . . . . rōō-zhā'.
Rouget de Lisle, or l'Isle . rōō-zhā' dŭ lēl.

Rougon-Macquart, Les . lä rōō-gôṅ'-mä-kär'.
Roulers, see Roeselare,
Rousselaere . . . . rōō-lä'.
Roumania, see Rumania . rōō-mä'-nĭ-à.
Roumelia, see Rumelia . rōō-mē'-lĭ-à.
Rousseau . . . . . rōō-sō'.
Rousselaere, see Roese-
lare, Roulers . . . rōōs-lär'.
Roussillon . . . . . *Fr.* rōō-sē-yôṅ',
    rōō-sēl-yôn'.
Roustam, see Rustam . . rōōs'-tàm. *Pers.* rōōs-tĕm.
Rouxville . . . . . rōō-vēl'.
Rovere, della . . . . dĕl-lä rō'-vä-rä.
Roveredo . . . . . rō-vĕ-rä'-dō.
Rovereto . . . . . rō-vä-rà'-tō.
Rovigo . . . . . . rō-vē'-gō.
Rowe . . . . . . rō.
Rowena . . . . . rō-wē'-nà.
Rowland . . . . . rō'-lànd.
Roxana, or . . . . rŏks-ăn'-ä, rŏks-ā'-nä.
Roxane . . . . . . *Fr.* rōks-ăn'.
Roy, Rammohun . . . räm-mō-hŭn' roi.
Roy Bareilly, see Rai Bareli roi bä-rä'-lē.
Roye . . . . . . rwä.
Royer-Collard . . . . rwä-yä'-kŏl-lär'.
Rozinante, see Rosinante rŏs-ĭ-năn'-tē.
Ruatan, see Roatan . . rōō-ä-tän'.
Rubaiyat (The) . . . rōō'-bĭ-yăt.
Rubens (Peter Paul) . . rōō'-bĕnz.
Rübezahl . . . . . rü'-bĕ-tsäl.
Rubicon . . . . . rōō'-bĭ-kŏn.
Rubinstein (Anton) . . rōō'-bĭn-stīn.
Rucelinus, see Roscelin . rōō-sĕ-lī'-nŭs.
Rucellai . . . . . rōō-chĕl-lä'=ē.
Rückert . . . . . rük'-ĕrt.
Rude . . . . . . rüd.
Rudesheim . . . . rü'-dĕs-hĭm.

Rüdiger . . . . rü'-dĭ-gĕr.
Rue de la Paix . . . . rü dŭ lä pā.
Rue de Rivoli . . . . rü dŭ rē-vō-lē'.
Rueil . . . . rü-ā'=yŭ.
Rue St.-Antoine . . . . rü săṅ-täṅ-twăn'.
Rue St.-Denis . . . . rü săṅ-dĕ-nē'.
Rue St.-Honoré . . . . rü săṅ-tō-nō-rā'.
Ruffini . . . . rŏŏf-fē'-nē.
Rufinus . . . . . . rōō-fī'-nŭs.
Rug . . . . rōōg.
Rügen . . . . rü'-gĕn.
Ruggiero, see Rogero . . rŏŏd-jā'-rō.
Ruhr . . . . rōōr.
Ruisdaal, or Ruisdael, see
Ruysdael . . . . . rois'-däl.
Ruk (I.) . . . . . rōōk.
Rum (I.) . . . . . rŭm.
Rumania, see Roumania . rōō-mā'-nĭ-ȧ.
Rumelia, see Roumelia . rōō-mē'-lĭ-ȧ.
Runeberg . . . . . rōō'-nĕ-bĕrċh.
Rungpoor, see Rangpur . rŭng-pōōr'.
Runjeet Singh . . . . rŭn-jēt' sĭngh.
Runnemede, or . . . . rŭn'-ĕ-mēd.
Runnimede, or Runny-
mede . . . . . . rŭn'-ī-mēd.
Rupert . . . . . . rōō'-pĕrt.
Ruprecht . . . . . rōō'-prĕċht.
Rurik . . . . . . rōō'-rĭk.
Rus . . . . rŭs.
Ruscuk, see Rustchuk . rōōs-chōōk'.
Russ . . . . . . rŭs.
Russia . . . . . . rŭsh'-ĭ=ȧ, rŏŏsh'-ĭ=ȧ.
Russian . . . . . rŭsh'ĭ=ȧn, rŏŏsh'-ĭ=ȧn.
Rustam, see Roustam and
Rustum . . . . . rōōs'-tȧm. *Pers.*
rōōs'-tăm'.
Rustchuk, see Ruscuk . rōōs-chōōk'.

Rustenburg . . . . . rōŏs'-tĕn-bōōrċh.
Rustum, see Roustam,
Rustam . . . . . . rōōs'-tŭm.
Rutherglen . . . . . rŭth'-ĕr-glĕn, rŭg'-lĕn.
Ruthven (Raid of) . . . rŭth'-vĕn. *loc.* rĭv'-ĕn.
Rutlam, see Ratlam . . rŭt'-lȧm.
Rütli, see Grütli . . . rüt'-lĭ.
Rutnagherry, see Ratnagiri rŭt-nȧ-gĕr'-ĭ.
Ruy Blas . . . . . . rü=ē' bläs.
Ruy Diaz . . . . . . rōō'-ē dē'-äth.
Ruyghur . . . . . . rī-gŭr'.
Ruysdale, see Ruisdaal,
Ruisdael . . . . . rois'-däl.
Ruyter . . . . rī'-tēr. *D.* roi'-tĕr.
Ryazan, see Riazan . . rē-ä-zän'.
Rydal . . . . rī'-dȧl.
Ryswick, or . . . . . rĭz'-wĭk.
Ryswijk . . . . . . *D.* rīs'-vĭk.

S

Saadi, see Sadi . . . . sä'-dē, sȧ-dē'.
Saale . . . . zä'-lŭ.
Saalfeld . . . . . . zäl'-fĕlt.
Saar . . . . zär.
Saarbrück, or . . . . zär'-brük.
Saarbrücken, see Sarre-
bruck . . . . . . zär'-brük-ĕn.
Saarburg . . . . . . zär-bürg'.
Saardam, see Zaarrdam . sär-dăm'.
Saavedra (Cervantes) . sä-ä-vä'-drä.
Saba, see Sabea . . . sā'-bä.
Saba (I.) . . . . . . sä'-bä.
Sábana Grande . . . . sä'-bä-nä grän'-dä.
Sabaoth . . . . . . săb'-ā-ŏth, sā-bā'-ŏtℓ
Sabbatic . . . . . . săb-ăt'-ĭk.
Sabea, see Saba . . . sȧ-bē'-ä.

Sabeans . . . . . . sā-bē'-ảnz.
Sabine (Cross Roads) . . sằ-bēn'.
Sabine (Mts.) . . . . sā'-bīn.
Sabine (Sir Edward) . . sắb'-ĭn.
Sabinella . . . . . . sä-bē-nĕl'-lä.
Sabines . . . . . . sắb'-īnz, sā'-bīnz.
Sabini . . . . sằ-bī'-nī.
Sabrina . . . . . sằ-brī'-nả, sā-brī'-nả.
Sacharissa . . . . . sắk-ả-rĭs'-ả.
Sacheverell . . . . . sằ-shĕv'-ĕ-rĕl
Sachs (Hans) . . . . zäks.
Sachsen . . . . . . zäk'-zĕn.
Sachsen-Altenburg, see
  Saxe-Altenburg . . . zäk'-zĕn-äl'-tĕn-bōōrċh.
Sachsen-Coburg-Gotha,
  see Saxe-Coburg-Gotha zäk'-zĕn-kō'-bōōrċh-gō'-tä.
Sachsen-Meiningen, see
  Saxe-Meiningen . . zäk'-zĕn-mī'-ning-ĕn.
Sachsenspiegel . . . . zäk'-zĕn-spē"-gĕl.
Sachsen-Weimar-Eisenach,
  see Saxe-Weimer-Eise- [näċh.
  nach . . . . zäk'-zĕn-vī'-mär-ī'-zĕ-
Sacile . . . . sä-chē'-lĕ.
Saco (R.) . . . . . . sô'-kō.
Saco (José Antonio) . . sä'-kō.
Sadducees . . . . . sắd'-yū-sēz.
Sadi, see Saadi . . . . sằ-dē'.
Sadi-Carnot . . . . . sằ-dē'-kär-nō'.
Sadowa . . . . . . sä-dō'-vä, sä'-dō-vä.
Saenz Peña . . . . . sä'-ānth pān'-yä.
Safed . . . . sä'-fĕd, sä-fĕd'.
Safed Koh, see Suffeed
  Koh . . . . sä'-fĕd kō.
Saffi, see Sufi, Sofi . . säf'-ĭ.
Saga Josoku . . . . . sä'-gä' zhä'-sō'-kĕ'.
Sagan . . . . zä'-gän. *Fr.* sä-gän'.
Sagar, see Saugor, Ŝaugur sä-gŭr'.

Sagasta (Praxedes Mateo)	sä-gäs'-tä.
Sage, Le, see Lesage . .	lē săzh'.
Saghalien, or Saghalin .	sä-gä-lē'-ĕn, sä-gä-lēn'.
Sagittarius	săj-ĭ-tā'-rĭ-ŭs.
Sagua La Grande . . .	sä'-gwä lä grän'-dā.
Saguenay	săg-ĕ-nā', sä-gĕn-ā'.
Sahara, see Zahara, Sahra,	
Sahhra	să-hä'-rä, sä'-hȧ-rä.
Saharanpur, see Seharun-	
poor	sȧ-här-ȧn-pōōr'.
Sahhra, see Sahara, Zahara	sä'-hrä.
Sahib	sä'-hĭb.
Sahra, see Sahara, Zahara	sä'-hrä.
Saïd (Port)	sä-ēd'. pop. sād.
Saida	sī'-dä.
Said Pasha	sä-ēd', pop. sād, pȧsh-ô',
	pȧ-shä', päsh'-ȧ.
Saigon	sī-gōn'. Fr. sā-gôṅ'.
Saigo Takamori	sī'-gō tä-kä-mō'-rē.
Saikio	sī-kē'-ō.
Sailly-Saillisel . . .	sä-yē'-sä-yē-zĕl'.
St. Albans	sänt, sĕnt ôl'-bȧnz.
St.-Amand, or	săṅ-tä-mäṅ'.
St.-Amand-Montrond . .	săṅ-tä-mäṅ'-môṅ-rôṅ'.
St.-Antoine, Faubourg .	fō-bōōr' săṅ-täṅ-twăn'.
Saint-Arnaud	săṅ-tär-nō'.
St. Augustine	sänt, sĕnt ô-gŭs'-tĭn,
	ô'-gŭs-tĭn.
St. Augustine (City) . .	sänt, sĕnt ô'-gŭs-tēn.
St. Barthélemy	Fr. săṅ bär-tāl-mē'.
St. Bernard	sänt, sĕnt bēr-närd',
	bēr'-närd. Fr.
	săṅ bĕr-när'.
St. Bernard de Menthon .	săṅ bĕr-när' dŭ môṅ-tôṅ'.
St. Cecilia, see Santa	
Cecilia	sänt sē-sĭl'-ĭ-ȧ.
St. Chad	sänt, sĕnt chăd.

St. Clair . . . . . . sānt, sĕnt klâr.
                      Eng. sĭng'-klâr.
St. Cloud . . . . . . sănt, sĕnt klowd'.
                      Fr. săṅ klōō'.
St. Croix, see Santa Cruz . sānt kroi'.
St. Cyr . . . . săṅ sēr'.
St. Denis . . . . . . sānt, sĕnt dĕn'-ĭs.
                      Fr. săṅ dĕn-ē'.
Sainte-Aldegonde . . . săṅt-äl-dē-gôṅd'.
Sainte-Beuve . . . . săṅt-bēv'.
Sainte-Chapelle . . . . săṅt-shä-pĕl'.
Sainte-Croix, see Santa
   Cruz . . . . săṅt-krwä'.
Saint Dizier . . . . . săṅ dē-zē=ā'.
St. Eloi . . . . . . săṅ-tĕl-wä'.
St. Étienne du Mont . . săṅ-tā-tē=ĕn' dü mŏṅ.
Ste. Geneviève . . . . săṅt zhĕn-vē=ĕv'.
Sainte-Gudule . . . . săṅt gü-dül'.
Sainte Lucie . . . . . săṅt lü-sē'.
Sainte Pélagie . . . . săṅt pā-lä-zhē'.
Saintes . . . . săṅt.
St.-Étienne . . . . . săṅ-tā-tē=ĕn'.
St. Eustache . . . . . săṅ tēs-täsh'.
St. Eustatius . . . . . sānt, sĕnt ū-stā'-shĭ-ŭs.
Saint-Évremond . . . . săṅ-tāvr-môṅ'.
St. Francis Xavier . . . sānt, sĕnt frăn'-sĭs
                      zăv'-ĕ-êr. *Sp.* ċhä-bē-âr'.
                      Fr. ksä-vē=ā'.
St. Gall, see Sankt Gallen sānt gôl. *Fr.* săṅ-gäl'.
Saint-Gaudens . . . . sānt, sĕnt-gô'-dĕnz.
                      Fr. săṅ-gō-dôṅ'.
Saint-Germain . . . . săṅ-zhĕr-măṅ'.
St.-Germain-des-Prés . săṅ-zhĕr-măṅ'-dā-prā'.
St. Germain l'Auxerrois . săṅ-zhĕr-măṅ' lōks-ĕr-wä'.
St. Gothard . . . . . *Fr.* săṅ gō-tär'.
St. Gotthard . . . . . sānt, sĕnt gŏth'-ärd.
                      Ger. sänkt gŏt'-härt.

St. Helena (Mother of Constantine)	sänt hĕl′-ē-nȧ.
St. Helena (I.)	sänt hĕ-lē′-nä.
Saint-Hilaire, Barthélemy	bär-tāl-mē′ săn̈-tē-lâr′.
Saint-Hilaire, Geoffroy .	zhō-frwä′ săn̈-tē-lâr′.
Saintine	săn̈-tēn′.
Saint-Ives, see St. Yves .	sänt, sĕnt īvz.
	Fr. săn̈-tēv′.
St. Jean d'Acre	săn̈ zhän̈ dä′=kr.
St.-Jean d'Angély . . .	săn̈ zhän̈′ dän̈-zhä-lē′.
St. John	sänt, sĕnt jŏn′. Eng. sometimes sĭn′ jŭn.
Saint Julien	săn̈ zhü-lē=ĕn̈′.
Saint-Just	săn̈ zhüst′.
St. Leger	sänt, sĕnt lĕj′-ẽr. Eng. sometimes sĭl′-ĭn-jĕr.
St.-Leu	săn̈-lē′.
St. Louis	sänt, sĕnt lōō′-ĭs, lōō′-ĭ. Fr. săn̈ lōō-ē′.
St. Lucia (I.) see Santa Lucia	sänt, sĕnt lōō′-shĭ=ȧ.
St. Malo	pop. sänt măl′-ō. Fr. săn̈ mä-lō′.
Saint Marceaux	săn̈ mär-sō′.
Saint-Mars	săn̈-mär′.
St. Martin	sänt, sĕnt mär′-tĭn. Fr. săn̈-mär-tăn̈′.
St. Michael	sänt, sĕnt mī′-kĕl.
St. Michel	săn̈ mē-shĕl′.
St. Mihiel	săn̈ mē-ĕl′.
St. Nicolas	Fr. săn̈ nē-kō-lä′.
St. Olaus	sänt, sĕnt ō-lä′-ŭs.
St. Omer	săn̈ tō-mâr′.
Saintonge	săn̈-tôn̈zh′.
St. Ouen	săn̈-tōō-ŏn̈′.
Saint Pancras	sĕnt păn′-krȧs.
St. Paul de Loanda . .	sänt, sĕnt pôl dĕ lō-än′-dä.

St. Pierre, de	dŭ săṅ pē=âr'.
St. Pierre, Bernardin de .	bĕr-när-dăṅ' dē săṅ pē=âr'.
St. Pol-de-Léon	săṅ pōl-dŭ-lā-ôṅ'.
Saint-Preux	săṅ-prē'.
St. Quentin	sänt kwĕn'-tĭn.
	Fr. săṅ kŏṅ-tăṅ'.
St. Roch	săṅ rōk.
St. Roque, see São Roque,	
see San Roque . . .	sänt, sĕnt rōk.
Saint-Saëns	săṅ-säṅs'.
St. Sebastian, see San Se-	
bastian	sänt, sĕnt sĕ-băs'-tē=àn.
St. Simon, de	dŭ sänt, sĕnt sī'-mŏn.
	Fr. dŭ săṅ sē-môṅ'.
St. Sulpice	săṅ sül-pēs'.
St. Vincent de Paul . .	sänt, sĕnt vĭn'-sĕnt dŭ pôl.
	Fr. săṅ văṅ-sän' dŭ pōl.
Saint Yves, see St. Ives .	săṅ tēv'.
Saïs	sā'-ĭs.
Saisiaz, La	lä sĕ-zē-äs'.
Sakai	sä'-kī.
Sakatal	sä-kä-täl'.
Sakhalien	säċh-ä-lēn'.
Sakuntala	sà-kōōn'-tà-là,
	shà-kōōn'-tà-là.
Sala (G. A.)	sā'-lä, sä'-là.
Saladin, see Salah-ed-Din	săl'-à-dĭn.
Salado de Tarifa . . .	sä-lä'-dō dä tä-r̓ē'-fä.
Salah-ed-Diu, see Saladin	Arab. sä'-lä-ĕd-dēn'.
Salamanca	săl-à-măn'-kà.
	Sp. sä-lä-män'-kä.
Salamis	săl'-à-mĭs.
Salammbô	sä-läm-bō'.
Salanio, or	sà-lä'-nĭ-ō, sä-lä'-nē-ō.
Salarino	sä-là-rē'-nō, sä-lä-rē'-nō.
Saldanha	säl-dän'-yä.
Salerno	sà-lĕr'-nō. It. sä-lĕr'-nō.

Sales (Francis of) . . . sālz. *Fr.* săl.
Saléza . . . . sä-lā'-zä.
Salian . . . . sā'-lĭ-àn.
Salic . . . . săl'-ĭk.
Salignac . . . . . . sä-lĕn-yăk'.
Salins . . . . să-lăn'.
Salisbury . . . . . sôlz'-bŭ-rĭ.
Salle, De la . . . . dŭ lä săl'.
Salmon (Falls) . . . săm'-ŭn.
Salm-Salm . . . . . zälm-zälm.
Salome . . . . . . să-lō'-mĕ, sā-lō'-mē.
Salon (The) . . . . sä-lôṅ'.
Salonica . . . . . săl-ō-nē'-kȧ.
Saloniki . . . . . . sä-lō-nē'-kē.
Salpêtrière, La . . . lä säl-pā-trē=âr'.
Salta . . . . säl'-tä.
Saltikoff, see Soltikoff . säl'-tē-kŏf.
Salvador . . . . . . säl-vä-dōr'.
Salvator Rosa . . . . säl-vä'-tōr rō'-zä.
Salvini . . . . säl-vē'-nē.
Salzburg . . . . . . zälts'-bōōrċh.
Salzkammergut . . . . zältz'-käm-ĕr-gōōt.
Samain, Albert . . . . äl-bâr' sä-măṅ'.
Samaná, Santa Barbara de sän'-tä bär'-bä-rä
    dä sä-mä-nä'.
Samar . . . . sä-mär'.
Samara (City) . . . . *Russ.* sä-mä-rä'.
Samarang . . . . . . sä-mä-räng'.
Samarcand, or Samarkand säm-är-känd'.
Samaveda . . . . . . sä-mä-vä'-dä.
Sambalpur, see Sumbul-
    pur . . . . sŭm-bŭl-pōōr'.
Sambre (R.) . . . . . sŏṅ'=br.
Samminiato, see San Min-
    iato . . . . säm″-mĭn-ĭ-ä'-tō.
Samoa . . . . sä-mō'-ȧ.
Samoan (Is.) . . . . . sä-mō'-àn, sä-mō'-än.

Samos	sā'-mŏs.
Samoset	săm'-ō-sĕt.
Samothrace	săm'-ō-thrās.
	Gr. săm-ō-thrā'-sē.
Samson et Dalila . . .	sän-sôn' nä dä-lē-lä'.
Samurai	sä'-moo͞o'-rä'-ē'.
San Ambrogio . . .	sän äm-brō'-jō.
San Antonio (City) . .	săn ăn-tō'-nĭ-ō.
San Antonio (Cape) . .	sän än-tō'-nē-ō.
Sanballat	săn-băl'-àt.
Sancho Panza	săng'-kō păn'-zä.
	Sp. sän'-chō pän'-thä.
San Clemente	sän klä-män'-tĕ.
San Cristóbal	sän krēs-tō'-bäl.
Sand, George	jôrj sănd. *Fr.* zhŏrzh sänd.
Sandalphon	săn-dăl'-fŏn.
Sandeau	sän-dō'.
Sandherr	sän-dâr'.
San Diego	sän dē=ā'-gō.
San Domingo, see Santo	
Domingo	sän dō-mēng'-gō.
Sandoval	sän-dō'-bäl.
Sandringham . . .	sănd'-rĭng-àm.
Sandys (Edwin) . . .	săn'-dĭs, săndz.
San Fernando	sän fēr-nän'-dō.
Sangallo	säng-gäl'-lō.
Sangar (Strait) . . .	sän-gär'.
San Giorgio	sän jŏr'-jō.
Sangir (Is.)	säng-gēr'.
Sangpo, see Sanpu . .	săng-pō'.
Sangraal	săng-grāl'.
Sangrado (Doctor) . . .	sän-grä'-dō.
Sangreal	săng'-grē-ăl.
Sanhedrim, or . . .	săn'-hē-drĭm.
Sanhedrin	săn'-hē-drin.
San Jacinto	săn jà-sĭn'-tō.
	Sp. sän ċhä-thēn'-tō.

San Joaquin . . . . . sän ċhō-ä-kēn'.
San José . . . . . . sän ċhō-sā'.
San José de Buenavista . sän ċhō-sā' dā
                       boo̅=ā-nä-vēs'-tä.
San Juan . . . . . . sän ċhoo̅=än'.
San Juan Bautista . . . sänċhoo̅=än'bä=oo̅-tēs'-tä.
San Juan de Puerto Rico . sän ċhoo̅-än' dā
                       poo̅-ĕr'-tō rē'-kō.
San Juan de Ulloa . . . sän ċhoo̅-än'dā o̅o̅l-yō'-ä.
Sankt Gallen, see Saint Gall sänkt gäl'-lĕn.
Sankt Goar . . . . . sänkt gō'-är.
Sankt Gotthard . . . . sänkt gŏt'-härt.
Sankt Jakob . . . . . sänkt yä'-kŏp.
Sankt Moritz . . . . sänkt mō-rĭts'.
San Luis de Apra . . . sän loo̅-ēs' dā ä'-prä.
San Luis Potosí . . . . sän loo̅-ēs' pō-tō-sē'.
San Marco . . . . . sän mär'-kō.
San Marino . . . . . sän mä-rē'-nō.
San Martin . . . . . sän mär-tēn'.
San Michele . . . . . sän mē-kä'-lä.
San Miguel . . . . . sän mē-gĕl'.
San Miniato, see Sammin-
  iato . . . . sän mē-nē=ä'-to',
                      mĭn-ĭ-ä'-tō.
San Onofrio . . . . . sän ō-nō'-frē-ō.
San Pietro in Vincoli . . sän pē=ā'-trō ēn vēn'-kō-lē.
Sanpu, see Sangpo . . . sän-poo̅'.
San Remo . . . . . . sän rä'-mō.
San Roque, see St. Roque,
  São Roque . . . . . sän rō'-kä.
San Salvador . . . . sän säl-väd-t̄hō'.
Sanscrit, see Sanskrit . . săn'-skrĭt.
San Sebastian, see Saint
  Sebastian . . . . . sän sä-bäs"-tē-än'.
Sans Gêne, Madame . . mă-dăm' sän zhĕn.
Sanskrit, see Sanscrit . . săn'-skrĭt.
Sansovino . . . . . . sän-sō-vē'-nō.

Sans Souçi	*Fr.* sŏṅ sōō-sē'.
San Stefano	sän stĕf'-ä-nō.
Santa Ana	sän'-tä ä'-nä.
Santa Cecilia, see St. Cecilia	sän'-tä chä-chēl'-ē-ä.
Santa Croce sull' Arno .	sän'-tä krō'-chĕ sŏŏl är'-nō.
Santa Cruz, see Saint Croix	sän'-tä krōōz.
Santa Cruz (Andres) . .	sän'-tä krōōth'.
Santa Cruz de la Palma .	sän'-tä krōōth' dä lä päl'-mä.
Santa Cruz de la Sierra .	sän'-tä krōōth' dä lä sē=ĕr'-rä.
Santa Cruz de Santiago .	sän'-tä krōōth' dä sän-tē=ä'-gō.
Santa Cruz de Tenerife .	sän'-tä krōōth' dä tä-nä-rē'-fä.
Santa Fé	sän'-tä fä.
Santal Parganas . . .	sän-täl' pär-gŭn'-ås.
Santa Lucia, see St. Lucia	*It.* sän'-tä lōō-chē'-ä.
	Sp. sän'-tä lōō-thē'-ä.
Santa Luzia	sän'-tä lōō-zē'-ä.
Santa Maria, La . . .	lä sän'-tä mä-rē'-ä.
Santa Maria degli Angeli	sän'-tä mä-rē'-ä däl'-yē än'-jä-lē.
Santa Maria del Carmine .	sän'-tä mä-rē'-ä dĕl kär-mē'-nĕ.
Santa Maria del Popolo .	sän'-tä mä-rē'-ä dĕl pō'-pō-lō.
Santa Maria in Ara Coeli	sän'-tä mä-rē'-äĭn ā'-rȧ sē'-lī.
Santa Maria in Cosmedin	sän'-tä mä-rē'-ä ĭn kŏs'-mĕ-dĭn.
Santa Maria Maggiore .	sän'-tä mä-rē'-ä mäd-jō'-rĕ.
Santa Maria Novella . .	sän'-tä mä-rē'-ä nō-vĕl'-lä.
Santa Maria sopra Minerva	sän'-tä mä-rē'-ä sō'-prä mē-nĕr'-vä.

Santander . . . . . . săn-tăn-dâr'.
        Sp. sän-tän-där'.
Sant' Angelo . . . . . It. sänt än'-jä-lō.
Santarem . . . . . . sän-tä-răṅ', sän-tä-rĕṅ'.
Santa Scala . . . . . sän'-tä skä'-lä.
Santayana . . . . . . sän-tä-yä'-nä.
Santerre . . . . . . säṅ-tĕr'.
Santillana . . . . . . sän-tēl-yä'-nä.
Santillane . . . . . . säṅ-tē-yăn'.
Santi, Raphael, see Ra-
   phael and Sanzio . . rä'-fä-ĕl sän'-tē.
Santiago . . . . . . săn-tē-ä'-gō.
        Sp. sän-tē=ä'-go.
Santiago de Chile . . . sän-tē=ä'-gō dä chē'-lä.
Santiago de Compostela, or sän-tē=ä'-gō dä
        kōm-pōs-tä'-lä.
Santiago de Compostella . sän-tē=ä'-gō dä
        kōm-pōs-tĕl'-ä.
Santiago de Cuba . . . sän-tē=ä'-gō dä kōō'-bä.
        Eng. kū'-bä.
Santiago de la Vegas . . sän-tē=ä'-gō dä läs
        vä'-gäs.
Santiago del Estero . . sän-tē=ä'-gō dĕl ĕs-tä'-rō.
Santillana . . . . . . sän-tēl-yä'-nä.
Santo Domingo, see San
   Domingo . . . . . săn'-tō dō-mǐng'-gō.
        Sp. sän'-tō dō-mēng'-gō.
Santo Espíritu . . . . sän'-tō ĕs-pē'-rē-tōō.
Santoveneo . . . . . sän"-tō-vä-nä'-ō.
Santuzza . . . . . . sän-tŏŏts'-sä.
San Yuste . . . . . . sän yōōs'-tä.
Sanzio, Raphael, see Ra-
   phael and Santi . . . rä'-fä-ĕl sänd'-zē-ō.
São Antão . . . . . . säṅ än-täṅ'.
São José do Rio Negro . säṅ zhō-zä' dōō rē'-ōō
        nä'-grōō.
Saona . . . . sä-ō'-nä.

Saône	sōn.
Saône-et-Loire	sōn-ä-lwär'.
São Paulo de Loanda . .	säṅ pow'-lōō dĕ lō-än'-dä.
São Roque, see Saint	
Roque	säṅ rō'-kä.
Sapho	sä-fō'.
Sapor, see Saphur and	
Shahpoor	sā'-pŏr.
Sapphic	săf'-ĭk.
Sapphira	să-fī'-rȧ.
Sappho	săf'-ō.
Saracen	săr'-ȧ-sĕn.
Saracenic	săr-ȧ-sĕn'-ĭk.
Saragossa, see *Sp.* Zaragoza	săr-ȧ-gŏs'-ȧ.
Saran, see Sarun . . .	sä-rŭn'.
Sarasate y Navascues . .	sä-rä-sä'-tä ē
	nä-väs'-kōō=ĕs.
Saratoff	sä-rä'-tŏf.
Sarawak	sä-rä-wäk', să-rȧ-wăk'.
Sarcey, Francisque . .	fräṅ-sēsk' sär-sä'.
Sardanapalus	sär''-dä-nä-pä'-lŭs.
Sardou	sär-dōō'.
Sarpedon	sär-pē'-dŏn.
Sarpi	sär'-pē.
Sarrail	săr-rä'=yŭ.
Sarrebruck, see Saarbrück	sär-brük'.
Sartain	sär-tän'.
Sarto	sär'-tō.
Sartoris	sär-tō'-rĭs.
Sartor Resartus	sär'-tôr rē-sär'-tŭs.
Sarum	sâr'-ŭm.
Sarun, see Saran . . .	sä-rŭn'.
Saskatchewan	săs-kăch'-ĕ-wȧn.
Saskia	säs'-kē-ä.
Sassari	säs'-sä-rē.
Sassenach	săs'-ĕ-năċh.
Sassoferrato	säs''-sō-fĕr-rä'-tō.

Satara, see Sattara . . . sä-tä'-rä.
Satire Ménippée, see
  Satyre Ménippée . . sä-tēr' mā-nē-pā'.
Satolli . . . . sä-tŏl'-lē.
Satsuma . . . . . . săt-sū'-mȧ, sät-sōō'-mä.
Sattara, see Satara . . . sä-tä'-rä.
Saturnalia . . . . . săt-ēr-nā'-lĭ=ä.
Satyre Ménippée, see
  Satire Ménippée . . sä-tēr' mā-nē-pā'.
Saugor, or . . . . . sô-gōr'.
Saugur, see Sagar . . . sô-gŭr'.
Sault Sainte Marie . . sōō sänt mā'-rĭ.
               Fr. sō sȧnt mä-rē'.
Saumarez, see Sausmarez sō-mä-rĕs'.
Saumur . . . . . . sō-mür'.
Sausmarez, see Saumarez sō-mä-rĕs'.
Sauternes . . . . . . sō-târn'.
Savaii, see Sawaii . . . sä-vī'-ē.
Savana la Mar . . . . *Sp.* sä'-bä-nä lä mär.
Savary . . . . sä-vä-rē'.
Savigny . . . . . sä-vēn-yē'.
Savile . . . . săv'-ĭl.
Savoie . . . . sä-vwä'.
Savoja . . . . sä-vō'-yä.
Savonarola . . . . sä″-vō-nä-rō'-lä.
Savoy . . . . să-voi'.
Savoyard . . . . . sā-voi'-ärd.
Sawaii, see Savaii . . . sä-wī'-ē.
Sawantwari . . . . . sä-wŭnt-wä'-rē.
Saxe (Marshal de) . . . săks.
Saxe-Altenburg, see Sach-
  sen-Altenburg . . . săks-ăl'-tĕn-bērg.
Saxe-Coburg-Gotha, see
  Sachsen-Coburg-Gotha săks-kō'-bērg-gō'-tȧ.
Saxe-Lauenburg . . . săks-low'-ĕn-bōōrch.
Saxe-Meiningen, see Sach-
  sen-Meiningen . . . săks-mī'-nĭng-ĕn.

Saxe - Weimer - Eisenach,
   see   Sachsen-Weimar-
   Eisenach . . . . . săks-vī'-mär-ī'-zĕ-näċh.
Say, Léon . . . . . . lä-ôṅ' sä.
Say (Viscount), or Saye   sä.
Scæan (Gate) . . . . sē'-àn.
Scaevola, Mutius . . . mū'-shĭ-ŭs sĕv'-ō-là.
Scafell, see Scawfell . . skä-fĕl'.
Scala, La . . . . . . lä skä'-lä.
Scala Santa . . . . . skä'-lä sän'-tä.
Scaliger . . . . . . skăl'-ĭ-jĕr.
Scamander . . . . . skā-măn'-dĕr.
Scanderbeg, see Skander-
   beg . . . . skăn'-dĕr-bĕg.
Scapa . . . . skä'-pä.
Scapin . . . . skā'-pĭn. *Fr.* skă-păṅ'.
Scapino . . . . . *It.* skä-pē'-nō.
Scaramouche . . . . skăr'-à-mowch. *Fr.*
                  skä-rä-mōōsh'.
Scarborough . . . . . skär'-bŭ-rŭ.
Scaria (Emil) . . . . skä'-rē-ä.
Scarlatti . . . . . . skär-lät'-tē.
Scarron . . . . . . skä-rôṅ'.
Scawfell, see Scafell . . skô-fĕll'.
Sceaux . . . . sō.
Schadow . . . . . . shä'-dō.
Schaffhausen . . . . shäf-how'-zĕn,
                  shäf'-how-zĕn.
Scharwenka (Philipp) . . shär-vĕng'-kä.
Schaumburg-Lippe . . . showm'-bōōrċh-lĭp'-pŭ.
Schedone . . . . . . skä-dō'-nä.
Scheele (C. W.) . . . . shēl. *Sw.* shĭl'-ĕ.
Scheherezade, see She-
   herezade . . . . . shä-hä"-rä-zä'-dä,
                  shĕ-hē'-rä-zäd.
Scheideck, or Scheidegg . shī'-dĕk.
Scheidemann . . . . shī'-dŭ-män.

Schelde, or	sċhĕl'-dĕ.
Scheldt	skĕlt. *pop.* shĕlt.
Schelling, von	fŏn shĕl'-lĭng.
Schenck	skĕnk.
Schenectady	skĕn-ĕk'-tȧ-dĭ.
Schérer	shä-rår'.
Scheurer-Kestner . . .	shĕr-âr'-kĕst-nâr'.
Scheveningen	sċhä'-vĕn-ĭng-ĕn.
Schiedam	skē-dăm', skē'-dăm.
	D. sċhē-dăm'.
Schiehallion	shē-hăl'-yŭn.
Schiller, von	fŏn shĭl'-lĕr.
Schipka (Pass), see Shipka	shĭp'-kä.
Schlegel, von	fŏn shlä'-gĕl.
Schlei, see Schley . . .	shlī.
Schleiermacher	shlī'-ĕr-mäċh"-ĕr.
Schlemihl, Peter . . .	*Ger.* pä'-tĕr shlä'-mēl.
Schleswig, see Sleswick,	
Slesvig	shlĕz'-vĭċh, shlĕs'-vĭċh.
Schleswig-Holstein . .	shlĕz'-vĭċh-hōl'-stīn.
Schley, see Schlei, Sley	
(Prussia)	shlī.
Schley (Winfield Scott) .	slī.
Schliemann	shlē'-män.
Schlüter	shlü'-tĕr.
Schmalkalden, see Smal-	
kald, Smalcald . . .	shmäl'-käl-dĕn.
Schnorr von Karolsfeld .	shnôr fŏn kär'-ŏls-fĕlt.
Schoeffer, see Schöffer .	shĕf'-fĕr.
Schoelcher (Victor) . .	*Fr.* skĕl-shâr'. *Ger.*
	shĕl'-ċhĕr.
Schöffer, see Schoeffer .	shĕf'-fĕr.
Schoharie	skō-hăr'-ĭ.
Schomberg, von	fŏn shŏm'-bĕrg.
	Fr. shôṅ-bâr'.
Schömberg	shĕm'-bĕrċh.
Schönberg-Cotta . . .	shĕn'-bĕrċh kŏt'-ä.

Schönbrunn	shĕn'-brŏŏn.
Schönefeld	shĕ'-nĕ-fĕlt.
Schongauer (Martin) . .	shōn'-gow-ĕr.
Schönhausen	shĕn-how-zĕn.
Schopenhauer . . .	shō'-pĕn-how''-ĕr.
Schouler	skōō'-lĕr.
Schouvaloff, see Shuvaloff	shōō-vä'-lŏf.
Schreiner (Olive) . . .	shrī'-nĕr.
Schreyer	shrī'-ĕr.
Schröder	shrē'-dĕr.
Schröder-Devrient . . .	shrē'-dĕr-dĕv-rē=ŏṅ'.
Schubert	shōō'-bĕrt.
Schumann	shōō'-män.
Schumann-Heink . . .	shōō'-män-hīnk'.
Schurz	shŏŏrts.
Schütt	shüt.
Schuyler	skī'-lĕr.
Schuylkill	skōōl'-kĭl.
Schwab (Chas.)	swäb.
Schwanthaler . . .	shvän'-täl-ĕr.
Schwartzkoppen . . .	shvärts'-kŏp-pĕn.
Schwarzenberg . . .	shvärt'-zĕn-bĕrċh.
Schwarzwald	shvärts'-vält.
Schwerin	shvä-rēn'.
Schwob (Marcel) . . .	shvŏb.
Schwyz	shvĭts.
Schytte	shĭt'-ŭ.
Scilly (Is.)	sĭl'-ĭ.
Scinde, see Sind . . .	sĭnd.
Scio, see Chios	sī'-ō, shĕ'-ō.
Scipio	sĭp'-ĭ-ō.
Scituate	sĭt'-yū-āt.
Sclav	skläv, sklăv.
Scone	skōōn, skōn.
Scopas	skō'-pȧs.
Scorpio	skôr'-pĭ-ō.
Scotti	skŏt'-tē.

Scriabine	skrē-ä'-bĭn.
Scribe, Eugène	ē-zhĕn' skrēb.
Scriblerus	skrĭb-lē'-rŭs.
Scudéri, or Scudéry . .	skü-dä-rē'.
Scuola di San Rocco . .	skōō=ō'-lä dē sän rŏk'-kō.
Scurcolla, or	skōōr-kŏl'-lä.
Scurcula, or	skōōr-kōō'-lä.
Scurgola, see Scurcolla .	skōōr-gō'-lä.
Scutari	skōō'-tä-rē.
Scylla	sĭl'-ä.
Sealkote, see Sialkot . .	sē-äl-kōt'.
Seattle	sē-ăt'-l.
Sebastian	sē-băs'-tĭ=àn. *Sp.*
	sä-bäs"-tē-än'.
Sebastiano del Piombo .	sä-bäs-tē=ä'-nō dĕl
	pē=ŏm'-bō.
Sebastopol, see Sevastopol	sĕb-'ăs-tō-pōl,
	sĕb-ăs-tō'-pōl.
Secchi (Angelo)	sĕk'-ē.
Sechuen, see Szechuen,	
Se Tchuen	sä-chōō-ĕn'.
Sedalia	sĕ-dä'-lĭ-ä.
Sedan	sē-dăn'. *Fr.* sē-däṅ'.
Sedgemoor	sĕj'-mōōr.
Sedlitz, see Seidlitz . .	sĕd'-lĭts.
Sée	sä.
Seeland	sē'-lănd.
Seetapoor, see Sitapur .	sē-tä-pōōr'.
Segan-fu, see Singan Fu,	
Sian-fu	sē-gän'-fōō.
Sego, see Segu	sā'-gō.
Segovia	sĕ-gō'-vĭ-ä. *Sp.*
	sä-gō'-vē-ä.
Segu, see Sego	sā'-gōō.
Ségur, de	dŭ sä-gür'.
Seharunpoor, see Saharan-	
pur	sĕ-här-ŭn-pōōr'.

Seidl, Anton . . . . . än'-tōn zī'-dl.
Seidlitz, see Sedlitz , . zīd'-lĭts.
Seine (R.) . . . . . . sān. *Fr.* sĕn.
Seine-et-Marne . . . . sĕn'-ā-märn'.
Seine-et-Oise . . . . sĕn'-ā-wäz'.
Seine-Inférieure . . . sĕn'-ăṅ-fā-rē̃=ẽr'.
Sejanus . . . . . . sĕ-jā'-nŭs, sē-jā'-nŭs.
Sekiang, see Sikiang . . sē-kē-äng'.
Seleucidae, or . . . . sē-lū'-sĭ-dē.
Seleucids . . . . . . sē-lū'-sĭdz.
Seleucus . . . . . . sē-lū'-kŭs.
Selim . . . . sē'-lĭm, sē-lēm'.
Sélincourt (Hugh de) . . sā-lăṅ-kōor'.
Seljuks . . . . sĕl-jōōks'.
Selle . . . . sĕl.
Selous . . . . sē'-lŭs.
Sembrich . . . . . . zĕm'-brĭċh.
Semele . . . . sĕm'-ĕ-lē.
Semering, see Semmering zĕm'-ĕr-ĭng.
Seminole . . . . . . sĕm'-ĭ-nōl.
Semiramide . . . . . sā-mē-rä'-mĭ-dĕ.
Semiramis . . . . . sĕ-mĭr'-à-mĭs,
sē-mĭr'-ā-mĭs.
Semites . . . . sĕm'-īts.
Semmering, see Semering zĕm'-ĕr-ĭng.
Semonides, see Simonides sĕ-mŏn'-ĭ-dēz.
Sempach . . . . . . zĕm'-päċh.
Sempione, *It.* for Simplon sĕm-pē̃=ō'-nĕ.
Senancour . . . . . sĕ-näṅ-kōor'.
Sendai . . . . sĕn-dī'.
Seneca . . . . sĕn'-ĕ-kä, sĕn'-ē-kà.
Seneffe . . . . sē-nĕf'.   [sĕn'-ē-gàl.
Senegal . . . . . . *n.* sĕn-ē-gôl'. *adj. and n.*
Sénégal . . . . . . *Fr.* sā-nā-găl'.
Senegambia . . . . sĕn-ĕ-găm'-bĭ-à.
Senekal . . . . . sĕn-ĕ-kăl'.
Senigallia, see Sinigaglia . sā-nē-gäl'-lē=ä.

Senlac . . . . sĕn'-lăk.
Senlis . . . . sôṅ-lē'.
Sennaar, see Sennar . . sĕn-när'.
Sennacherif . . . . . sĕ-năk'-ĕ-rĭb, sĕn-à-kē'-rĭb.
Sennar, see Sennaar . . sĕ-när'.
Señor . . . . sān-yōr'.
Señora . . . . sān-yō'-rä.
Sens . . . . sŏṅs.
Seonee, or Seoni . . . sē-ō'-nē.
Seoul, see Seul . . . sē-ōōl'.
Sepoy, see Spahi . . . sĕ-pô'-ē. pop. sē'-poi.
Septuagesima . . . . sĕp"tū-à-jĕs'-ĭ-mà.
Septuagint . . . . . sĕp'-tū-à-jĭnt".
Seraglio . . . . . . sĕ-räl'-yō.
Serajevo . . . . . . sā-rä'-yä-vō.
Serao, Matilde . . . . mä-tēl'-dä sā-rä'-ō.
Serapeion, or . . . . . sĕr-à-pē'-ŏn.
Serapeium, or Serapeum . sĕr-à-pē'-ŭm.
Séraphita . . . . . . sā-rä-fē-tä'.
Serapion, see Serapeion . sĕr-à-pē'-ŏn.
Serapis . . . . . . sĕ-rä'-pĭs, sē-rä'-pĭs.
Seres . . . . sĕr'-ĕs.
Sereth . . . . sĕr-ĕt'.
Sergius . . . . sēr'-jĭ-ŭs.
Serinagur, see Srinagar . sĕr"-ĭ-nà-gōōr'.
Seringapatam, see Sriran-
  gapatam . . . . . sē-rĭng"-gā-pā-tăm'.
Seringes . . . . . . sĕr-äṅzh'.
Serpukhoff . . . . . sĕr-pōō-ċhŏf'.
Serra, Junipero . . . . 'hōō-nĭp'-ā-rō sĕr'-ä.
Serrano y Dominguez . . sĕr-rä'-nō ē dō-mĭn'-gäth.
Serre . . . . sĕr.
Servetus . . . . . . sĕr-vē'-tŭs.
Servius Tullius . . . . sĕr'-vĭ-ŭs tŭl'-ĭ-ŭs.
Sesostris . . . . . . sē-sŏs'-trĭs.
Se Tchuen, see Se Chuen,
  Szechuen . . . . . sä chōō-ĕn'.

Setebos	sĕt'-ĕ-bŏs.
Seul, see Seoul . . .	sē-ōōl'.
Seurat	sēr-ä'.
Sevastopol, see Sebastopol	sĕv'-ăs'-tō-pōl.
	Russ. sĕv'-äs-tō'-pŏl.
Sevcik	sĕv'-chĭk.
Severus (Lucius Septimius)	sĕ-vē'-rŭs, sē-vē'-rus.
Sevier	sĕ-vēr'.
Sévigné, de	dŭ sä-vēn-yä'.
Sevilla, *Sp.*	sä-vēl'-yä.
Séville, *Fr.*	sä-vēl'.
Sèville	sĕv'-ĭl, sē-vĭl'.
Sèvres	sĕvr.
Sexagesima	sĕks-à-jĕs'-ĭ-mà.
Seychelles	sä-shĕl'.
Seydlitz	zīd'-lĭts.
Sfakus, or	sfä'-kŭs.
Sfax	sfäks.
Sforza	sfōrd'-zä.
Sganarelle	sgä-nä-rĕl'.
'S Gravenhaage, see The	
Hague	s-grä-vĕn-hä'-ċhĕ.
Shadrach	shā'-drăk.
Shafalus	shăf'-à-lŭs.
Shah	shä.
Shahabad	shä-hä-bäd'.
Shah Jahan, or Jehan . .	shä yà-hän', yĕ-hän'.
Shah Jehanpoor	shä yĕ-hän-pōōr'.
Shahpoor, see Sapor, and	
Shapur	shä-pōōr'.
Shakuntala	shă-kōōn'-tă-lä.
Shalmaneser	shăl-mà-nē'-zēr.
Shalott	shă-lŏt'.
Shanghai	shăng-hī', shăng-hä'=ĭ.
Shanking	shän-kĭng'.
Shansi	shän-sē'.
Shantow, see Swatow . .	shän-tow'.

Shan-tung	shän-tōōng'.
Shapur, see Sapor, Shah-	
poor	shä-pōōr'.
Sharezer	shă-rē'-zẽr.
Sharon	shâr'-ŏn.
Shawangunk	shŏng'-gŭm.
Shchedrin	shchĕd'-rĭn.
Shebat	shē-băt'.
Sheboygan	shĕ-boi'-gàn.
Shebuyeff	shĕ-bōō'-yĕf.
Shechem, see Sichem . .	shē'-kĕm.
Shechemite	shē'-kĕm-īt.
Shechinah, see Shekinah .	shē-kī'-nä.
Sheemogga, see Shimoga	shē-mŏg'-gä.
Sheeraz, see Shiraz . .	shē'-räz.
Sheherezade, see Sche-	
herezade	shä-hä''-rä-zä'-dä,
	shĕ-hē'-rä-zäd.
Sheik, or Sheikh . . .	shēk, shāk.
Sheila	shē̆'-là.
Shekinah, or Shechinah .	shē-kī'-nä.
Shelley	shĕl'-ĭ.
Shenandoah	shĕn-ăn-dō'-à.
Shen-si, Shen-See . . .	shĕn-sē'.
Sheol	shē'-ōl.
Sheraton	shĕr'-à-tŭn.
Sheriffmuir	shĕr-ĭf-mūr'.
Shiites	shē'-īts.
Shikarpur	shĭk-är-pōōr'.
Shikoku, see Sikoku . .	shē-kō'-kōō.
Shillaber	shĭl'-à-bẽr.
Shiloh	shī'-lō.
Shimoga, see Sheemogga	shē-mō'-gä.
Shimonoseki, see Simo-	
noseki	shĭm-ō-nō-sĕk'-ē.
Shinar	shī'-när.
Shingking	shĭng-kĭng'.

Shinto . . . . shĭn'-tō.
Shintoism . . . . . . shĭn'-tō-ĭzm.
Shipka, see Schipka (Pass) shĭp'-kä.
Shiraz, see Sheeraz . . shē'-räz.
Shiré . . . . shĕ'-rä.
Shirvan . . . . . . shĭr-vän'.
Shiva, see Siva . . . shĭ'-và.
Shogun . . . . shō-gōōn'.
Shokwado . . . . . . shō'-kwä'-do'.
Sholapur . . . . . . shō-lä-pōōr'.
Shoshone . . . . . . shō-shō'-nē, shō-shō-nē'.
Shrewsbury . . . . . shrūz'-bĕr-ĭ.
Shcherbacheff . . . shschĕr-bä-chĕf'.
Shuntien-fu . . . . . shōōn'-tē=ĕn'-fōō'.
Shushan . . . . . . shōō'-shăn.
Shuvaloff, see Schouvaloff shōō-vä'-lŏf.
Shylock . . . . . . shī'-lŏk.
Sialkot, see Sealkote . . sē-äl-kōt'.
Siam . . . . sĭ-ăm', sē-äm'.
Siamese . . . . . . sī-à-mēz', sī-à-mēs'.
Sian-fu, see Singan-fu; Se-
  gan-fu . . . . . . sē-än'-fōō.
Siasconset . . . . . . sī-ăs-kŏn'-sĕt. *pop.*
                        'skŏn'-sĕt.
Sibelius . . . . . . sē-bä'-lē-ōōs.
Sibola, see Cibola . . . sē'-bō-lä.
Siboney . . . . . . sē-bō-nä'=ē.
Sibuyan . . . . . . sē-bōō-yän'.
Sibyl . . . . sĭb'-ĭl.
Sicard . . . . sē-kär'.
Sichem, see Shechem and
  Sychem . . . . . . sī'-kĕm.
Sicilian . . . . sĭ-sĭl'-ĭ=àn.
Sicily . . . . sĭs'-ĭ-lĭ.
Sickingen, von . . . . fŏn zĭk'-ĭng-ĕn.
Sicyon . . . . sĭsh'-ĭ-ŏn.
Siddhârta, or . . . . . sĭd-här'-tä.

Siddhartha	sĭ-dhär'-thä.
Sidon, see Zidon . . .	sī'-dŏn.
Siegfried, see Sigfrid . .	sēg'-frēd. *Ger.* zēg'-frēt.
Siemaradski	zē-mȧ-räd'-skĭ.
Siemering	zē'-mä-rĭng.
Siena, see Sienna . . .	sē-ĕn'-nä.
Sienese	sē-ĕn-ēz', sē-ĕn-ĕs'.
Sienkiewicz	sē═ĕn-kē═ĕ'-vĭch.
Sienna, see Siena . . .	sē-ĕn'-ä.
Sierra de los Ladrones .	sē-ĕr'-rä dä lōs lä-drō'-nĕs.
Sierra Leone	sē-ĕr'-rä lē-ō'-nē. *loc.*
	lē-ōn'. *Sp.* sē-ĕr'-rȧ
	lä-ō'-nä.
Sierra Madre	sē-ĕr'-rȧ mä'-drä.
Sierra Maestra	sĕ-ĕr'-rä mä-ās'-trä.
Sierra Morena	sē-ĕr'-rȧ mō-rä'-nä.
Sierra Nevada	sē-er'-rȧ nĕ-vä'-dä.
	Sp. sē-ĕr'-rä nä-vä'-dä.
Sieyès	sē-yĕs', sē-ĕs', sē═ä-yĕs'.
Sigel, Franz	fräntz sē'-gĕl.
	Ger. zē'-gĕl.
Sigfrid, see Siegfried . .	sēg'-frēd. *Ger.* zēg'-frēt.
Sigismund (Emperor), see	[*Ger.* zē'-gĭs-mōͦnt.
Sigmund	sĭj'-ĭs-mŭnd.
Sigmaringen	zēg'-mä-rĭng"-ĕn.
Sigmund, see Sigismund .	sĭg'-mŭnd. *Ger.* zēg'-mōͦnt.
Signac	sēn-yăk'.
Signora	sēn-yō'-rä.
Signorelli	sēn-yō-rĕl'-lē.
Signoria	sēn-yō-rē'-ä.
Signory	sēn'-yō-rĭ.
Sigourney	sĭg'-ēr-nĭ.
Sigurd	zē'-gōōrd. *Fr.* sē-gür'.
Sikhs	sēks.
Sikiang, see Sekiang . .	sē-kē-äng'.
Sikoku, see Shikoku . .	sē-kō'-kōō.
Silenus	sī-lē'-nŭs.

Silesia . . . . . . sĭl-ē'-shĭ=à.
Silhet, see Sylhet . . . sĭl-hĕt'.
Siloah, or . . . . . . sĭ-lō'-ä.
Siloam . . . . sĭ-lō'-àm, sĭl-ō'-ăm.
Silva . . . . sēl'-vä.
Silvanus . . . . . sĭl-vä'-nŭs.
Silvester . . . . . . sēl-vĕs'=tr.
Silvio Pellico . . . . sēl'-vē-ō pĕl'-lē-kō.
Simancas . . . . . . sē-män'-käs.
Simbirsk . . . . . . sĭm-bērsk'.
Simeon Stylites . . . . sĭm'-ē-ŏn stī-lī'-tēz.
Simla . . . . sĭm'-là.
Simois . . . . sĭm'-ō-ĭs.
Simon de Montfort. . . sī'-mŏn dŭ mŏnt'-fōrt.
    Fr. sē-môṅ' dŭ môṅ-fŏr'.
Simon, Jules . . . . . zhül sē-môṅ'.
Simonides, see Semonides sĭ-mŏn'-ĭ-dēz.
Simonoseki, see Shimono-
  seki . . . . sĭm-ō-nō-sĕk'-ē.
Simplon, see Sempione . sĭm'-plŏn. Fr. săṅ-plôṅ'.
Sinai (Mount) . . . . sī'-nā, sī'-nā-ī, sī'-nī.
Sinaitic (Peninsula) . . sī-ṅā-ĭt'-ĭk.
Sinclair . . . . sĭn-klâr'. Eng. sĭng'-klâr.
Sind, or Sinde, or Sindh,
  see Scinde . . . . . sĭnd.
Singan-fu, see Sian-fu,
  Segan-fu . . . . . sēn-gän'-fōō.
Singapore . . . . . . sĭng-gà-pōr', sĭn'-gà-pōr.
Singhalese . . . . . sĭng-gà-lēz', or -lēs'.
Sinigaglia, see Senigallia sē-nē-gäl'-yä.
Sinn Fein . . . . . . shĭn fän.
Sinope, or . . . . . . sĭ-nō'-pē.
Sinub, Turk. . . . . . sē-nōōb'.
Sion, see Zion . . . . sī'-ŏn.
Sioux . . . . sōō.
Siraj-ud Daula, see Sura-
  jah Dowlah . . . . sē-räj'-ōōd-dow'-lä.

Sirdar	sēr-där'.
Sirius	sĭr'-ĭ-ŭs.
Sirsa	sēr'-sä.
Sisera	sĭs'-ĕ-rä.
Sismondi, de	dŭ sĭs-mŏn'-dĭ. *Fr.* dŭ sēs-môṅ-dē'.
Sissley	sēs-lē'.
Sistine, see Sixtine . .	sĭs'-tĭn.
Sisyphus	sĭs'-ĭ-fŭs.
Sitapur, see Seetapoor .	sē-tȧ-pōōr'.
Siut, see Assiut, Asyoot .	sē-ōōt'.
Siva, see Shiva	sē'-vȧ.
Sivan	sĭv'-ȧn.
Siward	sē'-wärd.
Siwash	sē-väsh'.
Six, Jan	yăn sēks.
Sixtine (Chapel), see Sistine	sĭks'-tĭn.
Sjögren	shē'-grĕn.
Skager-Rack	skăg'-ēr-răk', skăg'-ēr-räk.
Skaguay	skăg'-wā.
Skanderbeg, see Scanderbeg	skăn'-dēr-bĕg.
Skaneateles (L.) . . .	skăn'-ē-ăt'-lĕs.
Skeat	skēt.
Skiddaw	skĭd'-dô.
Skierniewice	skē=ĕr"-nē=ĕ-vēt'-sĕ.
Skobeleff	skō'-bĕ-lĕf.
Skrzynecki, Jan Boncza .	yän bŏn'-tsä skrĭzh'-nĕt-skĭ.
Skupshtina	skōōpsh'-tĭ-nä.
Slav, or Slave	släv, slăv.
Slavonic	slä-vŏn'-ĭk.
Slesvig (Dan.), see Schleswig	slĕs'-vĭg.
Sleswick, see Schleswig .	slĕs'-wĭk.
Sley, see Schlei	slī.

Slidell . . . . slī-dĕl'.
Slowacki . . . . . . slō-väts'-kĭ.
Slovak . . . . slō-văk'.
Slovene . . . . . . slō-vēn'.
Sluis, or Sluys . . . . slois.
Smalcald, or Smalkald,
see Schmalkalden . . smăl'-kăld.
Smalcaldic . . . . . smăl-kăl'-dĭk.
Smaldeel . . . . . . smălt'-āl.
Smectymnuus . . . . smĕk-tĭm'-nū-ŭs.
Smetana . . . . . . smĕ'-tä-nä.
Smillie . . . . smī'-lĭ.
Smith Cay . . . . . smĭth kä'=ē.
Smolensk . . . . . . smō-lĕnsk'.
Smuts . . . . smoŏts.
Sneyders, see Snyders . snī'-dĕrs.
Snorre, Snorri, or
Snorro Sturleson . . snŏr'-rā, snŏr'-rē, or
                        snŏr'-rō stoōr'-lā-sŏn.
Snowdon . . . . . . snō'-dŭn.
Snyders, see Sneyders . snī'-dĕrs.
Snyman (Gen.) . . . . snī'-măn.
Sobieski . . . . . . sō-bé=ĕs'-kē.
Sobranje . . . . . . sō-brän'-yĕ.
Socapa, La . . . . . lä sō-kä'-pä.
Socinian . . . . . . sō-sĭn'-ĭ-án.
Socinus . . . . . . sō-sī'-nŭs.
Socrates . . . . . . sŏk'-rà-tēz.
Södermanland . . . . sē'-dĕr-män-länt".
Sodom . . . . sŏd'-ŏm.
Sodoma, or . . . . . sō-dō'-mä.
Sodona . . . . sō-dō'-nä.
Soerabaya, see Surabaya . soō-rä-bī'-ä.
Sofala . . . . sō-fä'-lä.
Sofi, or Sophi, see Sufi,
Saffi . . . . sō'-fī.
Sofia, see Sophia . . . sō-fē'-ä.

Soho (Square) . . . . sō'-hō.
Sohrab, see Suhrab . . *mod. Pers.* sōō-hrôb'.
        Arab. sŏ-hrôb'.
Soignies . . . . . . swän-yē'.
Soissons . . . . . . swä-sôṅ'.
Sokoto . . . . sō-kō'-tō.
Sol . . . . sŏl.
Solace (The) . . . . . sŏl'-ās.
Solario (Antonio) . . sō-lä'-rē-ō.
Soldau . . . . zŏl'-dow.
Solebay . . . . . . sōl'-bā.
Solferino . . . . . . sŏl-fä-rē'-nō.
Solinus . . . . sō-lī'-nŭs.
Soltikoff, see Saltikoff . . sŏl'-tē-kŏf.
Solyman, see Suleiman . sŏl'-ĭ-màn.
Somaj . . . . sō-mäj'.
Somaliland . . . . . sō-mä'-lē-lănd.
Sombor, see Zombor . . sŏm'-bŏr.
Sombrero . . . . . . sōm-brä'-rō.
Somme (R.) . . . . . sŏm.
Sömmering . . . . . zēm'-mĕr-ĭng.
Somosierra . . . . . sō"-mō-sĭ-ĕr'-à.
Sonata Appassionata . . sō-nä'-tä
        äp-päs"-sē-ō-nä'-tä.
Sonata Tragica . . . . sō-nä'-tä trä'-jē-kä.
Sonderbund . . . . . zŏn'-dĕr-bōōnt.
Sonnambula, La . . . lä sŏn-näm'-bōō-lä.
Sonnino . . . . . . sŏn-nē'-nō.
Sontag . . . . sŏn'-tăg. *Ger.* zŏn'-täċh.
Soochow, see Su-chau . . sōō'-chow'.
Soodan, see Sudan, Soudan sōō-dän'.
Soodra, see Sudra . . sōō'-drä.
Sooloo, see Sulu, Joló . . sōō-lōō'.
Sopater . . . . . . sŏp'-ä-tēr, sō'-pà-tēr.
Sophia, see Sofia . . . sō-fī'-ä. *mosque,* sō-fē'-ä.
Sophia Dorothea . . . sō-fī'-ä dŏr-ō-thē'-ä
Sophrosyne . . . . . sō-frŏs'-ĭn-ē.

Sorbonne, La . . . . lä sŏr-bŏn'.
Sorel, Agnès . . . . . än-yĕz' sō-rĕl'.
Soria . . . . sō'-rē-ä.
Soriano . . . . sō-rē-ä'-nō.
Sorolla . . . . sō-rŏl'-yȧ.
Sorosis . . . . sō-rō'-sĭs.
Sosigenes . . . . . . sō-sĭj'-ē-nēz.
Sotatsu . . . . sō'-täts'-ē'.
Soubise . . . . . . sōō-bēz'.
Soudan, see Sudan . . . sōō-dän'.
Souche . . . . sōōsh.
Souchez . . . . . . sōō-shā'.
Soudanese, see Sudanese sōō-dăn-ēz', sōō-dăn-ēs'.
Soufflot . . . . sōō-flō'.
Soulé . . . . sōō-lä'.
Soult . . . . sōōlt.
Sousa . . . . sōō'-zȧ.
Southey . . . . . . sow'-thĭ, sŭth'-ĭ.
Southampton (City) . . sowth-hămp'-tŏn, or
                          sŭth-hămp'-tŏn.
Southampton (Earl of) . sŭth-ămp'-tŏn, or
                          sŭth-hămp'-tŏn.
Southwark . . . . . sŭth'-ērk.
Souvaroff, see Suvaroff,
  Suwaroff . . . . . sōō-vä'-rŏf.
Souvestre, Émile . . . ä-mēl' sōō-vĕs'=tr.
Souvigny . . . . . . sōō-vēn-yē'.
Soviet . . . . sôv-yĕt'.
Spagnoletto, Il . . . . ēl spän-yō-lĕt'-tō.
Spahee, or . . . . . spä'-ē, spä'-hē.
Spahi, see Sepoy . . . spä'-hĭ.
Spalato, or . . . . . spä-lä'-tō.
Spalatro . . . . . . spä-lä'-trō.
Spallanzani . . . . . späl-länd-zä'-nē.
Spandau . . . . . . spän'-dow.
Sparafucile . . . . . spä"-rä-fōō-chē'-lä.
Spartacus . . . . . . spär'-tȧ-kŭs.

Speichern, see Spicheren   spī'-ċhĕrn.
Speier, see Speyer, Spire .   spīr, spī'-ĕr.
Spencerian, or -serian . .   spĕn-sē'-rĭ-an.
Speranski, or Speransky .   spā-rän'-skē.
Spetzia, see Spezia . . .   spĕt'-zē-ä.
Speyer, see Speier, Spires   spī'-ĕr, spīr.
Speyerbach . . . . .   spī'-ĕr-bäċh.
Spezia, or Spezzia, see
   Spetzia . . . . . .   spĕt'-zē-ä.
Spica . . . .   spī'-kä.
Spicheren, see Speichern .   spē'-ċhĕr-ĕn.
Spielhagen . . . . .   spēl'-hä-gĕn.
Spinola, de . . . . .   dä spē'-nō-lä.
Spinoza . . . . . .   spē-nō'-zä.
Spion Kop . . . . . .   spē'-ŏn kŏp.
Spire, see Speier, Speyer .   spēr.
Spires, see Speyer, Spire .   spīrz.
Spiridon . . . . . .   spĭ-rĭd'-ĭ-ŏn.
Spitalfields . . . . .   spĭt'-àl-fēldz.
Spluga, or . . . . . .   splōō'-gä.
Splügen . . . . . .   splü'-gĕn.
Spohr (Louis) . . . .   spōr.
Spokan, or . . . . .   spō-kăn'.
Spokane . . . . . .   spō-kän'.
Spoleto . . . .   spō-lä'-tō.
Spontini . . . . . .   spŏn-tē'-nē.
Sporades . . . . . .   spŏr'-ā-dēz.
Spree . . . .   sprä.
Spurgeon . . . . . .   spŭr'-jŭn.
Spurzheim . . . . .   spōōrts'-hīm.
Spuyten Duyvil . . . .   spī'-tĕn dī'-vĭl.
Spytfontein . . . . .   spīt'-fŏn-tīn.
Squarcione . . . . .   skwär-chō'-nä.
Srinagar, see Serinagur .   srĭ-nà-gär'.
Srirangapatam, see
   Seringapatam . . . .   srĭ-răng"-gà-pà-tăm'.
Staal, de . . . . . .   dŭ stäl.

Stabat Mater . . . . stā'-băt mā'-tēr, stä'-bät mä'-tēr.
Stadtlohn . . . . . . stät-lōn'.
Stael-Holstein . . . . stä'-ĕl-hŏl'-stĭn.
　　　　　　　　　　 Fr. stä-ĕl'-ŏl-stăṅ'.
Stagira . . . . stä-jī'-rȧ.
Stagirite . . . . . . stăj'-ĭ-rīt.
Stagirus . . . . . . stä-jī'-rŭs.
Stamboul . . . . . . stäm-bōōl'.
Stambuloff . . . . . stäm-bōō'-lŏf.
Stanhope . . . . . . stăn'-ŏp.
Stanislas, see Stanislaus . stăn'-ĭs-lȧs.
Stanislas Lesczinski . . stăn'-ĭs-lȧs lĕsh-chĭn'-skē.
Stanislaus, see Stanislas . stăn-ĭs-lä'-ŭs.
Stanislaus (R.) . . . . stăn'-is-low.
Stanze . . . . ständ'-zĕ.
Starhemberg . . . . . stä'-rĕm-bĕrċh.
Statira . . . . stȧ-tī'-rȧ.
Staubbach . . . . . . stowb'-bäċh.
Stavanger . . . . . . stä-väng'-gĕr.
Stavropol . . . . . . stäv'-rō-pŏl.
Steen, Jan . . . . . yăn stän.
Steenkerke, or . . . . stän'-kĕrk-ĕ.
Steenkerken . . . . . stän'-kĕrk-ĕn.
Stefanie (L.) . . . . . stĕ-fä-nē'.
Stein, von . . . . . . fŏn stīn.
Steinau . . . . stī'-now.
Steinitz . . . . . . stīn'-ĭts.
Steinmetz . . . . . . stīn'-mĕts.
Steinwehr . . . . . . stīn'-vär.
Stelvio . . . . stĕl'-vĭ-ō.
Stendhal, De . . . . . dŭ stŏṅ-däl'.
Stéphanie . . . . . . stä-fä-nē'.
Stephano . . . . . . Tempest, stĕf'-ä-nō.
　　　　　　　　　　 Merchant of Venice,
　　　　　　　　　　 stĕf-ä'-nō.
Stephen Báthori . . . stē'-vĕn bä'-tō-rē.

Stepniak . . . . . . stĕp'-nē=äk.
Sterkstroom . . . . . stĕrk'-strōm.
Stettin . . . . stĕt-ēn'.
Steuben . . . . . . stū'-bĕn. *Ger.* stoi'-bĕn.
Steyn . . . . stīn.
Steyne . . . . stīn.
Stiberdigebit . . . . stĭ'-bĕr-dĭ-jĕb"-ĭt.
Stigand . . . . stĭg'-ånd.
Stilicho . . . . stĭl'-ĭ-kō.
Stilliano . . . . . . stēl-ē-ä'-nō.
Stinnes, Hugo . . . . hōō'-gō stĭn'-ĕs.
Stockholm . . . . . . stŏk'-hōlm.
Stoke Poges . . . . . stōk pō'-jĕs.
Stolypin . . . . . . stŏ-lĭp'-ĭn.
Stolzenfels . . . . . stŏlt'-zĕn-fĕlz.
Stormberg . . . . . stŏrm'-bĕrċh.
Stor-thing . . . . . . stōr'-tĭng.
Stötteritz . . . . . . stĕt'-tĕ-rĭts.
Stoughton . . . . . . stō-tŭn.
Stour . . . . stōōr.
Strabo . . . . strā'-bō.
Strachey, Lytton . . . lĭt'-ŭn strā'-chĭ.
Stradivarius . . . . . străd-ĭ-vā'-rĭ-ŭs.
Strakosch . . . . . . strä'-kŏsh.
Stralsund . . . . . . sträl'-sōōnd.
Strasbourg . . . . . *Fr.* sträs-bōōr'.
Strasburg, or . . . . străs'-bĕrg.
Strassburg . . . . . *Ger.* sträs'-bōōrċh.
Stratford-on-Avon . . . străt-fōrd-ŏn-ā'-vōn.
Strauss . . . . strows.
Stravinsky . . . . . . strä-vĭn'-skĭ.
Strelitz . . . . *Ger.* shtrā'-lĭts.
Strelitzes . . . . . . strĕl'-its-ĕz.
Strephon . . . . . . strĕf'-ŏn.
Strindberg . . . . . strĭnt-bĕrċh.
Stromboli . . . . . . strŏm'-bō-lē.
Strophades . . . . . strŏf'-ă-dēz.

Strozzi	strŏt′-zē.
Strumitza	strōō′-mēts-à.
Struve	strōō′-vŭ.
Stryj	strē.
Strypa	strē′-pä.
Stuhlweissenburg . . .	shtōōl-vīs′-ĕn-bōōrċh.
Stürmer	shtür′-mĕr.
Sturm und Drang . . .	shtōōrm ŏŏnt dräng.
Stuttgart	shtŏŏt′-gärt.
Stuyvesant	stī′-vĕ-sănt.
Stygian	stĭj′-ĭ-àn.
Stylites	stī-lī′-tēz.
Styr	stēr.
Styx	stĭks.
Suabia, see Swabia . .	swā′-bĭ-à.
Suabian, see Swabian . .	swā′-bĭ-àn.
Subiaco	sōō-bē=ä′-kō.
Subig (Bay)	sōō-bēg′.
Sublime Porte	sub-līm′ pōrt.
Su-chau, or Suchow, see	
Soochow	sōō′-chow′.
Suchet	sü-shā′.
Sucre, de	dā sōō′-krā.
Sudan, see Soudan, Soodan	sōō-dän′.
Sudanese, see Soudanese	sōō-dăn-ēz′, sōō-dăn-ēs′.
Sudermann	zōō′-dĕr-män.
Sudra, see Soodra . .	sōō′-drä.
Sue, Eugène	yū′-jēn sū. *Fr.* ē-zhān′ sü.
Suetonius	swē-tō′-nĭ-ŭs.
Suez	sōō′-ĕz, sōō-ĕz′.
Suffeed Koh, see Safed Koh	sŭf′-ēd-kō.
Suffren de Saint-Tropez .	süf-frĕn′ dŭ săṅ-trō-pĕss′.
	Fr. süf-frŏṅ′ du săṅ trō-pā′.
Sufi, see Saffi, Sofii . .	sōō′-fĭ.
Suhrab, see Sohrab . .	*mod. Pers.* sōō-hrôb′.
	Arab. sŏ-hrôb′.
Suippe	swēp.

Sukenobu . . . . . . sōō'-kä'-nō'-bĕ'.
Sul, Rio Grande do . . rē'-ō grän'-dä dōō sōōl.
Suleiman (Mosque of), see
  Solyman . . . . . sōō-lä-män'.
Sulla . . . . sŭl'-à.
Sully . . . . sŭl'-ĭ. Fr. sü-lē'.
Sully-Prudhomme . . . sü-lē'-prü-dŏm'.
Sultanpur . . . . . . sŭl-tăn-pōōr'.
Sulu, see Sooloo, Joló . . sōō-lōō'.
Suluk . . . . sōō-lōōk'.
Sumag . . . . sōō-mäg'.
Sumatra . . . . . . sōō-mä'-trä.
Sumbulpur, see Sambalpur sŭm-bŭl-pōōr'.
Sundi . . . . sōōn'-dē.
Sunna . . . . sŏŏn'-à.
Sunni . . . . sŏŏn'-ē.
Sun Yat Sen . . . . . sŏŏn yät sĕn.
Suppé, von . . . . . fŏn zŏŏp'-pä.
Surabaya, see Soerabaya sōō-rä-bī'-ä.
Surajah Dowlah, see Siraj-
  ud-Daula . . . . . sōō-rä'-jä dow'-lä.
Surat . . . . sōō-rät'.
Surikoff . . . . . . sōō'-rē-kŏf.
Surinam . . . . . . sōō-rĭ-näm'.
Susa . . . . sōō'-sà. It. sōō'-zä.
Sutlej . . . . sŭt'-lĕj.
Suvaroff, or . . . . . sōō-vä'-rŏf.
Suvla . . . . sōō'-vlà.
Suwalki . . . . . . sōō-väl'-kē.
Suwanee, or Suwannee . sū-wô'-nē.
Suwaroff, or . . . . . sōō-vä'-rŏf.
Suwarrow, see Suvaroff . sōō-vä'-rŏv.
Suzuki Harunobu . . . sōō'-zōō'-kē'
                hä'-rōō'-nō'-bĕ'.
Sverdrup . . . . . . svĕr'-drŏŏp
Swabia, see Suabia . . swä'-bĭ-à.
Swabian, see Suabian . . swä'-bĭ-àn.

Swansea . . . . . . swŏn'-sē.
Swartow, or . . . . . swär-tow'.
Swatow, see Shantow . . swä-tow'.
Swaziland . . . . . . swä'-zē-lănd.
Swedenborg . . . . swē'-dĕn-bôrg.
                Sw. svĭd'-ĕn-bōrg.
Swedenborgian . . . . swē-dĕn-bôr'-jĭ-àn.
Swegen, or . . . . . svä'-gĕn.
Swein, or . . . . . . swān.
Sweyn . . . . swān.
Sybaris . . . . sĭb'-à-rĭs, sĭb'-ā-rĭs.
Sybarite . . . . . . sĭb'-à-rīt.
Sybel, von . . . . . fŏn zē'-bĕl.
Sychar . . . . sī'-kär.
Sychem, see Sichem, She-
  chem . . . . . . sī'-kĕm.
Sycorax . . . . . . sĭk'-ō-răks.
Sydenham . . . . . sĭd'-ĕn-àm.
Sylhet, see Silhet . . . sĭl-hĕt'.
Sylva, Carmen . . . . kär'-mĕn sĭl'-vä.
Sylvester . . . . . . sĭl-vĕs'-tēr.
Sylvestre Bonnard . . . sĭl-vĕs'-tr bŏn-âr'.
Symonds . . . . . . sĭm'-ŭndz, sī'-mŭndz.
Symons . . . . . . sĭm'-ŭnz, sī'-mŭnz.
Symplegades . . . . . sĭm-plĕg'-à-dēz.
Synge . . . . sĭng.
Synod . . . . sĭn'-ŏd.
Synope . . . . sī-nō'-pē.
Syracuse . . . . . . sĭr'-à-kūs, sĭr'-à-kūz.
Syrinx . . . . sī'-rĭngks.
Szechenyi . . . . . . sä'-chĕn-yē.
Szechuen, see Sechuen,
  Se Tchuen . . . . . sä-chōō-ĕn'.
Szegedin . . . . . . sĕg'-ĕd-ēn.
Sziget . . . . sĭg'-ĕt.

T

Taafe, von	fŏn tä'-fŭ.
Taal	täl.
Tabago, see Tobago . .	tä-bä'-gō.
Tabard	tăb'-àrd.
Tabasco	tà-băs'-kō. *Sp.* tä-bäs'-kō.
Tablas	tä'-bläs.
Tabor	*Mt.* tä'-bŏr. *Boh.* tä'-bŏr.
Tacna	*pop.* tăk'-nà, täk'-nä.
Taddeo	täd-dä'-ō.
Tadema, Alma-	äl'-mä-tä'-dĕ-mä.
Tadmir	täd-mēr'.
Tadmor	tăd'-môr.
Taeping, see Tai-ping . .	tī-pǐng'.
Tafna	täf'-nä.
Tagal, see Tegal . . .	tä-gäl'. *D.* tä-ċhäl'.
Tagala	tä-gä'-lä.
Taganrog	*pop.* tăg-àn-rŏg', tä-gän-rŏg'.
Tagle, Sanchez de . . .	sän'-chĕs dä tä'-glä.
Tagliacozzo	täl-yä-kŏt'-zō
Tagliamento	täl-yä-män'-tō.
Taglioni (Filippo) . . .	täl-yō'-nē.
Tagore, Rabindranath . .	rä'-bǐn'-drä'-näth' tä'-gōr'.
Tagus, see Sp. Tajo, Port.	
Tejo	tä'-gŭs.
Tahamis	tä-ä'-mēs.
Tahiti	tä-hē'-tē.
Tahitian	tä-hē'-tǐ-àn.
Tahlequah	tä-lĕ-kwä'.
Tahoe	tä'-hō.
Tai, see Thai, or T'hai .	tī.
Tai-chau	tī'-chow'.
Taillebourg	tä=yŭ-bōōr'.
Taillefer	tä=yŭ-fâr'.
Taine	tän.

Tai-ping, see Taeping . . tī'-pĭng'.
Taiwan . . . . tī-wän'.
Tai-yuan . . . . . . tī-wän'.
Taj-e-mah (The) . . . täzh'-ĕ-mä'.
Taj Mahal, or Mehal . . täzh mä-häl', or mĕ-häl'.
Tajo, Sp. for Tagus . . tä'-ċhō.
Tajurrah . . . . . . tä-joo'-rä.
Takahira . . . . . . tä'-kä'-hē'-rä'.
Takala, see Tekele . . . tä-kä'-lä.
Takao, or Takow . . . tä-kä'=ō, tä-kow'.
Taku . . . . tä'-koo.
Talaut (Is.) . . . . . tä-lowt'.
Talavera de la Reina . . tä-lä-vä'-rä dä lä rä-ē'-nä.
Talbot . . . . tôl'-bŭt.
Talca . . . . täl'-kä.
Talfourd . . . . . . tôl'-fŭrd.
Taliaferro . . . . . . tŏl'-ĭ-vēr.
Ta Lien Wan, or Talien-
wan . . . . tä'-lēn'-wän'.
Taliesin . . . . . . täl'-ĭ-sĭn.
Tallard . . . . tä-lär'.
Talleyrand-Périgord . . täl'-ĭ-rănd. Fr.
                         täl-ā-răṅ'-pä-rē-gōr'.
Tallien . . . . tä-lē=ĕṅ'.
Talma . . . . täl'-mȧ, täl-mä'.
Talmud . . . . täl'-mŭd.
Talmudic . . . . . . täl-mŭd'-ĭk.
Talmudist . . . . . . täl'-mŭd-ĭst.
Tamalpais . . . . . . tăm-ȧl-pä'-ēs.
Tamanieb . . . . . . tä-mä-nē-ĕb'.
Tamar . . . . tā'-mär.
Tamaulipas . . . . . tä-mow-lē'-päs.
Tamboff . . . . . . täm-bŏf'.
Tamburlaine, or Tamber-
lane . . . . tăm-bĕr-lān'.
Tamerlane, see Timur-
Leng . . . . tăm-ĕr-lān'.

Tamils	tăm′-ĭlz, tä-mēlz′.
Tammuz	tăm′-ŭz.
Tamora	tăm′-ō-rà.
Tampico	tăm-pē′-kō. *Sp.* täm-pē′-kō.
Tamsui	täm-sōō′-ē.
Tanagra	tăn′-à-grä.
Tanais	tăn′-ā-ĭs, tā′-nā-ĭs.
Tananerivo	tä-nä″-nä-rē′-vō.
Tancred	tăng′-krĕd, tăn′-krĕd.
Tancrède	täṅ-krĕd′.
Tancredi	tän-krā′-dē.
Taneieff	tän-yä′-ĕf.
Taney (Robert)	tô′-nĭ.
Tanganyika (L.)	tän-gän-yē′-kä.
Tanger, *Fr.*, or	täṅ-zhä′.
Tanger, *Ger.*, see Tangier	täng′-ĕr.
Tangerine	tăn-jĕ-rēn′.
Tangier, or	tăn-jēr′, tän-jēr′.
Tangiers, or	tăn-jērz′, tän-jērz′.
Tanja, Native	tän′-jä.
Tanjore	tăn-jōr′.
Tan Kweilin	tän′-kwä′-lēn′.
Tannenberg	tän′-ĕn-bĕrch.
Tannhäuser	tän′-hoi-zĕr.
Tännyu	tän′-n-yū′.
Tantalus	tăn′-tà-lŭs.
Tao	tä′-ō.
Taoism	tä′-ō-ĭzm, tä′-ō-ĭzm, tow′-ĭzm.
Taparelli, Massimo	mäs′-sē-mō tä-pä-rĕl′-lē.
Tapia	tä′-pē-ä.
Tappan Zee	tăp′-àn-zā.
Tapti (R.)	tăp′-tē.
Tara	tä′-rà.
Taranto	tä-rän′-tō.
Tarapacá	*pop.* tă-rà-păk′-à.
	Sp. tä″-rä-pä-kä′.

Tarascon	tä-räs-kôn'.
Tarbes	tärb.
Tardieu	tär-dē=yē'.
Tarifa	tä-rē'-fä.
Tárlac, or Tarlac . . .	tär'-läk.
Tarn	tärn.
Tarn-et-Garonne . . .	tärn'-ä-gä-rŏn'.
Tarnopol	tär-nō'-pŏl.
Tarnovo, see Tirnova . .	tär'-nō-vō.
Tarpeia	tär-pē'-yä.
Tarpeian	tär-pē'-yȧn.
Tarquin	tär'-kwĭn.
Tarquinio	tär-kwē'-nē-ō.
Tarragona	tär-rä-gō'-nä.
Tarshish	tär'-shĭsh.
Tartar, see Tatar . . .	tär'-tär.
Tartarean	tär-tā'-rē-ȧn.
Tartarin	tär-tä-răṅ'.
Tartarus	tär'-tȧ-rŭs.
Tartufe, or Tartuffe . .	tär'-tŭf. *Fr.* tär-tüf'.
Tashkend, or Taschkend	täsh-kend'.
Tasmania	tăz-mā'-nĭ-ȧ.
Tasso, Torquato	tōr-kwä'-tō tăs'-ō.
	It. täs'-sō.
Tatar, see Tartar . . .	tä'-tär.
Tatiana	tät-yä'-nä.
Taubert	tow'-bĕrt.
Tauchnitz	towk'-nĭts.
	Ger. towċh'-nĭts.
Taughannock	tô-găn'-ŏk.
Tauler	tow'-lĕr.
Taunton	tänt'-ŏn.
Taunus	tow'-nōͦos.
Tauric	tô'-rĭk.
Taurida	tow'-rē-dä.
Taurus (Mt.)	tô'-rŭs.
Tavannes	tä-vän'.

Tavoy . . . . tä-voi'.
Tayabas . . . . . . tī-ä'-bäs.
Taygetus . . . . . . tā-ĭj'-ĕ-tŭs.
Taytay . . . . tä'=ē-tä'=ē.
Tchad (L.), see Chad,
    Tsad . . . . chäd.
Tchaikowsky . . . . . chī-kŏv'-skĭ.
Tcherepnin . . . . . chĕr-ĕp'-nĭn.
Tchernaya . . . . . . châr'-nī-ä.
Tchernigoff . . . . . chĕr-nē-gŏf'.
Tchernyshevsky . . . chĕr-nē-shĕf'-skē.
Tchitcherin . . . . . chĭch'-ēr-ĭn.
Tchu . . . . chōō.
Tchukchis . . . . . chōōk'-chēz.
Tean, see Teian . . . . tē'-àn.
Tebeth . . . . tĕ-bĕt'.
Teck . . . . tĕk.
Tecumseh . . . . . . tē-kŭm'-sĕ.
Te Deum . . . . . . tē dē'-ŭm.
Tegal, see Tagal . . . tĕ-gäl'.
Tegea . . . . tē'-jē-ä.
Tegetthoff . . . . . . tā'-gĕt-hŏf.
Tegnér . . . . tĕng-nâr'.
Teheran, or . . . . . tĕh-ĕ-rän'.
Tehran . . . . tĕh-rän'.
Tehri . . . . tĕh-rē'.
Tehuantepec . . . . . tā-wän"-tä-pĕk'.
Teian, see Tean . . . . tē'-àn.
Te Igitur . . . . . . tē-ĭj'-ĭ-tēr.
Teignmouth . . . . . tān'-mŭth.
Tejo, Port. for Tagus . . tā'-zhōō.
Tekele, see Takala . . . tā-kā'-lĕ.
Telamon . . . . . . tĕl'-ā-mŏn.
Tel or Tell El Kebir . . tĕl ĕl kĕb-ēr'.
Telemachus . . . . . tĕ-lĕm'-à-kŭs.
Télémaque . . . . . tā-lā-măk'.
Tellez . . . . tĕl'-yĕth.

Teman	tē'-măn.
Tembuland	· tĕm'-boo-lănd.
Téméraire	tā-mā-râr'.
Temesvár	tĕm'-ĕsh-vär.
Temora	tē-mō'-ra̕.
Tempe	tĕm'-pā, tĕm'-pē.
Tenasserim	tĕn-ăs'-ēr-ĭm.
Tencin	tŏṅ-săṅ'.
Tenebræ	tĕn'-ē-brē.
Tenedos	tĕn'-ē-dŏs.
Tenerife, or	tā-nā-rē'-fā.
Teneriffa, or	tā-nā-rēf'-fä.
Teneriffe	tĕn-ēr-ĭf'.
Teniers (David) . . .	tĕn'-yĕrz. *Fr.* tĕ-nē=âr'.
Tenniel	tĕn'-yĕl.
Teocalli	tē-ō-kăl'-ē.
Tepic	tā-pēk'.
Teplitz, see Töplitz . .	tĕp'-lĭts.
Terauchi	tā'-rä'=oo-chē'.
Terburg	tĕr'-bŭċh.
Terceira	tĕr-sā'-rä.
Terek	tĕr-ĕk'.
Tergnier	tĕrn-yā'.
Termonde	tār-mōṅd'.
Ternina, Fräulein Milka .	froĭ'-lĭn mēl'-kä tĕr-nē'-nä.
Terpsichore	tĕrp-sĭk'-ō-rē.
Terpsichorean	tĕrp″-sĭ-kō-rē'-a̕n.
Terracina	tĕr-rä-chē'-nä.
Terra del Fuego, see Tier-ra del Fuego	tĕr'-rä dĕl fū-ē'-gō.
Terrazas	tĕr-ä'-säs.
Terre, La	lä târ.
Terre Haute	tĕr'-ĕ-hōt. *Fr.* târ-ōt'.
Tertullian	tēr-tŭl'-ē=a̕n.
Teruel	tā-roo-ĕl'.
Teschen	tĕsh'-ĕn.
Tesla	tĕz'-lä.

Tête-Noire	tāt-nwär'.
Tethys	tē'-thĭs.
Tetrazzini	tā-träts-sē'-nē.
Tetuan	tĕt-ōō-än'.
Teucer	tū'-sēr.
Teufelsdröckh, Herr . .	hĕr toi'-fĕlz-drēk.
Teuton	tū'-tŏn.
Teutonic	tū-tŏn'-ĭk.
Teviot	tĭv'-ĭ-ŏt, tē'-vĭ-ŏt.
Tewfik Pasha . . .	tū'-fĭk păsh-ô', pȧ-shä'.
	päsh'-ȧ.
Texcoco, or	tās-kō'-kō.
Texel	tĕks'-ĕl.
Tezcuco	tās-kōō'-kō.
Thaba N'Chu, or Thaba	
Ntschu, or Thabanchu .	tä'-bänts-chōō.
Thaddeus	thăd'-ē-ŭs, thăd-ē'-ŭs.
Thai, see T'hi, Tai . . .	tī.
Thais	thā'-ĭs. *Fr.* tä-ēs'.
Thaisa	thā'-ĭs-ä.
Thalaba	thăl'-ȧ-bȧ.
Thalberg	täl'-bĕrċh.
Thales	thā'-lēz.
Thalia	thā-lī'-ȧ.
Thames, *Am.*	thāmz.
Thames, *Eng.*	tĕmz.
Thanatopsis	thăn-ȧ-tŏp'-sĭs.
Tharaud	tă-rō'.
Theætetus	thē-ē-tē'-tŭs.
Théâtre Antoine . . .	tā-ătr' äṅ-twăn'.
Théâtre Chauve Souris .	tā-ătr' shōv sōō-rē'.
Théâtre Comique . . .	tā-ătr' kō-mēk'.
Théâtre Français, Le . .	lē tā-ătr' fräṅ-sā'.
Théâtre Italien	tā-ătr' ē-tä-lē꞊ĕṅ'.
Thebaid (The)	thē'-bā-ĭd, thē-bā'-ĭd.
Thébaide, La	lä tā-bä-ēd'.
Thebais	thē-bā'-ĭs, thĕb'-ā-ĭs.

The Hague, see Den Haag,
La   Haye,   S'Graven
Haage . . . . . .   thē hāg.
Theiss, see Tisza, *Hung.*. .   tīs.
Thekla . . . .   tĕk'-lä.
Themis . . . .   thē'-mĭs.
Themistocles . . . . .   thē-mĭs'-tō-klēz.
Theobald (Lewis) . . .   thē'-ō-bôld, tĭb'-ăld.
Theocritean . . . . .   thē-ŏk"-rĭ-tē'-àn.
Theocritus . . . . .   thē-ŏk'-rĭ-tŭs.
Theodoric . . . . . .   thē-ŏd'-ō-rĭk.
Theodorus . . . . .   thē-ō-dō'-rŭs.
Theodosia . . . . .   thē-ō-dō'-sĭ-à, -shĭ-à.
Theodosius . . . . .   thē-ō-dō'-sĭ-ŭs,
                         thē-ō-dō'-shĭ-ŭs.
Theodota . . . . . .   thē-ŏd'-ō-tà.
Theodotus . . . . . .   thē-ŏd'-ō-tŭs.
Theophilus . . . . .   thē-ŏf'-ĭl-ŭs.
Theophrastus . . .   thē-ō-frăs'-tŭs.
Theotocupuli . . . . .   tā-ō"-tō-kōō-pōō'-lē.
Theresa . . . . . .   tĕ-rē'-sä.   *Ger.* tā-rā'-sä.
Thérèse . . . . . .   tā-rĕz'.
Thermidor . . . . . .   thēr-mĭ-dôr'.   *Fr.*
                         tĕr-mē-dōr'.
Thermopylæ . . . . .   thēr-mŏp'-ĭ-lē.
Thersites . . . . . .   thēr-sī'-tēz.
Theseion . . . . . .   thē-sē'-ŏn.
Theseum . . . . . .   thē-sē'-ŭm.
Theseus . . . . . .   thē'-sūs, thē'-sē-ŭs.
Thessalonica . . . . .   thĕs"-sà-lō-nī'-kà.
Thetis . . . .   thē'-tĭs.
Theuriet . . . . . .   tĕr-ē-ā'.
T'hi, see Tai, Thai . . .   tī.
Thiaucourt . . . . .   tē-ō-kōōr'.
Thiaumont . . . . .   tē-ō-mŏṅ'.
Thibaut . . . . . .   tē-bō'.
Thibet, see Tibet . . .   tĭb'-ĕt, tĭ-bĕt'.

Thibetan, see Tibetan . .   tĭ-bĕt'-àn, tĭb'-ĕt-àn.
Thielt . . . .   tēlt.
Thiepval . . . . .   t-yĕp-väl'.
Thiergarten, see Tier-
  garten . . . . .   tēr'-gär-tĕn.
Thierri, (or-ry) Amédée .   ăm-ā-dā'-tē-ĕr-ē'.
Thierry, Château . . .   shă-tō' tē-ĕr-ē'.
Thiers . . . .   tē-âr'.
Thing . . . .   Dan. tĭng.
Thionville . . . . .   tē-ôn-vēl'.
Thisbe . . . .   thĭz'-bē.
Thogji Chumo (L.) . .   thŏg'-jē chōō'-mō.
Tholuck . . . . . .   tō'-lŭk.   Ger. tō'-lŏŏk.
Thomas, Ambroise . .   än-brwäz' tō-mä'.
Thopas (Sir) . . . .   thō'-pàs.
Thor . . . .   thôr, tôr.
Thoreau . . . . . .   thō'-rō, thō-rō'.
Thorvaldsen, or often Thor-
  waldsen . . . . .   tŏr'-väld-zĕn,
               tôr'-wôld-sĕn.
Thoth . . . .   tōt, thŏth.
Thothmes . . . . .   thŏth'-mēz, tŏt'-mēz.
Thou . . . .   Fr. tōō.
Thouars . . . . . .   tōō-är'.
Thourout . . . . . .   tōō-rōō'.
Thrace . . . .   thrās. Class. thrā'-sē.
Thracian . . . . . .   thrā'-shĭ=àn.
Thrasybulus . . . . .   thrăs-ĭ-bū'-lŭs.
Thrasymenes . . .   thrā-sĭm'-ē-nēz.
Thrasymenus . . .   thrā-sĭ-mē'-nŭs.
Throndhjem, see Trondh-
  jem . . . .   trŏnd'-yĕm.
Thucydides . . . . .   thū-sĭd'-ĭ-dēz.
Thugut . . . .   tōō'-gōōt.
Thule . . . .   thū'-lē.
Thun (L.) . . . . . .   tōōn.
Thurgau, or . . . . .   tōōr'-gow.

Thurgovie, *Fr.* . . . . . tür-gō-vē′.
Thüringen . . . . . . *Ger.* tü′-rĭng-ĕn.
Thuringia . . . . . . thū-rĭn′-jĭ-à.
Thuringian . . . . . thū-rĭn′-jĭ-àn.
Thurn . . . . tōōrn.
Thursby . . . . . thĕrz′-bĭ.
Thyrsis . . . . . . thĕr′-sĭs.
Tibet, see Thibet . . . tĭb′-ĕt, tĭ-bĕt′.
Tibetan, see Thibetan . . tĭ-bĕt′-àn, tĭb′-ĕt′-àn.
Tibullus . . . . . . tĭ-bŭl′-ŭs.
Tiburzio . . . . . . tē-bōōrt′-zē-ō.
Ticao . . . . tē-kä′-ō.
Tichborne . . . . . tĭch′-bŭrn, tĭch′-bŭn.
Ticino . . . . tē-chē′-nō.
Ticinus (R.) . . . . . tĭ-sī′-nŭs.
Ticinus . . . . tĭs′-ĭn-ŭs, tĭ-sī′-nŭs.
Tieck . . . . tēk.
Tien-Tsin, or Tientsin . tē-ĕn′-tsēn.
Tiepolo . . . . tē-ā′-pō-lō.
Tiergarten, see Thier-
    garten . . . . . tēr′-gär-tĕn.
Tierra del Fuego, see
    Terra del Fuego . . tē=ĕr′-rä dĕl fwä′-gō.
Tiers État . . . . . . tĕrz ā-tä′, tē=âr′-zä-tä′.
Tietjens, see Titiens . . tēt′-yĕns.
Tiflis . . . . tĭf-lēs′.
Tighe (Mary) . . . . tī.
Tiglath-Pileser . . . tĭg′-lăth-pĭl-ē′-zēr.
Tigris . . . . tī′-grĭs.
Tilghman . . . . . . tĭl′-màn.
Tillemont . . . . . . tē=yŭ-môṅ′.
Tilly . . . . tĭl′-ĭ.
Tilsit . . . . tĭl′-sĭt.
Timæus . . . . . . tī-mē′-ŭs.
Timbuctoo, or Timbuktu . tĭm-bŭk′-tōō.
Timoleon . . . . . . tĭ-mō′-lē-ŏn.
Timon . . . . tī′-mŏn.

Timor	tē-mōr'.
Timotheus	tǐ-mō'-thē-ŭs.
Timour, or Timur, or. .	tē-mōōr'.
Timur Bey, or	tē-mōōr' bā.
Timur-Leng, see Tamer-	
lane	tē-mōōr'-lĕng.
Tinavelly, see Tinnevelli .	tǐn-à-vĕl'-ǐ.
Tinayre, Marcelle . . .	mär-sĕl tē-nār'.
Tindale, see Tyndale . .	tǐn'-dàl.
Ting-hae, or Ting-hai . .	tǐng-hī'.
Tinnevelli, see Tinavelly .	tǐn-ĕ-vĕl'-ǐ.
Tino (Gen.)	tē'-nō.
Tintagel	tǐn-tăj'-ĕl.
Tintern	tǐn'-tĕrn.
Tintoret, or	tǐn'-tō-rĕt.
Tintoretto, Il	ēl tǐn-tō-rĕt'-ō,
	tēn-tō-rĕt'-ō.
Tioomen, or Tioumen, see	
Tiumen, Tyumen . .	tē-ōō-mĕn'.
Tipitapa (R.)	tē-pē-tä'-pä.
Tippecanoe	tǐp'-ē-kà-nōō'.
Tipperah	tǐp'-ĕ-rä.
Tipperary	tǐp-ĕ-rā'-rǐ.
Tippoo Sahib, see Tipu	
Saib	tǐp-ōō' sä'-hǐb.
Tippoo Tib, or	tǐp-ōō' tǐb.
Tippoo Tip	tǐp-ōō' tǐp.
Tipu Saib, see Tippoo	
Sahib	tǐp-ōō' sä'-ǐb.
Tiresias	tǐ-rē'-sǐ-às.
Tirhakah	tĕr'-hà-kä.
Tirhoot	tǐr-hōōt'.
Tirlemont	tērl-mŏn'.
Tirnova, see Tarnovo . .	tēr'-nō-vä.
Tirpitz, von	fŏn tēr'-pǐts.
Tischendorf, von . . .	fŏn tǐsh'-ĕn-dôrf.
Tishri	tǐsh'-rǐ.

Tisiphone . . . . . tĭ-sĭf'-ō-nē.
Tissot . . . . tē-sō'.
Tisza, see Theiss . . . tĭs'-ä. *Hung.* tĭsh'-a̤.
Titan . . . . . . tī'-tán.
Titania . . . . . . tĭ-tā'-nĭ-a̤.
Titanic . . . . . . tĭ-tăn'-ĭk.
Tithonus . . . . . tĭ-thō'-nŭs.
Titian, see Tiziano . . tĭsh'-án, tĭsh'-ē=án.
Titicaca (L.) . . . . tĭt-ē-kä'-kä.
Titiens, see Tietjens . . tēt'-yĕns. *pop.* tĭsh'-yĕnz.
Tito Melema . . . . . tē'-tō mä-lä'-mä.
Tittoni . . . . . . tēt-tō'-nē.
Titurel . . . . . . tĭt'-ū-rĕl.
Tityrus . . . . . . tĭt'-ĭ-rŭs.
Tiumen, see Tioomen,
  Tyumen . . . . . tē-ōō-mĕn'.
Tivoli (Italy) . . . . tē'-vō-lē.
Tivoli (New York) . . tĭv'-ō-lĭ, tĭv-ō'-lē.
Tiziano Vecelli, It. . . tēt-sē=ä'-nō vä-chĕl'-lē.
Tobago, see Tabago . . tō-bä'-gō, tō-bä'-gō.
Tobias . . . . . . tō-bī'-a̤s.
Tobit . . . . . . tō'-bĭt.
Tobolsk . . . . . tō-bŏlsk'.
Tocqueville, de . . . dŭ tŏk'-vĭl. *Fr.* dŭ
                      tŏk-vēl'.
Togoland . . . . . tō'-gō-lănd.
Toison d'Or, La . . . lä twä-zôn' dōr.
Tokaj, or Tokay . . . tō-kä'. *Hung.* tō'-koi.
Tokio, Tokyo . . . . tō'-kē=ō.
Tokugawa Shogunate . . tō-kōō'-gä'-wä'
                       shō'-gŭn-āt.
Tolbooth . . . . . tōl'-bōōth.
Toledo . . . . . . tō-lē'-dō. *Sp.* tō-lä'-dŏ.
Tolentino . . . . . tō-län-tē'-nō.
Tolstoy . . . . . . tŏl'-stoi.
Tomaszov . . . . . tō'-mä-shŏf.
Tommaseo . . . . tŏm-mä-sä'-ō.

Tomsk	tŏmsk.
Tonga (Is.)	tŏng'-gä.
Tongaland, see Tongoland	tŏng'-gä-lănd.
Tong Chow, see Tung-chau	tŏng-chow'.
Tongking, see Tungking, Tonquin	tŏng-kĭng'.
Tongoland, see Tongaland	tŏng'-gō-lănd.
Tonkin, see Tonquin . .	tŏn-kēn'.
Tonnay-Charente . . .	tŏn-nā'-shä-rônt'。
Tonquin, see Tonkin . .	tŏn-kēn'.
Tonquin, Fr., see Tongking	tôn-kăn'.
Tonstall, see Tunstall .	tŭn'-stàl.
Toorkistan, see Turkestan	tōōr-kĭs-tän'.
Topeka	tō-pē'-kà.
Topete (Admiral) . . .	tō-pā'-tā.
Töplitz, see Teplitz . .	têp'-lĭts.
Toral	tō-räl'.
Torcello	tŏr-chĕl'-lō.
Tordesilhas, Port., or . .	tōr-dä-sēl'-yäs.
Tordesillas, Sp.	tōr-dä-sēl'-yäs.
Torgau	tŏr'-gow.
Torii	tō'-rē'-ē'.
Torino, see Turin . . .	It. tō-rē'-nō.
Torquato Tasso	tōr-kwä'-tō täs'-sŏ.
Torquay	tôr-kē'.
Torquemada	tōr-kä-mä'-dä.
Torregiano, see Torrigiano	tŏr-rā-jä'-nō.
Torres Vedras	tŏr'-rĕs vä'-dräsh.
Torricelli	tŏr-rĭ-sēl'-lĭ.
	It. tŏr-rē-chĕl'-lē.
Torricellian	tŏr-ĭ-sĕl'-ĭ-àn,
	tŏr-rĭ-chĕl'-ĭ-àn.
Torrigiano, see Tórregiano	tŏr-rē-jä'-nō.
Torso Belvedere . . .	tôr'-sō bĕl-vĕ-dēr'.
Tortola	tôr-tō'-lä.

Tortuga . . . . . . tŏr-tōō′-gä.
Tortugas . . . . . . tôr-tōō′-gäz.
Tosca, La . . . . . . lä tŏs′-kä.
Toscanelli . . . . . . tŏs-kä-nĕl′-lē.
Tosti . . . . tōs′-tē.
Tostig . . . . tŏs′-tĭg.
Totila, or . . . . . . tŏt′-ĭ-lä.
Totilas . . . . tŏt′-ĭ-lás.
Toul . . . . tōōl.
Toulmin . . . . . . tōl′-mĭn.
Toulmouche . . . . . tōōl-mōōsh′.
Toulon . . . . tōō′-lŏn.   Fr. tōō-lôṅ′.
Toulouse . . . . . . tōō-lōōz′.
Touraine . . . . . . tōō-rĕn′.
Tourcoing . . . . . . tōōr-kwăṅ′.
Tour d'Auvergne . . . tōōr dō-vârn′=yŭ.
Tour de Nesle . . . tōōr dŭ nāl.
Tourgee . . . . . . tōōr-zhā′.
Tourgueneff, or Tourgué-
    nief, see Turgenieff . . tōōr′-gĕn-yĕf.
Tournai, or Tournay . . tōōr-nā′.
Tourneur . . . . . . tĕr′-nĕr, tōōr-nĕr′.
Tours . . . . tōōr.
Tourville . . . . . . tōōr-vēl′.
Toussaint Louverture, or
    L'Ouverture . . . . tōō-săṅ′ lōō-vĕr-tür′.
Toxophilus . . . . . tŏks-ŏf′-ĭ-lŭs.
Toyoharu . . . . . . tō′-yō′-hä′-rē′.
Trachonitis . . . . . trăk-ō-nī′-tĭs.
Trafalgar (Battle of) . . trăf-ăl-gär′, tră-făl′-gär.
Trafalgar (Square) . . . trăfăl′-gär.
Trani . . . . trä′-nē.
Transbaikalia . . . . trăns-bī-kä′-lĭ-à.
Transkei . . . . . . trăns-kē′.
Transvaal . . . . . . trăns-väl′.
Trapani . . . . . . trä′-pä-nē.
Trapezunt, see Trebizond   trăp-ĕ-zōōnt′.

Trasimenus (L.) . . . trăs-ĭ-mē'-nŭs.
Tras-os-Montes, see Traz-
  os-Montes . . . . . träs'-ōs-mŏn'-tĕs.
Trastevere . . . . . träs-tä'-vä-rĕ.
Trauttmansdorff . . . trowt'-mäns-dŏrf.
Travailleurs de la Mer . trä-vī-yēr' dŭ lä mâr.
Travancore . . . . . trăv-àn-kōr'.
Traviata, La . . . . . lä trä-vē-ä'-tä.
Traz-os-Montes, see Tras-
  os-Montes . . . . . träz'-ōs-mŏn'-tĕs.
Trebbia . . . . . . trĕb'-ē-ä.
Trebizond, see Trapezunt trĕb-ĭ-zŏnd'.
Tregelles . . . . . . trĕ-gĕl'-ĭs.
Treitschke . . . . . trīch'-kä.
Trek . . . . trĕk.
Trelawney . . . . . trē-lô'-nĭ.
Tremont . . . . . . trĕ-mŏnt', trē-mŏnt',
                  trĕm'-ŏnt.
Trench . . . . trĕnsh.
Trenck, von . . . . . fŏn trĕngk.
Trentino . . . . . . trĕn-tē'-nō.
Trevannion . . . . . trē-văn'-yŭn.
Trevelyan . . . . . . trĕ-vĕl'-yàn.
Trevena . . . . . . trĕ-vē'-nä.
Treves . . . . trēvz.
Trèves . . . . trĕv.
Trevi (Fountain of) . . trä'-vē.
Trèvisa . . . . trĕ-vē'-sä.
Treviso . . . . trä-vē'-zō.
Trianon, Grand . . . . gräṅ trē-ä-nôṅ'.
Trianon, Petit . . . . pē̆=tē' trē-ä-nôṅ'.
Trichinopoli . . . . . trĭch"-ĭn-ŏp'-ō-lĭ.
Tricoteuses, Les . . . lä trē-kō-tēz'.
Tricoupis, see Trikoupis . trē-kōō'-pĭs.
Trier, *Ger.* . . . . . trēr.
Triest, or . . . . . . trē-ĕst'.
Trieste . . . . trē-ĕst'. *It.* trē-ĕs'-tä.

Trifanum . . . . . . trī-fā′-nŭm.
Trikala, or Trikkala . . trē′-kä-lä.
Trikoupis, see Tricoupis . trē-kōō′-pĭs.
Trimalchio . . . . . trĭ-măl′-kĭ-ō.
Trinidad . . . . . . trĭn-ĭ-dăd′.
　　　　　　　　　　　Sp. trē-nē-däd′.
Trinkitat . . . . . . trĭng-kĭ-tät′.
Tripoli . . . . trĭp′-ō-lĭ.
Tripolitan . . . . . . trĭ-pŏl′-ĭ-tàn.
Triptolemus . . . . trĭp-tŏl′-ē-mŭs.
Trisagion . . . . . . trĭ-sā′-gĭ-ŏn.
Tristan und Isolde . . . trĭs-tän′ ōŏnt ē-zŏl′-dŭ.
Triton . . . . trī′-tŏn.
Triumvirate . . . . . trī-ŭm′-vĭ-rāt.
Trivulzio . . . . . . trē-vōŏl′-dzē-ō.
Trocadero . . . . . . trō-kä-dā′-rō.
Trocadéro . . . . . . Fr. trō-kä-dā-rō′.
Trochu . . . . trō-shü′.
Troilus . . . . trō′-ĭl-ŭs.
Troilus and Cressida . . trō′-ĭl-ŭs and krĕs′-ĭ-då.
Trois Échelles . . . . trwä zä-shĕl′.
Trois Mousquetaires . . trwä mōōs=kĕ-târ′.
Trollope . . . . . . trŏl′-ŭp.
Trondhjem, see Thrond-
　　hjem . . . . . . trŏnd′-yĕm.
Trophimus . . . . . trŏf′-ĭ-mŭs.
Troppau . . . . . . trŏp′-ow.
Trosachs, or Trossachs . trŏs′-ăks.
Trotzky . . . . . . trŏts′-kē.
Troubadours . . . . . trōō-bä-dōōrz′.
Troubetzkoy . . . . . trōō-bĕts′-kō-ē.
Trouvères . . . . . . trōō-vârs′.
Trouville . . . . . . trōō-vēl′.
Trovatore, Il . . . . . ēl trō-vä-tō′-rĕ.
Troyes . . . . trwä.
Troyes, Chrestien de . . krä-tē=ĕṅ′ dŭ trwä.
Troyon . . . . trwä-yôṅ′.

Trübner . . . . . .   trüb'-nĕr.
Trueba, Antonio de . .   än-tō'-nē-ō dä trōō-ä'-bä.
Trujillo, or Truxillo . .   trōō-ċhēl'-yō.
Tsad (L.), see Chad,
   Tchad, Tschad . . .   tsäd.
Tsarevna, see Czarevna .   tsär-ĕv'-nä.
Tsarina, see Czarina . .   tsär-ē'-nä.
Tsaritsin . . . . . .   tsär-ēt'-sēn.
Tsaritza . . . . . .   tsär-ĭt'-zä.
Tsarovitch, see Czarevitch   tsär'-ō-vĭch.
Tsarowitz, see Czarowitz .   tsär'-ō-vĭts.
Tsarskoi Selo . . .   tsär-skō'-ĭ sä'-lō.
Tschad, see Chad, Tchad,
   Tsad . . . . . .   chäd.
Tschaikovsky . . .   tshī-kŏf'-skĭ.
Tsech, see Czech . . .   chĕk.
Tseng . . . . . .   tsĕng.
Tsigane . . . . .   tsē-gȧn'.
Tsimshian, or Tsimsian .   tsĭm-shē-än'.
Tsi-nan . . . . . .   tsē-nän'.
Tsing . . . . . .   tsēng.
Tsingtau (or -tao) Tsinan-
   fu . . . .   tsĭng'-tow' tsē'-näm'-fōō'.
Tsugaru Strait . . . .   tsōō-gä'-rōō strāt.
Tsunenobu . . . .   tsōō'-nä'-nō'-bē'.
Tsushima (Is.) . . . .   tsōō'-shē'-mä'.
Tübingen . . . . .   tü'-bĭng-ĕn.
Tucson . . . . . .   tōō-sŏn'.
Tuesday . . . . . .   tūz'-dä.
Tugela (R.) . . . . .   tōō-gä'-lä.
Tugendbund . . . .   tōō'-gĕnt-bōŏnt.
Tuh Chau . . . . .   tōō' chow'.
Tuileries . . . . .   twē'-lĕ-rĭz.   *Fr.* twēl-rē'.
Tula . . . .   tōō'-lä.
Tulle . . . . . .   tül.
Tullia . . . . . .   tŭl'-ĭ-ȧ.
Tully-Veolan . . . .   tŭl'-ĭ-vē-ō'-lăn.

Tuncha . . . . tŭn-chä′.
Tung-chau, see Tong Chow tōōng-chow′.
Tungking, see Tongking . tōōng-kĭng′.
Tunis . . . . tū′-nĭs.
Tunisie, *Fr.* . . . . . tü-nē-zē′.
Tunstall, see Tonstall . . tŭn′-stȧl.
Turcaret . . . . . . tŭr-kä-rä′.
Turcoman, see Turkoman těr′-kō-mȧn, tōōr-kō-män′.
Turenne, de . . . . . dŭ tū-rěn′. *Fr.* dŭ tü-rěn′.
Turgai, or . . . . . . tōōr-gī′.
Turgansk . . . . . . tōōr-gänsk′.
Turgenieff (or -iev), see
 Tourgueneff . . . . tōōr′-gĕn-yĕf.
Turgot . . . . tür-gō′.
Turiddu . . . . . . tōō′-rēd-dōō.
Turin, It. Torino . . . tū′-rĭn, tū-rĭn′.
Turkestan, or . . . . tōōr-kĕs-tän′.
Turkistan, see Toorkistan tōōr-kĭs-tän′.
Turkoman, see Turcoman těr′-kō-mȧn, tōōr-kō-män′.
Turquino . . . . . . tōōr-kē′-nō.
Tuskeegee . . . . . tŭs-kē′-gē.
Tussaud's . . . . . . tü-sōz′.
Tutuila . . . . tōō-tōō-e′-lä.
Tver . . . . tvâr.
Twickenham . . . . twĭk′-ĕn-ȧm.
Tybalt . . . . tĭb′-ȧlt.
Tyburn . . . . tĭ′-bērn.
Tychicus . . . . . . tĭk′-ĭ-kŭs.
Tycoon . . . . tī-kōōn′.
Tydeus . . . . tī′-dūs.
Tyndale, see Tindale . . tĭn′-dȧl.
Tynemouth . . . . . tīn′-mŭth, tĭn′-mŭth.
Typhon . . . . tī′-fŏn, tī′-fŏn.
Tyrol . . . . tĭr′-ŏl, tĭ-rōl′. *Ger.* tē-rōl′.
Tyrolean . . . . . . tĭr-ō′-lē-ȧn.
Tyrolese . . . . . . tĭr-ō-lēz′, tĭr-ō-lēs′.
Tyrone . . . . tĭ-rōn′.

Tyrrhene . . . . . . tĭr'-ēn.
Tyrrhenian . . . . . tĭ-rē'-nĭ-àn.
Tyrtaean . . . . . . tĭr-tē'-àn.
Tyrtaeus . . . . . . tĭr-tē'-ŭs.
Tyrwhitt . . . . . . tĕr'-ĭt.
Tyumen, see Tioomen,
  Tiumen . . . . . . tē=ōō-mĕn'.
Tzigane, La . . . . . lä tsē-găn'.
Tzigany . . . . . . tsĭg'-à-nĭ.

U

Uarda . . . . ōō-är'-dä.
Ubangi . . . . ōō-bäng'-gē.
Ubiquitarian . . . . ū-bĭk"-wĭ-tā'-rĭ-àn.
Uccello . . . . ōō-chĕl'-lō.
Uchatius . . . . . . ōō-ċhä'-tĭ-ōŏs.
Uclés . . . . ōō-klās'.
Udaipur, see Oodeypoor . ōō-dī-pōōr'.
Udall (Nicholas) . . . yōō'-dàl.
Udine . . . . ōō'-dē-nĕ.
Ufa . . . . ōō'-fä.
Uffizzi . . . . ōō-fēt'-sē.
Uganda . . . . . . ōō-gän'-dä.
Uggione, see Oggione . . ōōj-jō'-nĕ. [gä-rär-dĕs'-kä.
Ugolino della Gherardesca ōō-gō-lē'-nō dĕl'-lä
Uhland . . . . ōō'-länt.
Uhlans, see Ulans . . . ōō'-länz.
Uhrich . . . . Fr. ü-rēk'. Ger. ōō'-rĭċh.
Uitenhage . . . . . . oi-tĕn-hä'-ċhĕ.
Uitlander . . . . . . oit'-lăn-dĕr.
Ujiji . . . . ōō-jē'-jē.
Ukerewe . . . . . . ōō-kĕ-rē'-wĕ.
Ukiyo-ye . . . . . . ōō'-kē'-yo'-yä'.
Ukraine . . . . . . yū'-krān, ōō-krān',
                 ū'-krä-ĭn.
Ulalume . . . . . . ōō-lä-lōō'-mĭ.

Ulans, see Uhlans . . . ōō'-länz.
Ulfilas, see Ulphilas . . ŭl'-fĭ'-las.
Ulleswater . . . . . ŭlz'-wô-tēr.
Ulloa . . . . ŏŏl-yō'-ä.
Ulm . . . . ŏŏlm.
Ulphilas, see Ulfilas . . ŭl'-fĭ-las.
Ulpian . . . . ŭl'-pĭ-an.
Ulpianus . . . . . . ŭl-pĭ-ā'-nŭs.
Ulrica . . . . ŭl'-rĭ-ka. *It.* ŏŏl-rē'-kä.
Ulrich . . . . ŏŏl'-rĭch.
Ulrici . . . . ŏŏl-rēt'-sē.
Ulrike Eleonore . . . ŏŏl-rē'-kŭ ĕl"-ĕ-ō-nō'-rŭ.
Ultima Thule . . . . ŭl'-tĭm-à thū'-lē.
Ulundi . . . . ōō-lōōn'-dē.
Ulungu, see Urungu . . ōō-lōōng'-gōō.
Ulwar, see Alwar . . . ūl'-wär.
Ulysses . . . . yū-lĕs'-ēz.
Umar Khaiyâm, see Omar
  Khayyam . . . . . ōō'-mär kī-yäm'.
Umberto, Principe . . . prēn'-chē-pä ōōm-bĕr'-tō.
Umkomanzi . . . . . ŭm-kō-män'-sē.
Umritsir, see Amritsar . ŭm-rĭt'-sēr.
Unalaska, see Oonalaska ōō'-nà-lăs'-kà,
                   yū-nà-lăs'-kà.
Unao . . . . ōō'-nà-ō.
Un Ballo in Maschera . . ōōn bäl'-lō ēn mäs'-kä-rä.
Uncas . . . . ŭng'-kas.
Undine . . . . ŭn-dēn'. *Ger.* ŏŏn-dē'-nŭ.
Unitarian . . . . . . yū-nĭ-tā'-rĭ-àn.
Unser Fritz . . . . . ŏŏn'-zēr frĭts.
Unter den Linden . . . ŏŏn'-tĕr dän lĭn'-dĕn.
Unterwalden . . . . ŏŏn'-tĕr-väl"-dĕn
Unyoro, see Nyoro . . . ōō-nyō'-rō.
Upanishads . . . . . ōō-pă-nĭ-shădz'.
Upernavik, Upernivik . . ōō-pēr'-nà-vĭk.
Upolu (I.) . . . . . . ōō-pō-lōō'.
Upsal . . . . ŭp'-săl.

Upsala . . . . ŭp-sä′-lä.
Ur . . . . ēr.
Ural . . . . ōō′-rȧl, yū′-rȧl.
Urania . . . . yū-rā′-nĭ-ȧ.
Uranus . . . . yū′-rȧ-nŭs.
Urban . . . . ŭr′-bȧn.
Urbano, Pietro . . . . pē-ä′-trō ōōr-bä′-nŏ.
Urbanus . . . . . . ŭr-bā′-nŭs.
Urbino . . . . ōōr-bē′-nō.
Urfé, Honoré d' . . . . ō-nō-rā′ dür-fä′.
Uri . . . . ōō′-rĭ.
Uriah . . . . ū-rī′-ä′.
Uriel . . . . yū′-rĭ-ĕl.
Urquhart . . . . . . ēr′-kärt.
Urraca . . . . ŏŏr-rä′-kä.
Ursa Minor . . . . . ēr′-sȧ mī′-nŭr.
Ursula . . . . ŭr′-sū-lä.
Ursule Mirouët . . . . ür-sül′ mē-rōō-ā′.
Ursulines . . . . . . ŭr′-sū-lĭnz, ŭr′-sū-līnz.
Uruguay . . . . . . yū′-rōō-gwä.
                    Sp.ōō-rōō-gwī′.
Urundi . . . . ōō-rōōn′-dē.
Urungu, see Ulungu . . ōō-rōōng′-gōō.
Ushant . . . . ŭsh′-ȧnt.
Uskiub, see Uskub . . ōōs′-kē-ŭb.
Uskub, see Uskiub . . . ōōs′-kūb.
Usuramo . . . . . . ōō-sōō-rä′-mō.
Utah . . . . yū′-tä, yū′-tô.
Utamaro . . . . . . ōō′-tä′-mä′-rō′.
Ute . . . . yūt.
Utopian . . . . . . yū-tō′-pĭ-ȧn.
Utraquist . . . . . . yŭ′-trȧ-kwist.
Utrecht . . . . yū′-trĕkt. D. ü′-trĕċht.
Uvaroff . . . . ōō-vä′-rŏf.
Uzés . . . . ü-zäs′.
Uzziah . . . . ŭz-zī′-ä.
Uzziel . . . . ŭz-zī′-ĕl, ŭz′-zĭ-ĕl.

V

Vaal (R.) . . . . . . väl.
Vaca, Cabeza, or Cabeça de kä-bā'-thä dā vä'-kä.
Vaccai, or Vaccaj . . . väk-kä'=ē.
Vacuna . . . . vä-kū'-nä.
Vaga . . . . vä'-gä.
Vailima . . . . . . vī-lē'-mȧ.
Vaillant . . . . . . vä-yäṅ'.
Valais . . . . vä-lā'.
Val d'Arno . . . . . väl där'-nō.
Valdenses, see Waldenses väl-děn'-sēz.
Valdensian, see Walden-
sian . . . . väl-děn'-sĭ-ȧn.
Valdés . . . . *Sp.* bäl-děs'.
Valdéz . . . . *Mex.* väl-děs.
   Sp. bäl-děth'.
Valdivia . . . . . . väl-dē'-vē-ä.
Valée . . . . vȧ-lā'.
Valence . . . . . . *Fr.* vȧ-lŏṅs'.
Valencia . . . . . vȧ-lěn'-shĭ=ȧ.
   Sp. vä-lěn'-thē-ä.
Valenciennes . . . . . vȧ"-lŏn-sĭ-ěnz', *or*
   vä"-lěn-sĭ-ěnz'.
   Fr. vȧ-lŏṅ-sē=ěn'.
Valens . . . . vā'-lěnz.
Valentine . . . . . . văl'-ěn-tīn.
Valentinian . . . . . văl-ěn-tĭn'-ĭ-ȧn.
Valentinois . . . . . văl-ŏṅ-tē-nwä'.
Valera . . . . *Sp.* bä-lā'-rä.
Valère . . . . vȧ-lâr'.
Valeria . . . . vȧ-lē'-rĭ-ȧ.
Val-es-Dunes . . . . väl-ā-dün'.
Valhalla . . . . . väl-hăl'-ȧ.
Valjean, Jean . . . . zhäṅ văl-zhäṅ'.
Valjevo . . . . . . väl'-yä-vō.
Valkyrie . . . . . . väl-kē'-rē.

Valladolid . . . . . . văl-là-dō-lĭd'.
     Sp. bäl-yä-dō-lēt̄h'.
Vallandigham . . . . văl-lăn'-dĭ-gàm.
Vallière, La . . . . . lä văl-ē=âr'.
Vallombrosa . . . . . väl-lŏm-brō'-zä.
Valmy . . . . văl-mē'.
Valois . . . . văl-wä'.
Valona, see Avlona . . vä-lō'-nä.
Valparaiso . . . . . . văl-pà-rī'-zō, väl-pä-rī'-zō.
     Sp. bäl-pä-rä'=ē-sō.
Valtellina, or . . . . . väl-tĕl-lē'-nä.
Val Tellina, or . . . . väl tĕl-lē'-nä.
Valtelline . . . . . . väl-tĕl-lēn'.
Vámbéry . . . . . . väṅ'-bä-rē'.
Van . . . . vän.
Van Artevelde . . . . văn är'-tĕ-vĕl-dĕ.
Vanbrugh . . . . . . văn-brōō'.
Vandalic . . . . . . văn-dăl'-ĭk.
Vandamme . . . . . väṅ-däm'.
Van der Meulen . . . văn dĕr mē'-lĕn.
Vandyck, Vandyke . . . văn-dīk'.
Van Eyck . . . . . . văn īk'.
Van Gogh . . . . . . fän gŏgh. *Fr.* văn gŏf.
Van Hoeck . . . . . văn hōōk'.
Vanhomerigh, or . . . văn-ŭm'-ēr-ĭ.
Vanhomrigh . . . . . văn-ŭm'-rĭ.
Valjevo . . . . . . väl'-yä-vō.
Vanloo . . . . *Fr.* väṅ-lō'.
Vannucchi . . . . . . vän-nōōk'-kē.
Vannucci (Pietro) . . . vän-nōōch'-ē.
Van Ostade . . . . . văn ŏs'-tä-dĕ.
Vanozza . . . . . . vä-nŏt'-sä.
Van Schaick . . . . . văn skoik'.
Varanger Fjord, see Wa-
  ranger Fjord . . . . vä-räng'-gĕr fē=ôrd'.
Varangians . . . . . vä-răn'-jĭ-ànz.
Vardar . . . . vär-där'.

Varennes	vä-rĕn'.
Varicourt	vä-rē-kōōr'.
Vari, or Varj dei Porcari .	vä'-rē dä'-ē pōr-kä'-rē.
Varna	vär'-nä.
Varnhagen von Ense . .	värn'-hä-gĕn fŏn ĕn'-sŭ.
Varus	vä''-rŭs.
Varzin	vär'-tsĭn.
Vasa	vä'-sä.
Vasari	vä-sä'-rē.
Vasco da Gama	väs'-kō dä gä'-mä.
Vashti	văsh'-tī.
Vasili	vä-sē'-lē.
Vasnietsof (-ov) . . .	väs-n-yĕts'-ŏf.
Vasquez de Coronado, see	
Vazquez	Sp. bäs-kĕth' dä
	kō-rō-nä'-dō.
Vassilenko	väs-ĭ-lĕn'-kō.
Vassy	vä-sē'.
Vathek	văth'-ĕk.
Vatican	văt'-ĭ-kăn.
Vauban, de	dŭ vō-bäṅ'.
Vaucelles	vō-sĕl.
Vaucluse	vō-klüz'.
Vaucouleurs	vō-kōō-lēr'.
Vaud, Pays de	pä=ē' dŭ vō'.
Vaudois	vō-dwä'.
Vaudreuil	vō-drē'-yŭ.
Vaughan	vôn, vô'-àn.
Vauvenargues	vōv-närg'.
Vaux	vôks. Fr. vō.
Vazquez de Coronado, see	
Vasquez de Coronado .	Sp. bäth-kĕth' dä
	kō-rō-nä'-dō.
Ve-Adar	vē'-ä-där.
Vecchio	vĕk'ē-ō.
Vecellio	vä-chĕl'-ē-ō.
Veda	vä'-dȧ, vē'-dȧ.

Vedic	vā′-dĭk, vē′-dĭk.
Vega	vē′-gà. *Sp.* vā′-gä.
Vega Real	vā′-gä rā-äl′.
Vehmgerichte	fäm′-gä-rĭċh″-tŭ.
Veile	vī′-lĕ.
Veit	fīt.
Veitch (John)	vēch.
Velalcazar, see Benalcazar	bā-läl-kä′-thär.
Velasco	*Sp.* bā-läs′-kō.
Velasquez, or	*Sp.* bā-läs′-kĕth.
Velazquez	*Sp.* bā-läth′-kĕth.
Velletri	vĕl-lā′-trē.
Vendeans	vĕn-dē′-ànz.
Vendée, La	lä vŏṅ-dā′.
Vendémiaire	vŏṅ-dä-mē═âr′.
Vendidad	bĕn-dē-däd′, vĕn-dē-däd′.
Vendôme, de	dŭ vôṅ-dōm′.
Venern (L.), see Wenern	vā′-nĕrn.
Venetia	vĕ-nē′-shĭ═à.
Venezia	vä-nād′-zē-ä.
Veneziano	vä-nād″-zē-ä′-nō.
Venezuela	vĕn-ĕz-wē′-lä.
	Sp. vĕn-ĕth-wā′-lä.
Venice	vĕn′-ĭs.
Venlo, or Venloo . . .	vĕn-lō′.
Ventersburg	fĕn-tĕrs-bŭrċh.
Venters' Spruit	fĕn′-tĕrs sproit.
Ventose	vôṅ-tŏz′.
Venus Anadyomene . .	vē′-nŭs ăn″-à-dĭ-ŏm′-ĕ-nē.
Venus Callipyge	vē′-nŭs kă-lĭp′-ĭ-jē.
Vera Cruz	vā′-rä krōōz, *commonly*
	vĕr′-à-krōōz.
	Sp. vā′-rä krōōth′.
Veragua, or	vā-rä′-gwä.
Veraguas	vä-rä′-gwäs.
Verazzano, see Verrazano	vä-rät-sä′-nō.
Verboeckhoven	fĕr-bōōk′-hō-fĕn.

Vercelli	vĕr-chĕl′-lē.
Vercingetorix	vĕr-sĭn-jĕt′-ō-rĭks.
Verd (Cape), or Verde .	vērd.
Verdi	vâr′-dē.
Verdun	vĕr-dŭṅ′.
Vereshagin, or	vĕ-rē-shä′-gĕn.
Verestchagin, Vassili . .	*Russ.* vä-sē′-lē
	vä″-rä-shä-gĕn′.
Vergennes	vĕr-jĕnz′. *Fr.* vĕr-zhĕn′.
Vergil, see Virgil . . .	vẽr′-jĭl.
Vergniaud	vĕrn-yē=ō′.
Verhaeren, Émile . . .	ä-mēl′ vĕr-hä′-rĕn.
Verlaine	vĕr-lĕn′.
Vermandois	vĕr-mŏṅ-dwä′.
Vermelles	vĕr-mĕl′.
Verne, Jules	zhül vĕrn.
Vernet	vĕr-nä′.
Verneuil	vĕr-nē′-yŭ.
Vernéville	vĕr-nä-vēl′.
Verocchio, see Verrocchio	vä-rŏk′-kē=ō.
Verona	vä-rō′-nä.
Veronese (Paul) . . .	vä-rō-nä′-zĕ.
Veronese (adj.)	vĕr-ō-nēz′, vĕr-ō-nēs′.
Veronica	vĕr-ō-nī′-ká, vĕ-rŏn′-ĭ-ká.
Verrazani, see Verazzano	vĕr-räd-zä′-nē.
Verrazano, or	vĕr-räd-zä′-nō.
Verrazzano	vĕr-rät-sä′-nō.
Verrocchio, see Verocchio	vä-rŏk′-kē=ō.
Versailles	vĕr-sälz′. *Fr.* vĕr-sä′=yŭ.
Vertumnus	vĕr-tŭm′-nŭs.
Verulam (Lord)	vĕr′-ōō-lăm.
Verus	vē′-rŭs.
Verviers	vĕr-vē=ā′.
Vervins	vĕr-văṅ′.
Vesalius	vĕ-sä′-lĭ-ŭs.
Vesle	väl.
Vespasian	vĕs-pā′-zhĭ=án.

Vespucci, Amerigo . . .	ä-mä-rē'-gō věs-pŏŏt'-chē.
Vespucius, Americus, Lat.	à-mě'-rĭ-kŭs
	věs-pū'-shĭ=ŭs.
Veszprém, or	věs'-prām.
Veszprim	věs'-prĭm.
Vet (R.)	fĕt.
Vevay, or Vevey . . .	věv-ā'.
Via Æmilia	vī'-ä ē-mĭl'-ĭ-ä.
Via Appia	vī'-ä ap'-pĭ-ä.
	It. vē'-ä äp'-pē-ä.
Via Aurelia	vī'-ä ô-rē'-lĭ-ä.
Via Dolorosa	vī'-ä dŏl-ō-rō'-sä.
Via Mala	vē'-ä-mä'-lä.
Viardot-Garcia . . .	vē=är-dō'-gär-thē'-ä.
Viareggio	vē-ä-rĕd'-jō.
Via Salaria	vī'-ä sä-lä'-rĭ-ä.
Viatka, see Vyatka . .	vē-ät'-kä.
Viaud	vē=ō'.
Via Valeria	vī'-ä ṿä-lē'-rĭ-ä.
Vibert	vē-bâr'.
Viborg, see Wiborg . .	vē'-bŏrg.
Vicenza	vě-sĕn'-zä. It. vē-chĕn'-zä.
Vichy	commonly, vĭsh'-ĭ.
	Fr. vē-shē'.
Victor Amadeus	vĭk'-tôr ăm-à-dē'-ŭs.
Victor-Perrin	vēk-tōr'-pĕ-răṅ'.
Vidal (Pierre) . . .	vē-dăl'.
Vidocq	vē-dŏk'.
Vielé-Griffin	vē-lā'-grē-făṅ'.
Vienna	vĭ-ĕn'-à.
Vieques	vē-ä'-käs.
Viersen	fēr'-sĕn.
Vierzehnheiligen . . .	fēr"-tsän-hī'-lĭg-ĕn.
Vieux Colombier, Le . .	lē vē-ē' kŏl-ŏm-bē=ā'.
Vieuxtemps	vē=ē-tŏṅ'.
Vigan	vē-gän'.
Vigée-Lebrun	vē-zhā'-lē-brŭṅ'.

Vigero (Marquis), di . . dē vē-jä'-rō.
Vigneuilles . . . . . vē-nē'=yŭ.
Vignola . . . . vēn-yō'-lä.
Vignon, Claude . . . . klōd vēn-yôṅ'.
Vigny, de . . . . . . dŭ vēn-yē'.
Vigo . . . . vē'-gō.
Viljoen . . . . fĭl-yōōn'.
Villa Albani . . . . . vēl'-lä äl-bä'-nē.
Villa Aldobrandini . . . vēl'-lä äl"-dō-brän-dē'-nē.
Villa Borghese . . . . vēl'-lä bōr-gä'-zĕ
Villafranca, It., see Ville-
franche . . . . . . vēl-lä-fräng'-kä.
Villa Ludovisi . . . . vēl'-lä lōō-dō-vē'-zē.
Villa Medici . . . . . vēl'-lä mä'-dē-chē.
Villamil (Admiral) . . . vēl-yä-mēl'.
Villa Nazionale . . . . vēl'-lä nät"-zē-ō-nä'-lĕ.
Villani . . . . vēl-lä'-nē.
Villard . . . . vē-yär'.
Villa Real . . . . . . vēl'-lä rä-äl'.
Villari . . . . vēl'-lä-rē.
Villars . . . . vē-lär'.
Villebois- Mareuil . . . vēl-bwä'-mä-rē'=yŭ.
Villefranche, see Villa-
franca, It. . . . . . vēl-fräṅsh'.
Villehardouin . . . . vēl-är-dōō-ăṅ'.
Villemain . . . . . . vēl-măṅ'.
Villeroi . . . . vēl-rwä'.
Villers-Bretonneaux . . vē-yä' brä-tŏn-ō'.
Villers-Cotterets . . . vē-yä'-kŏt-rä'.
Villiers . . . . vĭl'-yērz.
Villiers de l'Isle Adam . vē-yä' dŭ lēl ä-däṅ'.
Villon . . . . vēl-yôṅ'.
Vilna, see Wilna . . . vĭl'-nä.
Vimeure . . . . . . vē-mēr'.
Viminal . . . . . . vīm'-ĭn-àl.
Vimy . . . . vē-mē'.
Vincennes . . . . . . vĭn-sĕnz'. Fr.văṅ-sĕn'.

Vincent de Paul	vĭn'-sĕnt dŭ pôl'.
	Fr. văṅ-sŏṅ' dŭ pŏl'.
Vincentio	vĭn-sĕn'-shĭ=ō.
Vinci, da	dä vĭn'-chē, dä vĭn'-chĭ,
	It. vēn'-chē
Vingt Ans Après . . .	văṅ täṅ zä-prä'.
Viola	vī'-ō-lä. *It.* vē-ō'-lä.
Viollet-le-Duc	vē-ō-lä' lĕ dük'.
Vionville	vē=ôṅ-vēl'.
Viotti	vē-ŏt'-tē.
Vira	vē'-rä.
Virchow	vēr'-chow. *Ger.* fēr'-ċhō.
Virgil, see Vergil . . .	vēr'-jĭl.
Virginia	vēr-jĭn'-ĭ=à.
Virginian	vēr-jĭn'-ĭ=àn.
Virginie	vēr-zhē-nē'.
Virgo	vēr'-go.
Visayan	vē-sä'-yän.
Viscaya, see Vizcaya . .	*Sp.* bēs-kä'-yä.
Vischer, Peter	pä'-tĕr fĭsh'-ĕr.
Visconti	vĭs-kŏn'-tē.
Visigoths	vĭz'-ĭ-gŏths.
Vistula	vĭs'-tū-lä, vĭst'-yū-lä.
Vita Nuova	vē'-tä nōō-ō'-vä.
Vitebsk	vē-tĕbsk'.
Vitellius	vĭ-tĕl'-ĭ-ŭs.
Viterbo	vē-tĕr'-bō.
Viti Levu	vē'-tē lĕv'-ōō.
Vitoria, or Vittoria . .	vē-tō'-rē-à.
Vitry	vē-trē'.
Vittoria Colonna	vē-tō'-rē-ä kō-lŏn'-nä.
Vittorio Emanuele . . .	vēt-tō'-rē-ō
	ā-män"-ōō-ā'-lä.
Viviani	vē-vē-ä-nē'.
Vizagapatam	vē-zä"gà-pà-täm'.
Vizcaya, see Viscaya . .	*Sp.* bĭth-kä'-yä.
Vizier	vĭz'-yĕr, vĭz-ēr', vĭz'-yēr.

Vladikavkaz . . . . . vlä″-dē-käv-käz′.
Vladimir, see Wladimir . vlăd′-ē-mēr. *Russ. and Polish,* vlä-dē′-mĭr.
Vladislav, see Wladislaw . vlä′-dĭs-läv.
Vladivostok . . . . . vlä″-dē-vŏs-tŏk′.
Vogelweide . . . . . fō′-gĕl-vī″-dŭ.
Vogesen, see Vosges . . vō-gä′-zĕn.
Vogler, Abbé, or Abt . . ăb-ä′ (äpt) fō′-glĕr.
Vogt . . . . fŏċht.
Vogüé . . . . . . vō-gü-ä′.
Voiture . . . . vwä-tür′.
Volapük . . . . . . vō-lä-pük′.
Volga . . . . vŏl′-gä.
Volhynia . . . . . vō-lēn′-yȧ.
Volsci . . . . . . vŏl′-sī.
Volksraad . . . . . fŏlks′-rät.
Vologda . . . . . vō-lŏg-dä′.
Von Essen . . . . . fŏn ĕs′-ĕn.
Volscian . . . . . vŏl′-shĭ=ȧn.
Volsung . . . . . vŏl′-sŭng.
Volta . . . . . . vŏl′-tä.
Voltaire . . . . . vŏl-târ′.
Voltas (Cape) . . . vŏl′-täs.
Volterra, da . . . . dä vŏl-tĕr′-rä.
Voltigeurs . . . . . vŏl-tē-zhĕr′.
Vondel . . . . . . vŏn′-dĕl.
Von Kluck . . . . fŏn kloͦk.
Von Spee . . . . . fŏn spä.
Voortrekkers . . . . fōr′-trĕk-ĕrs.
Vorarlberg . . . . fōr′-ärl-bĕrċh.
Voronetz, or . . . . vō-rō′-nĕts.
Voronezh . . . . . vō-rō′-nĕzh.
Vosges, see Vogesen . . vōzh.
Voynich . . . . . voi′-nĭch.
Vrede . . . . . . frä′-dĕ.
Vryburg . . . . . vrī′-būrg. *D.* frī′-bŭrċh.
Vrigny . . . . . . vrēn′-yē′.

Vroubel . . . . . . vrōō-bĕl.
Vryheid . . . . . . *D*. frī'-hīt.
Vuelta Abajo . . . . . *Sp*. bōō=ĕl'-tä ä-bä'-ćhō.
Vuelta Arriva . . . . *Sp*. bōō=ĕl'-tä är-rē'-bä.
Vuillard . . . . . . vwē-yär'.
Vulgate . . . . vŭl'-gāt.
Vyatka, see Viatka . . . vē-ät'-kä.

W

Wacace . . . . . . wä-shä'-shä.
Wace . . . . wäs.
Wacht am Rhein, Die . . dē väćht äm rīn.
Wadai . . . . wä-dī'.
Waddington . . . . . wŏd'-ĭng-tŭn.
            Fr. vä-dăṅ-tôṅ'.
Wadelai . . . . . . wä-dĕ-lī'.
Wady-Halfa . . . . . wä'-dē-häl'-fä.
Wagner . . . . . . wăg'-nēr. *Ger*. väg'-nĕr.
Wagnerian . . . . . wăg-nē'-rĭ-àn.
Wagram . . . . . . vä'-gräm.
Wahabee . . . . . . wä-hä'-bē.
Wahabis, see Wahhabees   wä-hä'-bēz.
Wahaby . . . . . . wä-hä'-bē.
Wahhabees, see Wahabis   wä-hä'-bēz.
Wahlstatt (Battle of) . . väl'-stät.
Wahnfried . . . . . vän'-frēt.
Wahrheit, Dichtung und . dĭćh'-tōōng ŏŏnt vär'-hīt.
Wahsatch . . . . . . wô-săch'.
Wailuku . . . . . . wī-lōō'-kōō.
Wakkerstroom . . . . văk'-ĕrs-strōm.
Walachia, see Wallachia . wŏ-lä'-kĭ-à.
Walcheren . . . . . väl'-ćhĕr-ĕn.
Waldeck . . . . . . wŏl'-dĕk. *Ger*. väl'-dĕk.
Waldemar . . . . . . wŏl'-dĕ-mär.
            Ger. väl'-dĕ-mär.
Walden . . . . . . wôl'-dĕn.

Waldenses, see Valdenses   wäl-dĕn'-sēz.
Waldensian, see Valdensian   wäl-dĕn'-sĭ=àn.
Waldersee . . . . . väl'-dĕr-zā.
Waldshut . . . . . . välts'-hōot.
Waldstätter, Die Vier . . dē fēr vält'-stĕt-ĕr.
Waldstein . . . . . . vält'-stīn.
Waldteufel . . . . . vält'-toi-fĕl.
Walewski . . . . . . vä-lĕv'-skē.
Walhalla . . . . . . väl-häl'-lä.
Walküre, Die . . . . dē väl'-kü-rŭ.
Walkyrie . . . . . . wäl-kĭr'-ĭ.
Wallachia, see Walachia . wŏl-lä'-kĭ-à.
Wallenstein . . . . . wŏl'-ĕn-stīn.
               Ger. väl'-lĕn-stīn.
Waller . . . . wŏl'-ēr.
Wallis, *Ger.* for Valais . väl'-lĭs.
Walloon . . . . . . wäl-ōōn'.
Walpole . . . . . . wôl'-pōl.
Walpurgis . . . . . . väl-pōōr'-gēs.
Walsingham . . . . . wôl'-sĭng-àm.
Waltham (U. S.) . . . wäl'-thàm.
Waltham (Eng.) . . . . wôlt'-hàm, wŏlt'-hàm.
Walther von der Vogel-
   weide . . . . . . väl'-tĕr fŏn dĕr
               fō'-gĕl-vī"-dŭ.
Wamba . . . . . . wäm'-bä.
Wan-chow-fu . . . . wän'-chow'-fōō'.
Waranger Fjord, see Var-
   anger Fjord . . . . vä-räng'-gĕr fē=ôrd'.
Warbeck . . . . . . wôr'-bĕk.
Wartburg . . . . . . värt'-bōōrċh.
Warwick . . . . . . wŏr'-ĭk.
Warwickshire . . . . wŏr'-ĭk-shĭr.
Wasulu . . . . . . wä-sōō'-lōō.
Waterloo . . . . . . wô-tĕr-lōō'.   *D.* vä-tĕr-lō'.
Watervliet . . . . . . wô-tĕr-vlēt'.   [vä-tō'.
Watteau . . . . . . *commonly,* wŏt'-tō.   *Fr.*

Wauchope (Gen.) . . .	wô'-chōp.
Waugh (Edwin)	wô.
Waukegan	wô-kē'-gȧn.
Waukesha	wô'-kĕ-shô.
Wavre	vävr'.
Wawre	vä'-vrĕ.
Weald (The)	wēld.
Wealden	wēld'-n.
Weber, von	fŏn vä'-bĕr.
Weeninx	wä'-nĭnks.
Wei-hai-wei	wä'-hī-wä.
Wei-ho	wä'-ē-hō.
Weimar	vī'-mär.
Weissenburg	vīs'-sĕn-bōōrċh.
Weissnicht-wo	vīs'-nĭċht-vō.
Welsbach	wĕlz'-bȧk. Ger. vĕlz'-bäċh.
Wellesley	wĕlz'-lĭ.
Wemyss (Castle) . . .	wēms, wē'-mĭs.
Wenceslaus	wĕn'-sĕs-lôs, wĕn'-sĕs-lȧs.
Wen-chau	wĕn-chow'.
Wenern, see Venern . .	vä'-nĕrn.
Wenzel	vĕnt'-zĕl.
Wepener	vä'-pä-nĕr.
Werder, von	fŏn vĕr'-dĕr.
Werdt, see Werth . . .	vĕrt.
Werra	vĕr'-rä.
Werrenrath	vĕr'-ĕn-rät.
Werth, see Werdt . . .	vĕrt.
Werther	wẽr'-tĕr. Ger. vĕr'-tĕr.
Wesel	vä'-zĕl.
Weser	wē'-zĕr. Ger. vä'-zĕr.
Wesleyan	wĕs'-lĭ-ȧn.
Westmoreland	wĕst'-mŏr-lȧnd.
Westphalia	wĕst-fä'-lĭ-ȧ.
Weyden, van der . . .	vȧn dĕr vī'-dĕn.
Weyler	wä'-lĕr.
Weyman	wī'-mȧn.

Weymouth	wā'-mŭth.
Whewell	hū'-ĕl.
Whitefield, or Whitfield .	hwĭt'-fēld.
Whydah, see Widah . .	hwĭd'-ä.
Wiborg, see Viborg . . .	vē'-bôrg.
Wickliffe, see Wyclif . .	wĭk'-lĭf.
Widah, see Whydah . .	wĭd'-ä.
Widdin, or Widin . . .	vĭd'-ĭn.
Widor	vē'-dōr.
Widukind, see Wittekind	wĭd'-ōō-kĭnd.
Wied	vēt.
Wieland	wē'-lănd. *Ger.* vē'-länt.
Wien	vēn.
Wieniawski	vē-nē-ŏf'-skē,
	vē=yā-nē-äv'-skĭ.
Wiertz	vērts.
Wiesbaden	vēs'-bä-dĕn.
Wigan	wĭg'-àn.
Wildenbruch	vĭl'-dĕn-brōōċh.
Wilhelm	vĭl'-hĕlm.
Wilhelmine	*Ger.* vĭl-hĕl-mē'-nŭ.
Wilhelmj	vĭl-hĕl'-mĭ.
Wilhelm Meister's Lehr-	
jahre	vĭl'-hĕlm mīs'-tĕrz'
	lâr'-yär"-ŭ.
Wilhelmshöhe	vĭl'-hĕlmz-hē-yŭ.
Wilhelmsthal	vĭl'-hĕlmz-täl.
Wilkesbarre, or Wilkes-	
Barre	wilks'-băr-ĭ.
Willamette	wel-ä'-mĕt.
Wilna, see Vilna . . .	vĭl'-nä.
Wiltshire	wĭlt'-shĭr.
Wimpffen (de)	*Fr.* văn-fŏń'. *Ger.*
	vĭmp'-fĕn.
Winburg	vĭn'-bŭrċh.
Winckelmann	wĭngk'-ĕl-măn. *Ger.*
	vĭngk'-ĕl-män.

Windischgrätz . . . . vĭn'-dĭsh-grâts.
Windsor . . . . . . wĭnd'-zôr.
Winkelried, von . . . . fŏn wĭng'-kĕl-rēd. *Ger.*
            vĭng'-kĕl-rēt.
Winnepesaukee, or Winni-
  piseogee . . . . . wĭn"-ē-pē-sô'-kē.
Wirth . . . . vē̤rt.
Witenagemot . . . . . wĭt'-ĕ-nä-gĕ-mōt".
Witte . . . . vĭt'-ŭ.
Wittekind, see Wittikind . wĭt'-ĕ-kĭnd.
Wittelsbach . . . . . vĭt'-tĕls-bäċh.
Wittenberg . . . . . wit'-ĕn-bērg. *Ger.*
            vĭt'-tĕn-bĕrċh.
Wittgenstein . . . . . vĭt'-gĕn-stīn.
Wittikind, see Wittekind . wĭt'-ĭ-kĭnd.
Wittstock . . . . . . vĭt'-stŏck.
Wituland . . . . . . vē'-tōō-lănd.
Witwaterstrand . . . . vĭt-vä'-tĕr-strănd.
Wladimir, see Vladimir . vlăd'-ē-mēr.
          Russ. vlä-dē'-mĭr.
Wladislaw, see Vladislav . vlä'-dĭs-läv.
Woden . . . . wō'-dĕn.
Wodenowski . . . . . vō-dĕn-ŏf'-skĭ.
Woerth, see Wörth . . . vē̤rt.
Woevre . . . . . . vĕvr.
Wöhler . . . . vē'-lĕr.
Wohlgemuth . . . . . vōl'-gä-mōōt.
Wolcott . . . . . . woŏl-kŭt.
Wolf, von, see Wolff . . *Ger.* vŏlf.
Wolfenbüttel . . . . . vŏlf'-ĕn-büt"-ĕl.
Wolff, see Wolf . . . . *Ger.* vŏlf.
Wolfgang . . . . . . vŏlf'-gäng.
Wolfram von Eschenbach vŏlf'-räm fŏn ĕsh'-ĕn-bäċh.
Wolgast . . . . . . vōl'-gäst.
Wolkonsky . . . . . vŏl-kŏn'-skē.
Wollaston . . . . . . woŏl'-ăs-tŭn.
Wollstonecraft . . . . woŏl'-stŭn-krăft.

Wolowski	vō-lŏv′-skē.
Wolseley	wŏŏlz′-lĭ.
Wolsey	wŏŏl′-zĭ.
Wolzogen	vōl-tsō′-gĕn.
Woochang, see Wuchan .	wōō-chăng′.
Woolwich	wŏŏl′-ĭch, wŏŏl′-ĭj.
Worcester (Eng.) . . .	wŏŏs′-tĕr, wōōs′-tĕr.
Worcester (U. S.) . . .	wōōs′-tĕr, wŏŏs′-tĕr.
Worcestershire	wŏŏs′ or wōōs′-tĕr-shĭr.
Worms	vŏrms.
Wörth, see Woerth . . .	vĕrt.
Wouverman, or Wouwer-	
man	wow′-vĕr-măn.
Wouvermans	wow′-vĕr-mănz.
Wrangel	räng′-gĕl. Ger. vräng′-ĕl.
Wrede	vrä′-dĕ.
Wren	rĕn.
Wriothesley	rŏts′-lĭ, rŏt′-ĕs-lĭ.
Wuchan, see Woochang .	wōō-chăn′.
Wun	wōōn.
Wundt	vŏŏnt.
Wurmser	vōōrm′-zĕr.
Wurtemberg	vür′-tĕm-bĕrċh.
Würzburg	vürts′-bōōrċh.
Wyandot, or Wyandotte .	wī-ăn-dŏt′.
Wyborg, see Viborg . .	vē′-bôrg.
Wycherley	wĭch′-ĕr-lĭ.
Wyclif, or Wycliffe, see	
Wickliffe	wĭk′-lĭf.
Wykeham	wĭk′-ȧm.
Wyndham	wĭnd′-ȧm.
Wyoming	wī-ō′-mĭng.
Wyss	vĭs.
Wythe	wĭth.
Wytschaete	wīts-ċhä′-tŭ.

X

Xalapa, see Jalapa . . .	ċhä-lä'-pä.
Xalisco, see Jalisco . .	ċhä-lēs'-kō.
Xanadu	zăn-à-dōō'.
Xanthippe, see Xantippe .	zăn-thĭp'-ē.
Xanthippus	zăn-thĭp'-ŭs.
Xanthus	zăn'-thŭs.
Xantippe, see Xanthippe ..	zăn-tĭp'-ē.
Xauxa, see Jauja . . .	'how'-ċhä.
Xaver	ksä'-vĕr.
Xavier	zăv'-ĭ-ēr. Fr. zăv-ē-ä'.
	Sp. ċhä-vē-âr'.
Xenia	zē'-nĭ-à.
Xenocrates	zĕn-ŏk'-rà-tēz.
Xenophon	zĕn'-ō-fŏn.
Xeres, see Jeres, or . .	'hā'-rĕs.
Xerez, see Jerez . . .	'hā-rĕth'.
Xerez de la Frontera, see	
Jerez de la Frontera .	'hā-rĕth' dā lä frŏn-tā'-rä.
Xerona, see Gerona, Jerona	'hā-rō'-nä.
Xerxes	zĕrk'-sēz.
Ximena, see Jimena . .	ċhē-mĕn'-ä.
Ximenez, see Jimenez .	zĭm-ē'-nēz.
	Sp. ċhē-mĕn'-äth.
Ximenez de Quesada . .	ċhē-mĕn'-äth dā kā-sä'-dä.
Xingú	shēn-gōō'.
Xorullo, see Jorullo . .	ċhō-rōōl'-yō.
Xucar, see Jucar . . .	'hōō'-cär.
Xury	zū'-rĭ.

Y

Yafa, see Jaffa, Japho . .	yä'-fä.
Yahoo	yä-hōō'.
Yahveh	yä-vä'.
Yaka	yä'-kä.

Yakama, or	yăk'-ā-mȧ.
Yakima	yăk'-ĭ-mȧ.
Yakonan	yă'-kō-năn.
Yakootsk, see Yakutsk,	
Jakutsk	yä-kōōtsk'.
Yakub Khan	yä-kōōb' khän.
Yakutsk, see Yakootsk,	
Jakootsk	yä-kōōtsk'.
Yalu	yä-lōō'.
Yana	yä'-nā.
Yang-chau	yäng'-chow.
Yang-tse-Kiang, or . .	yäng"-tsē-kĭ-äng'.
Yang-tze	yäng'-tsĕ.
Yanina, see Janina . .	yä'-nē-nä.
Yankton	yăngk'-tŭn.
Yap, see Guap . . .	yäp.
Yaqui	yä'-kē.
Yare	yâr.
Yarkand, or	yär-känd'.
Yarkend	yär-kĕnd'.
Yarmouth	yär'-mŭth.
Yaroslaff, or	yä-rō-släv'.
Yaroslavl, see Jaroslaff .	yä-rō-slä'-vl.
Yarra-Yarra	yä'-rä-yä'-rä.
Yarriba, see Yoruba . .	yä'-rē-bä.
Yasunobu	yä'-sōō'-nō'-bĕ'.
Yauco	yä'=ōō-kō.
Yazoo	yăz'-ōō.
Youghiogheny . . .	yŏ-hŏ-gā'-nĭ.
Youmans	yōō'-mȧnz.
Ypres	ēpr.
Ypsilanti	ĭp-sĭl-ăn'-tĭ.
Yradier	ē-răd-ē=ā'.
Yriarte, see Iriarte . .	ē-rē-är'-tā.
Ysaye	ē-zī'-yŭ.
Yser	ē-zĕr'.
Yseult, see Isolde, Iseult	ē-sēlt', ē-sōōlt'.

Ysoude, see Isoude . . ē-sōōd'.
Yssel . . . . ĭ'-sĕl.
Yuan Shi Kai . . . . yōō-än'-shē-kī.
Yucatan . . . . . . yōō-kä-tän'.
Yuen . . . . yōō-ĕn'.
Yugoslavia, see Jugoslavia yū'-gō slăv'-ĭ-å.
Yukon . . . . yōō'-kŏn.
Yungchau . . . . . . yōōng-chow'.
Yunnan-fu . . . . . yŭn-nän'-fōō'.
Yuste . . . . yōōs'-tä.
Yvetot, Le Roi d' . . . lĕ rwä dēv-tō'.
Yeats . . . . yāts.
Yeddo, see Jeddo, or . . yĕd'-dō.
Yedo . . . . yĕd'-ō.
Yegoroff . . . . . . yā'-gôr-ŏf.
Yaisen . . . . yā'-ĭ'-sĕn.
Yeishí . . . . yā'-ē'-shē'.
Yeisk, see Jeisk . . . . yā'-ĭsk.
Yeizan . . . . yā'-ĭ'-zăn'.
Yekaterinburg, see Eka-
    terinburg . . . . yĕ-kä''-tĕ-rēn-bōōrg'.
Yekaterinodar . . . . yĕ-kä''-tĕ-rē-nō-där'.
Yekaterinoslaff . . . . yĕ-kä''-tĕ-rē-nō-släv'.
Yelisavetpol, or Yelizavetpol yĕ-lē''-zä-vĕt-pŏl'=yĕ.
Yellala . . . . yĕl-lä'-lä.
Yemen . . . . yĕm'-ĕn.
Yenesei . . . . . . yĕn-ē-sā'-ē.
Yenikale (Strait) . . . yĕn-ē-kä'-lä.
Yeniseisk . . . . . . yĕn-ē-sā'-ĭsk.
Yesso, see Jesso, or . . yĕs'-sō.
Yezo . . . . yĕz'-ō, yā'-zō.
Yggdrasil, see Igdrasil . ĭg'-drȧ-sĭl.
Yguerne, see Igerna,
    Igerne . . . . . . ĭ-gērn'.
Y-lin . . . . ē-lēn'.
Yoga . . . . yō'-gȧ.
Yohchau . . . . . . yō-chow'.

Yokohama . . . . . yō-kō-hä'-mä.
Yonge . . . . yŭng.
Yonkers . . . . . yŏngk'-ērz.
Yonne . . . . yŏn.
Yorick . . . . . . yŏr'-ĭk.
York von Wartenburg . . yōrk fŏn vär'-tĕn-bōōrċh.
Yoruba, see Yarriba . . yō'-rōō-bä.
Yosemite . . . . . yō-sĕm'-ĭt-ē.
Youghal . . . . . . yôl, yô'-hȧl.

Z

Zaandam, see Saandam . zän-dăm'.
Zaardam, see Saardam . zär-dăm'.
Zab . . . . zäb.
Zabulon . . . . . zăb'-yū-lŏn.
Zacatecas . . . . . dzä-kä-tā'-käs,
                      sä-kä-tā'-käs.
Zacchaeus, or Zaccheus . zăk-ē'-ŭs.
Zacconi, Ermete . . . ĕr-mä'-tā dzäk-kō'-nē.
Zachariah . . . . . zăk-ȧ-rī'-ȧ.
Zadkiel . . . . . . zăd'-kĭ-ĕl.
Zadok . . . . zā'-dŏk.
Zahara, see Sahara, Sahhra zä-hä'-rä, zä'-hȧ-rä.
Zahn . . . . tsän.
Zama . . . . zā'-mȧ.
Zamacoïs . . . . . thä-mä-kō'-ĭs.
Zambales . . . . . zäm-bä'-lĕs. *Sp.*
                      thäm-bä'-lĕs.
Zambesi . . . . . zäm-bā'-zē, *pop.*
                      zăm-bē'-zĭ.
Zambezia . . . . . zăm-bē'-zhĭ=ȧ.
Zamboanga . . . . . zäm-bō-äng'-gȧ.
Zamora . . . . . . thä-mō'-rä.
Zampieri . . . . . dzäm-pē-ä'-rē.
Zand (R.) . . . . . zănt.
Zanguebar . . . . zäng-gä-bär'.

Zangwill	săng′-wĭl.
Zankoff	zän′-kŏf.
Zanoni	ză-nō′-nĭ.
Zante	zän′-tĕ, zän′-tā.
Zanzibar	zän-zĭ-bär′.
Zaragoza, see Saragossa .	thä-rä-gō′-thä.
Zarathushtra	ză-rȧ-thōōsh′-trȧ.
Zauberflöte, Die . . .	dē tsow′-bĕr-flē″-tŭ.
Zaylah, see Zeila . . .	zā′-lä.
Zealand, see Zeeland . .	zē′-lănd.
Zebedee	zĕb′-ĕ-dē.
Zebú, see Cebú	zē-bōō′. *Sp.* thä-bōō′.
Zebulon, or	zĕb′-ū-lŏn.
Zebulun	zĕb′-ū-lŭn.
Zechariah	zĕk-ȧ-rī′-ȧ.
Zedekiah	zĕd-ĕ-kī′-ä.
Zeebrugge	zā′-brŏŏg-ŭ.
Zeeland, see Zealand . .	zā′-länt.
Zeila, see Zaylah . . .	zā′-lä.
Zela	zē′-lä.
Zelaya	sä-lä′-yä.
Zenaida	zē-nä′-ĭ-dä.
Zeno	zē′-nō.
Zenobia	zĕ-nō′-bĭ-ȧ.
Zenta	zĕn′-tä.
Zephaniah	zĕf-ȧ-nī′-ȧ.
Zephon	zē′-fŏn.
Zeppelin	zĕp′-ĕ-lĭn. *Ger.* tsĕp′-ā-ıen.
Zephyrus	zĕf′-ĭ-rŭs.
Zerafshan	zĕr-äf-shän′.
Zerin	zĕ-rēn′.
Zerlina	dzĕr-lē′-nȧ.
Zermatt	zĕr-mät′, tsĕr-mät′.
Zerubbabel, see Zorobabel	zĕ-rŭb′-ȧ-bĕl.
Zeus	zūs.
Zeuxis	zūk′-sĭs.
Zhitomir, see Jitomir . .	zhĭt-ōm′-ēr.

Zidon, see Sidon . . . zī'-dŏn.
Ziethen, or Zieten . . . tsē'-tĕn.
Zimri . . . . zĭm'-rī.
Zincali . . . . zĭng'-kä-lē.
Zingara . . . . dzēn-gä'-rä.
Zingarelli . . . . . . dzēn-gä-rĕl'-lē.
Zion, see Sion . . . . zī'-ŏn.
Zipporah . . . . . . zĭp'-ō-rä.
Ziska, or . . . . . . zĭs'-kä.
Zižka . . . . zhĭzh'-kä.
Znaim . . . . tsnīm.
Zobeidah, or Zobeide . . zō-bā'-dä, zō-bī'-dä,
                          zō-bī-dā.
Zoë . . . . zō'-ē.
Zola . . . . zō'-lä. *Fr.* zō-lä'.
Zollverein . . . . . . tsŏl'-fā-rīn.
Zoloaga . . . . . . thō-lō-ä"-gà.
Zombor . . . . . . zŏm'-bŏr.
Zonurko . . . . . . zō-nōōr'-kō.
Zophiei . . . . zō'-fĭ-ĕl.
Zorilla, see Zorrilla . . thōr-rēl'-yä.
Zorn . . . . tsôrn.
Zorndorf . . . . . . tsôrn'-dôrf.
Zoroaster . . . . . . zō-rō-ăs'-tēr.
Zorobabel, see Zerubbabel zō-rŏb'-ā-bĕl.
Zorrilla, see Zorilla . . thōr-rēl'-yä.
Zorrilla y Moral . . . thōr-ēl'-yä ē mō-räl'.
Zouave . . . . zōō-äv'.
Zoutpansberg . . . . zowt'-pǎns-bĕrċh.
Zschokke . . . . . . tshŏk'-kŭ.
Zuccarelli . . . . . . dzŏŏk-kä-rĕl'-lē.
Zucchero . . . . . . tsŏŏk'-ā-rō.
Zuccoli . . . . tsŏŏk'-kō-lē.
Zug . . . . zōōg. *Ger.* tsōōċh.
Zuider Zee, see Zuyder
    Zee . . . . zī'-dĕr zē. *D.* zoi'-dĕr zā.
Zuinglius . . . . . . zwĭng'-glĭ-ŭs.

Zukertort	tsŏŏk′-ĕr-tōrt.
Zuleika	zū-lē′-kà.
Zulu	zōō′-lōō.
Zululand	zōō′-lōō-lănd.
Zumpt	tsŏŏmpt.
Zuñi	zōōn′-yē.
Zunz	tsŏŏnts.
Zurbaran	thōōr-bä-rän′.
Zurich, or	zōō′-rĭk.
Zürich, *Ger.*	tsü′-rĭċh.
Zurlinden (Gen.) . . .	zür-lĭn-dĕn′.
Zütphen	züt′-fĕn.
Zuyder Zee, see Zuider	
Zee	zī′-dĕr zē. *D.* zoi′-dĕr zā.
Zwartkopjesfontein . .	zvärt′-kŏp-yĕs-fŏn′-tīn.
Zweibrücken	tsvī′-brük-ĕn.
Zwickau	tsvĭk′-ow.
Zwingle	zwĭng′-gl.
Zwingli	zwĭng′-glē. *Ger.*
	tsvĭng′-lē.
Zwolle	zwŏl′-lĕ.